MOTHERHOOD IN BLACK AND WHITE

Motherhood in Black and White

Race and Sex in American Liberalism,

1930–1965

RUTH FELDSTEIN

Cornell University Press

Ithaca and London

Chapter 2 is revised and reprinted from *"Bad" Mothers: The Politics of Blame in Twentieth-Century America*, edited by Molly Ladd-Taylor and Lauri Umansky, by permission of New York University Press. © 1998 by New York University. All Rights Reserved.

Chapter 4 is revised and reprinted from *Not June Cleaver: Women and Gender in Postwar America, 1945–1960*, edited by Joanne Meyerowitz, by permission of Temple University Press. © 1994 by Temple University. All Rights Reserved.

First published 2000 by Cornell University Press
First printing, Cornell Paperbacks, 2000

Printed in the United States of America

Library of Congress Cataloging-in-Publication Data

Feldstein, Ruth, 1965–
    Motherhood in black and white : race and sex in American liberalism, 1930–1965 / Ruth Feldstein.
        p.   cm
    Includes bibliographical references and index.
    ISBN 0-8014-3414-9 (cloth) — ISBN 0-8014-8438-3 (pbk.)
    1. Motherhood—United States—History—20th century.   2. Mothers—United States—History—20th century.   3. Women—United States—History—20th century.
4. Liberalism—United States—History—20th century.   5. Racism—United States—History—20th century.   I. Title.

HQ759 F43 2000
306.874'3'0973—dc21
                                                                        00-022679

Cornell University Press strives to use environmentally responsible suppliers and materials to the fullest extent possible in the publishing of its books. Such materials include vegetable-based, low-VOC inks and acid-free papers that are recycled, totally chlorine-free, or partly composed of nonwood fibers. Books that bear the logo of the FSC (Forest Stewardship Council) use paper taken from forests that have been inspected and certified as meeting the highest standards for environmental and social responsibility. For further information, visit our website at www.cornellpress.cornell.edu.

Cloth printing   10   9   8   7   6   5   4   3   2   1
Paperback printing   10   9   8   7   6   5   4   3   2   1

CONTENTS

ACKNOWLEDGMENTS

It is with great happiness that I acknowledge the many people and institutions who have helped me as I have worked on this book. I feel fortunate that contacts with others have been not simply helpful but invaluable and that the stereotype of the lonely and isolated scholar does not apply.

Time to research and write has been a precious commodity. I received financial assistance from the American Association of University Women; the Center for Study of Race and Ethnicity at Brown University; the Woodrow Wilson National Fellowship Foundation; and Schlesinger Library, Radcliffe College. Thanks to the C. Boyden Gray Career Development Fund and the Junior Faculty Work-Study Program at Harvard University, I had the help of talented research assistants; Nathan Rein, Bradley Zakarin, and Kimberly Sims stared into microfilm machines for innumerable hours, checked facts, located illustrations, and tracked down details. Early on in this project, Kendra Lider-Johnson did very useful research for chapter 6.

This book owes a great deal to scholars and friends across disciplines. I have received invaluable criticisms and comments on work in progress from William Chafe, Susan Douglas, Mary Dudziak, Margaret Hunt, Molly Ladd-Taylor, Andrea Levine, John McGreevy, Elaine Tyler May, Nellie McKay, Harvard Sitkoff, Judith Smith, Rickie Solinger, and Lauri Umansky. A version of chapter 4 first appeared in *Not June Cleaver: Women and Gender in Postwar America, 1945–1960*, and I thank Joanne Meyerowitz and anonymous reviewers of that anthology for their astute questions. Carolyn Dean and John L. Thomas read the entire manuscript, and their perceptive comments helped me to transform a dissertation into a book. Generous colleagues at Harvard University have read drafts, have asked cogent questions about liberalism, and have shared perspectives on everything from political and cultural history to childcare. I thank Steven Biel, Catherine Corman, Lizabeth

Cohen, Kristin Hoganson, Lisa McGirr, and Laurel Thatcher Ulrich. Trevor Dickie offered computer assistance at a critical juncture.

Although I did not fully realize it at the time, I first began to think about the ideas in *Motherhood in Black and White* early in graduate school at Brown University. As a first-year graduate student, I listened to Mari Jo Buhle give a lecture about women in the Depression; with that, I began to consider how and why women in the private sphere came under close scrutiny in the 1930s. Two years later, John L. Thomas asked me a question during my preliminary examinations that made me translate vague ideas into a dissertation topic. In the years since, both have been the best kind of allies and the best kind of critics—offering incisive readings, probing questions, and enthusiastic support. I feel privileged to stand in a long line of scholars grateful to them both. I also benefited enormously from the input of Jacqueline Jones and Carolyn Dean. It was as a teaching assistant for Jacqueline Jones that I first learned about Mamie Till Bradley and began to think more seriously about relationships between black and white women and between gender and race. And, in draft after draft, revision after revision, Carolyn Dean has offered strategies for how I could sharpen my analytic frameworks.

"The group" has varied in membership over the years, but it has always been a place where I could think out loud and offer rough drafts to an incredibly talented community of scholars. I thank Lucy Barber, Gail Bederman, Elizabeth Francis, Linda Grasso, Dorothee Kocks, Donna Penn, Jessica Shubow, and Lyde Sizer. Several people deserve far more than acknowledgment. In and out of "the group," Melani McAlister, Uta G. Poiger, and, especially, Jane Gerhard have sustained me intellectually and emotionally. I have learned a great deal from their scholarship and from their feminism, and I could not have continued, at times, without their expansive support.

As well, I feel blessed to have a circle of friends and family too numerous to name who reminded me that there is a world beyond academia. My parents, Shirley and Donald Feldstein, fostered a wonderful combination of curiosity and respect for the past in my siblings and me. I thank them for encouraging me to ask questions. The extended family of Feldsteins, Nixons, and Suldans offered love, support, and babysitting.

Many people ask me what it is like to write a book that considers motherhood when I am a mother and historian. I cannot even begin to answer that complicated question without acknowledging the importance of reliable childcare in the lives of working parents. For providing loving, safe, stimulating, and fun care to my children, I thank Jennine Babine, Jenn Connor, Suzanne Evans, Daria Shoturma, Sarah Walls, Chris Williams, Gretchen Wurst, and, especially, Olivia Hunter. I thank Sara Feldstein Nixon and Max Feldstein Nixon for staying healthy the past few months, and for filling my life with a joy that I could not have anticipated. They, more than anyone, serve as reminders that there is a world of difference between ideologies of motherhood and the experience of mothering. Asa Nixon has supported me in more ways than I know. He has encouraged me to laugh and to work, and he has shown me, again and again, that risks are worth taking and that change is both possible and good. Asa first introduced the question, "is this a big thing or a little thing?" to our on-the-brink-of-tantrum children; but, in posing this question to them he has asked it of himself and of me, and this question has been invaluable. I thank him for making both the ordinary and extraordinary an adventure and a source of much happiness.

MOTHERHOOD IN BLACK AND WHITE

Introduction

W hen I ask students to describe the 1950s, they offer two types of adjectives and images. *Conservative, suburban, apathetic*, they begin. Stay-at-home mothers in aprons, fathers coming home from work, teenage girls in poodle skirts at high school dances—these are some of the images that come to the minds of those reared on reruns of *Happy Days* and *Leave It to Beaver*. But many of these same students also associate this period with the early years of the civil rights movement: they use adjectives like *rebellious, courageous*, and *dignified* to describe Rosa Parks in Montgomery, Alabama, the "Little Rock Nine" in Arkansas, and other icons of grassroots activism.

I began work on this book with similar associations. It was not clear to me what they had to do with each other. It was difficult to understand why, what Betty Friedan later called the "feminine mystique," flourished in the same era that the civil rights movement gained momentum. How was it that liberal ideas about race relations gained ascendance in the same period that conservative ideas about gender relations seemed so entrenched? As I considered this question, I realized that it encompassed more than the single decade of the 1950s. In the 1930s the New Deal transformed the political and cultural landscape of the United States in dramatic and subtle ways; one cannot think about the nature of postwar liberalism without first considering New Deal liberalism.[1] My second realization was that ideas about women as mothers—black women and white women—offered a key to understanding the relationship between race and gender that competing images of the 1950s brought to the fore. In these years, motherhood assumed meaning in relation to assumptions that Americans had about families, gender roles, racial difference, and the role of the federal government. Representations of women as mothers developed in conjunction with debates about who was a healthy citizen and what was a healthy democracy.

1

Motherhood in Black and White explores the relationship between liberalism and images of women as mothers in mid-twentieth-century America. From the 1930s to the 1960s, American liberalism reached a high-water mark in terms of influence and consensus. It was a time when the welfare state, an unfamiliar and contested concept in the 1930s, expanded and became a (seemingly) permanent fixture that by the early 1960s enjoyed bipartisan political support. It was a time when ongoing but largely local protests against racial injustice transformed into a national civil rights movement.

In these same decades, images of women who failed as mothers were also widespread. In the 1930s, and increasingly over the next two decades, experts on families, women, and child-rearing, as well as many politicians, popular commentators, and films, asserted that mothers were responsible for raising physically and psychologically fit future citizens. The citizen who made liberal democracy possible, according to a range of narratives, required adequate mothering in order to be both independent, productive, and cooperative with others. Mothers who smothered or dominated, who overprotected or rejected their offspring, raised future citizens unable to meet this ideal. This assumption persisted from the 1930s, when organized feminism was in a post-suffrage decline, into the 1960s, when second-wave feminism ascended. From Steinbeck's Ma Joad to Dr. Spock's *Baby and Child Care*, from Betty Friedan's analysis of white women in 1963 to Daniel Patrick Moynihan's analysis of black families in 1965, came the message that *good* mothers, white and black, were a precondition to healthy citizens and a strong democracy.

Women as good mothers constantly evoked the opposite: women as bad mothers. In 1939 E. Franklin Frazier, a sociologist, made the concept of a black "matriarchy"—black women who, in various ways, failed as mothers—central to his authoritative analysis, *The Negro Family in the United States*. *The Negro Family* opposed prejudice and challenged ideas about innate racial inferiority. At the same time (regardless of Frazier's politics or intentions), the book paved the way for what became a common assumption among progressive social scientists: that certain kinds of maternal behavior weakened black families and impeded racial progress. Three years after Frazier's influential text appeared, Philip Wylie wrote *Generation of Vipers*. In this widely read diatribe, Wylie explained that "moms" were white women who failed as mothers. "Moms" did such damage that they undermined the vitality and strength of the nation as a whole.[2]

Frazier and Wylie were anything but lone voices. Images of black women as "matriarchs" and white women as "moms" proliferated in the 1940s. By the postwar period, they had become staples in scholarly, political, and popular discourse. Even as "good" white mothers were celebrated as quintessentially American, mom-bashing became a national pastime. Even as civil rights activists applauded black " 'mamas' " as the "backbone" of the civil rights movement, indictments of black matriarchs were common among whites and blacks.[3]

Mother-blaming cannot be explained as simply a conservative backlash, or only as an expression of reactionary misogyny. One might easily (and at times correctly) reason that those who blame mothers for all of society's ills want to keep women in the home, bring feminism to a grinding halt, and preserve the status quo.[4] But it is perhaps even more important to consider how and why progressive thinkers have used mother-blaming, for in fact from the 1930s into the 1960s, many thinkers who favored increased social justice, an expansive liberal welfare state, and greater racial equality relied on mother-blaming in central ways. Further, Frazier's dominating and disorganizing "matriarchs" and Wylie's smothering, overprotective, and narcissistic "moms" had much in common. Even though scholars have rarely considered bad mothers across lines of race, it is crucial to see white and black motherhood as related to each other, and mother-blaming as relevant to changes in both race *and* gender relations.[5] Ideas about maternal failure that might seem focused only on gender actually advanced the racial liberalism that was a benchmark of mid-twentieth-century liberalism.

Motherhood in Black and White explores these unexpected intersections of race and gender. Why did images of both white and black women who failed as mothers surface so prominently in liberal scholarly, popular, and political thought from the 1930s through the 1960s? How did ideas about women as dangerous mothers affect discussions about who and what was a good American citizen? In what ways were indictments of white women as "moms" who "smothered" their children and of black women as "matriarchs" who "dominated" their children similar, and in what ways did race impel separate ideas about women? Perhaps most importantly, why did this conservative and prescriptive discourse about women's roles prevail in the same years that race moved into the mainstream of American liberalism to define a progressive mandate for the nation?

These questions illuminate a central though overlooked paradox in mid-twentieth-century American liberalism, a paradox my students evoked when they described the 1950s.[6] Like them, many people associate this period (particularly the post-World War II years, alternatively celebrated nostalgically as a "simpler time" or castigated as the "dark ages") with what I call "gender conservatism": an eclipse of organized feminism; a glorification of domesticity and nuclear families; and a celebration of traditional heterosexual gender roles in which the healthy male citizen was understood to be the paternal breadwinner, and the healthy female citizen was consigned to the role of wife and mother.[7] Donna Reed, films like *Penny Serenade*, early television shows like *I Remember Mama*—these were some of the popular figures and narratives that celebrated strictly demarcated gender roles, family values, and above all, motherhood.[8]

Of course, the postwar period was not one of monolithic conformity and political passivity, and not all women were ensnared in the "feminine mystique." Scholars have recently shown that the lives of many women did not conform to conservative gender ideologies.[9] Still, the symbolic significance of gender conservatism was considerable. It is perhaps *because* traditional gender roles did not capture the varied experiences and attitudes of Americans that gender conservatism assumed significance as an ideological norm, and stood in for a collective dream of social harmony.

Like my students, scholars and other commentators also associate these years with shifting attitudes and practices that contributed to civil rights activism. Black Americans migrated to cities in increasing numbers and gained access to some political power. Activists in the National Association for the Advancement of Colored People (NAACP) mounted legal challenges to segregation with increasing success from the 1930s onward. During the Depression and into the 1940s, alliances of blacks and whites formed—with mixed results at best—in urban labor unions, among rural tenant farmers, and in the offices of government officials.[10] Historical narratives about gender tend to locate World War II as a crucial dividing line—between an era of the independent Rosie the Riveter and the domestic suburban housewife—and narratives about race relations regard the war as a turning point as well. In patriotic rhetoric that became more common during and after World War II, racism was inherently un-American; it was a "dilemma," as Gunnar Myrdal put it in 1944, because it contradicted American democracy, or the "American creed."[11] While progress was neither given nor linear, social and political changes converged with changing attitudes about prejudice and, most importantly, with growing activism in African American communities across the country. This convergence culminated in the civil rights movement and passage of civil rights and voting rights legislation in the mid-1960s.

But gender conservatism and racial liberalism did not run parallel to each other by some ironic coincidence, nor was each simply a response to the traumas of World War II or an outgrowth of the prosperity that followed. Gender conservatism and racial liberalism were intimately connected. *Motherhood in Black and White* analyzes this often overlooked connection within liberalism itself. It does so by exploring two themes: first, the ways that ideas about masculinity and femininity shaped conceptions of the liberal welfare state; and second, the shift from biological to psychological theories of race, personality development, and gender role differentiation. More specifically, this book argues that conservative ideas about gender (and it counts mother-blaming among these) must be considered if we are to understand how and why liberal thinkers sought to improve race relations. Mother-blaming served particular functions and did particular kinds of work within liberalism.

Many discussions of motherhood focused on children of one sex or another. Some texts implied that "bad" mothers harmed daughters, as my analysis of the two versions of the film *Imitation of Life* (1934 and 1959) will suggest.[12] This perspective had an impact on female sexuality, in particular. These were decades when the "companionate marriage" ideal—marriages in which husbands and wives were supposed to share psychological companionship and sexual pleasure—gave way to a "sexual revolution" and images of sexually autonomous women who were neither mothers nor even married. In the face of these nascent changes, liberal thinkers reemphasized maternal failure and reinforced the equation between motherhood and womanhood; collapsing the terms into one and seeing daughters as future mothers helped to limit the parameters of acceptable female sexuality.[13]

Ultimately, however, most liberal narratives equated healthy and strong citizens with healthy and strong men, hence their primary concern was with sons, black and white. In maternal ideologies, women who failed as mothers were objects of concern because they raised *men* who (for different reasons at different moments) failed to meet the criteria of healthy citizenship. In other words, ideas about motherhood were a means through which ideas about normative masculinity *and* femininity took shape. Crucially, liberal discourse made this equation between citizenship and masculinity through discussions of women as mothers, discussions that appeared in diffuse venues. Maternal ideologies helped to produce ideas about what "normal" masculinity and femininity meant in a wide array of political and cultural arenas. Ideologies of motherhood are thus a lens through which to view gendered and racial conceptions of citizenship.[14]

Although *Motherhood in Black and White* begins with the 1930s, relationships between motherhood, citizenship, and race predated that decade. In the era of the American Revolution, for instance, the notion that white women were responsible for educating their sons to be "virtuous citizens" of the new republic—or "Republican Motherhood" as Linda Kerber has explained it—afforded women political status (if not rights) and was potentially empowering.[15] This endorsement of the value of motherhood was never devoid of racial meanings. In the eighteenth century, images of "savage" Native Americans countered those of Christian white women; increasingly over the nineteenth century Americans concluded that enslaved black women were either desexualized breeders of future slaves, or ever-promiscuous and sexually available "Jezebels," or "Mammies" who willingly cared for white children. These negative images of women and mothers served as both contrast and warning; they propped up and stabilized the idealization of white women as mothers.[16] Most often, black women (both before and after slavery) and poor working women (many of whom were immigrants) were simply excluded from dominant assumptions about "good" women and from celebrations of motherhood by virtue of their race and class. They had little access to notions of Republican Motherhood or to the sentimentalized white mother of the Victorian era, ensconced in the private sphere.[17]

If Americans celebrated certain white women as educators of good citizens well before the 1930s, they had also long been inclined to attack women who failed to meet established standards. Puritans, antebellum reformers, and intellectuals in the Progressive era, among others, leveled charges at certain kinds of women, black and white. Critics asserted that alleged witches, female abolitionists, middle-class professional women, and prostitutes harmed families and communities. Attacks depicted such "bad" women as either overly masculine and desexualized—and therefore unmaternal—or, conversely, as promiscuous and hypersexualized—and therefore unmaternal.[18]

Throughout the history of the republic, women had assigned their own meanings to motherhood. They extended into the public sphere prevailing assumptions that mothers were responsible for protecting citizens within the home. By drawing on associations between women and motherhood they made political demands ranging from abolition to temperance, from suffrage to antilynching to peace, and from segregation to desegregation.[19] This dynamic was particularly prevalent in the early twentieth century, when reformers who embraced "maternalist politics" fought for federal policies that would protect working women, many of whom were poor mothers. Women reformers were instrumental in the passage of state-run mothers' aid pensions in the years between 1910 and 1920; in the Supreme Court's 1908 ruling in favor of protective labor legislation (*Muller v. Oregon*); and in the passage of child welfare policies like the Sheppard-Towner Act of 1921—all forerunners to still more comprehensive welfare legislation of the 1930s. These efforts often involved coalitions among white and black women reformers. As the work of Linda Gordon, Sonya Michel, Gwendolyn Mink, and Robyn Muncy has demonstrated, gender and race shaped maternalist reform efforts; these and other scholars have shown that progressive welfare legislation institutionalized gender and racial hierarchies even as it afforded opportunities to some women.[20]

Much of this invaluable body of scholarship focuses on the years before the New Deal to show that women provided the building blocks for the American welfare state, and it demonstrates how and why women used ideas about motherhood in their political efforts. *Motherhood in Black and White* differs from this work in several respects. It focuses on how gender—meanings of masculinity and femininity—shaped ideas about race and the liberal welfare state more than it considers female or male reformers per se. Moreover, this study places ideas about motherhood in a broad cultural context in which "formal" politics and policies play but one part. Women reformers were hardly alone in using ideas about motherhood to build their vision of a healthy American democracy. Rather, ideas about motherhood were embedded in the very frameworks that progressive intellectuals and civil rights activists, mainstream Hollywood films and the popular press, and welfare legislation and political tracts used to construct meanings of citizenship. Finally, *Motherhood in Black and White* begins the story about gender, race, and American liberalism in the 1930s—where others often end it.

Three related changes altered the meanings of motherhood in the 1930s. First, experts in various disciplines came to a consensus that mothers were not only responsible for the physical, educational, and religious well-being of future citizens, but also were responsible for their children's *psychological* well-being. Although psychology had been relevant within intellectual circles since early in the century, it became a more influential framework through which progressive thinkers assessed social and political as well as personal issues by the 1930s. After World War II, psychological and political analyses increasingly overlapped. Categories like repression, neurosis, paranoia, insecurity, and frustration became vehicles for analyzing both personal and political problems, and for determining who and what was a healthy American citizen.[21]

A second difference apparent by the 1930s was that good and bad women were not as easily divided along private and public lines. The idealization of white motherhood in the nineteenth century was largely based on a series of divisions: mother-hood versus work, home versus workplace, private versus public, and of course, fe-male versus male.[22] Critiques of women abolitionists, temperance reformers, suf-fragists, prostitutes, and other working women had presumed that such women were "bad"—or more specifically, were dangerous, unwomanly, and unmaternal—precisely because they had left the (ostensibly) private sphere of the home and chal-lenged these divisions. Of course, class and race always affected these gendered dis-tinctions, and the division between the public and private was a privilege that many black and poor women across lines of race did not have. In fact, it was for precisely that reason that so many women in these categories were considered to fail as moth-ers, almost by definition.

By the 1930s "bad" women were not just "out there." Experts no longer labeled women dangerous, bad, unwomanly, and unmaternal simply because they tried to wield power in the public sphere. Now experts criticized women and labeled them bad mothers because of their behavior in the home. Women became suspect be-cause they wielded too much power in the private sphere *as mothers*. In this context, dangerous women and bad mothers stood in for each other even more; the cate-gories of "woman" and "mother" blurred. Ideas about motherhood thus affected all women, across lines of race, and regardless of their reproductive status.

Third, the Depression triggered a profound crisis in liberalism, which in turn affected ideas about masculinity and femininity and about families and mother-hood in new ways. Economic instability in the 1930s at once rendered precarious the received models of liberalism and masculinity. Historically, wage earning, inde-pendence, citizenship, and masculinity were interdependent sources of authority.[23] The Depression threatened to sever these links because long-term unemployment affected the manufacturing and industrial labor force where white men dominated most dramatically. A belief in progress, individual initiative and economic mobility, and equality of opportunity to all those who worked hard—the very foundations of American democracy and a liberal capitalist work ethic—was under assault when year after year men could not find work, feed their kin, or keep their homes.[24] New Deal liberalism developed to address these concerns in ways that made maternal behavior central. Because of its attempt to speak to the "common man"—white and black—New Deal liberalism would have effects on ideas about women as mothers that reverberated for the following three decades.

As a result of these three changes—the growing role of psychology within liberal discourse, the focus on women's behavior in the private sphere, and the perceived interrelated crises of liberalism and masculinity that the Depression set in mo-tion—the specter of maternal failure loomed large and had more dire political *and* personal implications. Black and white mothers emerged as dangerous in specific ways in the 1930s because they were perceived as the linchpin of a host of social, political, and personal problems that the emergent liberal welfare state was trying to solve.

As psychology became a more prominent aspect of liberal thought from the 1930s onward, damaged citizens and damaged men had something in common:

both suffered from the effects of bad mothers and dysfunctional families. The private sphere had let them down as a wellspring of both mental and political health.

This personalization of the political made prejudice a more pressing and accessible issue for many American liberals. White Americans simply could not psychologically bear the "American dilemma" indefinitely, Gunnar Myrdal's influential work declared. At the same time that the focus on damaged personalities propelled race more forcefully onto a liberal agenda, it deflected attention from systemic racial inequalities. Psychosocial theories of race de-emphasized political and economic considerations and drew attention to the role women played in producing men whose masculinity was not intact and who therefore could not function effectively as citizens.

The relationships between motherhood, race, and gendered views of citizenship varied over time. Still, as liberalism was renegotiated in different periods from the New Deal through the Great Society, and as civil rights moved into the mainstream of American liberalism through these renegotiations, liberal narratives used white and black maternal pathology to explain social ailments. They represented maternal failure as a causal factor in problems that beset the nation, weakening American citizens and American democracy.

One goal of the following chapters is to examine this logic, to analyze why many liberal Americans who were committed to social justice, a greater degree of racial equality, and some degree of action on the part of the federal government to ensure civil rights and social security often *needed* to emphasize the dangers women posed in order to make their progressive arguments. A related goal is to analyze race and gender as mutually constructing categories. Doing so illuminates the intersections between racial liberalism and gender conservatism.

Chapter 1 locates the re-figuring of images of motherhood in the Depression and explores their relationship to New Deal liberalism. In New Deal liberalism, white and black mothers were key to the ability of families to withstand the Depression and emerged as equally important to achieving more harmonious race relations. Chapters 2 and 3 analyze the proliferation of "matriarchs" and "moms" in the 1940s and 1950s. These chapters demonstrate that mother-blaming did not develop only as part of a conservative postwar backlash against women. Mother-blaming was central to analyses of prejudice that were influential before and after World War II, and it shaped the anticommunist liberalism that became so influential after the war. As New Deal liberalism became Cold War liberalism, motherhood and the dangerous effects of femininity on men were linked to the new problems of domestic communism and overconsumption in a prosperous society. In this Cold War climate, relationships between class, motherhood, and race shifted considerably from what they had been in the 1930s. But the gendered components of liberalism continued to have racial dimensions, and the racial components of liberalism continued to have gendered dimensions.

Chapters 4 through 6 chart ideas about women in relation to a growing civil rights movement, a consumer-oriented ethos, and the Great Society. In the early days of the civil rights movement it became clear that female behavior might affect men, the political demands activists made, and gender relations among activists; in this context, I will consider the pivotal murder of Emmett Till in 1955 and the sit-ins of 1960–61. Assumptions about motherhood remained relevant into the 1960s as a liberal civil rights agenda fractured and as liberal feminism developed into a national movement. According to *The Negro Family: The Case for National Action*, a report that Daniel Patrick Moynihan offered in 1965, bad black mothers who were "matriarchs" created the "tangle of pathology" that perpetuated black poverty and dysfunctional families. White mother-blaming also persisted from the 1950s into the 1960s, playing a role, for example, in Betty Friedan's landmark *The Feminine Mystique*, the bible of liberal feminism published in 1963.[25] It was only in the mid- to late 1960s that the psychosocial dimensions of liberalism which tied political health and racial harmony to stable families and traditional gender roles started to erode.

Together, the chapters demonstrate how ideas about maternal failure inform intersections of gender and race in liberal discourse. Each is a vignette, or snapshot of sorts, with different players, sources, and topics. Chapters 1 and 5, for example, explore two different film versions of *Imitation of Life*. In both versions, a white woman and a black woman struggle together to be good mothers to their daughters. But I consider the Depression-era film and the later Cold War remake in a broad context that includes passage of the Social Security Act in 1935 and sit-ins in 1960. Chapters 4 and 5 link political and cultural concerns within liberalism to murders and subsequent trials which became national spectacles and in which motherhood played a central role. Different episodes and configurations of stories allow us to see both changes and continuities in American liberalism.

A discussion of such large categories as race and liberalism requires some attention to definition. With regard to race, this book assumes that both whiteness and blackness are racial categories whose meanings shifted over time.[26] Race and gender always intersected to give ideas about motherhood their meaning: enduring images of the white suburban mother in her apron, baking cookies and going to PTA meetings, are as marked by whiteness as images of the strong and nurturing black mother, caring for her own and for white children, are marked by blackness. Yet this book's focus on blackness and whiteness engages with the racial dichotomy that dominated these decades and these sources; it does not encompass or accurately reflect the multiracial nature of American society.[27] As well, even though it is important to use gender and race together to understand depictions of women, these categories are neither structurally nor analytically equivalent. However similar the descriptions of black and white women as matriarchs and moms were, these representations nonetheless had different effects on women whose experiences diverged and whose access to power was unequal. This book considers how liberal ideologies mobilized racial and gendered images of motherhood by pinpointing similarities *and* differences between moms and matriarchs.[28]

To speak of liberal ideologies or *liberalism* is to refer to a wide-ranging political, social, scholarly, and popular discourse that was historically specific and changed over time. Liberalism was never singular, and liberals were never a monolithic group. Nevertheless, certain assumptions consistently recurred in the liberal texts in this study, from films to political manifestos: the assumption that progress was possible; the conviction that social and political problems could be remedied through rational intervention; and the expectation that the federal government could play a role in remedying these problems in ways that helped a collective body politic while simultaneously strengthening *individual* citizens within it.[29] These tenets of liberalism were shaped by gender and race, even—or perhaps particularly—when they appeared to be universal. It is by charting changes as well as continuities in liberal discourse that the gender and racial underpinnings of this universalism become clear. The fact that people as diverse as E. Franklin Frazier and Lillian Smith articulated these beliefs, and that events like the murder of the black teenager Emmett Till and films like *Imitation of Life* expressed them, does not mean that all of these were equally or identically "liberal." But this diversity is meaningful; it is the contradictions in any discourse that give it, in the words of one scholar, "a tenacious power over people's thoughts and actions."[30] That is because significant recurrences alongside contradictions convey how and why ideas dispersed and assumed dominance.

To speak of liberal *discourse*, then, is to refer to this *process*: one through which different texts from various social, cultural, and political arenas produced, circulated, and sometimes contested intertwined assumptions about gender, race, and liberalism. As historians who have been influenced by discourse theory have explained, discourse means more than literal language. It refers to a system of ideas and practices, including individual behavior and institutional policies, which help to produce material reality.[31] With this methodological perspective, this study incorporates a range of sources that have often been treated separately, from "high" to "low" culture, from political to popular culture, and from intellectual ideas to social practices and policies. It considers intersections between scholarly debates *about* women, gendered and racial assumptions in welfare policies *toward* women, and popular representations *of* women. *Motherhood in Black and White* analyzes paradigmatic texts that proved particularly influential at the time and in subsequent decades—E. Franklin Frazier's *The Negro Family in the United States* and Arthur Schlesinger Jr.'s *The Vital Center* are two examples. But it also recovers certain voices and texts that have been overlooked or marginalized. For example, Mamie Till Bradley, an activist in her own right, figures in civil rights histories, if at all, only as Emmett Till's mother rather than as a political figure herself. *Because* of the ways that images of mothers in these different kinds of narratives overlapped, they assumed ideological and political power. Representations of women as mothers that at first might seem to be beyond the realm of politics implicitly and explicitly helped to shape liberal policy, just as policies were also texts or narratives that reflected and produced cultural assumptions about liberalism.[32]

This methodological framework also serves as a reminder that aspects of individual or group identities that are easy to take for granted or that seem "natural" and unchanging do in fact get produced. If categories that are so tied up with an individual's identity—like being a mother, being black, or being white, for example—are less than natural, if they take shape in particular ways at specific moments, then individuals themselves are part of this process, a process that is never wholly hegemonic or without dissent. It is worth adding, however, that the focus here is not on women who negotiated the minefield that ideas about motherhood presented to them.[33] Instead *Motherhood in Black and White* accounts for how and why this minefield—a common matrix of thought about the dangers "bad" mothers posed to the nation—developed in scholarly, popular, and explicitly political arenas in relation to liberalism.

This book is best understood, then, as a cultural history of the central role that racialized representations of motherhood played in mid-twentieth-century liberalism. The sources that this study juxtaposes *constituted* liberal discourse, as it was repeatedly renegotiated from the New Deal through the Cold War and into the Great Society. Indeed, a history of American liberalism looks very different when the contradictions of race and gender at the heart of liberal discourse receive consideration, and when gender becomes part of the story of liberalism's relationship to race.

CHAPTER ONE

"The Women Have a Big Part to Play"

Citizenship, Motherhood, and Race in New Deal Liberalism

At the end of John Steinbeck's best-selling Depression-era novel *The Grapes of Wrath*, the young woman in the family of displaced "Okies" draws a starving man to her breast to nurse him. It is a powerful image. The woman's baby was stillborn, and she is very frail. The girl-turned-woman, Rose of Sharon, and her mother, the strong and ever-sustaining Ma Joad, conceive of this idea at nearly the same moment: after the starving man's distressed son has approached them, and as their menfolk stand by, "helplessly gazing at the sick man."[1] This concluding action is only the most vivid in a novel which suggests in myriad ways that female behavior enabled beleaguered families—and beleagured men specifically—to survive the assaults of an unprecedented Depression.

In the 1930s, a time of economic, social, and political uncertainty, the family as an "ultimate community" was in crisis. *The Grapes of Wrath* foregrounded this sense of crisis as well as the widespread assumption that women determined how and if families would cope with the turmoil of the Depression. Eleanor Roosevelt was just one among many who believed that, "the women have a big part to play if we are coming through it successfully."[2]

Ma Joad may have helped those around her survive this "great crisis," but other fictional women behaved differently. The film *Gold Diggers of 1933*, for example, featured acquisitive women who used their sexuality to trap rich men. In the opening number, the women appeared dressed as gold coins and sang "We're in the Money." The decade's most famous film heroine, Scarlett O'Hara, struggled through the Civil War and Reconstruction, often at the expense of her family and her femininity. Most Americans assumed that women's actions were potentially destructive to families. In 1936, 82 percent of respondents in a Gallup Poll agreed that married women who worked outside the home were "thieving parasites" who took "jobs that rightfully belong to the God-intended providers of the household."[3]

12

It seemed that women might—or crucially, might not—live up to Eleanor Roosevelt's vision of them.

The assumption that women had a big part to play during the Depression surfaced in a variety of novels, films, documentary studies, and other narratives in the 1930s. But this notion of women sustaining families was particularly relevant to liberalism, as it was reconceived and reinvigorated in that decade. If families were to overcome hunger, displacements, and rampant unemployment, and if liberal democracy itself was going to overcome challenges from the left and from the right, then gender relations in which Ma Joads and Rose of Sharons outnumbered gold diggers were imperative. As Barbara Melosh argues, in liberal discourse specifically, "heightened concern for family stability . . . found cultural expression in a reaffirmation of traditional gender ideology."[4]

Both Ma Joad and the gold digger conveyed profound anxieties about masculinity. The Depression and the widespread unemployment it spawned was a crisis for families, in the view of many Americans, precisely because of its effects on men. " 'I ain't no good anymore,' " says an unemployed, homeless, and otherwise ineffective Pa Joad. " 'Funny! Woman takin' over the fambly. . . . An' I don' even care.' "[5] In passages such as this, Steinbeck was among those who indicated that unemployment was more than an economic problem; because it threatened male authority, in and out of the home, it transformed the fabric of family and national life in its entirety.

Although citizenship always had gendered dimensions, the relationship between masculinity, citizenship, and liberalism had heightened significance in the 1930s.[6] The Depression undermined traditional understandings of masculinity in ways that were linked to assaults on liberalism in this period. Liberals themselves were not certain that an emerging welfare state could provide a safety net without eroding authority and individual initiative among men, or that "relief" from the federal government would help families get back on their feet rather than further emasculating American men. Nor was it clear whether New Deal liberalism inspired confidence among a largely male unemployed workforce, many of whose families were hungry and homeless.[7] Amidst this sense of diminished manhood and alongside a perceived crisis in liberalism, the family came to function as a yardstick for measuring political health more than as a private or self-enclosed unit. Resolving a perceived crisis in the family required resolving a perceived crisis of masculinity, and both of these moves were necessary to bolster liberal democracy.[8]

If liberal discourse required stable and traditional gender relations in the 1930s, it also increasingly deemed stable race relations a precondition to political security. A number of changes contributed to a political and intellectual reassessment of race. Black voters, many of them recent migrants to northern and western cities, shifted their support to the Democratic party in dramatic numbers during the decade.[9] As white liberal politicians became more aware of the potential power of black voters, more worked, even if only rhetorically, to include black citizens in their version of the New Deal. "In no national election since 1860," observed *Time* magazine, "have politicians been so Negro-minded as in 1936." Eleanor Roosevelt was perhaps the most prominent white public figure to speak out on behalf of civil rights, but by Franklin Roosevelt's second term other New Dealers did so as well.[10]

International events made the implications of racial hatred still more troubling. The rise of fascism and the Nazi party in Europe reinforced fears that a depression could foster a uniquely dangerous social and political situation; political events abroad suggested that large-scale economic downturns and the expression of violent racial hatreds were related. Riots in Harlem in 1935 were among the disturbances that brought such fears home. They provided glaring "proof" that economic instability could have frightening repercussions, and that racism was neither a regional aberration restricted to the South nor a non-American phenomenon.[11] American liberals committed to guarding against political extremes on the right and the left felt compelled to consider race relations as part of their more comprehensive social agenda.

Thus in the altered landscape of the 1930s there was a growing sense among liberals that a secure democracy required stable race relations (of a certain kind) and stable gender relations (of a certain kind). These ideas about gender and race were not unrelated, however—to each other, or to the anxieties about the survival of families that John Steinbeck tapped into so powerfully in *The Grapes of Wrath*. What *kind* of gender and race relations would reinforce political stability according to liberal discourse requires further consideration.

Analyzing the role of mothers in liberal depictions of families from the 1930s illuminates relationships between race and gender within New Deal liberalism. Liberals in the 1930s facing what they felt was a crisis in liberalism and in masculinity sought to redefine the relationship between families, government, and capitalism as part of their project. But liberal texts that engaged with intensified concerns over families contained a paradox. Although social scientists, writers, and politicians worried that men no longer able to serve as breadwinners weakened families and the nation, many analyses shifted attention away from the behavior of men and to the *mis*behavior of women. As a result, black and white women who were either "good" or "bad" mothers figured prominently in liberal discourse. Their behavior was one potential solution to interrelated political and gender instability.

Three different types of liberal narratives about families—popular, scholarly, and political—all hinged on images of women as either good or bad mothers. *Imitation of Life* was a successful and overtly antiracist film released in 1934. This popular melodrama targeted female audiences and featured white and black women who sacrificed to save their families and be good mothers. In the work of progressive social scientists who studied white and black families, "good" mothers were few and far between; indeed, when women misbehaved, they endangered citizenship, the health of families, and race relations. Debates about social security legislation are a third arena illuminating intersections of gender and race in New Deal liberalism. Male and female politicians and reformers offered images of women as either good or bad mothers as they created landmark New Deal policies designed to help struggling families and safeguard future citizens.

These popular, scholarly, and political texts were hardly identical or consistent.

Some praised women who worked for wages, while many others condemned working women. Yet all these texts—the film, progressive scholarship, and policies—were part of a liberal discourse linking political and personal problems (as well as solutions) to each other.[12] All these texts maintained that dire economic conditions or racial inferiority were not permanent conditions but were subject to progress. All struck a balance between affirming the importance of the individual and that of collective measures. And ultimately, all located sources of political problems, including economic stress and racial inferiority, not in a socioeconomic political system but in families. There, white and black women's behavior assumed a new significance. Images of white and black mothers shaped debates about what responsibilities an American welfare state should assume and framed the tensions between an activist and a restrained state that underscored New Deal liberalism.

But what were the tensions in New Deal liberalism? What did concerns about families, black and white, have to do with these tensions? And did the New Deal offer anything new, or better, to black or white women, or to black men?

New Deal liberalism was designed not only to bring about an economic recovery (though surely that was important). It also sought to restore confidence—in families, capitalism, liberal democracy, and American citizens. Given this multiplicity of goals, it is not surprising that the reconfiguration of liberalism in the 1930s had many, sometimes contradictory facets. With its emphasis on individual liberty and *self*-help, New Deal liberalism owed much to classical liberal theory. Many liberal politicians and the policies they enacted emphasized independence and self-reliance and ultimately excluded Americans who did not seem to fit into these categories. Yet liberalism in the 1930s simultaneously carved out a far greater role for the state to ensure *collective* liberty and to provide all American citizens with a safety net.[13] The power of New Deal liberalism stemmed from the ways it bridged these contradictions and negotiated these tensions.[14]

Perhaps because of the contradictory nature of New Deal liberalism, it has been difficult to assess its impact on black and white women, or on black men. Scholars have shown that many women grew more politically active during the Depression, and some amassed a greater degree of political and social power. Professional women helped create social security legislation, working-class housewives organized successful collective actions, and other working women participated in radical politics. Popular culture, from New Deal-sponsored photography to Hollywood films, celebrated female strength and fortitude.[15] But these "successes" could not alter the fact that as unemployment and economic distress swept through the country, the conditions in which most women lived worsened. White and black rural women were among the thousands of displaced migrants who did not know where they would sleep from night to night, or how they would feed their families. Thousands of white working women were fired from their jobs because of a widespread panic that they were "taking" jobs from men. Public attacks on women escalated, and organized feminism was discredited.[16] For every courageous and praiseworthy

Ma Joad there was at least one money-hungry gold digger or conniving Scarlett O'Hara.

Some scholars of American race relations have emphasized how the 1930s marked a turning point in the liberalization of race relations. As New Deal policies appealed to black Americans, the white "solid south" became less solid. Members of Roosevelt's "Black cabinet" received significant coverage in the black press, while in popular culture, images of African American men and women were increasingly dignified.[17] But the same New Deal liberalism that assisted some black Americans also institutionalized discriminatory labor practices against black men and women. Rural black families suffered disproportionately as a result of agricultural policies. And even progressive representations of African Americans in political and popular culture continued to assume racial deviance or subordination.[18]

Analyzing how white and black women as mothers functioned in liberal discussions of families can clarify the relationship between these apparent gains and losses. Ideas about motherhood underlay the formation of a more racially inclusive New Deal liberalism. The paradox is that these same ideas helped to explain how and why race remained marginal to New Deal liberalism. Ultimately, identifying women as good or bad mothers became one means of resolving social disorder and affirming liberalism during the Depression.

"How Can You Hurt Your Mother Like This?": Good Mothers and Prosperity in *Imitation of Life*

Americans flocked to the movies in the 1930s. Although profits declined briefly after the stock market crash, by 1934 business had revived and attendance was up. Previously closed theaters reopened during this golden age of Hollywood, as "talkies" replaced silent films. In confusing times, movies were more than merely an escape. Films brought audiences together and "at least appeared to help them comprehend their own world," as one historian has explained. A variety of genres captured the attention of moviegoers: gangster films like *The Public Enemy* (1931) and romantic screwball comedies like *Bringing Up Baby* (1938); horror films like *King Kong* (1933) and socially aware films like *The Grapes of Wrath* (1940).[19]

And then there was the "woman's film" or melodrama. Melodramas targeted female audiences specifically; part tragedy and part social realism, they evoked tears and centered on motherhood, female self-sacrifice, and the private sphere.[20] Critically scorned, many were enormously popular moneymakers. The film *Imitation of Life*, released in 1934 and based on a novel by Fannie Hurst, was one such success story. *Imitation* was the "most shameless tearjerker of the Fall," according to the *New York Times*. Yet, with an air of near puzzlement, the *Times* review noted that audiences "seemed to find it a gripping and powerful if slightly diffuse drama which discussed the mother love question, the race question, the business woman question, the mother and daughter question and the love renunciation question."[21]

The Universal production that fans loved and critics mocked received an Oscar nomination for best picture in 1934.

As the *Times* indicated, *Imitation* was a film that brought together pressing personal and social questions and filtered them through the lives of women. What appeared to be simply a sentimental maternal melodrama was unusual in the ways that it affirmed both financial security *and* interracial harmony. It did so by focusing on black and white motherhood, an uncommon emphasis in films generally, and especially in a genre typically the province of white women. Emblematic of a widespread focus on motherhood and yet relatively unique in its pairings—of black and white women, and of typically "segregated" themes of race and gender—*Imitation of Life* is worth a close look.[22]

Audiences who paid about twenty-five cents to see *Imitation of Life* in 1934 encountered two protagonists: the white, widowed Bea Pullman and the black, unmarried Delilah.[23] The women form a household together in the 1920s. Delilah gains a home and takes care of Bea's daughter and her own child, while Bea sells maple syrup door to door. Bea transforms Delilah's family pancake recipe into a marketable commodity and, against many odds, opens a restaurant. Soon after, the entrepreneurial Bea makes "Aunt Delilah's" a packaged mix. She runs the "family" business, and Delilah cares for the children and makes pancakes.

The film then jumps ten years ahead into the 1930s. A flashing neon "Aunt Delilah" announces that thirty-two million boxes of pancake mix have been sold in one year. The women's interracial home moves from the back of an Atlantic City storefront to a fashionable New York City townhouse. Signs of a flourishing consumer and producer economy are everywhere—from the elegant clothes that Bea now wears, to the boxes upon boxes of mass-produced pancake mix moving along on conveyor belts. Bea falls in love and plans to marry, but her daughter falls in love with her fiancé. Meanwhile, the light-skinned black daughter, in an effort to "pass," runs away from home to work as a cashier.[24] The two heartsick mothers must address these problems. Delilah dies, but her prodigal daughter, weeping and loyal, returns during the funeral. To preserve her relationship with her own daughter, Bea ends her romance and returns to the business she had considered selling.

Through Bea Pullman, director John Stahl countered negative portrayals of white women common to the 1930s and carved out a middle space between Ma Joad and the gold digger. The film never shows Bea as money-hungry or promiscuous. She is neither a spoiled and selfish Scarlett O'Hara nor an earth mother like Ma Joad. Bea works alongside men and succeeds in the public sphere, but her business acumen does not even jeopardize her femininity. When she first meets her potential mate, her feminine allure belies his assumptions about "big businesswomen," and he is smitten.

In certain respects, the film also departs from one-dimensional and explicitly racist depictions of black women. Delilah, initially an unemployed and homeless single mother, saves enough money for her daughter to attend a "Negro college" and for a grand funeral. Hurst herself argued that the film considered "the Negro as part of the social pattern of American life," and many in contemporary audiences, as well as subsequent film scholars, agreed. A columnist in *The Crisis* asserted that "as propaganda favoring the American Negro in his struggle for recognition as a human being, no picture has been as effective." Stories that circulated in the black press about how actress Louise Beavers resisted racism in the script and on the set amplified the view of Delilah as challenging the status quo.[25] Though Delilah speaks with a heavy dialect, flips pancakes with aplomb, and calls her fellow mother "Miss Bea," she is an "anti Aunt-Jemima," in the words of one critic, and utters "the film's most political sentences."[26]

Imitation of Life may not overtly demonize its women as did other Depression-era narratives, yet failure is an ever-present possibility for both Bea and Delilah. Director John Stahl affirms the potential for female success only by invoking the possibility of maternal failure and by punishing both women to varying degrees. The daughters' problems, which come to dominate the plot, do not emerge out of the blue: the film fixes their origins in the two mothers. In Delilah's case, desexualized hypermaternalism contributes to her daughter's deviant racial desires and efforts to pass. Observers in the 1930s reacted to the ways that Delilah literally envelops her young daughter into her vast expanse, failing the girl as a result. According to one critic in 1934, "the mother had a way of forcing herself on her daughter."[27] Bea hardly forces herself on her daughter; instead her multiple interests beyond the home, including her loyalty to Delilah, contribute to the young woman's inappropriate sexual desires for her mother's mate. "I hate to run away like this," says Bea (again) when she asks her fiancé to look after her daughter while she and Delilah hunt for the light-skinned daughter who has run away.[28] Though the sources of failure differ and the relationship between the women is unequal, the potential for mothers' failures cuts across lines of race and class. Both women get in the way of the development of appropriate femininity in their daughters.

Even if the white woman's untraditional behavior yields economic security and apparent harmony, it does so only as the result of ongoing racial hierarchies. The white Bea is a female—and feminine—Horatio Alger whose success neither hurts her family nor takes jobs from men. Yet she is able to be a relatively unconventional heroine only as this seemingly antiracist film squashes challenges to the racial order. The interracial harmony that the film seems to offer is but another imitation. The women may share a desire for a secure home, for example, but a spiral staircase in the townhouse splits their domestic haven. After one intimate chat, Bea ascends to her room, while Delilah descends to hers, leaving only a view of the staircase that separates them.[29] Even at the outset, Bea takes in both Delilah and her daughter with words that simultaneously diminish and widen the divide between them. Delilah, says the slender Bea, is "just 200 pounds of mother fighting to keep her baby"—another instance in which Delilah's maternity, body, and physicality define her identity in racially specific ways.[30] When Bea forces Delilah to pose—smiling

Bea Pullman (Claudette Colbert) assures Delilah (Louise Beavers) that her runaway daughter will return by reminding Delilah of what all mothers share: "A few hard knocks and she'll come running back to her mother. That's what mothers are for." Courtesy of the Museum of Modern Art / Film Stills Archives.

broadly in a large white hat and apron—for a photograph as the icon of the new business, she commodifies Delilah's body and the image of her as a nurturing black mother. Again and again, assurances of racial place through motherhood mitigate this "Boston marriage" of two unmarried working women.

The successful pancake business that Bea builds and Delilah so literally embodies reflects New Deal liberalism's emphasis on a national consumer economy and the increasing mechanization of household production in the 1930s.[31] It also, however, conveys New Deal liberalism's more "humane" goals for race relations and the role of women in this ethos. It is Bea, after all, who insists—over Delilah's protests—that her "partner" receive a whopping 20 percent share of the booming business.

Consequently, when the two daughters are poised to reject their mothers, there is more at stake than simply mother-daughter relationships. The young women threaten this interracial female community in which the white woman controls the finances and the black woman flips pancakes; they threaten the *interdependent* racial, economic, and gender order. In failing to elicit appropriate expressions of femininity in their daughters, Bea and Delilah endanger the social fabric more generally.

Despite the social ramifications of the daughters' protests, the film codes these conflicts as maternal and private. The black daughter repeatedly tries to reject her subordinate racial place, but Bea transforms her sociopolitical protest into a maternal issue: "How can you hurt your mother so?" she asks. "How can you make her suffer this way?" Delilah urges her daughter to "submit" to blackness and does not implicate anyone or anything in her pain. "It ain't her fault, Miss Bea," she explains. "It ain't yourn, and it ain't mine. I don't know rightly where the blame lies. It can't be our Lord's. Got me puzzled." Both women see the desire to imitate whiteness as an individual problem that would disappear if the young woman attended a Negro college. Both resolve their daughters' conflicts in ways that reinforce the sense that these are merely personal problems that mothers should take care of within the family.

The end of *Imitation of Life* confirms this vision. Delilah's funeral separates the black and white women and reunites mothers and daughters along lines of race. Having broken her engagement, Bea is once again single. When she notes in the final scene that the black daughter is at the Negro college, the film further reasserts racial difference; the flashing neon Aunt Delilah in the final frame links the resolution of personal conflicts to the now restabilized racial and economic order. *Imitation* ends as it begins: with Bea and her daughter together in their again all-white single-sex home. All the characters know their place and their race. Like Delilah, Bea restores harmony—though at far less cost.

Imitation of Life displaced overlapping political anxieties regarding race relations, gender roles, and economic health onto the two mothers. In some respects, both Bea and Delilah consequently emerged as sympathetic, if not heroic. The genre itself offered its largely female audiences capable women who set and met goals. This critically scorned woman's film that triggered "stentorian sobbing" from the urban "matinee trade" assumed political significance in part because of the ways that women actually solved social problems.[32] Mothers in the film were sources of potential social disorder but not of pathology exclusively. At the same time, however, Bea and Delilah consistently suppressed any political protest regarding race and gender relations. This burden lay particularly heavily on Delilah, who had to die in order for these problems to be resolved and contained. Further, *because* this text made adult women the repositories for social problems, the Depression, unemployment, and institutionalized racism were subtexts. Small wonder that Delilah remained puzzled about who or what to blame.

Far from Hollywood and afternoon matinees, motherhood remained a preoccupation. Could anyone achieve the American dream of wealth through hard work? What role should white and black mothers play in this dream? What would happen to migrating black women in the urban north? These questions generated alternative and contradictory answers in studies of white and black families.

They are "Aggressive and Very Efficient" and "Take Sex More Lightly": Scholars Look at White and Black Families

In 1938 Robert Lynd declared that "our contemporary world is losing its confidence in the inevitability of Progress." In fact, wrote the sociologist and author of the best-selling *Middletown*, a study of middle-America in the 1920s, "men's ways of ordering their common lives have broken down so disastrously as to make hope precarious." Lynd, a "part-time New Dealer," offered a solution to this crisis: committed intellectuals who took up relevant social issues could make hope less precarious for themselves and for others. Their scholarship could help Americans cope with the strain and uncertainty in their lives.[33]

Sentiments like Lynd's help to explain why research on white and black families and communities escalated in the 1930s. During the Depression, social activism, intellectual endeavors, and artistic experimentation were increasingly intertwined.[34] Studies of families were part of an impulse to document the "real" in ways that mattered and that were original. Some projects attempted to relieve the strain and uncertainty that Lynd noted by offering reassurance and by suggesting that ordinary folk were coping with unemployment or downward mobility. Others focused on hardships and tensions within families to signal all that was wrong beyond the immediate world of any one family and to highlight the need for comprehensive reforms on the part of the federal government. But whether they soothed or sounded an alarm, liberal intellectuals who took up these issues implied that progress was possible. They avoided abstractions and engaged contemporary problems as part of their belief that individual behavior and social conditions could improve. Studies of families employed approaches that ranged from photojournalism to statistical profiles. Amidst this diversity was the conviction that effective social science research and state policies could reinforce each other—and be a source for social reform and progress.[35]

Since early in the twentieth century, eminent scholars—including Franz Boas, Robert E. Park, Ernest W. Burgess, and Edward Sapir, among others—had influenced a generation of social scientists with approaches that were cultural, relativist, and psychological. They and their students emphasized the need for accurate data and scientific expertise. Yet anthropologists, sociologists, and others also went beyond empiricism and scientism to consider how individual personalities developed within larger networks of intersubjective relationships, communities, and cultures. A considerable amount of scholarship in the 1930s built upon these foundations, exploring the social and psychological effects of the Depression *in relation to each other*. Disciplinary divides did persist, of course. Nevertheless, experts from a variety of disciplines incorporated an eclectic blend of sociological, anthropological, and psychological perspectives to investigate families and communities.[36] Many studies of white families and unemployment, for instance, were based on home visits and extensive psychiatric-oriented interviews of family members rather than simply statistical data. Though less avowedly psychological, Robert and Helen Lynd and their field staff submerged themselves in "Middletown" life for over a year before writing the follow-up study, *Middletown in Transition*. Margaret Hagood, a sociologist, spent sixteen months in the homes of white tenant farmers in her effort to capture their voices and perspectives in *Mothers of the South*.[37]

When Lynd described socially relevant research, he called for scholarship that would "deal with the white-hot core of current controversy, where passions are most aggravated and counsel most darkened."[38] The stark racial imagery of these words may have been unintentional, but it was illuminating. For liberal scholars of American race relations—that "white-hot" topic where "passions" had indeed "darkened"—were among those actively involved in interdisciplinary family and community studies. Both Robert Park and Ellsworth Faris had done influential race relations research at the University of Chicago in the 1920s; in the decade that followed, former students and others took race relations research in new directions. The social sciences appealed to racial liberals in the interwar years; an ethos of scientific objectivity allowed them to integrate a commitment to social reform and a desire for professional authority.[39]

John Dollard, a social psychologist, and E. Franklin Frazier, a sociologist, were among the most influential scholars who studied black families and communities in the 1930s. They did so in pathbreaking studies that challenged beliefs in biologically based racial hierarchies and assumptions of innate black inferiority. In doing so, both rejected a crucial foundation for the second-class citizenship historically foisted upon African Americans.[40]

John Dollard joined the interdisciplinary Institute of Human Relations at Yale University in 1932. He had recently completed graduate work at the University of Chicago and analytic training at the Berlin Psychoanalytic Institute. In 1935 Dollard, who was white, "headed for this open country" of the South, as he later put it, for a five-month sojourn in a community he dubbed "Southerntown." The result was *Caste and Class in a Southern Town*, a work that drew on Freudian and socioeconomic theories to analyze relations between blacks and whites of different classes and castes. Caste, he and other theorists explained, was the divide that separated racial groups into social systems regardless of material conditions or economics.[41] Dollard argued that no inherent qualities kept blacks either impoverished or insecure. Rather, caste and class barriers together helped to produce the inferior status in which Southerntown's blacks lived. "This is not just another book on the Negro," wrote Robert Park, who praised *Caste and Class*. It was a "magnificent study," wrote another reviewer, and in the judgment of one historian, the book was "the decade's most influential case study of race relations in a single community."[42]

E. Franklin Frazier was one of several black graduate students who studied sociology under Robert Park and Ernest Burgess at the University of Chicago in the 1920s (he and Dollard overlapped there). Frazier received his graduate degree in 1931, while he was teaching at Fisk University in Nashville. In 1934 the already prominent black sociologist became chair of the sociology department at Howard University, the leading all-black university in the country at the time. Like his mentors, Frazier believed that assimilation was possible in the urban north; at the height of the Depression, he also advocated interracial unionism and denounced institutionalized racism in New York City agencies.[43] In *The Negro Family in the United States* Frazier synthesized and extended his earlier work, offering a sweeping historical analysis of black families from Africa through contemporary migrations into urban areas. By charting the fate of black families' interactions with dominant white society since slavery, Frazier offered two major arguments: that many—though not all—black families had been stripped of the cultural resources necessary to cope with racism; and that differences between races could eventually diminish. He drew on subjective "life histories" as well as demographic data to explain that environment rather than biology or race per se played a significant role in social problems that included crime, poverty, and more.[44]

This "most important contribution" was significant for its universalism as well as its empirical rigor, according to Frazier's many fans. Despite its title, *The Negro Family in the United States* shed light on "the understanding of the family in general. It is in fact, the most valuable contribution to the literature on the family" in twenty years, wrote Ernest Burgess. As several reviewers noted, with its attention to differences among black Americans, Frazier's study would "check the too frequent tendency to assume that it is possible to generalize about the Negro." *The Negro Family in the United States* won the Anisfeld Award as the most significant work on race relations in 1939.[45]

These studies by Dollard and Frazier, with their psychosocial, sociohistorical, and always interdisciplinary analyses, influenced decades of liberal antiracist scholarship. Historians continue to disagree over Dollard and Frazier's intentions and politics, as well as the long-term implications of *Caste and Class* and *The Negro Family in the United States*. These books set the terms of debates among liberals about black families and black-white relations that are with us still, and they influenced progressive intellectuals from the 1940s into the 1960s especially.[46]

Thus political, intellectual, and personal reasons compelled liberal intellectuals interested in white and black families to heed Lynd's call for relevant research. An overview of literature on white families and closer scrutiny of Dollard and Frazier's work on black families reveal why gender mattered in this liberal discourse.

Relationships between men and women proved to be an important clue for progressive scholars who investigated white families as a way to gauge the strength or weakness of American democracy in the Depression. Traditional gender roles in which the woman was supportive wife and mother, and the man retained at least some qualities associated with the independent wage earner and father, provided evidence that families remained "organized" or "integrated."[47] In *Middletown in Transition* Lynd argued that even though the Depression had brought "latent conflicts" regarding "men's and women's roles" to the fore, the "different and secondary role" of Middletown's white women was "largely unchanged" since 1925. Mirra Komarovsky, a sociologist, made a similar point when she suggested that unemployed men lost status in their families only in *previously* "unsatisfactory marriages." And according to Margaret Hagood's study of tenant farmers, even in rural families struggling to make ends meet, it was "almost universal . . . that the wife doesn't 'tote the pocketbook.' "[48] Such observations suggested that male authority in the home could withstand the stresses that unemployment posed and could persist even when families received relief.[49] Further, by defining "normal" families as "white families only" which included "father, mother and the child," many scholars obscured the racial specificity of their subject; in fact, they were producing ideas about who and what was an acceptable or normal family and who and what was a healthy citizen.[50]

Reassurance was not always possible for experts in the 1930s, as many concluded that male authority had declined in white families. To describe such men, they used images and terms associated with femininity. Evidence for "disorganization" in one such family was a father who "cried in relating his situation to the case worker." Experts who deemed families unable to cope with the Depression cast fathers as "high-strung" or as lacking "emotional stability."[51] According to these studies, many unemployed white men could not achieve the necessary balance between a desire for individual independence and the need for group solidarity. Some exhibited too extreme a commitment to abstract notions of independence. The father who refused to go on relief but became violent because of economic tensions was selfish or immature. Other men exhibited extreme passivity, a lack of autonomy, and disinterest in work; such behavior also hurt families. Regardless of which extreme men occupied, their identities as men specifically, and not just their livelihoods, were in jeopardy.[52]

The feminization of men had interpersonal as well as economic sources. Progressive scholars implicitly and explicitly suggested that overly aggressive and ungenerous white women (often referred to as simply "mothers") were catalysts for synonymous crises of masculinity and family. Many a wife "thinks it is her husband's fault that he is unemployed" and undermined him by withholding sex, according to one observer.[53] Women assuming "masculine" prerogatives were particularly "disorganizing." Two experts invoked the tragedy of an unemployed man who killed his wife and then himself. The case history began, "In the Beczkowski family the mother was aggressive and very efficient." It was *she*—and not the labor market—who wreaked psychological havoc: "When her husband lost his job, she could not believe that he was unable to find work. . . . The mother became suspicious of her husband. Mr. Beczkowski became very much discouraged . . . He felt that she did not care for him. The crisis came one evening when he asked his wife for $10 with which to leave the city. When she refused to give him the money, he shot and killed her, then himself."[54]

Many white women were less drastically implicated in "disorganization." Yet scholars consistently invoked female behavior as a factor that contributed to family problems ranging from divorce and anxious children to physical dislocations.[55]

Given how many Americans assumed that married women who worked outside the home harmed their families, it is not surprising that many experts also criticized working women. According to Robert Lynd, such women were also superficial. "It appears to be for more than bread alone that its [the town's] married women leave their home to work," he wrote. Images of women and girls as sexualized and as insatiable consumers, (desiring "rouge and brightly covered fingernails," for example) recurred in this literature and echoed popular if inaccurate assumptions that women's earnings were supplemental.[56] Experts did point to exceptions, noting that some white mothers who worked outside the home (like the fictional Bea Pullman) helped their families adjust to economic hardships. They praised "the shifting of roles as well as of family functions" and suggested that the Depression potentially made families more thrifty, loyal, intimate, and democratic.[57] Yet even praise for alternative arrangements suggested that unorthodox gender roles were acceptable only if they were temporary and did not undermine the more fundamental and enduring nature of masculinity and femininity.[58]

In general, ideas about normative gender roles pervaded discussions of white families. Some experts argued that gender roles had not changed all that dramatically. Others assigned blame for changes to "bad" women who were either overly masculine or frivolous. Some conflated unstable families with "femininity" in men. These approaches were not mutually exclusive.

Even though the Depression had motivated many social scientists to study families, their point of view minimized the seriousness of long-term socioeconomic conditions. Whether mothers drove their partners to suicide or to overly-expensive apartments, whether they worked hard outside the home or harder inside the home, in many of these texts political and economic issues remained something of a backdrop. It was primarily women (their personality disorders or their strengths) who prevented or enabled families to respond to the external stresses of the Depression. Either political and personal troubles had been exaggerated—evidence being the endurance of patriarchal gender arrangements—or they were "just" the fault of women and did not reflect a national crisis.

At the same time, analyzing families and communities in this manner legitimated New Deal federal assistance and the large-scale planning so important to the administration in the early 1930s. Margaret Hagood's study of tenant farm women, *Mothers of the South* (1939) was a summons to action. In light of the urgency of the problems she saw among tenant farm families, there was "no basis for laissez-faire optimism." For Hagood and others, scholarly research and New Deal policies were potential tools with which to restore families, masculine authority, and the nation to health. As Lynd explained, the "interjection of Federal planning into the local scene" was a source of hope. Centralized intervention showed that "some problems cannot be coped with on a basis of self-sufficient local autonomy."[59] Just as men should not be overly independent from other family members, families themselves should not be overly independent from the federal government. In this liberal scholarly discourse, constructing women as relevant to family instability allowed intellectuals to affirm the viability of families and of masculine autonomy, as well as the viability of New Deal liberalism.

This gendered logic was also a salient feature of Dollard's and Frazier's landmark antiracist analyses of black families, even though their work, too, was not primarily concerned with women. Constructing women as "bad mothers" buoyed arguments in *Caste and Class* and *The Negro Family in the United States* that under the right circumstances black men could be independent wage earners and, by extension, would be productive citizens and have stable families.

In *Caste and Class* Dollard interwove psychological categories and analyses of individuals (and their dreams) with economic categories and social analyses. Repression, displacement, frustration—these were the watchwords for the damaging effects of a Jim Crow class/caste system. The stakes were high in Dollard's psychosociological analysis: Jim Crow placed the psychic, social, political, and economic health of blacks *and* whites at risk. *Caste and Class* exposed the dangers that the southern caste system posed, and it illuminated the psychological and economic pleasures that the racial hierarchy afforded. With this approach Dollard demonstrated the need for change even as he suggested how difficult it would be to achieve.

Gender shaped this analysis in several ways. Like studies of white families, *Caste and Class* associated rationality, independence, and wage earning with masculinity. Dollard entered "Southerntown" determined to gather information in an objective and systematic manner. If anything, he acknowledged his suspicions of prejudiced whites. Nevertheless, he identified almost immediately with the hardworking, rational, white male. White townspeople treated him with "immediate courtesy," whereas he regarded friendly blacks as "devious." The former's "well-painted . . . and neat" homes were but one indication that a "sense of discipline and order is more apparent."[60] By contrast, his very first impressions of " 'nigger town,' " were that "here the houses are small and cheap": "Walking along the street, one sees the flash of a big white bed . . . A well-cropped lawn is a rarity, as is a well-built house. . . . Behind the houses the frequent privies testify to the fact that these people are not wholly included in our modern technology."[61]

The bed as the site for sex was the first object Dollard allowed his readers to see in blacks' homes. It was a sign of the dirtiness, disorder, and familial disorganization so important to his analysis of many black families. In another instance, Dollard suggested that picking cotton was "backbreaking" and poorly paying work for blacks. Yet he could only conclude that white landowners were "as automatically caught in this socio-economic situation as are the colored." He argued that only "those who have correct working habits involving abstinence and foresight" could receive "economic justice." Those who "do not have these habits, as the lower-class Negroes do not, would have to be trained by force to have them."[62] The value that Dollard placed on abstinence, foresight, and other "correct working habits"—qualities that he and others associated with white men in the workforce—emerged despite his progressive analysis of labor.

Significantly, Dollard did not regard the absence of these qualities in black men as inevitable. Instead, he explained black men's temporary deficiencies by drawing on Freudian analyses of family dynamics. Because so many black men could not support their families, he noted, black women had to work for wages. As women worked, they became economically independent, which caused a "weak, mother-centered family" and made "the hold of the Negro man on his woman . . . institutionally very weak."[63]

In contrast to the desexualized black woman in *Imitation of Life, Caste and Class* relied on images of hypersexualized black women. For Dollard, all too often, "economic independence carries with it the usual correlate of sexual independence"; as a result, black women often dominated black men emotionally. Further, many reacted "more responsively and permissively" to white men's "overtures." In fact, he said, such black women "take sex more lightly altogether."[64]

The antiracist Dollard cautioned that "the image of the Negro woman as inveterately sexual may or may not correspond with the facts." Despite this disclaimer, he reinforced the stereotype. For instance, when he explained asssumptions among whites that black women were "as accessible as animals in heat and always ready for sexual gratification," he presented this "belief" as one of several possible perspectives. Even more significantly, *Caste and Class* emphasized the psychological dimensions of sexual relationships between white men and black women in ways that deemphasized power relationships. Middle-class blacks who regarded sex between white men and black women "as virtual assaults" were "defensive"; they underestimated "wishes for pleasure." "Undoubtedly," Dollard concluded, "wishes for transitory gratification are a factor in the accessibility of Negro women." By contrast, "one cannot take a cavalier attitude toward the problem of attacks on white women by Negroes; they undoubtedly do occur and under circumstances that are especially terrifying."[65]

Caste and Class was less concerned with black women, inveterately sexual or not, than it was with the effects such women had on men. Dollard explained that black men responded to black women with feelings of jealousy, rage, and frustration and behaved in one of two ways: some men repressed their rage, and some displaced it onto other blacks. Repression was evident in deferential behavior, laziness, and political apathy. It contributed to a poor work ethic and to a "renunciation of protest or aggression against undesirable conditions of life." Black men who displaced their rage onto other blacks also weakened the black community. Both responses, repression and aggression, (and they could coexist) increased "Negro disunity" and impeded productive social change.[66]

Healthy black men and healthy black communities, suggested *Caste and Class*, would only develop if men assumed greater control in their families. But black wives and mothers often stood in the way of that development. Although *Caste and Class* did not focus extensively on "matriarchy," it assumed that as a result of maternal behavior, sons could not learn to exercise authority. The absence of healthy masculine aggression recurred one generation to the next. "It is not very likely," wrote Dollard, "that the children will develop along lines different from their parents." In another instance, in the absence of data, Dollard simply asserted that if more "extensive histories of lower-class Negroes were gathered . . . it seems very likely that the role of the mother would emerge much more strongly and that of the father less strongly than in the middle class group."[67]

Caste and Class did not discriminate in at least one respect: Dollard offered less-than-flattering assessments of white and black women. In an effort to understand how and why prejudice developed in whites, he focused on white men's relationships with white women. He explained that prejudiced white men suffered from Oedipal traumas and from childhood "controls on sexuality" that their repressed mothers had imposed. "Impulses everywhere meet with taboo and control." The white adult was "a record of these frustrations"—and sought an outlet for them. Black men provided an outlet for white men's frustrations and black women provided one for their sexual desires. Indeed, virile white men "would hardly be expected to pass this challenge [of a black woman] by."[68]

Dollard's characterizations of white women differed substantially from those of black women. In asserting that white women were sexually repressed, he reasserted black women's ostensible sexual expressiveness and "freedom"; *Caste and Class* set these two models of racialized female sexuality in opposition to each other, and used the one to define the other.[69] At the same time, however, Dollard's analysis rendered women *across lines of race* central to emotional problems in men and social problems in the region.

Caste and Class marked an important step forward in studies of black families. Dollard was not trying to assign blame. He was well aware that many "normal outlets for aggression" were unavailable to southern black men. When he observed that it was "part of wisdom for the Negro to suppress his resentment," he dismantled the image of the black man as innately passive. Dollard also acknowledged the dire economic factors that compelled black women to engage in wage work, and he was sympathetic to the stresses black female domestics experienced.[70] Yet he *still* suggested that this labor made women dominant in harmful ways. He still regarded apparently excessive submission in black men with suspicion—and as evidence for both psychic and political instability. He simply could not untangle assumptions about gender from his psychological and economic analyses. Along with many other liberals in the 1930s, he assumed that healthy economies and healthy families *must* be organized around a male wage earner and that certain kinds of mothers were obstacles to this process. Unlike many of his contemporaries he applied this gendered vision of citizenship to black men.

Like John Dollard, E. Franklin Frazier was committed to salvaging black masculinity and black men as citizens, and he did so in ways that evoked the dangers of femininity and maternal failure. Frazier too defined independence, initiative, and rational self-control as evidence for healthy masculinity and viewed dependence, passivity, and irrational emotionalism as signs of femininity in men. In *The Negro Family in the United States* the "Negro problem" was that only "a favored few" black men were sufficiently masculine. Historical circumstances had contributed to these deficiencies. Emancipation was a "crisis" because it was "bound to create disorder and produce widespread demoralization." Some ambitious Negroes did succeed after the Civil War. In contrast to the "drifting masses" who were "left without any restraint," successful Negro men were wage earners, landowners, and heads of families. They controlled "wild desires" with "character," "self-direction," and a "permanent interest in marriage." They balanced individual needs with collective interests. And a "feeling of solidarity and some community of interest" emerged precisely because of "the subordination of the woman in the economic organization of the family."[71]

The majority of African Americans, as Frazier characterized them in *The Negro Family in the United States*, were " 'exulting in the unrestraint of the liberty.' " During transitional periods particularly, "unrestraint," or negative freedom, had severed bonds between men and families and ruptured the balance between individual desire and communal social controls. This concept of "unrestraint" guided Frazier's analysis of black migration in a chapter he titled "In the City of Destruction." Physical mobility had "emancipated" migrants "from the most elementary forms of social control." It contributed to the disunity, chaos, and demoralization of black families in the urban north.[72]

In discussing the variables that made black families "disorganized" and made it difficult for black men to develop healthy masculine identities, Frazier focused on maternally organized families. Historically, he explained, black women had tended to dominate the family; they were also sexually active. In the rural South, this behavior had not necessarily been destructive because it was accompanied by "a more fundamental interest" in children and networks of women who helped each other.[73] It was in the shift from the rural South to the "city of destruction" that motherhood became a source of crisis, according to Frazier. When "the simple folkways of these peasant folk" broke down, poor and dominant black mothers emerged as a primary cause of ongoing inequality and as transmitters of "loose behavior" from generation to generation. What had been "The Matriarchate"—matrifocal rural families where extended kin networks of dominant and sexually active but capable women cared for children—became "Outlawed Motherhood," a far more problematic matriarchy.[74] Poor single women who were "outlawed" mothers in urban settings were corrupt and corrupting, diseased and infectious. The increase in syphilis "undoubtedly originated through the contacts which the men had with women in logging camps and cities. . . . As the women in these rural communities move about and come into contact with the outside world, illegitimacy loses its harmless character. . . . It becomes a part of the general disorganization of family life, in which the satisfaction of undisciplined impulses results in diseases and in children who are unwanted and uncared for."[75]

Frazier located promiscuity as a cause of social disorder in black women. It was *women* for whom "sexual contacts continued to be of a more or less casual nature."[76] In discussing urban prostitution, *The Negro Family in the United States* did not dwell on male patrons of prostitutes but quoted women prostitutes generously: " 'I kept having guys. I'm honest, I like it. I sure can give it and I can take it, too.' " Or, " 'I don't lay every pair of pants that come along . . . I only grab a drunk if he looks like his pockets are loaded with dough.' " While some women prostitutes, according to Frazier, had been psychologically scarred by their own mothers, others demanded that "their 'daddies' keep them entertained by taking them to the cinema and the cabarets.' "[77]

Thus, in this declension history of migration, black women and femininity sig-

This illustration from *The Negro Family in the United States* linked traditional gender arrangements to racial progress: the bare-chested and muscular black man holds a tool and is in the foreground, while the black woman in the background looks down on a baby. Copyright © Hilda Wilkinson Brown, courtesy of Lilian Thomas Burwell.

nified the vice and sexual deviance that enveloped many black neighborhoods. Consider the linkages and juxtapositions in the following passage, in which Frazier described the streets of Negro communities:

> painted and powdered women, resembling all the races of mankind, with lustful songs upon their lips, rub shoulders with pious old black charwomen. . . . Strutting young men, attired in gaudy clothes and flashing soft hands and manicured fingernails, jostle devout old men clasping Bibles. . . . one sees men and women with tired black faces staring vacantly into a future lighted only by the hope of a future life, while beside them may sit a girl with her head buried in a book on homosexual love. . . . [78]

In Frazier's view, the postmigration mother clearly transmitted degeneracy. She did not do so genetically or biologically but instead inflicted damage in more complex ways. At times she did not want or care for her illegitimate children; Frazier described the mother who "sometimes kills her unwanted child by throwing it in the garbage can." Some mothers sustained the "elemental maternal sympathy" common in rural communities. Still, even this "elemental" love could be "detrimental to the welfare of the children" because it made it more difficult for the next generation to form nuclear families in which men had authority.[79]

A contradictory attitude toward black motherhood structured *The Negro Family in the United States*, one similar to that in *Imitation of Life*. The rural matriarch remained an ideal of sorts for Frazier; her literal and figurative death in the urban north anticipated social problems. At the same time, the southern rural mammy had to be relegated to the past. In the urban north of the 1930s, she created turmoil more than she offered tranquility. In any case, it was black women who perpetuated female dominance and promiscuity, masculine weakness and, through the production of disorganized families, ongoing racial inequities.

Though their methods differed (Dollard was far more psychoanalytic, for example), both Dollard and Frazier combined analyses of gender, race, motherhood, and sexuality in such a way as to equate female sexuality with female dominance, and both with racial inequalities. *Caste and Class* and *The Negro Family in the United States* were among the books that drew causal relationships between sexuality, women, and racial inferiority. Ironically, Dollard's and Frazier's progressive views on race—a disavowal of biologically based theories of race and personality—allowed them to make these connections. Replacing insidious scientific theories of racial difference with environmental and psychosocial analyses, they reasoned that black women as mothers created the inferiority of feminized African American men; black women's bodies and behavior required regulation for race relations to improve. Now the old paradigm which had suggested that African Americans were feminized pervaded a new discourse on race which emphasized environment, culture, and personal histories over biology. Now women's behavior rather than innate factors caused this feminization.[80]

Despite the bleak images of black families and race relations that dominated *Caste and Class* and *The Negro Family in the United States*, neither book was wholly pessimistic. Dollard and Frazier held out hope, just as studies of white families did. Frazier argued that the "city of destruction" might also be a "city of rebirth." Black families' disorganization might give way to a reorganization based on working-class identities and self-respect. As class-based identities developed and assimilation progressed, racial differences would diminish.[81]

Constructions of women as bad mothers facilitated a sense that change was possible: if maternal dominance diminished, healthy gender relations could develop in black families. Black men could be independent wage earners and productive citizens who controlled their wives, and race relations would then improve as well. Making motherhood a problem of (male) citizenship enabled *Caste and Class* and *The Negro Family in the United States* to argue that a civilized black population could come to participate more fully in American life. To varying degrees, both Dollard and Frazier demanded that the vision of citizenship evident in discussions of white families and New Deal policies be more racially inclusive.

Focusing on the private sphere of the family and ensuing depictions of dangerous women helped make this racially inclusive vision possible. Yet, as in *Imitation of Life*, this framework took little account of concrete political demands. Even as Dollard drew attention to the discriminatory racial division of labor, his own logic made him skirt the inequities he had exposed. As he concluded, "the race issue can be faced only after the more fundamental family problems have been solved."[82]

The movie characters Bea and Delilah and their business and domestic partnerships appear more reassuring when considered in the context of the recurring anxieties expressed by scholarly studies of the time. The worst fears in studies on families were not realized in the film. *Imitation*'s portrait of Bea suggested that a working white woman could overcome poverty and maintain an organized family. Bea's sumptuous clothes and home did not make her one of the frivolous consumers that Lynd and others derided. Her material well-being attested to her femininity and to her participation in the country's healthy consumer economy.

Delilah, too, invoked yet departed from images of black women in the scholarly discourse. Country ways—a strong dialect and belief in the power of a rabbit's foot—positioned her as one of the female migrants about whom Frazier was so clearly anxious in *The Negro Family in the United States*. Her daughter's "pappy" had "beat his fist against life," a quality that echoed scholarly descriptions of unrestrained black men and perhaps explained Delilah's status as a single mother. Yet, in the midst of the Depression, Delilah affirmed the alleged universalism of the American Dream: the possibility of some degree of social mobility for those who worked hard, and the possibility of interracial "harmony"—as long as she remained subordinate to Bea. The gospel-singing Delilah was not among the "painted and powdered women . . . with lustful songs upon their lips" who populated Frazier's urban landscape. Nor was she a displaced black sharecropper moving across the eastern seaboard in search of temporary work, or a black woman at an urban street corner "slave market" waiting for a white woman to offer lunch and thirty-five cents for six hours of work.[83] Both women's stories were similar enough to contemporary life to evoke anxiety, yet different enough to offer reassurance.

In scholarship about families, as in *Imitation of Life*, ideologies about gender and race were entwined. It was through *gendered* hierarchies that progressive experts like Dollard and Frazier offered reassurance about race relations and affirmed their liberal belief in progress. And it was through *racial* hierarchies that *Imitation of Life* offered reassurance about gender relations and affirmed that same belief.

These representations of white and black families developed amidst more widespread efforts on the part of New Dealers to solve social problems and restore faith in families and government. National reform policies that affected families, like progressive scholarship, were based on the belief that concerned and committed experts could strengthen families. Even as *Imitation of Life* focused on the potential for women to be good mothers, New Deal policies mobilized competing images of women as good or bad mothers as part of its reform agenda.

"To Rear Them into Citizens": Good and Bad Mothers in the New Deal

Imitation of Life and progressive scholarship about families were liberal testaments to the possibility of personal and political health. They achieved their aims by privatizing pathology and presenting images of women as either good or bad mothers. This privatization accomplished a great deal: these texts at once obscured social inequities of power even as they emphasized the economic and social obstacles that families faced and summoned a newly activist federal government to address them.

New Deal policies produced related meanings of family and citizenship. The New Deal created and reflected ideas about what kinds of families and citizens the federal government should assist, and on what basis they should receive such assistance. Gender and race were critical to these constructed meanings of families and to related images of women as mothers and of men as husbands/fathers/citizens.[84] Images of masculinity and femininity come into focus in the Social Security Act of 1935 and related legislation.[85] But discussions of race among New Dealers also produced gendered conceptions of citizenship and family. Understanding New Deal social security legislation and racial politics in relation to each other illuminates the inclusiveness as well as the limitations of New Deal liberalism and clarifies the role that ideas about motherhood and masculinity played in both.

On August 9, 1935 Congress passed the Social Security Act. The eleven titles in this landmark legislation included Unemployment Insurance and Old Age Insurance (OAI) as well as Public Assistance and Aid to Dependent Children (ADC). Liberals who supported this bill believed that the federal government had the power and the responsibility to make life better for more citizens "on a permanent and not an emergency basis," according to one. An activist federal government was providing an estimated thirty million additional Americans—men, women, and children—with a safety net as it addressed the needs of the elderly, the sick, the unemployed. "An important milestone has certainly been passed," wrote *The New Republic*.[86]

Seeking to heighten the sense that this was a historic moment and a positive step forward for the country, President Franklin Delano Roosevelt used several different pens as he signed the bill on August 14. (He later bestowed presidential pens on those who had helped get the legislation passed.) Roosevelt was well aware that this legislation was controversial. Editorials suggested that the "objectives at which the bill aims are now generally accepted by enlightened opinion," but critics abounded.[87] Many argued that the bill gave the federal government far too much power—that "undigested Congressional bills with uneconomic tendencies" hurt business and could even undermine "the thrift habits of our people." Others felt the legislation had not gone far enough. Some critics were more specific: "The Negro stands definitely to lose more than his white brother."[88]

As some speculated at the time, this liberal legislation was not nearly as universal as it may have first appeared. FDR vetoed noncontributory benefits that would have entitled all citizens, as individuals, to receive social insurance funds. He opted for a contributory program that allowed only former workers in certain kinds of jobs to receive benefits. They earned these benefits based on their years in the workforce. Consequently, a bifurcation between old age insurance to which wage earners were "entitled"—or *social security*, as it came to be known—and assistance for needy but potentially less deserving Americans—or *welfare*, as it came to be known—was built into the Social Security Act.[89] As Linda Gordon and Nancy Fraser have explained, social insurance created "the misleading appearance that beneficiaries merely got back what they put in." In contrast, ADC reinforced images of dependence and "created the appearance that claimants were getting something for nothing."[90]

This bifurcation seemed natural enough because the men and women who designed social insurance and public assistance programs assumed that a welfare state and a family-wage system should go hand in hand. In the family wage ideal, male heads of households were supposed to support their families, or " 'tote the pocketbook,' " as Margaret Hagood put it.[91] Not surprisingly, then, family wage-oriented policies allowed male heads of households to benefit the most from the Social Security Act, privileging male wageworkers and certain kinds of wage work.

The emphasis on a family wage had several effects on white and black women. For one, OAI and Unemployment Insurance excluded domestic and agricultural workers. Consequently, the scope of insurance policies was limited to the industrial workforce where white men dominated.[92] Second, entitlement programs in the Social Security Act that strengthened white male wage earners in the industrial workforce came on the heels of other initiatives that did target women workers. In 1932, amidst widespread critiques of working white women, Congress passed the Federal Economy Act. Officially, section 213 of this legislation prohibited any two family members from working for the civil service. Under this law, which remained in effect until 1937, over one thousand married women employees were fired. Many state laws and unofficial policies accomplished on a local level what this act did nationally; school boards, in particular, often fired women teachers if they married.[93]

Race and class determined the impact that these and other policies had. The Federal Economy Act, for example, primarily eliminated middle-class white women from the ranks of the civil service. By contrast, other policies effectively compelled less financially secure black women to remain in the workforce. Some southern New Deal administrators restricted federally funded (and better-paying) work programs to whites, insisting that black women continue to work as cotton-pickers, laundresses, or domestics.[94]

A Social Security Act that excluded women in some respects and regulated them in others took shape in relation to images of women as good or bad mothers. This was most evident in the Aid to Dependent Children program. ADC alternatively valorized and vilified mothers. According to one report, ADC was "designed to release from the wage-earning role the person whose natural function is to give her children the physical and affectionate guardianship necessary not alone to keep them from falling into social misfortune, but more affirmatively to rear them into citizens capable of contributing to society."[95]

As this passage suggested, the federal government established a program to provide assistance to needy women with children because it assumed that the task of mothering was a crucial one—for individual families and for the country as a whole. With an even greater reach than mothers' pensions and other reforms earlier in the century, ADC affirmed the power of motherhood and the work that women did in the home. By offering economic assistance, it also provided more options to needy women with children, including, for example, those of not marrying and leaving an abusive relationship.[96]

But these protections presumed that mothering was women's "natural" role. Accordingly, ADC could penalize women who did not fit this image of motherhood or who were "unnatural." As in *Imitation of Life*, ideas about (and policies certifying) good mothers worthy of ADC took shape against those that pertained to bad mothers. For example, Congress declared the moral character of potential recipients a basis for considering eligibility; numerous provisions rendered some kinds of mothers more deserving than others. As Grace Abbot, a longtime reformer and advocate for poor women argued, if programs assisting mothers were to succeed, "it is necessary to establish by investigation the need of the mother and her moral and physical fitness to maintain the home." Under such guidelines, in the years between 1935 and 1939, widows were far more likely to receive ADC on behalf of their children than were divorced, deserted, or never-married women with needy children.[97] Throughout the 1930s and into the 1940s, the program funded children only. ADC did not directly allocate funds to support the dependent child's mother even though it failed to assist her to become a wage earner. Such a woman might, after all, spend federal funds unwisely and selfishly—on consumer goods for herself, perhaps. She might become comfortable or independent without a male breadwinner.[98]

Moreover, New Deal liberals implemented the assistance program in racially specific ways. Because the New Deal permitted states to establish local guidelines, state administrators were able to exclude black women from the ranks of ADC; they were more likely to do so systematically in southern states where the black population was highest.[99] "Suitable home" and "employable mother" rules were among the provisions that local white administrators used to disqualify black women and keep them in a poorly paying workforce. One white woman public servant, writing in the 1930s, revealed that very few black women received ADC because of "the unanimous feeling on the part of the staff and board that there are more work opportunities for Negro women. . . . The attitude that 'they have always gotten along,' and that 'all they'll do is have more children' is definite . . . [lay boards] see no reason why the employable Negro mother should not continue her usually sketchy seasonal labor or indefinite domestic service rather than receive a public assistance grant."[100]

This passage echoed several significant themes and images that consistently recurred from *Imitation of Life* through liberal research on black families: the strong black woman whose commitment to her family and ability to "get along" or "succeed" was suspect; the sexualized black mother who bore unnecessary and uncared-for children; and the working black woman who was not a deserving mother because she worked, but whose labor was nonetheless undercut through references to its "sketchy" and "indefinite" nature (not "real" work). Here one sees how such images had a concrete impact on women.

The chasm between so-called deserving and undeserving women widened in 1939, when Congress passed amendments to the original Social Security Act. At that point, wives and widows became entitled to receive financial assistance from the federal government through Old Age Insurance (OAI) rather than through ADC. This left ADC to provide for families headed either by unmarried, divorced, or deserted women.[101] According to the advisory council that recommended the transfer of widows from the ranks of ADC assistance to social insurance, ADC was simply "insufficient to maintain normal family life or to permit the children to develop into healthy citizens. . . . Social insurance offers an improved method of dealing with the problem." The majority of women who benefited from this "improved method" were white; less than 2 percent of all women who received OAI in 1940 were black. And the council did not speculate about how women who remained dependent on "insufficient" ADC payments would offer their children a "normal" family life or raise them into independent "healthy citizens." This group consisted of white and black women with children who, by definition, were not "normal": either they had never been married, were divorced, or were married to unemployed men. These women might well raise children who themselves would be dependent. They might—or might not—be allowed to receive aid, or "welfare," from the federal government.[102]

The New Deal consolidated these assumptions and made discrimination against black women a given, based on the exclusion of domestic and agricultural labor from key pieces of protective labor legislation—including the original Social Security Act. As a result of these exclusions, 90 percent of working black women gained nothing from this pioneering legislation. Within New Deal liberalism, black women were seen—and equally significantly not seen—as outside a sexual division of labor, as Jacqueline Jones has explained.[103] Their work, like that of Delilah, was effaced yet taken for granted, their status as mothers both presumed and maligned.

To be sure, New Deal policies discriminated against black men as well as black women.[104] But the New Deal affected black men and women differently. The circle of New Dealers who opposed racism to varying degrees, including Harold Ickes, Will Alexander, and Aubrey Williams, among others, was able to make the masculine and individually based vision of citizenship inherent in the Social Security Act available to black men in some crucial respects. The model of citizenship that New Dealers offered African Americans potentially included black men in a "universal" community of citizens. As an editorial in the NAACP magazine *The Crisis* explained, the "specific benefits" that blacks could expect from the New Deal derived from its attention to "the man in the street above everything else, whether that man is black or white."[105]

Indeed, according to antiracist New Dealers, focusing on racial difference was counterproductive—particularly relative to questions of economic reform that they preferred.[106] They argued, moreover, that blacks should work to overcome their own tendency to perceive themselves as different. Sounding very much like John Dollard, Will Alexander explained that only when black industrial workers overcame *their* "assumption of separateness" and stopped perceiving themselves as "Negro workers" would "inferiority complexes which are the result of generations of segregation and discrimination . . . be rooted out."[107] Ickes offered a vision of ostensibly color-blind citizenship based on wage earning in a speech titled "The Negro As A Citizen," which he gave to the NAACP in 1936. He avowed, "Under our new conception of democracy, the Negro will be given the chance to which he is entitled—not because he will be singled out for special consideration, but because he preeminently belongs to the class that the new democracy is designed especially to aid."

Ickes sanctioned inclusion as long as it did not veer into a desire for "special consideration."[108] Clark Foreman, the "Negro adviser" in the administration, expressed similar sentiments. He responded to black leaders critical of discriminatory labor practices in National Recovery Administration codes by arguing that the government should "ignore" black workers "as a racial group"; blacks stood to gain the most if they would "act as workers and consumers."[109]

The ideal "Negro as a citizen" that antiracist New Dealers envisioned was a wage earner who was neither too submissive nor too aggressive and was a productive member of the national community. Invoking the very same (intertwined) criteria for citizenship and masculinity that experts on families did, Ickes praised black citizens with a strong sense of individuality, who were "forthright" and "self-respecting." He applauded "Negro leaders" for "not asking the Government to coddle them." Yet Ickes also offered accolades to leaders' "faith," "loyalty," and "lack of resentment." He reminded African Americans that "hatred is a venom which . . . incapacitates the person who generates it." Like scholars writing about white families, Ickes sought to balance independence and the need for community. And, in terms very similar to those of John Dollard and E. Franklin Frazier, Ickes and other antiracist New Deal liberals sanctioned assertiveness in black men as long as it never veered into excessive anger—or premature demands for integration, for that matter. After all, "meek submission" Ickes explained in a speech to the Urban League, was "one of the great virtues of the Negro race as well as one of its great faults."[110]

The racially inclusive universalism of New Deal liberalism rested on these gendered constructions of citizenship. Political historians and other scholars have long observed that the "new deal" for blacks stopped well short of support for race-based policies. They have demonstrated that despite the significant shift of African Americans to the Democratic Party in the 1930s, explicit questions of race relations were never central to the liberal agenda. In just one of many examples, the administration's lack of support for a federal antilynching bill was notable. To the extent that New Deal liberals addressed discrimination at all, they did so through their focus on economic reform.[111] The political realities of urban black voters versus southern white Democrats who dominated important committees contributed to this pattern of supporting rights for blacks while avoiding concrete race relations policies.

Yet more than political opportunism was involved here. Again, gender is a key to understanding the inclusiveness and restrictiveness. Because of the ways that New Deal liberalism accommodated the "forgotten man" and seemed to speak to African Americans as individuals who could participate in liberal capitalism and improve race relations, it simultaneously thwarted efforts to improve the lives of African Americans as a racial group. Although the New Deal may have "had little to offer blacks in particular," this lack of particularity and de-emphasis of racial difference was significant because it encompassed Americans across lines of race.[112] This inclusiveness reflected both the actual and the symbolic attention that the New Deal gave to citizens in need and helps to explain the popularity of the Democratic administration among African Americans.

The resonance of New Deal liberalism's alleged inclusiveness inhered in making racial difference an individual and private issue and in making citizenship evoke attributes of gender. If racial differences resulted from individual personalities and families, they were not a national problem or responsibility. There was a reason, then, that the social and economic problems African Americans confronted required no specific attention or intervention on the part of the federal government. This liberal ethos echoed the message in *Imitation of Life*, where Delilah worked and saved money for her elegant funeral while living in Bea's basement but could only say that she didn't "know rightly where the blame lies" and accept segregation. It also expressed itself in John Dollard's declaration that "the race issue can be solved only after the more fundamental family problems have been solved." Progressive social policies, like progressive scholarship, reproduced images of hardworking men as a seemingly inclusive category—and as the key to the success of the family, the race, and the liberal welfare state.

Dividing white and black women into "good" and "bad" mothers expressed and re-solved the intertwined crises of liberalism and families in the 1930s. According to liberal discourse, a perceived crisis in masculinity and potentially dangerous women posed personal as well as social problems. These problems required some attention from an activist welfare state. At the same time, because mothers were supposed to solve these problems (as in *Imitation of Life*), a more restrained view of the welfare state developed, particularly with regard to questions of race. Thus, casting women as good or bad mothers was one means of resolving social disorder and affirming the possibility of progress—including racial progress—in the 1930s. Representation of white and black women served this common function across lines of race, even though the images themselves were racially specific. Gendered imagery in liberal discourse helps to explain how and why (paradoxically) a newly activist state remained restrained, and how race, in particular, was circumscribed within New Deal liberalism.

The frightening "bad mother" as a mirror image to the nurturing "good mother" steeped in domesticity is a cultural stereotype that is easy to associate with the political right and that many scholars link to post-World War II America.[113] Important sources for this familiar stereotype in the modern era lay in the 1930s, however. In this period concerns about the survival of the family converged with concerns about the survival of liberal democracies and with an increase in psychologically informed analyses. In this context, images of women as mothers became central to liberal narratives that fo-cused on the need for economic mobility, family harmony, and financial security.

In the 1940s the tendency to represent women as bad mothers became even more widespread, as did efforts to understand social issues in psychological terms. By understanding how these impulses were part of New Deal liberalism, we can un-derstand how and why they assumed greater currency after the Depression. We can also consider the relationship between images of white women as "moms" and black women as "matriarchs" and the functions that these images served in the con-text of World War II, postwar prosperity, and the burgeoning of racial liberalism.

CHAPTER TWO

Racism as Un-American

Psychology, Masculinity, and Maternal Failure in the 1940s

A dramatic voice-over introduces *Home of the Brave* as a film about "one American." Released in 1949, *Home* chronicles the wartime relationships between this "one American"—a wounded black private, Pete Moss—and his fellow white soldiers, all of whom have been on a dangerous mission together. Over the course of the film, a white psychiatrist cures Moss of various ailments. Not only does Moss recover from hysterical paralysis and amnesia, he also overcomes his own "disease" of "sensitivity" and forges positive relationships with white men. By the end, the black soldier even understands that many white peers "make cracks" about him because "down deep underneath, they feel insecure and unhappy too." As Moss notes with a sense of wonder and conviction, "everybody's different. But so what? Because underneath, we're all guys."[1]

Home of the Brave was part of diverse and widespread efforts among antiracists in the 1940s and 1950s to expose the psychic toll that prejudice exacted, on both African American "victims" and on white Americans "suffering from" prejudice. This dual focus—on whites ostensibly afflicted with prejudice as well as on blacks subjected to prejudice—helped to redefine racism as undemocratic and un-American. In the New Deal era, liberalism had largely subordinated problems of race to questions of class, economics, and individual opportunity. By contrast, in the 1940s and 1950s liberals came to view prejudice as a psychological problem *and* a problem of citizenship; with this shift, race relations became a more dominant component of liberalism.

Ideas about gender, and about motherhood specifically, played a role in this psychologically informed racial liberalism. Images of black and white women as mothers were central to the process through which "racism as un-American" became a dominant liberal paradigm. This chapter centers on the work of liberal social scientists, critics, and public intellectuals, for the scholarly arena articulated the shifting

40

emphasis in liberalism in particularly clear terms. Some progressive intellectuals explored the psychological *sources* of prejudice in whites, while others studied the psychological *effects* of it on blacks. It is worth keeping in mind, however, that the idea of racism as un-American and the related focus on the psychological damage inflicted by prejudice cut across disciplines and genre. As *Home of the Brave* indicates, it permeated popular and political discourse.[2]

A psychologically oriented racial liberalism was gendered in two ways. First, this discourse suggested that certain kinds of mothers created racial prejudice in whites and perpetuated ostensible pathology in blacks. Second, progressive experts were concerned that racial hatred weakened American masculinity. They were preoccupied with white and black *sons* whose mothers failed them psychologically and who, therefore lacked the codes of masculinity necessary for healthy and productive citizenship.[3] Prejudice, enabled by white and black mothers, undermined the ideal male citizen—the citizen who, like the protagonist of *Home of the Brave*, could say with confidence that "we're all guys."

Masculinity and the Birth of "Momism"

Quite aside from questions about race relations, concerns about masculinity were endemic in the war and post-World War II years and had everything to do with motherhood. For instance, it was a perceived and alarming weakness in the "American man" that led the journalist Philip Wylie to write *Generation of Vipers* in 1942, the book in which he gave birth to the term, or more accurately to the "condition," of "momism." Wylie used Freudian and Jungian theory to explain the apathy that he saw in men; he concluded that the "mealy look of men today is the result of momism." According to *Generation*, "moms" were (implicitly) white women whose apparent maternal love masked their narcissism and desire for power. Their "policy of protection" led to a "possession of the spirit of a man" akin to "slavery." Not content to describe "moms" as all-powerful "middle-aged puffin[s]" guilty of "parasitism" and of destroying their "captive sons," *Generation* also charged them with being like Hitler, controlling the American economy, and manipulating the war to advance their agenda.[4]

In 1947, five years after Wylie wrote *Generation*, and as the country was shifting from a war against fascism to a Cold War against communism, Marynia Farnham, a psychiatrist, and Ferdinand Lundberg, a journalist and sociologist, took up similar themes in *Modern Woman: The Lost Sex*. Like Wylie, Farnham and Lundberg believed that women created men's deepest problems. Neurotic modern women who rejected their "natural" roles were responsible for an "epidemic of neurosis" and were "the principal transmitting media of the disordered emotions that . . . are reflected in the statistics of social disorder." Their frequent failures as mothers contributed to a "slaughter of the innocents."[5]

Generation of Vipers and *Modern Woman* were both enormously popular. In 1950 the American Library Association selected *Generation* as one of the major works of nonfiction in the first half of the century; the award-winning book went through twenty printings by 1955 and elicited thousands of responses from readers. Farnham and Lundberg, quoted and interviewed widely, became leading authorities on the "lost sex." Inadequate mothers, Lundberg said in 1949 (he estimated approximately 33 percent of all mothers), constituted "just about the No. 1 problem of the country." Even critics engaged with such ideas because of their influence.[6] Both books helped to transform the white "bad mother" from a convenient scapegoat during the Depression to a menacing, sexually deviant, and ubiquitous figure in a time encompassing war, increased prosperity, and uneasy peace.

Images of bad white mothers mushroomed in advice manuals, scholarly treatises, films, and cartoons in part because they could explain virtually all that was wrong with the country—and with men. During the war, for example, experts argued that women raised sons who were unfit soldiers; after the war experts suggested that women made it harder for veterans to adapt to civilian life, or raised men who were susceptible to communism.[7] Moreover, any number of activities or attitudes could cause women to fail in the role they were supposedly destined to occupy. Women who were bad mothers were too indulgent or they were too strict; they were frivolous and obsessed with consumption, or they were "drab" and obsessed only with their children.[8] Wylie, Farnham and Lundberg, and others popularized competing and overlapping theories of "maternal overprotection" and "maternal rejection" that psychiatrists had developed from the 1930s onward.[9]

One quality was consistently attributed to women who failed as mothers: sexual dysfunction. Women might be frigid or they might be promiscuous, but they were inevitably sexual failures. Their failures as women and their failures as mothers were one and the same, and experts equated both with failures at sex. In certain respects, the 1940s were marked by a degree of sexual liberation. Issues of sexuality entered public discourse more easily, and notions of female sexual pleasure gained some degree of acceptance. Experts qualified this liberation when they tied female sexual pleasure not only to marriage and heterosexuality, but to motherhood. As Farnham and Lundberg explained, "for the sexual act to be fully satisfactory to a woman, she must, in the depths of her mind, desire, deeply and utterly, to be a mother." They went on to avow that the woman who could not realize this desire did not understand that her role in sex was "passive. It is not as easy as rolling off a log for her. It is easier. It is as easy as being the log itself."[10]

Such excesses make it tempting to regard "momism" as a conservative impulse, or as a *reaction*—to the anxieties that shifting gender mores generated.[11] During World War II, for example, greater numbers of white married women worked for wages, and women's opportunities for both heterosexual and homosocial relationships increased. Mother-blaming was one way to contain these changes. After the war, the threat of white maternal rejection bolstered efforts to "free" the workforce for returning white veterans as experts urged working women to relinquish their jobs for the sake of their children. An emphasis on maternal failure also intersected with a postwar culture of conformity, when cold war witch-hunts triggered fears of the enemy within.

The bad mother, however, was a contradictory and even ironic figure. Certainly, texts like *Generation* and *Modern Woman* revealed overt misogyny and efforts to regulate women. Nevertheless, it is important to consider both the premises on which mother-blaming was based and what its ethos enabled. For one, images of women as bad mothers functioned in close relation to a celebration of motherhood that also prevailed in this period. Wylie and Farnham and Lundberg would in all likelihood have agreed with the popular anthropologist Ashley Montagu when he argued that women had the responsibility for teaching "*men how to be human.*" Montagu's *The Natural Superiority of Women* as well as advice literature, films, and early television shows offered images of good mothers—fulfilled women who by nurturing their children nurtured their husbands and, ultimately, themselves.[12] "What does a woman see when she uses lipstick?" asked an ad for *McCalls*. The words of the question appeared in the mirror of a compact. The answer: "she sees herself, of course—but herself in relation to what others, especially those closest to her, think about her . . . *When Jim Jr.'s Cub Scouts say, 'Hey, your Mom's O.K., I'll be more thrilled than I was at my first prom* . . . this is the way she lives today—in close togetherness with her family."[13]

Glorified images of motherhood were not limited to white women. "Goodbye Mammy, Hello Mom," declared *Ebony* in 1947, heralding the alleged postwar retreat of black women to the home. A commentator in the black press gave thanks that "Junior" has "been getting his bread and butter sandwiches regularly after school" and had found "that rip in his blue jeans mended when he goes out to play." This celebration of black motherhood was not identical to that of white motherhood. In fact, an emphasis on black women as good mothers countered white-defined racial stereotypes.[14] Nevertheless, this pro-maternal ethos narrowed women's options even when (as was the case for black women) it was marshaled to resist racism.

Indeed, however different they appeared, "good" and "bad" mothers, white and black, were closely related and evoked similar anxieties. Praise for mothers and criticism of them insisted on the centrality of women to the private sphere and on the centrality of the private sphere as a source of psychological health. Moms, mothers, and matriarchs—these were three prominent icons in the 1940s through which psychology, gendered ideals, and racial liberalism converged to redefine masculinity and to redefine the ideal American citizen.

Despite associations between momism and conservative or reactionary impulses, mother-blaming was not incapable of constituting liberal intellectual discourse.[15] Momism was not born amidst a post-World War II backlash, and it was not restricted to middle-class white women who needed to be "contained" in the suburban domestic sphere. Mother-blaming, we have seen, had been important to liberal analyses of families in the 1930s. It became still more common in major liberal analyses of prejudice and authoritarianism in the 1940s and 1950s.

"Frustration and Aggression": Psychology, Families, and the Fight against Prejudice

After writing about "Southerntown" in the 1930s, John Dollard remained interested in relationships between social systems and individual personality development. In 1939 he and a team of researchers at Yale University involved in what became known as culture and personality research published *Frustration and Aggression*. This study articulated an extremely influential paradigm: that "*aggression is always a consequence of frustration.*" The collaborators argued that dangerous expressions of aggression between people and between nations (they cited lynching and war on the first page) must be understood in the context of irrational frustrations that developed in childhood.[16]

Although *Frustration and Aggression* met with criticism as well as praise, even its critics noted the "brilliant experimental work" the authors brought to the project.[17] In the coming years, the notion that frustration caused aggression and had insidious ramifications became a common point of departure among scholars and others. A range of intellectuals argued that frustration turned into excessive aggression and contributed to crime, juvenile delinquency, and a host of other social ills. Or it turned into insufficient aggression, or submission, and contributed to passivity, poor work habits, and still other social ills. Analyzing personal sources of frustration became a precondition for understanding behavior that was "*distinctively* democratic, fascist, or communist."[18]

Psychosocial frameworks oriented around frustration and aggression provided sociologists, anthropologists, psychiatrists, and others with nonbiological methods to explain how individual and national identities developed. If they could figure out how emotionally stable individuals took shape, then perhaps they could ensure social stability. Progressive experts self-consciously wanted to make the leap from studying individual identities to assessing national characters, citizens, and political systems. Throughout the 1940s prestigious and popular works linked childhood experiences of frustration and aggression to the kind of citizen the child would become.

The focus on childhood brought motherhood to the attention of experts concerned about future citizens. In *Childhood and Society*, for example, Erik Erikson outlined the developmental stages through which autonomous identities formed; as he pinpointed the obstacles to that process, he focused considerable attention on the mother-child dynamic. Benjamin Spock's *Baby and Child Care* became the bible for thousands of parents seeking information about "permissive" childrearing. Spock's approach promoted democratic methods for raising psychologically healthy citizens who were neither too compliant nor too recalcitrant. But as Spock explained, it was as a result of effective mothering that the three-to-six year-old boy curbed his aggression and "acquires much of his desire to be cooperative with men, brave in danger, courteous to women, faithful to a job, just as his father is."[19] Erikson and Spock may have used far less sensational language than did Philip Wylie, but like him, they and other liberal intellectuals hoped to avoid the "mealy look of men today" that Wylie had identified in *Generation of Vipers*.

International events in the 1940s made race a more prominent category in discussions of frustration and aggression. As German armies spread through Europe, Americans concluded that unhealthy aggression was an emotional disorder that was politically dangerous well beyond American borders. These were years of the Holocaust and genocide, when the dangers of excessive racial and ethnic hatred emerged starkly. As atrocities inflicted in the name of "racial purity" became known, intellectuals and others asked how individuals had ever developed these violent hatreds and how willingly cruel, excessively aggressive, and authoritarian personalities came into being. (They did so even as some experts worried that American soldiers were not sufficiently aggressive to counter these dangers.)[20]

Fighting a war against National Socialism also compelled many to consider American racism as a point of comparison. Wartime race riots and a segregated military only reinforced such comparisons. The war made many people wonder, with fear, if what happened "over there" could ever happen here.[21] Americans sought assurance that democracy in the United States was secure, and one source of such assurance lay in rejecting and combating prejudice. Antisemitism and discrimination against African Americans increasingly occupied similar analytic space, and in many instances white liberals considered them to be virtually interchangeable.[22]

At the same time, National Socialism profoundly discredited biologically based theories of personality development and racial difference.[23] This delegitimation of biologically based theories at precisely the moment when issues of race assumed such urgency created an opening of sorts. It was in this space that interdisciplinary psychosocial research came to dominate studies of prejudice.

Psychology in the 1940s was at once a rational science grounded in empirical data, and a discipline concerned with irrational emotions. Psychoanalytic categories provided a way for sociologists, anthropologists, political scientists, and others to link analyses of individuals and their emotions with analyses of society and states. These categories also allowed experts to examine the discriminators and the discriminated against and to envision a society freed from the dangers of excessive hatred, violence, and aggression. This "ice-cold scientific research," wrote one psychiatrist, could determine why "a certain kind of person . . . *needs to hate*."[24] Fascism, the Holocaust, and the "new" enemy in the postwar period—communism in the Soviet Union—gave added political weight to concerns about aggression and its relation to race. The danger of racial hatred was difficult to ignore. Race relations thus assumed a more prominent place in liberal discourse and could not be suppressed as it had been within New Deal liberalism in the 1930s.[25]

Émigré intellectuals, many of them affiliated with the Institute of Social Research in Germany and then New York, contributed to an increased focus on psychology, frustration and aggression, and prejudice.[26] T. W. Adorno as well as Erich Fromm, Wilhelm Reich, and others analyzed antisemitism, authoritarianism, and prejudice in both Europe and the United States by integrating psychology, critical theory, and Marxist-oriented analyses. Their work, particularly *The Authoritarian Personality* (1950), a study of American authoritarianism in which Frankfurt School theorists and American social scientists collaborated, had a significant influence on those concerned with prejudice against African Americans. So too did

Swedish economist Gunnar Myrdal's landmark analysis of American race relations, *An American Dilemma* (1944).[27]

Scholars interested in the effects that prejudice had on African Americans also used psychosocial approaches and drew on a frustration-aggression paradigm. Among these were sociologist and former New Dealer Charles Johnson, in his study of rural black youth in the South, *Growing Up in the Black Belt* (1940); Horace Cayton and St. Clair Drake in their community study of urban Chicago, *Black Metropolis* (1945); and Abram Kardiner and psychoanalyst Lionel Ovesey in their psychoanalytic case studies of blacks in Harlem, *The Mark of Oppression* (1951).[28] These and other experts continued to draw attention to the socioeconomic dimensions of racial inequality evident in both Frazier's *The Negro Family in the United States* and Dollard's *Caste and Class*, but their interdisciplinary analyses were attentive to the psychological dimensions of prejudice as well.

Intellectuals interested in prejudice often read and reviewed each other's work, cited each other, and attended conferences and seminars together.[29] Overlapping circles of colleagues (and competitors) worked at universities and foundations in the New York area, at Yale, at the University of Chicago, and at centers for scholarship and activism in the South like Fisk University in Nashville. Perhaps even more significantly, shared concerns and assumptions circulated among this liberal cohort even when specific ties between individuals were less concrete. In using psychology to explain both personality formation and political stability, scholars seeking to understand the sources and effects of prejudice, like those concerned with frustration and aggression generally, viewed the family as the point of intersection between the private individual and the social citizen. A near-consensus emerged that childhood experiences were important in understanding the sources of prejudice in whites and the effects of prejudice on blacks; events in childhood had a role in determining the kinds of citizens white and black men could be. Finally, this body of work reflected a liberal belief in progress and in the potential for interracial harmony that was more insistent than were many Depression-era studies.[30]

It is worth emphasizing that this focus on psychology and family dynamics was progressive. It created a paradigm that replaced biological theories of race with psychological theories of racism. At the same time, this progressive impulse directly and indirectly implicated white and black women in both the dangerous production of racism and its dangerous effects.

From the "Negro Problem" to the "White Problem": The Origins of Racism and Maternal Failure

In 1948 an article about "race hate" appeared in both *Cosmopolitan* and *Negro Digest*. "What can be done—in homes and schools and churches—to fight a danger which, in its way, may be as threatening as the atomic bomb?" asked the author, a psychiatrist.[31] As the article suggested, violently prejudiced Americans had a problem that contradicted tenets of democracy. They were unfit, or at best unstable, cit-izens who endangered national security.

One particularly influential scholar who tried to figure out just what could be done about this danger was the Swedish economist Gunnar Myrdal. When the Carnegie Corporation brought Myrdal to the United States in 1938 to conduct a comprehensive study of American race relations, he worked for several years with a staff of white and black, northern and southern social scientists.[32] The result was the two-volume *An American Dilemma* (1944), a social history that offered a tremendous amount of detail about African Americans. But the "American" of the title—the one afflicted with the "dilemma"—was a white man. His dilemma, moreover, was fundamentally psychological: the "ever-raging conflict" in whites between the liberal "American creed" and "group prejudice" was at the crux of Myrdal's analysis. It was white America that was *"free to choose whether the Negro shall remain her liability or become her opportunity."* What one scholar has called "the most influential study of American race relations from its publication in 1944 to the end of the 1960s" helped to transform the "Negro problem" into an American problem by considering the interrelated moral, psychological, and political effects of prejudice in whites.[33]

The popularity and underlying optimism of *An American Dilemma* grew out of the focus on whiteness and an (ensuing) belief in change. This and other work on prejudice implicitly assumed that if racial prejudice was a disorder and an aberra-tion that contradicted other experiences and values, then it could also be avoided. Myrdal believed in progress, despite centuries of discrimination, because he con-cluded that whites could not tolerate discrepancies between prejudice and the lib-eral American creed; they could not live indefinitely with the feelings of guilt these discrepancies evoked. "People want to be rational," Myrdal asserted. It was also "significant," he noted, that "today even the white man who defends discrimina-tion frequently . . . says that it is 'irrational.' "[34]

Interest in the "dilemma" of white Americans increased in the 1940s and 1950s—in part as a result of the enormous influence of *An American Dilemma*, in part as a result of the degree to which biological theories of racial difference were discredited, and in part as fears of fascism during World War II fed into fears of communism during the Cold War. Myrdal explicitly related the fight against preju-dice in the United States to the fight against fascism abroad, viewing the United States as the democratic country capable of resisting both.[35]

In 1950, authors of *The Authoritarian Personality* extended the exploration of fascism and prejudice in relation to democracy. They attempted to strengthen democratic institutions by understanding how and why men developed distorted personalities within the United States. Under the direction of T. W. Adorno, and sponsored by the American Jewish Committee for its Studies in Prejudice series, this collaborative project combined psychoanalytic case studies and family histories of two thousand Californians with qualitative and quantitative analyses. With this approach, American social psychologists and émigré theorists hoped to determine "what within the individual organism responds to certain stimuli in our culture with attitudes and acts of destructive aggression." The authors assumed that prejudice "could not be derived solely from external factors, such as economic status, group membership, or religion."[36] Readers reacted to this approach with appreciation. "At last," wrote one reviewer, there were "books on prejudice produced after careful research. . . . After many years of pious hopes some groups have decided to try the scientific method in attacking prejudice." Today scholars agree that despite methodological flaws *The Authoritarian Personality* was a—if not the—"major social psychology contribution of the 1950s" (comparable in influence only to Alfred Kinsey's reports on human sexuality, according to one), and that it paved the way for many other related studies on prejudice.[37] Several years later, for example, the Harvard social psychologist Gordon Allport drew on scholarship about prejudice, race relations, and family dynamics that had preceded and followed *The Authoritarian Personality* in his influential, synthetic volume *The Nature of Prejudice*, which remained a popular resource for years.[38]

These and other researchers depicted white mothers as playing a crucial role in the childhood experiences through which frustrations, and ultimately prejudice, either developed or receded. In *The Authoritarian Personality*, for example, Adorno and collaborators used the "F-scale" (with F signifying "fascist") to link types of personalities likely to submit to an authoritarian leader to certain types of families and family dynamics. They argued that mothers of prejudiced children were either excessively "sacrificing, kind, submissive," or "domineering, dictatorial, and self-centered." Maternal behavior thus helped to create the negative childhood experiences through which feelings of frustration and consequent prejudice developed. As Gordon Allport explained, "Mothers of prejudiced children, far more often than the mothers of unprejudiced children" were strict disciplinarians. They tended to punish children for masturbating, and they responded with anger and rejection to temper tantrums.[39]

Several themes recur in this literature. First, even when the mother was not herself prejudiced, she played a role in the production of prejudice in sons and affected the future political behavior of citizens. The woman's position as mother was more important than were her political opinions about race relations.[40] Second, there was no one kind of behavior that mothers could avoid or cultivate in order to have prejudice-free offspring. Mothers who generated in their children frustration that was later expressed as prejudice were *both* "henpeckingly dominant"*and* overly "sacrificing." They were alternatively (and/or simultaneously) rejecting and overprotective.[41] This spectrum of "bad mothers" was quite similar to that associated with reactionary momism. Moreover, the rare "good" mothers in this antiracist literature struck that necessary balance between maternal rejection and overprotection: they were "sociable, lovable [and] understanding," yet they had interests beyond the home and were not consumed by childrearing.[42] In championing families "centered about a mother whose primary function is to give love rather than to dominate, and who is not too weak or too submissive," *The Authoritarian Personality* echoed Benjamin Spock's *Baby and Child Care*. In both instances, maternal moderation was key to democratic families in which future citizens themselves learned to moderate their aggression.[43] Mother-blaming circulated from general discussions of the mother-child relationship seemingly unconcerned with race into progressive discussions of prejudice, families, and authoritarianism.

Third, the considerable focus on the relationship between fathers and prejudice among experts implicated mothers. *The Authoritarian Personality* repeatedly emphasized that too "distant" or too "stern" a father made sons more inclined toward prejudice and authoritarianism. In such instances, researchers argued, the son longed to "assert his strength against those who are weaker" precisely because his own father was so harsh. Still, the assumption that mothers were ultimately responsible for childrearing was so pervasive that discussions of patriarchal authority always implied that mothers had not done their job; women frequently contributed to the gender disarray that excessive paternal domination or paternal neglect signaled. The prejudiced man susceptible to authoritarianism, explained Adorno, "longs for strong authority" because his cloying mother made it impossible for his father to assert himself. Analyses of prejudice expected healthy men (fathers and sons) to be emotional, expressive, and able to admit their fears and their fleeting desires for dependence. These qualities were only appropriate, however, in certain quantities.[44] Masculinity and patriarchal authority—whether in dangerous decline or in frightening ascendance—were difficult to separate from distortions of maternal authority that helped to bring about this decline or ascendance.

As these examples suggest, studies of prejudice and its sources saw women as causal agents: women caused prejudice *and* a damaged masculinity in their sons. In case study after case study, the prejudiced male whom experts discussed in detail had failed to resolve his Oedipal issues. By not separating from his own mother, he remained overly identified with femininity. In many instances, this fixation on femininity caused a " 'sissy complex' " in effeminate boys, setting up a dangerous dynamic because their "outward submissiveness" masked an "inward aggressiveness." A fixation on femininity also led boys to overcompensate; *unsuccessful* attempts to identify with masculinity were evident in an "overaggressiveness toward the outer world" and toward "socially sanctioned scapegoats" in particular. Again and again, it was "mother domination" that made it difficult for white boys to forge a healthy masculine identity. Boys whose mothers had dominated them, explained Gordon Allport, confused "sheer aggression with masculinity" and could not forge a healthy heterosexual masculine identity as a result.[45] This discourse explicitly and implicitly invoked fears of homosexuality, doing so in ways that conflated sexual and gender deviance, and linked both to prejudice. In other words, prejudice was, in part, a problem of gender.

Racism in white men, experts concluded, emerged as a result of feelings of sexual inadequacy, "impotence" (a word that abounds in this discourse), and unresolved Oedipal conflicts—all of which white mothers helped to create. These intersections between motherhood, masculine aggression, and prejudice crystallized in the work of Lillian Smith.

Lillian Smith was a white southern woman, an essayist and novelist, and, in a period of entrenched segregation, an ardent integrationist. Born in a small town in northern Florida, she lived her adult life on a mountaintop in Georgia. She edited a magazine devoted to southern literature and culture, ran a summer camp for girls, and wrote fiction and nonfiction. Her first published novel, *Strange Fruit* (1944), was a story about a doomed interracial romance between a white man and a black women; the best-seller generated significant controversy in the north and in the South. Smith continued to explore segregation as a psychocultural problem in the coming years.[46]

Smith consistently analyzed whites and condemned segregation in unqualified terms. In 1944 she wrote a short essay for *The New Republic* titled "Addressed to White Liberals." There she asserted that the "white man himself is one of the world's most urgent problems today." Smith supported integration and an end to a racial caste system that, she argued, caused both white and black children to grow up with "distorted, twisted personalities."[47] Like Wylie and Farnham and Lundberg, and like others concerned with the sources of prejudice in whites, Smith positioned psychology on the border between private and political life. For her it was a means of evaluating the political, emotional, and moral shortcomings of prejudiced white Americans. Even more so than Myrdal, Smith sought to create a sense of urgency about American race relations by framing it as a "white problem" rather than as a marginal question that merely affected blacks or a single region. She placed questions of race within the parameters of, and as central to, liberalism.

Smith's analysis was admirable on several levels. Using psychology to analyze segregation enabled her to challenge directly the assumption that American race relations should be understood in terms of the "Negro problem." She argued that "we have looked at the 'Negro problem' long enough": "Now the time has come for us to right-about-face and study the problem of the white man: the deep-rooted needs that have caused him to seek those strange, regressive satisfactions that are derived from worshipping his own skin-color. . . ."[48]

Smith also used the notion of a "white problem" to counter prevailing views among her white liberal peers that "segregation must change slowly." She argued—and in this regard she was quite unusual—that those who supported "gradual reform" denied racism's suffocating effects on whites as well as blacks. They denied the fact that the lines between the prejudiced and the ostensibly unprejudiced often blurred, and that democracy and oppression existed in close proximity to each other. These denials constituted a collective withdrawal from reality, she argued, akin to that of an individual schizophrenic. While liberal white Americans had started to conclude that violent expressions of prejudice were a problem, few besides Smith considered "peaceful" segregation in these same terms.[49]

Finally, by focusing on frustration as a crucial component of the "white problem," Smith placed discriminatory attitudes and the psychological dimensions of prejudice on equal footing with discriminatory behavior and the practical dimensions of prejudice. "Man," she argued, is not simply an "economic or political unit." Therefore, "racial problems cannot be solved by putting a loaf of bread, a book and a ballot in everyone's hand."[50] Although Smith felt that legislative measures were important, her article, published shortly after Franklin Roosevelt established the Fair Employment Practices Commission to protect African Americans from discrimination in defense industries, suggested that external changes alone could not eliminate discrimination.

If Smith's emphasis on the psychological dimensions of prejudice stood out with regard to the conclusions she drew, it should be clear by now that the perspective itself was not unique. At a time when experts like Benjamin Spock or Margaret Ribble, author of *The Rights of Infants,* argued that literal, physical attention to children did not preclude maternal rejection, antiracist intellectuals argued that legal attention to minorities did not preclude prejudice. In both instances, conscious and unconscious attitudes were as important as behavior; in both, disease imagery was conspicuous. In this context, questions about class and economic opportunities were not the focus of liberal frameworks as they had been in the 1930s.

Published in 1949, *Killers of the Dream,* Smith's collection of essays and memoirs, elaborated on these themes, in ways that placed gender at the center of the analysis. In this controversial book, Smith analyzed what she called the "sex-race-religion-economics tangle" of southern life.[51] "The mother who taught me what I know of tenderness and love and compassion taught me also the bleak ritual of keeping Negroes in their 'place,'" she declared. According to Smith, racism in southern white men developed out of their boyhood experiences with white and black women. She explained this dynamic in greater detail and with more personal references than had Dollard's *Caste and Class* a decade earlier. White mothers taught their children that both African Americans and their own sexual feelings had to be "segregated." These women were themselves repressed by a "patriarchal-puritanic system which psychically castrated" them, and in turn, they "psychically castrated" their offspring. They "armored their children against their fantasies" and sexual desires and inoculated them with a "hypodermic needle" that was "tainted" with racial hatred. In these ways, withholding white mothers interwove sexual desire and blackness and cast both as dangerous. "Our mother's voice" taught five-year-olds that "masturbation is wrong and segregation is right, and each had become a dread taboo that must never be broken." By contrast, black women who were mammies to young white boys, said Smith, were unrepressed; they were excessively nurturing and physically and emotionally available to their young charges.[52]

Smith concluded that, as adults, white men had conflicting sets of desires based on their encounters with white and black mothers. They desired black women, emotionally and sexually, because these were the women who had been available to them as children. But they feared and hated the objects of their desire because their mothers had reinforced associations between blackness, sex, and sin. White men also ostensibly placed their wives on a pedestal even as they distanced themselves from these desexualized reminders of their own mothers. As a result of these conflicting needs, white men sought to maintain power over African Americans who had been cast since childhood as feared and hated objects, even as these same men sought out sexual relationships with black women. Finally, white men projected their own "sins" and desires onto "the Negro male" and then used images of black men as sexual predators to maintain the racial caste system. In this way, they channeled their childhood frustrations *and* preserved their power in the racial caste system. White women were left isolated and resentful, emotionally and sexually frustrated. They were primed to repeat the cycle and inculcate prejudice in the next generation.[53]

In the storm of response that met *Killers of the Dream*, the role that psychology played seldom went unnoticed. Fans praised Smith's psychological insights; her focus on guilt, family dynamics, and the "dual mother symbol" was "provocative stuff," wrote the *New York Times*. (According to *Labor Action*, this perspective was not "a minimization of economics.") To critics, like the reviewer in the *Atlanta Constitution*, Smith's argument was "as warped as the Freudian cast with which she covers it."[54] Readers had less to say about how Smith's psychological perspective related to women.

And yet, Smith's analysis and imagery duplicated disturbing aspects of "moms" and "matriarchs" in many important respects. She may have had nothing but scorn for *Generation of Vipers*, but like Wylie, she positioned white women in terms of frigidity and repression. Like E. Franklin Frazier in *The Negro Family in the United States*, she positioned black women in terms of sexuality and physicality. And Smith depicted all mothers, black and white, as potentially infectious, damaging, and alternatively overprotective and rejecting. She used the very same criteria Wylie and Frazier did to evaluate—and indict—mothers. In her antiracist work, mothers were either too emotionally giving or too emotionally restrained, too preoccupied with or too removed from their children's needs, and they were plagued by sexual frustrations. For Smith as for Farnham and Lundberg in *Modern Woman: The Lost Sex*, feminists who were known for "rejecting their womanly qualities . . . cropping their hair short, walking in heavy awkward strides" and who reflected a "kind of fibroid growth of sick cells" were particularly disordered and disordering. Even as Smith wondered if "sometimes we blame Mom too much for all that is wrong with her sons and daughters" and analyzed the cultural context for feelings of female inferiority, she concluded that mothers "did a thorough job . . . of leaving in their children an unquenchable need to feel superior to others."[55]

These psychosocial frameworks and the focus on prejudiced whites underscored what was both most progressive *and* most reactionary in *Killers of the Dream*. Smith's analysis of the origins of prejudice depended on a psychological analysis of childhood. As a result, her gendered logic—what one might even call misogyny in some instances—was a necessary component of her unwavering resistance to segregation. She invoked images of maternal pathology, but these were an essential element of the courageous stand that she took against segregation; they were essential, too, to the ways she located race as the primary category within liberalism.

These contradictions cannot necessarily be resolved, and that is, perhaps, precisely the point. Smith's work is emblematic of intersections between reactionary misogyny and racial progressivism that proliferated in the 1940s and 1950s. The psychological frameworks that underscored antiracism in this period required a logic that assumed mothers were important to the production of *interrelated* social, psychological, and political problems.

This discourse affirmed a vision of an ideal citizen cured of the "disease" of prejudice and free from the effects of femininity. This ideal citizen was an autonomous male and was sufficiently—though not excessively—aggressive. As a result of his own upbringing, he was rational though emotional. He was independent yet able to cooperate with his family and with other men, black and white. He understood, as did the protagonist in *Home of the Brave*, that what matters is "we're all guys." This same standard of citizenship was a model for black men and surfaced in literature that focused on the psychological effects of racism on African Americans. It too developed through a gendered logic that required images of maternal pathology.

The "Trouble Lies in the Original Relationship with His Mother": The Effects of Racism and Black Maternal Failure

Fewer scholars studied the effects of prejudice on blacks as compared to those who analyzed its origins in whites from the 1940s into the postwar years. This owed, in part, to the ways that World War II generated anxiety about authoritarianism and prejudice in white Americans, and it illustrates the degree to which the pivotal "American dilemma" became essentially a white problem. Funding was simply less available to scholars who studied African Americans.[56] Those who were interested in the impact of prejudice on blacks also used psychology to understand how healthy American identities developed and to chart the variables that could interfere with this development in blacks. Prejudice, explained sociologists, anthropologists, psychologists, and others, not only hurt African Americans economically and politically: it also undermined their self-esteem. Moreover, the feelings of inferiority and self-hatred that prejudice generated, or the "mark of oppression," in the words of Abram Kardiner and Lionel Ovesey, originated in childhood and persisted into adulthood.

Experts who studied the development of African American personalities studied diverse regions, age groups, and classes. Charles S. Johnson was one of the most prominent African American scholars in this period. He had studied sociology with Robert Park at the University of Chicago, edited the New York-based Urban League's journal, *Opportunity*, in the 1920s, and was a researcher and consultant for New Deal agencies in the 1930s. He also served on the American Youth Commission that the American Council on Education established to study black youth in the 1930s and 1940s (as did Frazier and Dollard, among others). In *Growing Up in the Black Belt* (1940), Johnson, then chairman of the social science department at Fisk University, examined the economic and social barriers that young blacks faced in the rural South. He also drew attention to the psychic costs exacted by these barriers. Johnson organized this sociological and statistical overview of rural black youth around personality profiles and family histories; the study concluded with a "Memorandum on a Psychiatric Reconnaissance" by analyst Harry Stack Sullivan.[57]

St. Clair Drake, an anthropologist, and Horace Cayton, a sociologist, turned their attention to a different place and population. Their two-volume *Black Metropolis: A Study of Negro Life in a Northern City* (1945) focused on adult African Americans in segregated urban Chicago—"Bronzeville," as they called it. *Black Metropolis*, dedicated to Robert Park and funded in part by the Works Progress Administration, analyzed the effects of the Depression and World War II on urban blacks across lines of class. Drake and Cayton, themselves black, looked at the institutional, associational, and personal structures of residents' lives in this city and community. They offered personal profiles and anecdotes alongside statistical data; the novelist Richard Wright wrote in his introduction to the volume that with such an approach "sincere art and honest science were not far apart." Drake and Cayton hoped to reach a wide audience, and they did. *Black Metropolis*, in the words of one scholar, "was soon to become a sociological classic." Reviewers praised Drake and Cayton for challenging the notion of fixed status groups within the black community and for challenging assumptions that urban blacks who lived in segregated areas lacked healthy communities.[58]

Other studies were more psychoanalytic. In the case histories that constituted *The Mark of Oppression* (1951), Abram Kardiner, an anthropologist and psychiatrist, and Lionel Ovesey, a psychiatrist, studied external sources of prejudice in direct relation to internal sources of racial self-hatred in African Americans living in Harlem. Kardiner had studied with Franz Boas and was an analysand of Freud in the 1920s. Beginning in 1933, he organized an interdisciplinary seminar with the anthropologist Ralph Linton that met at the New York Psychoanalytic Institute and then Columbia University; for years many of the most prominent scholars in culture and personality research attended. Throughout his career Kardiner worked to integrate psychoanalysis and anthropology and emphasized the mother-child relationship as the "template" for the child's later development. The terms, categories, and images that Kardiner and Ovesey used in *The Mark of Oppression* were not unique; they overlapped considerably with those that Erik Erikson, an ego psychologist, used to discuss "black identity" in *Childhood and Society*, to cite just one example.[59]

It has made sense for scholars to consider the differences between various studies of African Americans. After all, Drake and Cayton were committed to offering a vision of a black community that was vital, if beset by problems. They mapped out interlocking systems—of neighborhoods, transportation, organizations, and individuals—in this community. By contrast, Kardiner and Ovesey's personality profiles in *The Mark of Oppression* were more atomized. Drake and Cayton believed that black culture was intact, while Kardiner and Ovesey assumed that for all intents and purposes there was no such thing as a viable black culture. And while Charles Johnson was skeptical about the psychological argument that all southern blacks were gripped by fear and the desire to escape, Horace Cayton embraced psychoanalytic theories of racial prejudice.[60]

Given such differences, the commonalities across these works are particularly noteworthy. Indeed, the diversity can obscure the fact that even more so than in the 1930s, psychological categories permeated race-relations literature. These categories allowed experts to render black experiences and black identity in universal and environmental terms, rejecting biologically based frameworks that presumed essential difference. "Differences" in "the family life of Negroes" could "hardly be called 'racial traits,' " argued one scholar.[61] As Richard Wright explained in his introduction to *Black Metropolis*, "the authors have presented much more than the anatomy of Negro frustration; they have shown how *any* human beings can become mangled, how *any* personalities can become distorted when men are caught in the psychological trap of being emotionally committed to the living of a life of freedom which is denied them."[62]

This body of scholarship also shared a paradox. Studies of African Americans from the 1940s and into the postwar years affirmed the potential for blacks to function as healthy citizens; liberal experts used psychological categories with growing regularity to make such claims. At the same time, the scholarship highlighted the emotional damage caused by prejudice and the degree to which this damage was a personal and political problem. These positive affirmations and exposés of damage were not mutually exclusive, but reinforced each other.

Despite the variations in their work, liberal scholars, black and white, echoed the message of *Home of the Brave*: interracial cooperation and psychic health required each other; both, moreover, required black men who were appropriately yet not excessively aggressive. Scholars directly and indirectly prescribed for black men codes of masculinity associated with white middle-class men. These codes presumed that healthy self-esteem facilitated moderate aggression in the public sphere, and controlled emotional satisfaction in the private sphere. Early on in *The Mark of Oppression*, Kardiner and Ovesey asserted, without qualms, that "our constant control is the American white man. We require no other control system."[63]

Experts who studied the effects of prejudice pinpointed a vicious cycle. Discrimination generated feelings of frustration that subjects often internalized. Such feelings made it more difficult to resist discrimination. More specifically, internalized frustration interfered with the development of healthy black American men who had jobs and headed families—who could, by definition, participate successfully in American society. Frustration, then, was both effect *and cause* of further inferiority.

Authorities concluded that black men all too frequently failed to attain the "constant control" that the white man represented, and lacked the ideal proportion of restrained, yet energizing, aggression. Many men were not sufficiently aggressive. One was weak and inclined toward "submissiveness" in his private and public life, preferring "empty dreams of escape" to hard work; another sought "escape" with "chronic drunkenness."[64] Still other men could not control their excessive aggression. In *Growing Up in the Black Belt*, Charles Johnson explained that some, often unemployed, black men sought "self-assurance in free sexual activity, in a reputation for physical prowess or for being a bad man, and in other forms of anti-social behavior."[65] A psychological paradigm that emphasized

In the film *Home of the Brave* the black man, Pete Moss (James Edwards), and the one-armed white man, Mingo (Frank Lovejoy), both learn that "everybody's different. But so what? Because underneath, we're all guys." Here and elsewhere, interracial harmony, psychic health, and masculinity required each other. Courtesy of the Museum of Modern Art / Film Stills Archives.

low self-esteem underlay these references to abusive, drunken, or passive and dreamy men.

Underaggressive men given to submission and overaggressive men given to sexual and other excesses were similar in one crucial respect to prejudiced white men: all three groups failed to meet standards of healthy masculinity. Whether black men's "compensatory gratifications" included gambling or drinking, whether they were unemployed, impotent, or otherwise unable to assert themselves, their masculinity itself (or their "magical powers" as providers, as Kardiner and Ovesey put it), was on the line.[66]

Experts influenced by psychology in the 1940s and 1950s were not content merely to document this state of affairs. How, asked Kardiner and Ovesey in *The Mark of Oppression*, did the weak or violent, submissive or aggressive man "get this way?" The "trouble," they answered, "lies in the original relationship with his mother."[67] The mark of oppression that incapacitated so many black men developed as a result of institutionalized racial exclusions *combined with* family dynamics. Liberal intellectuals who studied the effects of prejudice on African Americans paid far more attention to socioeconomic issues than did those interested in the development of prejudice in whites. However, experts located many of the sources for the problems black men experienced in the home—where, they argued, black mothers played a role in the low self-esteem that perpetuated racial inferiority.

The notion that black mothers could damage black families and black men was not new, and many themes evident in literature on black families during the Depression persisted in pre- and post-World War II studies. Following Frazier and Dollard's lead, the discourse referred frequently to poor and "disorganized" families that were "more often dominated by the woman than by the man." This emphasis on "disorganized" families in which poor women were *economically* dominant (or "held the purse strings") reflected a continuity of thought among white and black intellectuals about what was wrong with black family life. "Since she pays the piper, she usually feels justified in calling the tune," wrote Drake and Cayton.[68]

Yet ideas about black motherhood shifted and assumed particular currency in the 1940s and 1950s. In this period, liberal scholars melded pre-existing ideas about black women's economic domination with the psychological terms and images that filtered through so many arenas. The "momism" that Philip Wylie and others used to critique weak white men appeared here as a concern about the psychological damage black mothers could cause. This was particularly apparent in *The Mark of Oppression*. In one case study, Kardiner and Ovesey explained that the mother of "B. B." had "devoted all of her time" to her son and "was the real 'boss' of the household"; they concluded that the adult B. B. retained an infantile neediness and a "struggle for the maternal breast." Here and elsewhere, a centuries-old tradition of black women as quintessential maternal figures intersected with contemporary theories about maternal rejection and maternal overprotection. As Drake and Cayton put it in *Black Metropolis*, black women alternated between a destructive "defensive hardness" and an equally unhealthy "lavish tenderness" toward their partners and offspring.[69] Families could be "disorganized" if there were illegitimate children present, or if there were boarders and extended family members present. A mother who cared for her child in a dirty home was disorganizing, but so was the mother who was not the primary caretaker in a clean home.[70] Still other women failed as mothers because, like Wylie's "moms," they were too concerned with the "primacy of pleasure" and "hedonistic" superficial goals. And, like Farnham and Lundberg's "lost sex," black women were inclined toward "sex irregularity": both "frigidity" and promiscuity were frequent problems that black mothers exhibited, according to experts.[71]

Because all too many black women did not mother successfully, they failed to raise sons equipped to resist racial prejudice. Mothers helped to determine whether black men internalized or displaced their feelings of frustration; they determined whether compensatory behavior in adult black men included underaggressive "apathy" or overaggressive "living for the moment." As Erik Erikson explained, maternal behavior in black women yielded three possible "types" of black identities. These were "mammy's oral-sensual 'honey child,' " the "evil . . . dirty,

anal-sadistic, phallic-rapist 'nigger,' " and the "clean, anal-compulsive, restrained
. . . but always sad 'white man's Negro.' "[72]

As a result of psychological theories of race and personality, relationships between class, race, and motherhood were renegotiated in this period. In the 1930s,
Frazier had reserved the bulk of his criticism for poorer urban blacks; it was primarily recent migrant women through whom he had forged links between femininity, vice and consumption, and disorganization. In *The Negro Family in the United
States*, these were the women who perpetuated matriarchal patterns of mothering
that endangered racial progress and prevented assimilation. Depression-era studies
of black and white families had often linked traditional gender relations, respectability, and financial security as intertwined goals. Families that met these
goals also "solved" the problems of motherhood and the weak men mothers produced. This approach was consistent with a liberal emphasis on economic issues,
the family wage, and individual economic opportunities in this period.[73]

These economic dimensions did not disappear in the 1940s and 1950s. To offer
a positive view of rural blacks, for example, Charles Johnson asserted that "upper-
and middle-class [black] families usually follow what might be called a patriarchal
setup like that of white families." Similarly, in *Black Metropolis*, Drake and Cayton
pointed to middle-and upper-class black men who had an "ordered and disciplined
family life." Such men saw "individual competition" as a *"racial* duty as well as a
personal gain," noted the authors, reinforcing the equation between economic security, racial progress, and patriarchal black families.[74]

At the same time, as psychology became the centerpiece of race-relations research and other studies of American identity in the 1940s, upward mobility became a less definitive "solution" to racial problems, and class was a less definitive
barometer for measuring racial health.[75] As a result, "bad" mothers were not only
those who were poor and single. Experts began to suggest that middle-class black
mothers might also do damage. Charles Johnson scorned the widow who used her
husband's insurance policy to build and furnish an elaborate house. Her constant
striving for status symbols made her oblivious to the fact that her daughters were
"bored and indifferent," "sad and broken targets of ridicule," and that they wanted
to drop out of school and leave home. In *Black Metropolis*, Drake and Cayton argued that a middle-class black mother who stressed to her children "the need for
being prepared to be a good citizen" placed too much pressure on them. "The
whole atmosphere of middle-class life is one of tension"; it was marked by a "striving and straining" that destabilized black families and harmed children emotionally.[76] Here and elsewhere, scholars criticized middle-class blacks by focusing on the
behavior of women.

Bad mothers who were middle-class made the most frequent appearances in *The
Mark of Oppression*. Kardiner and Ovesey researched and wrote this study well after the Depression and World War II, amidst anxieties about the effects of affluence
in a consumer-oriented society. Their concerns with consumerism were embodied,
as such concerns often were, in the figure of the materialistic woman. They suggested that women with economic security and wage-earning husbands could still

be rejecting, "loveless tyrants," or overprotective. For example, "A. T." was a middle-class woman who married "mainly for economic reasons," for whom sex was "ridden with fear and disgust," and who applied unrealistic "perfectionist standards" to her son.[77]

Kardiner and Ovesey also asserted that middle-class black women were likely to emulate white women and want their sons to be like white men. One such subject rejected her son when his behavior fit "prejudicial anti-Negro stereotypes"; her maternal rejection reflected an attempt "to deny her Negro identification."[78] Erik Erikson confirmed this pattern but noted that black mothers of all classes might be guilty of maternal rejection based on a problematic relationship with whiteness. When black mothers (of any class) used "sudden correctives . . . to approach the vague but pervasive Anglo-Saxon ideal," they created "violent discontinuities" that harmed their children. The "Negro's unavoidable identification with the dominant race" was damaging, explained Erikson, because it led to self-hatred. Certain kinds of maternal behavior prevented children from developing a "lasting ego identity" so necessary for full participation in American life.[79]

Progressive analyses of racism's effects that focused on the private sphere of the home—and on mothers—served several functions. By arguing that undesirable qualities long regarded as innate (such as laziness or shiftlessness in black men) developed, in part, through interactions between the individual and his family, liberal scholars suggested that racial progress was possible. To change family dynamics would be to counter the underlying feelings that created undesirable behavior.

In fact, one important goal of progressive literature was to dismantle racial stereotypes of black men and to show that blacks "too" could be masculine and, by extension, could be respectable citizens. Johnson described an eighteen-year-old southern black farmer whose "teachers call him ambitious and energetic" despite his poverty and limited options. *Black Metropolis* explained that lower-class "roving" black men were compelled to leave home by discriminatory hiring practices and a "search for better or supplementary jobs" and not out of indifference to their families. To rehabilitate the reputation of these men, the authors noted that "lower class men do not necessarily refuse to live with or even marry a girl who has had an illegitimate child." In the words of Gunnar Myrdal, there were "exceptions to the general observation that the average Negro family is more disorganized than the white family."[80]

In some instances, this literature challenged racist myths about black men through representations of black women. In *The Mark of Oppression*, for example, Kardiner and Ovesey argued that black men were *not* the overly aggressive sexual predators that whites imagined: "The most surprising fact about the sex life of the Negro—of all classes—[and here they referred to men only] lies in its marked deviation from the white stereotypes . . . the Negro is hardly the abandoned sexual hedonist he is supposed to be." Yet how did they explain this surprising "deviation"? They argued that black men raised in a "female dominated household" had feelings of "frustrated dependency and hostility." Their unhealthy relationships with mothers recurred with other women and interfered with healthy heterosexuality.[81] In order to counter stereotypes of black men, the authors needed to emphasize psychic distress and female dominance, and in the process they reinforced stereotypes of black women.

Thus black women in this literature "carried connotations of other crises," as Hazel Carby has explained in her analysis of black women migrants.[82] These were *overlapping* crises of black masculinity and race relations. It is important to note that if maternal behavior threatened black masculinity, the tendency to demonize black women as mothers also facilitated an affirmation of black masculinity. By explaining deficiencies in black men and in race relations with psychological frameworks that drew attention to maternal failure, scholars reaffirmed black men's potential. Mother-blaming made the effects of prejudice comprehensible and suggested that it was possible and necessary for the individual self as well as society to develop differently.[83]

Psychological frameworks allowed experts to turn inward and consider the emotional effects of prejudice on African Americans. As these frameworks became more commonplace than they had been in the 1930s, a liberal consensus on race that looked outward to demand social change also gained currency. Charles Johnson was hardly a racial militant, yet he concluded that young rural blacks were not complacent: "If one cannot safely predict progress in race relations, he can at least predict change." In *Black Metropolis* Drake and Cayton depicted resistance in unions, in party politics, and in "race" organizations. "At a time when entire peoples are being liquidated," they concluded, the "theory of 'gradual gains' for Negroes has little meaning." And Kardiner and Ovesey distanced themselves from those who might use their arguments about psychic scars to defend the status quo; they concluded *The Mark of Oppression* with strong support for integration.[84] Studies of African Americans that were more attentive to the interior lives of blacks (whether in their own homes or psyches) were also more insistent on the need for change with regard to race relations.

Raising Citizens

All forms of maternal pathology caused one of two basic problems: sons who were either insufficiently aggressive, inhibited, and sexually passive and repressed; or sons who were too aggressive, insufficiently cooperative, and violent. In either case, adult men confirmed the damage that mothers, black and white, inflicted, and made it clear that emotional conditions were at the root of social and political problems. Mothers jeopardized the very codes of masculinity and citizenship that liberals deemed essential to American strength *and* interracial health in this period. Bad mothers, then, were bad precisely because they raised damaged citizens.

Even when "matriarchs" and "moms" appeared to be most similar, race shaped indictments of mothers. Female sexuality, for example, was crucial to assessments of motherhood across lines of race. Indeed, this biracial discourse reformulated normative female sexuality by linking it to motherhood.[85] Liberal scholars, however, were more likely to associate white women with frigidity and black women with promiscuity, although both disorders were evident in all women. "Good" mothers had to achieve a balance between stereotypes and extremes that were historically racially specific and that continued to be evoked in racialized ways: between the frigidity with which white women remained associated and the promiscuity with which black women remained associated. Further, there was one type of maternal failure specific to black women: identifying with whiteness. Although race and gender intersected in images of all women, gender remained the point of entry and the lens through which experts saw white maternal failure, while race remained the point of entry and the lens through which experts saw black maternal failure. If "momism" produced what was in part a racial problem (prejudice) as a result of gender disorders in white women, then "matriarchy" produced what was in part a gender problem (unmanly black men) as a result of racial disorders in black women.

It is of course, more than ironic that studies of the effects of racism directly and indirectly evaluated African Americans against a "white control group" at the very same time that experts indicted black women for being too preoccupied with white standards. This contradictory logic indicates the degree to which black women were in a double bind and how difficult it was for them to escape charges that they failed as mothers and as women. We can begin to see that black and white women figured into a developing liberal consensus on race in different ways, despite the fact that the threat of maternal failure transcended race. The marginalization of black women within liberal discourse would increase as Cold War liberalism took shape. What did persist in the shift from New Deal to Cold War liberalism was a focus on the internal life of American citizens. This focus would continue to implicate both white and black women.

CHAPTER THREE

"Politics in an Age of Anxiety"

Cold War Liberalism and Dangers to Americans

"**P**olitics in an Age of Anxiety": The young historian Arthur Schlesinger Jr. chose this phrase as the title for the first chapter of *The Vital Center: The Politics of Freedom*. Published in 1949, *The Vital Center* explained why liberalism needed to be "new" in the aftermath of a war against fascism and in the midst of a Cold War against communism. The book was a manifesto of sorts that placed its author at the forefront of a "broad intellectual movement" known as vital center or anticommunist liberalism. In the words of one reviewer, Schlesinger's book had announced "the spirit of an age to itself."[1]

Schlesinger argued that liberalism with a commitment to a "vital center" was the only way to avoid the dangerous and irrational extremes that communism and fascism each represented. Older expressions of liberalism, he explained, particularly in the Popular Front era, had failed to stem either destructive tide. By contrast, a commitment to a vital center would provide true freedom: it would yield stronger individual American citizens and a more secure democracy for all Americans collectively. With this framework, Schlesinger and others established the terms that many scholars continue to use as they study postwar liberalism: fierce anticommunism coupled with some commitment to New Deal reforms.[2]

Schlesinger may have regarded new liberalism as the way to combat the postwar "age of anxiety," but insecurity pervaded *The Vital Center* and, he observed, seeped through postwar society: "Western man in the middle of the twentieth century is tense, uncertain, adrift. We look upon our epoch as a time of troubles, an age of anxiety."[3] The United States had emerged from World War II victorious, prosperous, and the world's strongest superpower. Yet it was unclear how—or if—this position would be sustained, and what it would require of American citizens and the government. No consensus existed as to what the country's role should be as a global power—what its responsibilities were in the physical and political reconstruction of European democracies, and in what ways could it counter aggression and the repression of rights in the Soviet Union. It was equally unclear how the government should exercise power at home. The federal government had expanded enormously during the Depression and the war. Some concluded that this expansion should be checked in a time of peace and prosperity, but others felt that a growing federal government should continue to regulate the economy. And in defeating fascism the United States had defeated National Socialism's campaign for "racial purity," but ongoing prejudice and segregation within its own borders remained a divisive issue. The postwar period may well have inaugurated the "American Century" as Henry Luce put it in 1948, but a widespread sense of doubt offset the exuberant confidence the phrase evoked. Or, as Schlesinger wrote, "frustration is increasingly the hallmark of this century."[4]

The language in Schlesinger's blueprint for postwar liberalism is but one indication that psychological frameworks were not the exclusive domain of Freudians, race relations experts, and other scholars who worked beyond the explicitly political realm. During World War II and into the Cold War, it was increasingly apparent that the pragmatic approaches on which liberals engaged in party politics had long relied could not explain the irrationality that surrounded them—from the Holocaust to the atom bomb, and from virulent racial prejudice to the new evils that anticommunist liberals perceived in the Soviet Union. Psychology provided liberals with a way to get past what Henry Steele Commager, in his review of *The Vital Center*, described as the "inadequacy of reason" and allowed them to consider "the causes of fear and the bases of hope."[5]

Psychological frameworks were central to renegotiations of liberalism from the New Deal into the Cold War, and this more psychologically-oriented liberalism depended in crucial ways on ideas about both gender and race. The psychologically fit and masculine citizen that progressive intellectuals like Benjamin Spock and others endorsed was an ideal that had concrete political ramifications; this ideal shaped changing liberal conceptions of citizenship and of government activism in the late 1940s and 1950s. As well, in the early years of the Cold War, gendered psychological frameworks provided the means to create racially progressive political imperatives—well before the heyday of the civil rights movement in the early 1960s.

Intersections between psychology, gender, and race in Cold War liberalism had ambiguous effects. Efforts to promote strong citizens and a strong state bolstered calls for greater activism in some instances. But this same goal served as a brake on government activism in other instances. Three different arenas illustrate this paradox and indicate how Cold War liberalism took shape in relation to gender and race. These are social welfare legislation, civil rights advances, and anticommunist liberalism.[6] Analyzing them together demonstrates that punitive welfare policies that became more common in the 1940s and 1950s, civil rights advances in these same years, and anticommunist liberalism of which *The Vital Center* is emblematic were related in important ways. In all three areas, a vision of masculinity as neither too frustrated nor too aggressive was the normative ideal for citizenship. In all three, femininity (or certain kinds of women) emerged as threats to this norm. And in all three, assumptions circulated that were similar to those in progressive scholarship. Both the language and the logic that made images of dangerous women productive for intellectuals like Lillian Smith and T. W. Adorno infused liberal political discourse as well.

"The Special Ways of Life That Make Up the Civilization": Social Security, Gender, and Liberalism

In overlapping intellectual circles in the 1940s and 1950s, women stood in for anxieties about masculinity. Philip Wylie's diatribe against American apathy, Abram Kardiner and Lionel Ovesey's case studies that explored the effects of discrimination, and Lillian Smith's reflections on the sources of prejudice—all of these projected men's personal, racial, and political problems onto women, and did so in and through their descriptions of motherhood.

An overview of key aspects of social security legislation from the 1940s and 1950s reveals a related set of dynamics. Despite an overall expansion in the liberal welfare state after World War II, the hierarchy of "social insurance" (primarily old age insurance and unemployment insurance) and "welfare" or "assistance" (primarily Aid to Dependent Children) became even more rigid than it had been in the 1930s. Images of white and black women who mothered effectively or ineffectively, and related images of feminized men, exacerbated this stratification.

A social vision that offered a modicum of state-sponsored security to all citizens became a reality for a greater number of Americans following the Second World War. "Social security's postwar triumph," according to one scholar, made key aspects of the welfare state "noncontroversial."[7] In ways that few liberals might have anticipated in the 1930s, crucial aspects of New Deal liberalism—and the notion of an activist federal government itself—were institutionalized, if not extended, in the 1940s and 1950s. This is not to say that liberal policies were uncontested. The Supreme Court had invalidated New Deal programs as early as the late 1930s. A decade later, Republicans stymied much of Truman's Fair Deal. Nevertheless, numerous policies reflected liberalism as a more commonplace feature of political life. Programs in which social insurance increased in the 1940s included congressional passage of the Servicemen's Readjustment Act (1944), the National School Lunch Program, National Mental Health Act, and the Employment Act (all in 1946), and, in the coming years, a federal housing project and a school milk program.[8]

Alan Brinkley has explained that a consensus on the role of the federal government emerged in the 1940s as liberals embraced a more restrained view of the state. By 1945 "American liberals . . . had reached an accommodation with capitalism." They did so, in part, by "defining a role for the state that would, they believed, permit it to compensate for capitalism's inevitable flaws and omissions without interfering with its internal workings."[9] The Truman administration and other liberals were poised to bolster the "economy of abundance" visible by the war's end; they were less interested in comprehensive economic reforms and extensions of federal government powers than New Deal liberals in the early 1930s had been. It was only at this point that New Deal reforms were "elevated to the status of a national consensus" that in many respects cut across party lines.[10]

The Social Security Act of 1950 is a notable example of how the liberal welfare state expanded in an effort to strengthen the economy, compensate for capitalism's flaws, and widen the safety net for American workers and their families. The bill increased both the range of recipients who received social security insurance and the amount of aid that recipients received. As a result, an additional ten-and a-half million people received coverage—including "regularly employed" agricultural workers and many self-employed workers, among others. The coverage was nearly 80 percent higher than it had been. According to supporters, these and other policies that extended social security to insured workers and their families realized the underlying goals of an American welfare state. "Even conservatives" agreed that the increases in social security were necessary, wrote *The New Republic.*[11]

While the Social Security Act of 1950 was more concerned with insurance than assistance, it consolidated on a national level growing assumptions that Aid to Dependent Children (ADC), and more importantly, its recipients themselves, were suspect. It reinforced the connection between ADC as an unworthy aspect of the welfare state and certain kinds of mothers as themselves unworthy. This connection was already evident in the 1930s, especially after needy widowed mothers started to receive insurance (OASI) instead of assistance (ADC) in 1939. But in the 1940s and 1950s this split between social insurance and ADC increased, with "public concern for the children" accompanying "censure of the parents," as two commentators put it.[12]

The Social Security Act of 1950 included the Notification of Law Enforcement Officers (Noleo) amendment, which stipulated that welfare administrators had to notify police when they gave ADC to families in which fathers had "deserted." Noleo was designed to secure paternal support and lower the welfare caseload. By making men accountable, the amendment worked to give the "illegitimate child" more legal protection.[13]

The Noleo amendment may have been designed to counter the "sorry and worthless citizens among us" by compelling men to support their families, but in practice it affected women more immediately than men. The amendment expanded the role of the state in women's lives by allowing officials to police their behavior: it was women who, in the process of applying for assistance, had to provide welfare administrators with information about missing men; it was women who lost the crucial principle of client confidentiality; and it was women who were required to name (potentially abusive) biological fathers of their children, rendering these men criminals. At least one ADC supporter focused more on the emotional lives of noncompliant women than on the risks they incurred by reporting missing men. When a woman was reluctant to locate the missing father of her children "because she feels hurt and hostile," the case worker "has the responsibility of helping the mother work through these feelings in order that the mother may be able and willing to offer assistance in locating the father."[14] In an era of a rampant "Red

Scare"—as the Supreme Court validated loyalty oath requirements and House Un-American Activities Committee (HUAC) members encouraged witnesses to "name names"—this kind of surveillance was not unusual. Indeed it was remarkably consistent with the overall desire to maintain the health of the country and its citizens in this period and with efforts to diminish the dangers that seemed to lurk everywhere.

The Social Security Act of 1950 expanded insurance overall while the Noleo amendment regulated assistance. Both components of this legislation presumed that stable and responsible masculinity was the foundation for "normal" families and a strong democracy. In such families, men were wage earners and had authority, and the state did not have to support dependent citizens.

Similar assumptions about normal families fostered local attacks on ADC, or "relief." State-specific programs to curtail assistance gained momentum in the late 1940s and early 1950s—in the very same years that Congress passed landmark national social security legislation and a consensus developed about the need for and value of social insurance. Critiques of ADC dominated public and professional discussions of welfare, as even long-time liberal advocates resorted to defensive if not critical tones. There was a sense of being "under a certain amount of fire," and that ADC was "forced into a soul-searching phase."[15]

Structural and socioeconomic changes contributed to the sense of alarm about the place of assistance in American society. After a decline in welfare rolls in the years 1942 to 1945, demands on ADC escalated substantially in the postwar period, and so too did the costs of the program. Rising divorce rates among white and black families, decreasing work opportunities for women, and the beginnings of a cross-class baby boom were among the reasons for this growth. Terminating allowances to former servicemen also increased demands on ADC.[16] In this atmosphere, the notion that ADC depleted government resources gained credibility despite the fact that recipients received a fraction of allocations relative to unemployment and other forms of social insurance; in 1950, for example, ADC payments comprised approximately fifty million dollars, and insurance comprised approximately two-hundred-and-ninety million dollars.[17]

Critics were not merely concerned about cost. They regarded ADC as both symptom and cause of a more pervasive decline, one that, in different ways, E. Franklin Frazier and Philip Wylie had named in *The Negro Family in the United States* and *Generation of Vipers*: in families organized around a strong male, in monogamy, and in self-reliance among men. According to opponents of ADC, the program sapped the vitality of both the American economy and the American family.[18]

In their concern for citizenship, both critics and defenders of assistance focused on the effects ADC had on masculinity and on men in the workforce. Supporters defended assistance by pointing to boys from recipient families who were "outstanding in athletics"; one was even "captain of his football team." By contrast, opponents noted that relief was "sapping" men's "will to work."[19] In an effort to promote more healthy and independent men, Maine anticipated the Noleo amendment by several years. In 1947 it became the first state to establish a special "investigation process" designed to locate a man or another relative in a woman's life who could support her in lieu of the government program. Over the next decade, seven states and eighteen large cities followed Maine's lead and established surveillance-like programs oriented around paternal support.[20]

In postwar discussions of welfare as in Depression-era studies of families, observers described men whom they regarded as weak or otherwise damaged in terms associated with femininity. One interviewer was dismayed when a man on relief who admitted to being lazy giggled upon making that admission. Another man who refused to support his estranged wife was "a shiny-haired sharpie, dressed like a sport." Still another physically and emotionally ill man "had strong wishes not only to be dependent but even to be a woman."[21] Women themselves, especially those who were dependent on relief and not on husbands, also rendered men less appropriately masculine. One unmarried mother who received assistance, "abruptly ordered" her son to quit his part-time job. Given that the government cut her assistance check by more than the amount that her son brought in, this may have been a reasonable and strategic survival strategy. Nevertheless, one observer concluded that "in his home there is no incentive, because his mother forbids him to work. So he, too, may grow up to be a parasite; his mother's check might well be his passport to a life of indolence." Some discussions were more clinical: because ADC encouraged passivity, a single mother "derived gratification from coddling and infantilizing Jimmy [her son] to an extreme. . . . her excessive need for affection operated against a constructive parental relationship with the child."[22]

In general, the language in this discourse was less Freudian than Philip Wylie's in his critique of weak and "mealy" white men in *Generation of Vipers*, T. W. Adorno's in his discussions of inadequate and "distant" fathers in *The Authoritarian Personality*, and Abram Kardiner's in his description of "hedonistic" or "violent" black men in *The Mark of Oppression*. Yet the ideas about masculinity were nearly identical. The normative masculine ideal that emerged in scholarly and political narratives presumed that men who lacked financial resources and could not support their families—economically or emotionally—were weak and irresponsible. Because they did not live up to the ideal of masculinity, they failed as men and as citizens. With such emphasis on personal failure, psychological damage, and immorality, little attention was paid to the socioeconomic system or to the discriminatory wages and limited opportunities that black men, in particular, faced.[23] Significantly, in contrast to the 1930s, when images of feminized men made a liberal welfare state seem imperative, similar images now "proved" how problematic a welfare state could be.

As a way to promote visions of responsible masculinity and to contain anxieties about the decline of nuclear families organized around a male wage earner, the discourse on welfare disciplined women in their homes and their bodies. Members of state commissions, local administrators, and journalists were among those who agreed that ADC "is breaking up families, encouraging desertion, divorce, immorality, and neglect of children." Many concluded that recipients were "shiftless, lazy, immoral, degenerate, dishonest, and radical, and must, therefore, be treated with harshness and firmness."[24]

There were several consistent features in discussions of ADC and in efforts to restrict assistance, despite local variations.[25] For one, this discourse represented economically needy women as potentially undeserving and in need of surveillance because their mothering had detrimental effects on future citizens. According to one state official, ADC offered " 'no plan to create a pleasant home for the un-happy children; only to send money each month to a person who, in too many cases, could never qualify as a responsible guardian for anyone's welfare.' "[26] Second, uncontained female sexuality was seen as contributing to maternal failure. Women who were unmarried and sexually active were either emotionally unbal-

In the 1940s and 1950s, the dangers of ADC became more associated with black women. An article titled "The Relief Chiselers are Stealing Us Blind" included a photograph of a black family outside their home. An article titled "The Case for Federal Relief" included a photograph of a white family with a social worker inside their home. Used with permission of the *Saturday Evening Post*.

anced or greedy (or both). "It is entirely possible," wrote one administrator evidently trying to be generous, "that the prospect of financial assistance is an implicit part of the irresponsibility inherent in the psychological makeup of those involved in illicit relationships."[27]

Third, and perhaps most importantly, images that originated with black "matriarchs"—particularly independence from men and potential promiscuity—were central to the negative meanings that ADC accrued. Congress continued to allow states to consider the "moral character" of caretakers in determining ADC eligibility in the postwar period; state policies supported moral means tests to curb women's dependency on the government. "Unsuitable homes" ineligible for ADC included those in which women took in male boarders (a practice through which women earned much-needed money), had more than one illegitimate child, or would not name the fathers of their children. By the early 1960s, twenty-three states had stringent "suitable home" policies that made it more difficult for needy women to receive assistance.[28] It is not hard to hear the echoes of assessments that experts had offered of black families. Similar behavior, after all, had produced family "disorganization" among African Americans according to experts like E. Franklin Frazier and Gunnar Myrdal.[29]

Yet it is crucial to be aware that throughout the 1940s and 1950s the majority of women who received ADC were white.[30] The symbolic racial connotations of welfare did not derive from its numerical racial composition. Demographic factors begin to explain why a program that provided money to more white than black women became associated with black women. In part as a result of efforts to make ADC more equitable, the number of black families receiving this relief increased over the course of the 1940s. This relative liberalization accompanied the shifting over of many widowed white women to social insurance. Negative meanings of welfare escalated as the overall percentage of widowed (mostly white) women receiving ADC shrank, and the overall percentage of black women and unmarried women across lines of race receiving ADC rose.[31]

Statistics alone do not clarify how or why ADC was increasingly—and *conjointly*—stigmatized and racialized. As ADC came to support a greater number of families that departed from a white nuclear two-parent model, more and more people concluded that the program itself *caused* this allegedly deviant behavior. Critics and supporters of ADC invoked images of black women as matriarchs as they repeatedly drew links between the program, promiscuity, and illegitimacy. "ADC fosters illegitimacy," was a common assertion.[32] Many welfare workers themselves came to believe, wrote one liberal official, the all-too-common accusation that "you can't get a maid anymore because all the maids are home . . . living from ADC." An article on ADC in the popular *Saturday Evening Post* depicted "filth in the two-room shack," illegitimate children who "stared vacantly" out the window, sexually active women "whose adventures left me a little stunned," alongside photos of poor black children "in wretched hovels." The author reaffirmed the links between blackness, dirt, sexuality, and femininity that John Dollard had forged in *Caste and Class in a Southern Town*.[33] Charges against ADC affected all women through their discursive relationship to black women.

Welfare administrators in southern states continued to use eligibility requirements to try to keep black women specifically from claiming ADC as a right to which they were entitled. The state welfare director in Georgia, for example, declared that "limiting aid to children of unwed Negro mothers" would save the state thousands of dollars. "Some of them," he explained, "finding themselves tied down with one child are not averse to adding others as a business proposition." In 1951 Georgia was the first state to cut unmarried women who had more than one child from ADC rolls.[34] If women deviated from normative ideas about appropriate motherhood and appropriate female sexuality, the state could regulate their behavior and deny them funds.

When Mississippi reduced its allocations to ADC in the early 1950s, the language in the provisions drew attention to relationships between emotional development, citizenship, sexuality, and race that were evident in other discussions of assistance in this period: " . . . among the recognized functions of the family are the passing on from one generation to another of the special ways of life that make up the civilization of the nation and the development of socially desirable character traits."

Elaborating on the sources and effects of healthy or unhealthy citizenship, a Mississippi policy statement continued: "Flagrant and continued violation of the moral and social standards of the community usually result in emotional and sometimes actual physical damage to the child. . . . Involved here also is the failure of the family to develop and to assist the child to develop sound relationships between the members of the family and the outside community." Provisions stipulated that "casual relations and the birth of an illegitimate child" constituted evidence that "the parent must be termed promiscuous" and the home unsuitable. Unmarried mothers—the "parents" in need of ADC who gave birth to these children—were unable to pass on the values so crucial to American "civilization."[35]

Mississippi's effort to punish "promiscuous" behavior was neither unique nor racially neutral. Two-thirds of ADC recipients in Mississippi were black; even before the new provisions went into effect, all needy families in Mississippi received grants a third less than the national average.[36] Thus restrictions that technically cut across lines of race in practice targeted black families primarily. They did so through images of "promiscuous" behavior historically linked to black femininity. At the same time, southern states were not alone in their efforts to regulate all poor women, white and black, by invoking the racial and gender deviance most closely tied to black women. "Immorality, promiscuity, and unwed motherhood seem to be rewarded" by ADC, declared a New Jersey grand jury seeking to curb benefits to all women with tendencies toward "connivance" and "promiscuity."[37] These sets of associations between gender, sexual, and racial pathology—evident in Mississippi, New Jersey, and elsewhere—cemented the relationship between ADC and black femininity in ways that made all women in need, white and black, seem undeserving.

Finally, despite the fact that ADC was initially designed to give poor women the opportunity to care for their children, there were increasing calls for women on assistance to work in the wageforce. Race shaped this postwar welfare reform as well. Arkansas, for example, defined women as "employable mothers" and therefore ineligible for welfare during planting or harvest time—precisely the period when landowners wanted black women to work as laborers.[38] But regardless of race, poor mothers compelled into wagework were excluded from the celebration of domesticity that fueled the "feminine mystique." The postwar backlash that drove many white middle-class white women out of the workforce did not include women who were dependent in the wrong ways: on government relief instead of on male wage earners.

With masculinity and citizenship as ostensibly motivating forces, the Noleo amendment, "substitute parent" provisions, and other discussions of ADC placed women who were mothers under a microscope, particularly with regard to their sexual behavior. In many places, evidence of a man in her life became yet another way to disqualify a mother from aid. Local laws allowed special units to investigate the finances and, without warning, raid the homes of potential recipients in search of a "substitute father."[39] Several states sought to disclose to the public the names of recipients and the amount of relief that they received. Only such measures would determine true eligibility and make the ADC caseload less "contaminated with in-eligibles."[40] If Farnham and Lundberg projected their concern about the "general citizen" and masculine authority onto neurotic modern women who failed as moth-ers in *Modern Woman: The Lost Sex*, then social welfare legislation projected con-cerns about masculinity and public spending onto "dependent" women who failed as mothers. The same fears recurred: that femininity in men or women them-selves—most often mothers—could psychologically damage citizens and thereby weaken the nation.

Attacks on a welfare system increasingly equated with black women must be seen in relation to civil rights struggles. Ironically, what scholars have regarded as efforts to make ADC more racially equitable during the 1940s made the program vulnerable to opponents of civil rights. Punitive welfare policies that restricted black women's access to public money were a means of resisting African Ameri-cans' demands for equal rights as citizens. Rickie Solinger has explained that "body-centered attacks on childbearing black women as proxies for a race resisting white supremacy" prevented "black women from claiming the means to physical sustenance that the federal government, via ADC legislation and allocations, had deemed their right."[41] Or, in the words of an editorial in the *Arkansas Gazette* in 1959, "Nobody . . . wants to be put in the light of defending both bastardy and Negroes in the same breath."[42] Mississippi established restrictive welfare policies that denied ADC to thousands of black women, for example, in 1954—in the same period that the Supreme Court ruled against segregated education in *Brown v. Board of Education*. This state's efforts to regulate ADC "parents," the majority of whom were black women, came on the heels of this landmark Supreme Court decision.

In sum, discussions of welfare shared a great deal with liberal psychosocial stud-ies of families—especially an approach to citizenship that encouraged interventions into women's lives. In the context of the welfare state, a liberal emphasis on envi-ronment, private life, and psychological development could have positive results. Expansive social insurance policies in the postwar years did help some mothers (mostly widowed and white) and their children. But with regard to assistance, the notion that maternal behavior affected the psychic and political health of future cit-izens reinforced efforts to limit the scope of government assistance, and widened the gap between deserving and undeserving citizens. A strong government was re-strained and less active; it was strong because it did not extend excessive largesse to undeserving women incapable of raising citizens.

In this same period in which social insurance expanded and assistance was stig-matized and racialized, liberal assumptions that racial prejudice was an emotional failure on the part of whites were gaining credibility. To counter what was under-stood as the disease of prejudice, liberals more frequently sought to *expand* the role of the government. But their efforts shared many of the same premises evident in debates about welfare that sought to *contract* state activism.

Combating the "Disease" of Prejudice: Civil Rights Activism during the War and the Cold War

Even before Gunnar Myrdal analyzed racism as white Americans' "dilemma," liberal Americans had begun to regard extreme expressions of prejudice as un-American, unpatriotic, and undemocratic. With fascism and war spreading in Europe, efforts to promote national unity increased; images of interracial cooperation were increasingly integral to such efforts. As Mary McLeod Bethune explained in 1944, "racial advancement and national unity" required blacks and whites to share "together more fully in the benefits of freedom—not 'one as the hand and separate as the fingers,' but one as the clasped hands of friendly cooperation."[43]

By the late 1940s, many liberals who considered race relations through the prism of the Cold War concluded that overt prejudice was antithetical to the democratic ethos that the United States had to promote nationally and internationally. Liberal politicians, activists, and scholars concluded that excessive or violent prejudice reflected an irrational lack of restraint dangerously similar to totalitarianism; moreover, it was a propaganda tool with which the Soviet Union discredited American democracy. "Basic civil rights is the core of our struggle with communist totalitarian forces," wrote Senator Hubert Humphrey, a Democrat, in 1950.[44]

It was in this context that the federal government gradually took a stronger stand against discrimination. Government activism—evident in the establishment of the Fair Employment Practices Committee (FEPC), desegregation of the military, and several Supreme Court rulings—was also based on an ideal citizen who was productive, emotionally stable, and sufficiently masculine.[45] A brief overview suggests how gender underscored these civil rights initiatives designed to expand citizenship.[46]

After the war in Europe began, production in American war-related defense industries accelerated rapidly. By the early 1940s, defense industries were booming and unemployment among whites had declined dramatically. This stable and productive American workforce had political and economic value: it reinforced images of American "preparedness" and patriotism. For the most part, however, industries and labor unions excluded African American men and women. Policies of exclusion changed in late June 1941, when Franklin Roosevelt issued Executive Order 8802, which established the FEPC and outlawed discriminatory hiring practices by defense industries. It was noteworthy because it offered African Americans seeking employment official protection from the federal government.[47]

The significance of Executive Order 8802 also stemmed from the events that led up to FDR's decision to issue it. The president's order came in direct response to pressure from black activists. A. Philip Randolph, the charismatic leader of the Brotherhood of Sleeping Car Porters, coordinated the March on Washington Movement (MOWM) in the spring of 1941. He and other leaders threatened to bring up to one hundred thousand African Americans to the still-segregated city of Washington, D.C. to protest discrimination. Initially they refused the administration's requests to cancel the march. The prospect (or threat, in the eyes of many) of thousands upon thousands of black protesters descending on the nation's capital compelled FDR to issue the executive order.[48]

The March on Washington Movement was an important campaign in the evolution of the modern-day civil rights movement. Clearly, it made a method of protest— nonviolent mass action—visible and credible. It also constructed citizenship in ways that were important to racial liberalism for years to come. Randolph announced the march with a "Call to Negro America" that carefully balanced gendered images of aggression and restraint. The march would be, he wrote, a "mass action that is orderly and lawful, but aggressive and militant."[49]

Supporters drew on these dual images of order and aggression in the months to come. They noted that the march offered black Americans an opportunity to demonstrate their patriotism and to show white Americans that "colored people mean business." At the same time, they emphasized that this willingness to make demands was neither reckless nor unrestrained. The MOWM " 'was not planned, developed, and fostered by irresponsible, wild-eyed crackpots,' " according to Randolph, but was " 'composed of sane, sober, and responsible Negro citizens.' "[50] Adam Clayton Powell Jr., a New York minister, explained that there "was no chip on the shoulders of marching blacks, though resentment still ached in their hearts . . . they were disciplined." Randolph and others also argued that the MOWM promoted psychological well-being. The all-black movement "develops a sense of self-reliance. . . . It helps to break down the slave psychology and inferiority-complex in Negroes." The campaign was important because "blacks were no longer children but a mature minority."[51]

This focus on active yet restrained and mature black citizens drew on ideas about gender mores as well as race relations. For activist racial liberals as for antiracist scholars, a certain kind of masculinity became a sign of racial health and a resource for protest. In rejecting passivity and deciding to march, "the American black man has decided henceforth and forever to abandon the timid role of Uncle-Tomism in his struggle for social justice" wrote the *Chicago Defender*. Adam Clayton Powell Jr. recalled that "great national organizations were ready in 1941. The Urban League had cast off its swaddling clothes, the NAACP stood in the full virility of manhood."[52] The view of citizenship in the MOWM duplicated the assumption so central to antiracist research on black families: that establishing appropriately aggressive black men as active and productive participants in the labor force was necessary for racial progress.

Ideas about class and respectability were important to racial protest. The MOWM promoted a vision of orderly and restrained black citizens; this emphasis on respectability drew on ideas about class-appropriate behavior. But these ideas about class were themselves gendered. Organizers envisioned women and children, as well as men, marching in Washington and planned to have separate groups of fathers, mothers, boys, and girls.[53] Such divisions conveyed the sense that black citizenship and gender-role differentiation went hand in hand; apparently, black citizens, like their white counterparts, shared a commitment to American family values, including distinct roles for men and women. Sex segregation also reinforced images of respectability, precluding charges that the protesters were unruly or promiscuous. In other words, the MOWM promoted class-related images of respectability by drawing on ideas about gender.

The MOWM and subsequent presidential action anticipated a change in antiracism. Certainty the Fair Employment Practices Committee that resulted from the MOWM was hardly a revolutionary step forward. In certain respects, in fact, the executive order that created the FEPC was consistent with the suppression of racial difference characteristic of New Deal liberalism. The FEPC outlawed discrimination, but like previous White House directives, its argument was based on "effective use of scarce manpower" rather than on the need for racial justice. Over time, FEPC possessed no enforcement powers and little funding. The executive order did not touch upon the issue of segregation in the armed forces.[54] It was, effectively, a federal policy that ostensibly upheld equality and interracial cooperation but demanded little. At the same time, with this executive order, the federal government intervened actively to undermine racial discrimination.

Racial liberalism oriented toward some degree of government intervention became more widespread—and more publicized—after the war. The assumption that prejudice was a disease gained political currency in the Truman administration. Several initiatives from the late 1940s and early 1950s further entangled healthy citizenship, appropriate restraint, and interracial cooperation in ways that were gendered.[55] In 1946, for example, Truman appointed the fifteen-person President's Committee on Civil Rights. That year, whites had brutally beaten and murdered several black veterans and others. These and other atrocities received significant publicity, generating protests that drew as many as fifteen thousand people. Protesters were abundantly aware that black veterans had fought for their country abroad—albeit in a segregated and sometimes virulently racist military—and demanded a response from the federal government.[56]

In 1947 the committee issued *To Secure These Rights: The Report of the President's Committee on Civil Rights*. This final report indicated that focusing on prejudice as a psychological disease could foster support for greater government activism on race-related issues. In its condemnation of prejudice, *To Secure These Rights* repeatedly employed the psychological vocabulary and conceptual frameworks prevalent in liberal race-relations research. Prejudice was a "disease" that hurt all Americans. It contributed to "a sense of frustration" (in minorities) "which is wholly alien to the normal emotions of a free man." The report also advocated that the government attempt to prevent prejudice from developing in whites.[57] The disease of prejudice weakened the country and required a "strong need for federal safeguards." The committee recommended renewing the FEPC, passing anti-poll tax and antilynching legislation, and desegregating the military, among other measures. Members based these recommendations on the assumption that such actions on the part of the federal government were "sound in instinct and reason." They were necessary responses to hysterical "outrages" across the nation.[58] In other words, outrages on the part of white Americans afflicted with prejudice required immediate attention from the federal government because those who committed such actions were irrational and defied standards of healthy citizenship. It is not surprising, perhaps, that the Group for the Advancement of Psychiatry was among the liberal organizations, white and black, that heralded the report. This national organization of psychiatrists endorsed the President's Committee "as an aid to mental health in America"; protecting civil rights thwarted the "near-hysteria" of prejudice, and was "vital to the mental health of our citizens."[59]

What was perhaps the most concrete civil rights success on a national scale in these years—the desegregation of the armed forces—provides the most vivid example of how a gendered vision of citizenship and fears of irrational excess characterized the cautious racial reforms common in the early years of the Cold War. In the midst of the presidential campaign of 1948, in which Truman's chances of success seemed slim and in which northern black votes were vital, the president issued Executive Order 9981 ordering military desegregation. Truman's order, though not detailed, provided the foundation for full integration of African Americans into the military.[60]

In the years of activism that preceded and followed Truman's order, supporters of military integration offered a range of arguments. During the war, they drew attention to Nazi racial policies and repeatedly emphasized that it was hypocritical for the United States to fight a war against racism with segregated armed services. In an editorial, "Hitlerism at Home," the *Pittsburgh Courier* charged that "the War Department has bowed from the beginning of the national emergency to the doctrine of white supremacy and racial separatism with a zeal that Dr. Joseph Goebbels would regard as commendable." The call for a "double V"—against fascism abroad and prejudice at home—was quite popular; with this slogan, antiracists designated prejudice as un-American.[61]

In addition to employing antiracist and democratic rhetoric, advocates of military desegregation, white and black, mobilized attributes of masculinity to promote their cause.[62] As was the case with the MOWM, proponents argued that black men were sufficiently masculine—in terms of their patriotism, aggression, and discipline—to serve in the military as equal citizens. One officer attested that volunteer black soldiers exhibited "the aggressive spirit that pervades all ranks and ratings of the Navy." Another general asserted that "the colored soldier individually can be made into a good combat man." These officers and others concurred with Myrdal's assessment that black men were "just the opposite of war dodgers and traitors: they pray to have the right to fight and die for their country."[63]

In challenging longstanding racist military practices, advocates of integration challenged myths that had historically diminished black manhood. "The stereotype of the shiftless, ambitionless plantation hand did not characterize the Negro soldier," concluded one group of researchers. Supporters affirmed black men's potential as loyal soldiers who followed orders but who also "exhibited ambition for personal advancement themselves." Some even took on the myth of the black man as a sexual predator. Venereal disease was more common among black than white soldiers, researchers explained, not because black men were inherently sexually aggressive but because of the women they encountered. Black men stationed abroad "had difficulty in associating with better classes of local women—especially after a few months of experiences with American troops had familiarized local populations with American racial attitudes."[64]

Arguments in favor of military integration did not focus only on African American men. Another way to discredit segregation was to consider the negative impact it had on whites in the military. Desegregation would reduce prejudice in whites, and morale and efficiency would improve in an integrated military. All in all, as the President's Advisory Commission on Military Training asserted, programs that "forced our young manhood to live . . . in an atmosphere which emphasized or bred class or racial differences" would "nullify the important lesson in citizenship which such training could give."[65] In subtle and not so subtle ways these arguments implied that *not* to integrate the military was risky—to whites—in light of the effects of segregation on Negro manhood. "The low morale of Negro servicemen," explained one observer, "expresses itself in apathy, passive resistance . . . sporadic aggression and actual rebellion." While dissatisfied black soldiers were "not revolutionaries plotting the overthrow of the present social system," according to one group of observers, "there was a readiness to protest which was quite inconsistent with the stereotype of happy-go-lucky indifference." As an article titled "The Negro's New Belligerency" explained, even optimists were "alarmed by the Negro's increasing belligerency and by the unmistakable rise of counter-antagonisms among the whites."[66] Like racism in American society generally, segregation in the military affected white and black soldiers emotionally and politically—as citizens, as men, and as soldiers. But it could have particularly dangerous effects on white Americans *because* of its effects on black men.

Finally, antiracists used ideas about families and mothers as part of their political campaign. Some explained black men's deficiencies as soldiers in terms of their upbringing and environment. Poor soldiering was not the result of innate or inherent racial differences. For instance, there were more "neuropsychiatric" black than white soldiers because "Negro children are more likely than white to have had an unhappy childhood." Psychoneurotic black men "were more likely to say that they were punished without cause." This argument echoed that of the military psychiatrist Edward Strecker. In his popular tract *Their Mothers' Sons*, Strecker explained that many white soldiers were psychologically unfit because of their mothers.[67] Ideas about black women as good mothers also played a role in efforts to desegregate the military. Black women positioned themselves as loyal women and mothers "with husbands, sons, brothers, etc., who are likely to be lost," in their campaign against a segregated military. As one woman wrote in 1947, "we as mothers oppose a bill which would betray our sons and the best interests of our nation."[68]

Service in the American military figured as a "reward" to black men who were appropriately aggressive, restrained, and masculine; it was a source of possible transformation for those who were not.[69] The battle for military desegregation, which continued into the Korean War, was part of a more widespread vision of American citizenship in which national strength, restrained yet aggressive masculinity, and, increasingly, interracial cooperation all stood in for each other.

With the exception of military desegregation, the government did not implement the recommendations from *To Secure These Rights*. Nevertheless, the related preoccupation with prejudiced attitudes and excessive aggression in *To Secure These Rights* was evident in other areas. In the 1940s and 1950s the NAACP legal defense fund waged legal battles against segregation; in several instances, the administration offered amicus curiae briefs in support of these civil rights cases. Legal successes included *Shelley v. Kraemer* (1948), a ruling that state-sponsored covenants prohibiting the sale of land to nonwhites were unconstitutional; *Henderson v. United States* (1950), a ruling against segregated railroad dining cars; and the famous ruling against school segregation in *Brown v. Board of Education* (1954).

As scholars have noted, these cases legally codified scholarly research by highlighting how discrimination damaged the self-esteem of black children.[70] In *Briggs v. Elliott* in 1951 and the more famous *Brown v. Board of Education* in 1954, Justices concurred with the brief arguing that segregation contributed to a "defeatist attitude" in unhealthfully passive black children. An editorial in *Life* avowed that discrimination in schools "results in heavy social waste and damage to individuals." As one psychologist put it, with its emphasis on the inferiority complex, *Brown* was "the greatest compliment ever paid to psychology by the powers-that-be."[71]

But *Brown* and other cases implied that prejudice could have more than merely a psychological impact. As Mary Dudziak, a legal historian, has demonstrated, some cases "raised the specter of black radicalism in the U.S." Black Americans who suffered from prejudice and felt inferior as a result might, like black soldiers, act out; they could not be counted on to be good citizens. According to the Justice Department brief in *Henderson v. United States* (1950), "a society professing equality but practicing segregation . . . furnishes justification and reason for the latent urge to rebel, and frequently leads to lasting bitterness or total rejection of the American creed and system of government."[72]

These images of psychological damage and rebellion drew on anxieties about masculinity. Indeed, fears of radicalism were related to fears of certain types of men. As was the case in discussions of military service, *Henderson* legitimated judicial activism by pointing to the damage that frustrated and aggressive black men could inflict on the "American creed"—and on white citizens. It was potentially rebellious or bitter black men—the alter ego of the passive Sambo figure—who so worried whites and had done so for over a century. Such men now figured largely in antiracism, in films like *Home of the Brave*, in scholarship by eminent intellectuals, and in recommendations for policies and court rulings. Racial liberals invoked centuries-old stereotypes in order, ultimately, to counter them, and to affirm the potential of black men who departed from them.

Inherent to racial liberalism in this period was the sense that the government needed to promote the development of black manhood. But antiracist logic that promoted an empowered masculinity was infused with images of femininity as dangerous to the ideal citizen. It can be difficult to remember that this civil rights activism gained momentum in the same period that attacks on ADC did. Representations of black women who raised insufficiently masculine black men and ongoing assumptions among liberals that black families were "disorganized" were contemporaneous with affirmations of black citizenship.

In fact, ideas about masculinity evident in civil rights activism and ideas about femininity in welfare legislation were crucially related. Social welfare legislation coded black mothers as dangerous because they were sexual, independent from men, and dependent on the state. These women, then, were part of the problem that black men—who so needed the jobs that FEPC might provide and who so needed the training and male camaraderie that an integrated army offered—faced.

Accordingly, restrained masculinity was as important in the bids for civil rights in this period as it was in discussions of ADC. Similar fears of excesses and irrationality structured racial liberalism and discussions of welfare. In *To Secure These Rights*, court cases, and elsewhere, perceptions of excessive prejudice and deviant behavior in whites strengthened support for government activism. By contrast, perceptions of excessive sexuality and other deviant behavior in women (particularly mothers and even more particularly black mothers) underlay calls for the federal government to provide less assistance to those unworthies. In both cases, there was a sense that these excesses had a rippling effect that went beyond the individual and the private sphere and affected society as a whole. In both areas, liberals worried about overly aggressive citizens who might "rebel" or overly passive Americans who lacked the "special values" of American civilization.

There was, however, a crucial difference in reactions to these dangerous excesses: in social security legislation, the problem of uncontained female sexuality served to limit liberalism. This occurred as ideas that had assumed meaning in relation to black women were projected onto all women. By contrast, for racial liberals, the problem of uncontained prejudice motivated liberal activism, at least on some occasions. Common concerns about unrestrained citizens who might hurt the liberal welfare state prompted efforts to restrict welfare on the one hand and to expand civil rights on the other. Further, punitive policies made women political objects, whereas interventionist civil rights policies that affected all African Americans but promoted an ideal masculinity made men political subjects.

Clearly, a psychosocial approach to race was not consistently a galvanizing force. The notion of prejudice as a psychosocial problem, along with related concerns about masculinity and aggression, made it easier, at times, for liberals to minimize the need for structural reforms. Even when resisting racial discrimination became more prominent on the liberal agenda, and despite the condemnation of prejudice and the recommendations for legislation and other reforms in *To Secure These Rights*, the postwar years were marked by a relative absence of concrete government action.[73] It is worth recalling that *because* the black private in the postwar film *Home of the Brave* resolves his feelings of frustration, he is able to conclude, "we're all guys." It is this realization, rather than a significant policy change, which enables him to participate in the interracial, masculine community. This conflation of political health, psychological well-being, and a secure gender identity can help us to understand liberal anticommunism.

"New Virility" and "The Sin of Racial Pride": Gender, Race, and Anticommunist Liberalism

Arthur Schlesinger Jr. said relatively little about race relations in *The Vital Center* and had even less to say about gender or welfare. Nevertheless, the images of femininity as dangerous that were important to discussions of welfare, and the images of inappropriate aggression as an emasculating psychological disorder that were important to discussions of race relations, intersected in anticommunist liberalism. What one reviewer called a "passionate, witty, brilliantly executed" defense of liberalism relied on paradoxical codes of masculinity and citizenship that insisted on sufficient but not excessive aggression.[74] *The Vital Center* suggests that in anticommunist liberalism even more than in debates about welfare and civil rights, this paradox was evident in the demand for state intervention as a sign of American strength in some instances, alongside a demand for state restraint as a sign for strength in others.[75]

Schlesinger's quest for a vital center was quite literal: he insisted that the ideal state and its citizens must be "vital"—sufficiently strong, active and even aggressive when necessary, yet anchored in a "center" characterized by unity and restraint, a rejection of extremes, and cooperation. This quest for moderation and strength, in both citizens and states, was profoundly shaped by psychologically oriented analyses. One reviewer observed that new liberals like Schlesinger were "less doggedly rationalist. . . . Freud renewed their belief in the irrationality of the will; Hitler and Stalin revealed to them the hideous excesses of which men are still capable."[76] In an effort to understand this irrationality, anticommunist liberals turned a psychological gaze outward *and* inward, demanding self-scrutiny. Schlesinger offered chapters on "the failure of the right" and "the failure of the left," but he also probed lines of continuity between these dangers and liberalism. The internal enemies that anticommunist liberals feared included the "individual's own psyche."[77]

Elaine Tyler May has noted that this postwar political discourse rested on entrenched and "well-articulated assumptions about masculine power."[78] Schlesinger repeatedly interwove images of femininity and political weakness and contrasted them with images of masculinity and national strength. Pragmatic new liberalism, for example, was the antidote to a political right that was "subject to spasms of panic and hysteria" and to the "shrill" left liberal of the 1930s and 1940s. He chastised old liberals for their "soft not hard" approach to communism and their "impotence."[79] The old liberal or fellow traveler, Schlesinger elaborated, had a "feminine fascination with the rude and muscular power of the proletariat . . . immersing himself in the broad maternal expanse of the masses."[80] "Vigorous" new liberalism, by contrast, offered "passion" and would bring "a new virility into public life."[81] The theologian Reinhold Niebuhr, a strong influence on Schlesinger, evaluated political systems using similar language and values. The "hard utopianism" of communism was obviously threatening, according to the anticommunist Niebuhr. But he also regarded the "soft utopianism" of overly "sentimental" liberal democracies as potentially insidious.[82]

Recurring references to virility and impotence, and to hardness and softness were not coincidental, and nor were diagnoses of politics in terms of paranoia and insecurity. Gendered language and imagery were an essential part of the psychological analysis of politics so salient to Cold War liberalism. They were the means through which *The Vital Center* made sense of the world. The vocabulary had productive value in that it allowed Schlesinger, and other liberals, to analyze dangers that Americans faced at home and abroad and to formulate responses to these dangers. For instance, Schlesinger's extensive discussion—and condemnation—of American communism did not make sense without an understanding that feelings of frustration were politically dangerous because they undermined masculinity. American communists were "lonely and frustrated people, craving social, intellectual and even sexual fulfillment they cannot obtain in existing society." Communism, he explained, was a "disease" and a seductress; it was repellent yet compelling—much as prejudice was in Lillian Smith's *Killers of the Dream*. Schlesinger depicted the political dangers that totalitarianism posed with potent sexual and psychological imagery. Totalitarianism was a "psychosis" that offered "profound psychological appeal" but "perverts politics" into "something secret, sweaty and furtive like nothing so much . . . as homosexuality in a boy's school."[83]

Furtive homosexuality was perhaps the ultimate symbol of the damage that could occur if sexuality permeated the political realm, and Schlesinger was one among many liberals who used images of homosexuality to define weak and feminized men.[84] Fears of homosexuality figured in liberal discourse in the 1940s and 1950s in ways that rendered heterosexual sex a precondition to political progress. The particular goals varied: for Lillian Smith in *Killers of the Dream*, healthy heterosexuality help white boys to grow up free from prejudice; for Abram Kardiner and Lionel Ovesey in *The Mark of Oppression*, healthy heterosexuality helped mature black men improve race relations. For Schlesinger, it could ensure a strong democracy that celebrated pluralism but was untainted by communism. In these and other liberal projects, the wrong kind of sexuality was politically dangerous because the wrong kind of men—and citizens—embraced it. This perspective on sexuality was part of liberalism itself and was not a vestige of conservatism pasted on to otherwise progressive political visions. Thus Schlesinger did not only express political anxieties with language that was gendered; anxieties about masculinity were integral to this political vision. Further, in equating political strength and a certain kind of masculinity on the one hand, and political weakness and femininity on the other, *The Vital Center* relied on sets of associations that circulated widely in this period.[85]

To meet the multiple dangers that communism posed, anticommunist liberals supported activist measures on the part of the federal government. Despite some dissent within its then-small ranks, the Americans for Democratic Action (ADA), an organization dedicated to anticommunist liberalism, supported the Truman Doctrine granting military aid to Greece and Turkey announced in March 1947 and responded with even more enthusiasm to the Marshall Plan for Western Europe announced that June. Shortly after the Soviet Union exploded an atomic weapon in September 1949, the United States joined the North Atlantic Treaty Organization (NATO), committing arms and money to this mutual defense pact.[86] Schlesinger felt that these virtually unprecedented peacetime deployments of American money and troops signaled strength and were aspects of "containment" that protected nations against "totalitarian aggression" on the part of the Soviet Union. Building on distinctions between "soft" old liberalism and the vital center, he noted that with its tough "maturity" and "cold correctness," new liberalism could meet the true evils of totalitarianism.[87]

Words like *aggression, security*, and *insecurity*, and images of neurosis or mental health were frequent terms through which anticommunist liberals interpreted American-Soviet relations. The Soviets were excessive and irrational—the wrong kind of aggressors. The United States, with its "firm resistance" and belief in cooperation, could resist excessive physical and psychological aggression on the part of communists. These were fundamental premises in the emerging foreign policy of Cold War liberalism.[88] For example, when Clark Clifford, special counsel to President Truman, supported an American military expansion that even included biological warfare, he did so by juxtaposing America's quest for security and "preparedness" to "aggressive militaristic imperialism" in the Soviet Union. U.S. actions reflected strength and preparedness and were mobilized in the name of cooperation and international security. The "primary objective" of American foreign policy, Clifford asserted, was "to convince the Soviet leaders that it is in their interest to participate in a system of world cooperation."[89]

But *The Vital Center* rejected government activism that veered into unrestraint and irrational aggression. Just as Schlesinger endorsed government activism by projecting images of sufficient *aggression*, strength, and masculinity onto the state, so, too, he endorsed government inaction by projecting images of *self-restraint*, strength, and masculinity onto the state. To do so, he evoked anxieties about gender. For example, Schlesinger scorned HUAC investigations as "witch hunts" and "promiscuous and unprincipled attacks" that ignited dangerous "hysteria" and harmed American "vitality."[90] Conversely, if HUAC was excessive, investigations into the loyalty of government employees and the firing of "suspect" employees were sound responses. "If irresponsible power is the source of evil," reasoned

Schlesinger, "and irresponsible impotence, the source of decadence, then responsible power . . . is the source of wisdom."[91] Within Cold War liberalism, decadence, promiscuity, and hysteria signified undesirable political extremes and either excessive or insufficient aggression. Historically, both gender and race had shaped the meanings of promiscuity, decadence, and irrationality, and the gendered terms common in *The Vital Center* were simultaneously racial markers.[92] Schlesinger worried that frustrated and feminized citizens could weaken American democracy, as did racial liberals intent on social change. Racial liberals in this period equated racial health with normative masculinity, a logic echoed by Schlesinger in articulating anticommunist liberalism and by critics of ADC in stigmatizing and racializing welfare. Postwar liberalism invoked images of impotence or hystericia, relying on interrelated gender and racial ideologies to do so. Similar terms underscored ideas about what endangered liberal democracy.

Even though *The Vital Center* was most concerned with the dangers that communism posed, it revealed that the issue of race relations was on the liberal agenda by 1949, even among those who did not regard it as all-important. In a larger discussion of freedom, Schlesinger asserted that it "is fatal not to maintain an unrelenting attack on all forms of racial discrimination," arguing that the "sin of racial pride still represents the most basic challenge to the American conscience."[93] Like the President's Commission on Civil Rights, *The Vital Center* considered racist attitudes, specifically racial pride in whites, as an obstacle to progress.

Despite his perspective on prejudice, Schlesinger came to a conclusion quite different from that of the presidential report. Whereas *To Secure These Rights* called for immediate action, *The Vital Center* supported only moderate or gradual reforms: "For most Americans . . . the basic principles of civil rights are now clearly defined" and accepted, Schlesinger explained—"at least in principle." Consequently, he wanted to avoid policies that were too extreme. The attitudes of whites had changed because they had accepted those basic principles of civil rights; that factor, rather than the ongoing realities of and discrimination in the lives of African Americans and inequities of power between groups was the important piece in Schlesinger's brief discussion. In fact, "even the South on the whole accepts the objectives of the civil rights program as legitimate, even though it may have serious and intelligible reservations about timing and method."[94] By validating white southerners' reservations, *The Vital Center* corroborated the views of "moderate" white southerners like Virginius Dabney, editor of The Richmond *Times Dispatch*, who accused "extremist" blacks of "demanding an overnight revolution in race relations" that would unleash violence and incite "interracial hate."[95]

Because anticommunist liberalism required civil rights to fall within the parameters of a vital center, it marginalized civil rights. Despite their stance against racism, few Cold War liberals, for example, opposed the Council of Industrial Organizations' expulsions of eleven progressive unions accused of communist infiltration—all with strong records for interracial organizing and leadership. By segregating questions of civil rights from "hard" anticommunism and subordinating the former to the latter, anticommunist liberals positioned themselves within a liberal center. They embraced antiracism more readily than New Deal liberals had and made questions of race relations more central to their agenda. Yet they distanced themselves from components of New Deal liberalism—for example the labor movement—through which black men and women had actually gained increased wages and leadership positions. With its emphasis on universality and freedom, vital center liberalism recognized and accommodated the principles of civil rights; the ADA was instrumental in getting a civil rights plank included in the Democratic Party platform at the national convention in 1948.[96] However, a desire to minimize conflict coupled with fears of excessive aggression on the part of recalcitrant white southerners rendered this commitment to principles largely symbolic.

Schlesinger's brief discussion of civil rights in *The Vital Center* indicates that a psychological focus on the sources and effects of racism could have conservative implications even though it emanated from liberal and antiracist scholarly research. *The Vital Center* reflected many of the overlapping tendencies to de-emphasize racial difference, focus on attitudes, and reinforce codes of masculinity that were evident in civil rights policies in this period. Schlesinger argued that the vital center must accommodate many peoples; he also drew attention to the harm that prejudice caused to all citizens, white and black. Nonetheless, because this paradigm for thinking about race minimized the power most whites held over most African Americans, it could not account for the impact that racial differences actually had. By making prejudice an individual, psychological problem, Cold War liberalism advocated moderation and restraint in government activism with regard to civil rights: to diminish the possibility of domestic conflict (particularly in the South) and to highlight the potential unity of all citizens.[97]

These limits confined vital center liberalism even though Schlesinger and others valued dissent (or "unmolested inquiry") and pluralist liberal politics. The liberal celebration of difference was carefully circumscribed; diversity and dissent were valuable, as long as they were neither extreme nor divisive.[98] In vital center liberalism, dissent was contingent upon bolstering masculinity and upon the erasure, in many respects, of race. The paradox of Cold War liberalism in all these different areas—from scholarly work to political tracts, from welfare policies to civil rights activism—stemmed from the ways that it endorsed difference and condemned prejudice at the same time that it regulated difference and limited racial reforms.

Using psychological frameworks to help define the healthy citizen yielded more than one result. As racial prejudice became a psychological problem that afflicted white and black Americans, civil rights seemed to assume greater urgency on a national liberal agenda. But another result of exploring emotional life in order to interpret social problems was to individualize and feminize pathology—be it poverty or racism or domestic communism—in ways that linked seemingly unrelated, but in fact, overlapping debates. When social security legislation, civil rights initiatives, and anticommunist liberalism are analyzed together, they reveal that fears of eviscerating frustration and unhealthy aggression in American citizens were widespread among liberals in the 1940s and 1950s. Gender anxieties were integral to the liberal project of reasserting national strength as the country moved from Depression to war to Cold War, *particularly* when national strength now included interracial harmony and psychological well-being. Together, these phenomena explain how visions of restrained masculinity became virtually synonymous with citizenship, and why femininity generally, bad mothers, and qualities tied to black women most specifically were dangerous to this model of liberal citizenship. A common matrix of thought characterized these liberal narratives: black and white women, and qualities associated with femininity, produced politically undesirable qualities, which in turn produced equally undesirable behavior in men.

If the "personal is political" was the rallying cry of the late 1960s, in the immediate postwar period the "political is personal" was perhaps a guiding principle. It was through this rendering of politics as personal and psychological that the "good" and "bad" mother—black and white—did political work in the reconfiguration of liberalism. In the next chapter we will consider one black woman's efforts to assign her own personal and political meanings to motherhood in the aftermath of the very public Supreme Court decision *Brown v. Board of Education*. We will see the effects she had on the related questions of who was a healthy American citizen, and who was a good mother. And we will see the effects racial ideologies of motherhood within liberalism had on her.

CHAPTER FOUR

"I Wanted the Whole World To See"

Constructions of Motherhood in the Death of Emmett Till

T he murder of fourteen-year-old African American Emmett Till in the summer of 1955 was grisly. Late Saturday night on August 28, Roy Bryant,
twenty-four years old, and his half-brother J. W. Milam, thirty-six years
old, kidnapped Emmett Till, a native of Chicago, at gunpoint from his relatives'
cabin in Money, Mississippi. Several days after the abduction, a white teenager
found Till's body in the nearby Tallahatchie River. Till had been brutally beaten
and shot in the skull, and one eye was gouged out. In the hope of weighting the mu-
tilated body in the water, Till's murderers had tied a hundred-pound cotton gin fan
to his neck with barbed wire. Till allegedly had whistled at Carolyn Bryant, Roy
Bryant's wife and the mother of two young sons. The two white men felt compelled
to avenge what they perceived as a racial and sexual transgression.[1]

Authorities in Mississippi arrested, indicted, and tried Bryant and Milam for
murder. During the five-day trial in September, three television networks daily
flew footage from Mississippi to New York for the nightly news.[2] "Will Mississippi
Whitewash the Emmett Till Slaying?" asked *Jet* magazine in a photo essay depict-
ing Till in life and death. On Friday, September 23, the all-white, all-male jury deliberated for only sixty-seven minutes before returning a verdict of not guilty. Less
than two months later in November, a grand jury chose not to indict Milam and
Bryant on charges of kidnapping. They were free men.[3]

This brutal murder transfixed the country, and the subsequent acquittals exacerbated the horror and collective anger that the killing evoked. In the weeks before
and after the trial, dozens of rallies with crowds of over ten thousand protesters
were held around the country. Till's relatives and others involved in the trial told of
their experiences, raised funds for the NAACP, and urged voter registration. "Not
since Pearl Harbor has the country been so outraged as by the . . . [Till] lynching
. . . and the unconscionable verdict," commented one magazine.[4]

Till's murder occurred in the mid-1950s, one year after the Supreme Court had observed in its landmark *Brown v. Board of Education of Topeka* ruling that segregation damaged the self-esteem of black children. This period was one of growing defensiveness and violence on the part of some white southerners; the postwar moment in which Arthur Schlesinger Jr. could write that "the South on the whole accepts the objectives of the civil rights program as legitimate" had passed. Shortly after the *Brown* ruling, White Citizens' Councils, which were "respectable" and largely middle-class white supremacist organizations, sprang up throughout the region. The Councils grew amidst fears that the federal government was going to "interfere" too aggressively in the southern racial caste system; they also reflected efforts to intimidate African Americans who claimed rights as citizens. In Mississippi alone, two other black males were shot to death between May and August 1955; both had registered to vote.[5]

The year 1955 was also one of cautious optimism in many black communities. The activism that had led to the March on Washington Movement and the FEPC in the early 1940s, to the President's Committee on Civil Rights and military desegregation in the late 1940s, and to a string of successful civil rights court cases in the 1940s and 1950s was growing. The African American newspaper the *Chicago Defender* celebrated its fiftieth anniversary in 1955 with an eighty-page edition that "epitomizes the position of the American Negro today in relation to his native country. All of the elements that have gone into his development and progress in the United States are embodied in this issue . . . a hefty, tangible symbol of our democracy." The year would end with the onset of the Montgomery bus boycott, a campaign that would break segregated public transportation in that city of the deep South and bring an obscure black minister, Martin Luther King Jr., to national attention.[6]

Of course, the year of Till's murder was marked by many other events and attitudes, seemingly unrelated to support for or opposition to racial liberalism. There was an ongoing consensus in the mid-1950s that mothers were responsible for the psychological and physical well-being of their children—an assumption that shaped both progressive scholarship and repressive social security legislation, as we have seen. Self-identified liberal Americans were among those who emphasized that a "good" woman was one whose primary concerns were her home and family and who was, perhaps most importantly, a nurturing mother. In a commencement address at Smith College in May 1955, liberal Democrat Adlai Stevenson urged each graduate to become a mother and inspire "in her home a vision of the meaning of life and freedom . . . help her husband find values that will give purpose to his specialized daily chores."[7] Television moms like June Cleaver projected images of good white mothers onto recently acquired screens across the country; these representations of motherhood retained their power despite increases in women's labor-force participation and the alternative gender roles that popular culture offered. African American periodicals and fiction also continued to celebrate motherhood and domesticity. Roi Ottley, a columnist, praised black mothers for caring for and disciplining their children successfully, arguing that they were more effective than "modern" white mothers.[8]

Mamie Till Bradley, a thirty-three-year-old African American woman who lived, worked, and raised her child in Chicago, was a part of these seemingly unrelated currents in race relations and gender roles.[9] The interdependence between traditional ideas about gender roles and progressive ideas about race relations came into sharp focus as antiracists and racists reacted to the murder of her son, Emmett Till.

Assumptions about black and white women as mothers were not incidental to the widely publicized murder of Emmett Till—an episode that many people cite as critical to the birth of the civil rights movement.[10] To analyze reactions to the southern-born and Chicago-bred Mamie Bradley is to discover that motherhood itself was a battleground on which the meaning of Till's death was fought. Both racists and antiracists, conservatives and liberals invoked, constructed, and relied upon meanings of motherhood to formulate their related views on race relations and American citizenship, on families and gender roles, and on the role of the federal government vis-a-vis race relations.

Historians and commentators interested in the Till case have analyzed it in terms of the racial, regional, and class conflicts that Till's death brought to the fore. Initially, many white southerners condemned the murder and praised the speedy indictment of the two men they now labeled "white trash" or "peckerwoods." In the days immediately following Bryant and Milam's arrest, local lawyers intentionally named fees that they knew the men could not afford, and the two had no legal counsel. When white southerners rejected the alleged murderers, they seemed to confirm Gunnar Myrdal's prediction in *An American Dilemma* that because "people want to be rational," support for violent expressions of prejudice would diminish.[11] But this position was short-lived. As many white southerners concluded that the South itself was under attack and on trial, and as blacks around the country mobilized politically to protest the murder, an all-white alliance developed to defend Milam and Bryant and to protect power relations in the region. Within a week of the murder, all five attorneys in Sumner, Mississippi, agreed to collaborate in Bryant and Milam's defense; a "defense fund" raised $10,000 for the two. The impact of the case, scholars have argued, stemmed in part from the way that one region of the country felt itself set against another.[12]

Because Bryant and Milam murdered Till for his ostensible advances toward Carolyn Bryant, discussions of the murder have explored the gendered dimensions of Till's alleged racial transgression. Yet scholars often analyze gender in terms of the white woman, Carolyn Bryant; she becomes the only woman who is relevant to these events. Similarly, discussions of race and the political mobilization that the murder generated tend to focus on black men; either Till or Moses Wright, Till's uncle and a prominent witness in the trial, become the only blacks (and heroes) who are relevant to these events. These frameworks obscure the relationships among gender, race, and class and the ways in which these fluid categories interacted in liberal reactions to this event. Consequently, a central figure in understanding how meanings of Till's death developed has been largely effaced: Mamie Till Bradley.[13]

Mamie Till Bradley was central to the politicization of her son's murder. She chose to open his casket to the world and thus helped make his death an international civil rights issue. Bradley actively involved herself in the events that followed the murder, including the funeral, the trial, and the political mobilization the murder spurred. In the process, she defined her own subjectivity as a black woman and a black mother.[14] Bradley is one of the many women who demonstrate that liberal scholars like E. Franklin Frazier and others who represented black women as potentially damaging did not speak for black women themselves. Restrictive welfare policies that cast suspicion on all needy women through images associated with matriarchy did not keep women from making demands on the nation-state. Nor could civil rights activism that privileged masculinity keep black women from claiming their own rights as citizens and mothers. Bradley explicitly politicized motherhood on a number of levels. She challenged black women's exclusion from celebrations of white motherhood, an exclusion evident in social insurance legislation that privileged white widows. She also challenged black and white women's marginal status in a gendered liberal political discourse, a marginalization that was manifest in the Cold War liberalism that Arthur Schlesinger Jr. articulated. Her actions exposed the ways in which liberal conceptions of citizenship relied upon normative ideas about masculinity and upon unquestioned assumptions about race and gender.

The story of Mamie Till Bradley demonstrates that women's interventions into a liberal discourse on motherhood could have multiple meanings and consequences. In claiming her role as a grieving mother, Bradley injected motherhood more forcefully into the political landscape of liberalism and defined herself as a political subject. But she could not control the terms of the debate or the ways in which she became a symbol. Not surprisingly, perhaps, those who defended the murderers invoked assumptions about "natural" (white) motherhood that privileged Carolyn Bryant and excluded Mamie Till Bradley. They did so in order to preserve citizenship and the racial caste system as these were defined in the South. However, in its political battle for black citizenship, the NAACP, too, sought to contain Bradley and define the meaning of motherhood. As had been the case since the 1930s and was increasingly apparent in the 1940s, liberal claims to citizenship that included African Americans were also gendered. The racial liberalism that took shape after Till's murder depended on divisions between a public and rational masculinity and a private and emotional femininity. In their quest for civil rights, liberals needed first to define, and then to marginalize, Mamie Till Bradley when she did not adhere to certain gender roles. In short, because Bradley acted as she did—as a woman, mother, and African American, in the public and private spheres—she became an object to be positioned, defined, and contained by those across the political spectrum.

"A Mother's World Came to an End": The Meanings of Respectable Motherhood

Representations of Till's death revolved around contested meanings of motherhood and respectability. Who or what was a "natural" or a "good" mother? What sources of authority did this role confer and who was excluded from this category?

Who was and who was not respectable? Could either the African American and northern Mamie Till Bradley or the white, southern, less financially stable Carolyn Bryant be cast as respectable?

Powerful as these categories were, their meanings were not fixed, and motherhood did not confer automatic authority on either Mamie Bradley or Carolyn Bryant. Indeed, precisely because motherhood was considered the ultimate form of womanhood, any woman might be judged and found wanting based on her maternal capacities. Over the course of the 1950s, experts in psychology, sexology, sociology, and other interdisciplinary areas continued to interpret motherhood as the source for a range of social and political problems ranging from communism and homosexuality to juvenile delinquency and feelings of racial inferiority.[15]

Nevertheless, white motherhood afforded women potential power and demanded at least rhetorical loyalty.[16] The (mostly white) widowed mothers who were entitled to receive social insurance were just one example of how the state rewarded white mothers who seemed good, or deserving. In the same week that thousands waited in line to view Till's body, reviewers praised Herman Wouk's novel *Marjorie Morningstar*, the tale of an aspiring actress turned mother and homemaker. She "fulfilled her destiny," sang one voice in the chorus of praise, and was a model for women everywhere—"their lives at last disposed into the state which becomes them." Even critiques of white mothers retained a basic belief in mothers' potential importance as civilizers of men.[17]

Carolyn Bryant had access to this image of motherhood as the ultimate state of womanhood. She did so despite the fact that she was hardly the typical (white) suburban housewife/mother. The glorification of domesticity and motherhood that Betty Friedan later named as oppressive might have been restricted to upwardly mobile women in suburbia; symbolically, however, this ideology of womanhood accommodated *all* white women across lines of class.[18] *Mama*, for example, a popular television program on CBS, celebrated a working-class Norwegian immigrant family, especially the hard-working and domestic "mama" of the title. A 1956 issue of *Look* magazine devoted to American women lauded "this wondrous creature" who "married younger than ever, bears more babies and looks and acts far more feminine than the emancipated girl of the 1920s or even 1930's. *Steelworker's wife and Junior Leaguer alike* do their own housework."[19] Carolyn Bryant, twenty-one years old in 1955, was married and had two young sons. She worked in her home as well as in the small country store she and her husband struggled to maintain. She too, then, was a "wondrous creature."

For whites, and especially for financially insecure southern whites like Roy and Carolyn Bryant, this gender ideology was deeply intertwined with race relations. Both white men involved in Till's murder were notches above the sharecroppers and tenant farmers of both races who populated the rural South; still, Roy and Carolyn Bryant owned a small country store that could not support the family of four, and Roy Bryant engaged in a variety of other jobs to make ends meet.[20] Whiteness established the code by which "protecting" white womanhood permitted violence against African Americans. Relying on idealized images of white womanhood to strengthen white racial dominance was not new in 1955. In this period, however, white southerners like Bryant and Milam were drawing on a gendered logic and a prevailing emphasis on motherhood to contest an increasingly ascendant racial liberalism. For Bryant and Milam, their rights as citizens and men were shaped by images of respectable womanhood, as well as by race and class. In part as a result of representations of Carolyn Bryant as a "good" white woman and mother, the two men emerged from the trial as worthy citizens in the eyes of many. The paradox is that these same gender codes and divisions between "good" and "bad" women shaped the liberal discourse on race that the men opposed.

African American motherhood was far more fraught with potential pitfalls. As evidenced in the stigmatization and racialization of ADC in the 1940s and 1950s, the negative qualities associated with "matriarchy" cast a wide net. Despite women's efforts to support and care for their families, liberal scholars often continued to argue that they were "disorganizing," and that this "matriarchy" interfered with racial progress. As scholars who opposed racism continued to rely on the authoritative work of E. Franklin Frazier, and as the liberal welfare state itself consolidated assumptions that black women were suspect, matriarchy and black pathology became ever-interwoven concepts. The absence of traditional gender roles among blacks was synonymous with "the Negro's cultural inferiority and therefore inequality."[21]

In this context, Mamie Till Bradley's credentials as a mother, and as a working single mother especially, were highly contested. For defenders of Till and for liberal supporters of civil rights, constructing Mamie Bradley as a respectable mother was a means through which African Americans could assert their right to the American credo of equal rights for all. The message was that if Till came from a family that loved him, that cried for him—a "good" family—then his murder, and racial discrimination generally, violated American political values because it violated this healthy private sphere. The degree to which Till had been successfully mothered would corroborate his innocence and his "Americanism" as well as the legitimacy of those who opposed his murder. His identity as an innocent victim depended on his position as a son raised in a stable family by a good mother.

Mamie Till Bradley worked as a voucher examiner in Chicago's Air Force Procurement Office and earned $3,900 annually, well above the median income of black families in this period. Bradley could afford the $11.10 ticket for her son to take the segregated train for a vacation in Mississippi.[22] That the urban-bred Till was killed while vacationing in the country, a wholesome teenage experience gone awry, was not lost on sympathetic whites. "The boy's mother could not send him to the mountains, nor to the seashore," editorialized *Commonweal*. "His uncle is poor and his home is a cabin, but to the boy from Chicago's streets, a vacation in Mississippi sounded fine." Race had intruded into the vacation, continued this editorial, and "tragically, a mother's world came to an end and thousands of Negroes stood in line to see what a vacation in Mississippi had done to one of their sons."[23] In 1955 a vacation was a desirable and potent symbol, signifying respectability, a healthy family life, and a strenuous work ethic that entitled one to leisure. Situating the teenager on vacation was a way of assigning a respectable, moral middle-class ethos to Till and his mother; garnering sympathy from liberal whites depended in part on erasing race and foregrounding this middle-class lifestyle.

Within Chicago's black community, where visiting southern kin had a long history, other criteria determined respectability. As Kardiner and Ovesey had implied in *The Mark of Oppression*, economically secure black women were not necessarily good or respectable mothers. Comments in the black press intimate the tightrope that black women had to walk to be respectable. For example, the Association of Mannequins' tenth annual "Ten Best-Dressed Women" awards in Chicago honored "those women of the Race who have achieved an appearance that is fashionable and appropriate. . . . such women help to hold high the standard of good grooming . . . they deserve the accolade of best dressed, *regardless of financial status*." One columnist criticized the black woman who worked because she "flaunts her independence and makes it clear that she can take care of herself. She resents and resists any inclinations to lean upon a man. . . . She hardly ever cries."[24] A woman's competitive salary, then, was dangerous, even if it might enable a seemingly respectable middle-class lifestyle, because it endangered equally important qualities associated with respectable femininity. Too much independence, too much self-control, too much interest in status—these were just some of the qualities that Mamie Till Bradley had to avoid in order to "earn" the politically necessary designation of respectable mother.[25]

Contemporary coverage of Till's funeral, the trial of Bryant and Milam, and protest rallies indicates that Bradley's status as a mother and a respectable, feminine woman was as precarious as it was essential to a condemnation of the murder. Reestablishing the innocence and respectability of both Emmett Till and his mother was crucial to racial liberals in the face of accusations that Till had violated racial and sexual boundaries in his supposed aggression against a white woman and mother. Bradley needed to confirm her role as a respectable mother along multiple valences: to emerge as protective of Emmett, yet not emasculating; fashionable and well-groomed, yet not ostentatious and luxury-laden; hardworking, yet not ambitious; and "universal" enough to attract the sympathy of whites without distancing herself from the black community.

"Mother Breaks Down": Constructing Mamie Till Bradley

Mamie Bradley learned on Wednesday, September 1, that her son's corpse had been discovered in the Tallahatchie River. Till's body immediately became the physical sign of what Mississippi wanted to forget and Bradley wanted remembered. Although the sheriff of Tallahatchie County ordered that Till be buried in Mississippi immediately, Bradley insisted that her son's body be returned to Chicago. "We [relatives] called the governor [William Stratton, governor of Illinois] we called the sheriff. . . . We called everybody we thought would be able to stop the burial," she later explained. To the sympathetic white and black press in the north, it was "the grieving mother of a Chicago boy" who "barely averted" this "hasty burial."[26]

When the casket arrived in Chicago, Bradley insisted that it be opened so that she could know for sure it held her son. And at that point, when she saw Till's beaten and bullet-ridden body, she decided he would have an open-casket funeral. She wanted to "let the people see what they have done to my boy!"[27] Till's body lay first at Rayner Funeral Home and then at Roberts Temple of the Church of God in Christ until the burial on Tuesday, September 6. Thousands stood in long lines winding around the block outside the church to view the disfigured corpse dressed in a suit and three enlarged photographs of Emmett Till in life. A public-address system broadcast the Saturday memorial service to crowds outside the church. Bradley postponed the burial for a day to accommodate the many who wanted to pay their respects. Estimates of attendance varied, from ten thousand to six hundred thousand, but there was little dispute that "the memorial service for young Till" had mobilized Chicago's "Negro community as it has not been over any similar act in recent history."[28]

Emmett Till's funeral blurred the boundaries between public and private. As a result of the open casket, his body and the individual pain he endured became the locus for a collective political mobilization of African Americans demanding citizenship for all blacks. The symbolic construction of Mamie Till Bradley during the funeral also provided a basis on which antiracists protested Till's murder. Sympathetic accounts of the funeral and protest rallies offered images of her that reconciled the various positive meanings of motherhood and respectability. She was represented not just as a mother, but as "Mrs. Mamie Till Bradley," "a cautious, God-fearing, law-abiding mother."[29] Photographs showed her flanked by ministers or in familial domestic settings—"the elm-shaped stretch of St. Lawrence Avenue where Bobo [Emmett's nickname] lived. It is a family neighborhood where many own the buildings where they live."[30] Descriptions of Till as "polite and mild-mannered . . . with a near-perfect attendance at Sunday School" enhanced the image of Bradley as a good mother. A neighbor shared an anecdote about the dutiful son who "was going to surprise his mother with a cake." One photograph even pictured Mamie Bradley holding a dog; according to the caption, "Mike [the dog] keeps nightly vigil in the boy's room, not knowing that his young master will never play with him any more."[31] What could be more all-American than the boy and his dog?

Mamie Bradley's patriotism was another component in her construction as a worthy mother whose son's rights had been violated. This theme was consistent with other civil rights battles, like that over military desegregation. *Newsweek* reported Bradley's "concern that the murder would be used by the Communists for anti-American propaganda." (According to one account, Bradley "found it necessary to play sick . . . as a means of ducking 'Red' rallies.")[32] Patriotism emerged most explicitly in ubiquitous accounts that the "bereaved mother" was the widow of a war hero. "Private Louis Till must have turned in his grave last week" began one account of the murder. Bradley had suffered "a double tragedy . . . for the boy's father had died abroad as a soldier in World War II." Louis Till's alleged heroic death was the cornerstone to a dramatic and much-quoted editorial in *Life*, which avowed that southerners who condoned the murder were "in far worse danger than Emmett Till ever was. He had only his life to lose, and many others have done that, including his soldier father who was killed in France fighting for the American proposition that all men are equal."[33]

But being religious, familial, and patriotic was not enough to make Mamie Bradley an appropriate symbol of exemplary motherhood and womanhood. Frequent references to Bradley as "the attractive Chicago woman" served multiple functions.[34] A repeated emphasis on Bradley's stylish appearance and physical appeal contested standards of womanhood and beauty that had historically excluded black women. Mamie Bradley as a good mother who was also attractive was an alternative to both the hefty and desexualized Mammy-like Delilah in the 1934 *Imitation of Life* and the heavily made-up prostitute waiting for her welfare check as portrayed in postwar critiques of ADC.[35] Photographs and physical descriptions of both Emmett Till and Mamie Bradley were integral to coverage of the case. Their bodies became icons and, in evoking horror and pleasure respectively, were agents in the politicization of the murder.

Images of Bradley as "well-dressed" and attractive simultaneously reassured potential opponents of segregation and white supremacy that she was "feminine," had not usurped any "male" prerogatives, and was ladylike—all without being overtly or excessively sexual.[36] Descriptions of her appearance and body and references to her as "Till's Mom" tended to appear at precisely those moments when she was most public—during speeches or her testimony at the trial, for example—and "proved" that while she might make her private grief a public and political issue, she was not questioning the feminine private role as her primary source of identity. In New York, "Mamie Bradley hardly had time to powder her nose from the time she stepped off a plane until after the rally."[37] Bradley had brought both long-denied racial violence and motherhood into the public and political sphere. These transgressions needed to be contained, even by her liberal supporters.

Bradley's emotionalism and her consequent dependence on men or male-dominated institutions were the crucial components in assuaging doubts regarding her respectability and motherhood. From the outset, her weakness, even hysteria, and her need to defer to men confirmed her femininity, religiosity, and her "authenticity" as an American woman and mother. "Mother Breaks Down" announced the *Chicago Tribune*. "Mother's Tears Greet Son Who Died a Martyr" proclaimed the *Chicago Defender*. She was a woman "limp with grief"; an accompanying photograph showed her in a wheelchair, "sobbing" and "near collapse."[38] Bradley's physical weakness was politically valuable because it highlighted traditional gender roles within the black community. It was an important resource in the mobilizations that the trial generated, even though the emphasis on her body's limits suggested that she was not a part of the active political community around her seeking power.

Subsequent analyses of the funeral are more readily understandable given these contemporary accounts. Although studies of the murder acknowledge that Mamie

This full-page photo spread reinforced the sense that Mamie Till Bradley, or the "grieving mother," was weak and dependent on others. Courtesy of the *Chicago Defender*.

Bradley insisted on the open-casket funeral, many suggest that this was simply an emotional decision. In *The Vital Center* Arthur Schlesinger Jr. had coded emotion as a feminine and irrational quality that could have dangerous effects on male citizens; this dominant liberal framework has precluded consideration of Bradley as a political player.[39] Evidence indicates, however, that this emotionally infused decision was neither haphazard nor apolitical. "Lord you gave your only son to remedy a condition, but who knows, but what the death of my only son might bring an end to lynching!" Bradley said when she first saw the body at Illinois Central Station. In the days before the burial she explained that she "wanted people 'to realize the threat to Negroes in the Deep South and to what extent the fiendish mobs would go to display their hate.' "[40] In opening the casket, then, Bradley showed that an ability to be politically aware and even calculating in an effort to resist racial prejudice could coexist with her personal grief.

Segregationists and others drew on these same values—religion, family, patriotism, and femininity—to paint a very different picture of Mamie Bradley. The funeral was not a true religious event infused with political meaning; it was a fund-raising spectacle that attracted "curiosity seekers" because "against the advice of undertakers" Bradley had insisted that the casket be opened. This amounted to "macabre exhibitionism," according to a one southern newspaper. In these accounts, "Mamie Bradley of Chicago" (versus "Mrs. Mamie Bradley") was (at best) a pawn of NAACP "rabble rousers," and the funeral was cheap "exploitation." The journalist William Bradford Huie wrote of the funeral that "cash was collected at the bier in wastebaskets: Mamie Bradley received five thousand dollars the first week. . . . The explosion was a godsend to the NAACP." Accusations that the NAACP exploited Till's death cast suspicion on Bradley's status as a mourning mother.[41] Such accounts assigned to Bradley the same negative qualities attributed to "conniving" mothers on ADC who sought money from the government. Bradley, like these needy women, was not entitled to sympathy or political legitimacy.

Milam and Bryant's defenders also drew on images of patriotism. Accusations ranged from charges that the NAACP was "Red-inspired" to charges that communist-NAACP collaborators had staged the murder to make the South and the United States look bad abroad. After Milam and Bryant had been acquitted, southern reporters learned that the army had hanged Louis Till in Italy for alleged murder and rape; Mississippi senators James O. Eastland and John Stennis obtained the information from the War Department and released it. Although the details remained unclear and some accused the senators of using "secret army files," this news was the "most explosive of the developments" in the Till case, according to the *New York Times*. "Till's Dad Raped 2 Women, Murdered a Third in Italy," shouted an oversized headline on the front page of one Mississippi paper. Given racist stereotypes of black men, many concluded that if Louis Till had been hanged for the rape of white women, then his son must certainly have been guilty of making unwanted advances toward Carolyn Bryant. "One must consider the atmosphere young Till was raised in," said a Georgia congressman.[42] This news imperiled Emmett's innocence as well as Bradley's claims to respectable motherhood and family stability.

Within an anti-civil rights discourse, images of Carolyn Bryant as a victim, the wife of a hero, and the mother of young children provided the necessary antithesis to the rendering of Mamie Bradley as greedy, unfeeling, and unwomanly. One reporter, for example, placed Mamie Till Bradley at Emmett's public funeral where "a collection was still being taken up at his casket" in the same story that placed Carolyn Bryant "in seclusion"—with her two sons of course. Carolyn, according to her mother-in-law, "went all to pieces after the incident. She has been unable to sleep and has to take sedatives."[43]

Opposing images of Mamie Till Bradley or Carolyn Bryant as the good or the bad woman, and, in turn, as victim or perpetrator, were central to indictments and defenses of the murder. In the *Chicago Defender*, for example, a photograph of Mamie Bradley, the "grief-stricken mother," and innocent victim, was set against a photograph of Carolyn Bryant with the caption "The Cause of It All." A similar argument led at least one southern white woman to conclude that Till had died because his mother "permit[ed] her boy to visit. . . . She should have had better sense than to let such a child come here."[44] Citing either woman as the "cause" of Till's murder deflected attention from Roy Bryant and J. W. Milam and exemplified how women could become the site for social anxieties.

A segregationist discourse in which Mamie Bradley appeared as greedy and unmaternal on the one hand, and hysterical and unrefined on the other, spun together racial and gender stereotypes that coded emotionalism as inherently feminine, and as an essentially "negro" quality.[45] This race/gender analogue conceptualizing African Americans as a weakly and "feminine" race was, by the 1940s and 1950s, a model that many racial liberals challenged with their emphasis on appropriately masculine black men and appropriately feminine women. According to liberal constructions of Bradley, emotionalism was an inherently and exclusively feminine quality that signified racial health—because it was present in this respectable black woman. This liberal interweaving of emotionalism, irrationality, and gender strengthened an antiracist position but rested on sexist stereotypes that minimized black women's strength and political agency. In other words, these frameworks restricted Bradley, even as they gave her a way to make political demands. Only ostensible dependence enabled Bradley to transgress certain boundaries. It was permissible for her to go to Mississippi for the trial or to attend protest rallies, since she had done so under the advice of her "advisors," was "accompanied by her father," and had deferred to the NAACP to prevent communist-front organizations from "trying to line her up for big meetings." She might speak at a New York rally in a "calm intelligent voice," but she would be uttering words from her "heart" and as the "Victim's Mother." And, even as she planned a civil suit against the Bryants and raised funds for the NAACP, supporters commended her because she was "placing her crusade in the hands of the NAACP."[46] These contradictory configurations of race and sex, and the degree to which emotionalism was a sign for race or for gender, would be even more pronounced during the trial of Roy Bryant and J. W. Milam—a trial in which far more was being judged than the actions of two men.

"Who Else Could Identify That Child?": Black Motherhood on Trial

The murder trial of Roy Bryant and J. W. Milam began on September 19, 1955, in Sumner, Mississippi. Above a Coca-Cola billboard, a sign welcomed some seventy reporters to a town with a population of 527: "Sumner, A Good Place to Raise a Boy."[47] Here, for five brutally hot days, competing notions of womanhood, motherhood, and respectability—what it actually meant to raise a son successfully—occupied center stage and helped to determine the outcome of the trial. Few had expected a conviction of two white men for the murder of a black teenager. Criteria for the acquittal revolved around ideologies of motherhood that excluded Mamie Till Bradley.

The state presented its case against Bryant and Milam first. Special prosecutor Robert Smith III and District Attorney Gerald Chatham offered six witnesses who confirmed that the two white men had kidnapped Till. With Mamie Bradley's testimony, they state confirmed the identity of the body found in the river three days later. Two "surprise witnesses" filled in some of the intervening time, testifying that they had seen Till with Milam and Bryant in a truck and had heard them beating the youth in a barn.[48] Moses Wright, a sixty-four-year-old preacher and sharecropper, "Uncle Mose" to defense attorneys and simply "Mose" to the prosecution, stood up in the witness chair and, with his "Dar he" and an outstretched arm, identified Milam and Bryant as Till's abductors. Wright's willingness to do so was "symbolic of the increase in Negro militancy throughout the south," according to one account.[49]

Then the team of defense attorneys offered their case. Four key witnesses for the defense first reminded the all-male, all-white jury of Till's alleged advances toward Carolyn Bryant and then claimed that the body was not Till's. These strategies simultaneously cast doubt on Till's death and implied that in any case it had been deserved. Sheriff Harold Strider asserted that the body had been in the water for "at least ten days, if not fifteen," so it could not be Till's. "Experts"—L. B. Otken, a physician, and H. D. Malone, a mortician—agreed and elaborated; the former testified that no one could identify this body because *even* the race of the body was a mystery.[50]

The notion that good mothers could be white or black informed liberal representations of Mamie Bradley during the trial. Bradley's willingness to testify reinforced the sense that she was a mourning mother committed to doing her political duty and to honoring her dead son's memory. On these terms, coming to Mississippi was not easy, or even necessarily safe. As her (male) "spokesperson" conveyed to the press and to the district attorney, she would not travel to Mississippi without official protection. One headline proclaimed "Mother Arrives With Her Pastor." Accounts that Bradley communicated through a spokesperson, frequently appeared with two male relatives "who stood like bodyguards," and demanded protection for herself all suggested that she was a respectable woman who, even in these unusual circumstances, adhered to traditional gender roles.[51]

Bradley's position was in fact highly untraditional. By insisting on physical protection, Bradley effectively drew attention to a long history of black women's physical vulnerability at the hands of white men.[52] She also challenged assumptions about black women's promiscuity that pervaded liberal discourse; moreover, she bridged the chasm between chaste (or frigid) white mother and promiscuous black mother.

White supremacists and other civil rights opponents repeatedly challenged the view that a black woman could be a good or worthy mother. Some Southern newspapers suggested that Bradley's wariness about coming to Mississippi stemmed from maternal indifference. According to the *Memphis Commercial Appeal*, District Attorney Chatham had to remind Bradley, repeatedly, of her duties as a mother: "it is important to the state's case that she appear," said one telegram. "Your failure to make yourself available as a witness for the state is not understandable."[53] Supporters of Milam and Bryant would permit no rivals to their racially specific version of womanhood. One southern paper noted that Bradley, "the fashionably dressed Negro woman . . . caused a sensation [among the press] when she walked into the courtroom flanked by her father and advisers" and consequently "swept an expression of almost painful dislike across the faces of local spectators."[54]

Contrasts between Mamie Till Bradley and Carolyn Bryant escalated throughout the trial and were central to competing views of who—and what—was on trial. The captions below adjacent head shots of "Mrs. Carolyn Bryant" and "Mrs. Mamie Bradley" in the *Pittsburgh Courier*, for example, were "doesn't like whistles" and "would avenge her son." While "Mrs. Bradley" was "plump and dimpled," the "coldly attractive" Carolyn Bryant appeared in "a family portrait which can be described in one word: unhappy." A liberal Parisian weekly labeled Carolyn Bryant a "cruel shrew," and another French paper said she was "a crossroads Marilyn Monroe."[55]

Those hoping to preserve the racial status quo relied on positive representations of Carolyn Bryant to convey the message that the white nuclear family was on trial and must be preserved at all costs. Cooperative if embarrassed, Carolyn Bryant wore a "black dress with a white collar" on the stand and "demurely told a court" that "a Negro man" (the fourteen-year-old Till) had grabbed her. One defense attorney positioned himself as Till to re-create the alleged scene between them. Even though Judge Curtis L. Swango ruled that most of Carolyn Bryant's testimony was inadmissible to the jury, the defense regarded her as its "key witness," for her very presence reminded jury members of the threat Till allegedly posed to the "pretty brunette."[56] *Newsweek* successfully condensed the multiple attributes of respectable white motherhood into one sentence: "It was Bryant's wife, Carolyn, an attractive, dark-haired mother of two, whom Emmett was accused of insulting."[57]

Carolyn Bryant was central in the campaign to underscore her husband's innocence and to cast him, too, as a respectable and upstanding citizen. She was also important to the curious elision of class during the trial. "Wives Serious, Children Romp as Trial Begins," declared one headline, in a story with detailed attention to Milam and Bryant playing peek-a-boo with their "four handsome sons" as attorneys selected the jury. While white guards frisked African Americans at the door of the jammed courtroom and made them sit at a segregated, crowded bridge table, Milam and Bryant came to the courtroom with "their wives and children" in a new "green 1955 Chevrolet" and sat "quietly and without handcuffs." The two men received daily shaves at the barbershop; on breaks from the steaming courtroom they lunched with the prominent Tallahatchie County sheriff, Harold Strider, "at an air conditioned cafe."[58] In many respects, the gender roles assigned to these families during the trial defused class tensions and provided Bryant and Milam access to middle-class values and ideals of masculinity—albeit temporarily.[59] The men became symbols of all that was good about the middle-class white family and appropriately masculine citizens. They were veritable commercials for *Father Knows Best:* clean-cut, pillars of their communities, quintessential family men, war veterans, and "heroes." That segregationists managed to shape the trial into a tale about the white nuclear family tragically imperiled by Emmett Till was evident in coverage of the acquittal: the not-guilty verdict marked a "happy ending" and was "a signal for Roy Bryant and his half brother J. W. Milam to kiss their wives." The sheer repetition of these accounts, of the two lighting cigars, of the women, each "the mother of two small sons," smiling radiantly, served to celebrate the reconstituted white families.[60]

Mamie Bradley's testimony was the crucial space in which motherhood's meaning as universal or racially specific was negotiated. Because the defense challenged the identity of the body, her identification based on her authority as "the boy's mother" was pivotal; she was, in effect, the "expert" for the prosecution.[61] Bradley testified on Thursday, September 22, that she had known the body was that of her son because she had "recognized Emmett's hair line, his hair, the general shape of his nose and his teeth. Especially his teeth, because I used to tell him daily to take care of his teeth." The jury could not discount Bradley's identification, argued Robert Smith in his closing statement, because "the last thing in God's creation a mother wants is to believe that her son is dead." Prosecutor Gerald Chatham concurred. "Who else could identify that child?" he asked dramatically. "Who else could say 'That's my boy'?"[62] Black women "too," the prosecution's argument went, loved and cared for their offspring and recognized their bodies almost viscerally.

Upon closer inspection, "the grief-stricken mother's" authority was in fact predicated on ideas about race.[63] As had been the case throughout the funeral and the rallies, Bradley had to "prove" that she had been a good mother to Till and had raised him "correctly." Mamie Bradley testified that she had warned Till "to be very careful" in Mississippi, cautioning him to "say 'yes sir' and 'no, ma'am.' " She also said that she had urged him "to humble himself to the extent of getting down on his knees" to whites if necessary.[64] This portion of her testimony was widely quoted in the white press, north and south, and indicated that Bradley had to prove herself a credible mother not in universal but in these racialized and racist terms. Assigning guilt to Bryant and Milam required proof that Mamie Till Bradley had raised her son to "know his place"—or, to know his race—and that being polite and respectful was itself constructed by race.[65]

Bradley's emotional fortitude during her testimony was also subjected to considerable debate. The *New York Times* wrote that "young Till's mother . . . stoutly maintained that the dead body sent to her was that of her son. . . . Mrs. Bradley was a composed and well-spoken witness," who, when shown photographs of her son's body, simply "removed her glasses and wiped at her eyes."[66] In choosing to maintain her composure throughout these public and hostile proceedings, Bradley may well have chosen to reject stereotypes of all women and African American men and women as emotional and lacking control, as well as to preserve her privacy.

Nevertheless, many racial liberals and others who condemned Milam and Bryant represented Bradley as a highly emotional "tragic figure" and did not mention self-control. Positive accounts emphasized that she had "wept on the witness stand as she identified a police picture of the body of her son. . . . She ran her hand quickly across her eyes as tears trickled down her cheeks." In these accounts, her inability to control her emotions confirmed her maternal authority. "The boy's mother, Mrs. Mamie Bradley, a $3,600 civil-service employe [sic], weepingly told the jury that she was certain the body was that of her son," wrote *Newsweek*.[67] Those fighting racism needed to position Bradley as a "naturally" emotionally distressed woman expressing her private emotions in order to corroborate her position as a "good" mother. To Till defenders and civil rights supporters, private emotion in women was a sign for gender difference, "evidence" of Bradley's womanliness and of respectable gender difference among African Americans generally.

Once again, Bradley's efforts to define herself as a subject were open to manipulation on all sides. The trial made clear that cross-racial assertions of maternal power might have radical implications in the Jim Crow South but might also circumscribe Mamie Till Bradley.

The jury of white southern men "chose to believe" that the body was not Till's as a way to acquit Milam and Bryant and preserve power relations in Mississippi. They rejected Bradley's identification of the body and rejected a definition of "natural" motherhood that included black women, privileging instead the rational, "scientific" testimony of the experts. "What could a black mother say that would be of any value?" asked *L'Aurore*, a French daily.[68] Moreover, the jury dismissed Bradley's testimony based on what they perceived as a *lack* of authentic expression of maternal grief. "If she had tried a little harder," said the foreman of the jury, J. A. Shaw, in an interview, "she might have got out a tear." In this interview with Shaw, in fact, Bradley emerged as a manipulative, defeminized black woman who did not cry "naturally" and had thus forfeited her moral and maternal authority to identify her son's body.[69] This depiction was consistent with racist representations of the funeral and the protest rallies: Bradley was not a "natural" mother because she did not express or experience true grief; she was, instead, a public performer of sorts, capitalizing on her son's death. This version of Mamie Bradley as morally undeveloped and unwomanly drew on constructions of motherhood shaped by race and gender, and it bore considerable similarity to depictions of women who did not deserve ADC.

In sum, during the trial, Bradley's potential power as a respectable African

American mother was simultaneously subversive and reactionary. Her authority as a mother challenged notions of good mothers as necessarily white, but it also relied upon racial stereotypes that required Till to be "humble" and upon gender stereotypes that required mothers to be emotionally overwrought. And the jury rejected even these conditional sources of power. "Where else," asked liberal critic I. F. Stone, "would a mother be treated with such elementary lack of respect and compassion?"[70] Racially specific constructions of motherhood prevailed in Sumner, most powerfully evoked in photographs of the reconstituted Bryant and Milam families. Significantly, Mamie Bradley chose not to be in the courtroom when the jury returned the verdict. "I was expecting an acquittal," she said, "and I didn't want to be there when it happened." Her absence indicated her continuing rejection of the values through which the verdict had been offered and her refusal to be contained—even in the walls of the courtroom. By absenting herself, Bradley further exposed the inequities of the southern judicial system; or, in the words of one front-page editorial, the unpunished murder of blacks now lay "Naked Before the World!"[71]

"What Is True Story About Mrs. Bradley?": The Tide Turns

Protest rallies continued for six to eight weeks after the acquittal of Bryant and Milam, with their focus shifting from the case itself to the ongoing battle for African American citizenship and civil rights. It was time to "stop being emotional and start being smart," according to the NAACP's executive secretary, Roy Wilkins. At a protest rally in New York, Thurgood Marshall, a lawyer, urged the crowd to register to vote and to "worry about those who are alive."[72]

The murder had triggered a "New Negro Militancy" manifest in a comprehensive set of political demands. The NAACP placed a nearly full-page advertisement in the *New York Times* on October 3 titled "Help End Racial Tyranny in Mississippi." The ad detailed a "slaughter of personal rights" that included "Three Unpunished Murders—Open Defiance of Supreme Court School Decree" and "Over 900,000 Mississippi Negroes Without an Effective Voice in Their Government." It concluded that Till's murder "climaxed a series of blows to American ideals that has horrified the country." Within a month, the ad generated $5,500 in donations and multiple requests for similar fund-raising appeals from newspapers across the country.[73] The "program of action" that black leaders endorsed in the trial's aftermath called for Congress to address unequal voting practices and to pass civil rights legislation, and for the Justice Department to investigate the murder and to enforce the Supreme Court's ruling on desegregation in schools.[74]

The sympathetic construction of Mamie Bradley as a good mother—respectable, all-American, feminine, and deferential—did not persist alongside this growing liberal bid for equal rights and government activism. On November 8, the NAACP publicly severed its relationship with Mamie Bradley. The rupture occurred as rumors about the propriety of Till-related fund-raising drives percolated, immediately after a grand jury refused to indict Milam and Bryant on kidnapping charges, and on the eve of Bradley's NAACP-sponsored west coast speaking tour. Roy Wilkins publicly condemned Bradley's request for remuneration, declaring that the "NAACP does not handle such matters on a commercial basis." Shortly thereafter, the NAACP attorney William Henry Huff resigned as Bradley's legal representative. Reporters wondered, "Will Mamie, NAACP Kiss, Make Up?" The organization quickly made the separation—or divorce, as the romance metaphors implied—official when it arranged for Moses Wright to replace Bradley on the west coast tour.[75]

The conflict triggered a transformation in constructions of Mamie Till Bradley within the African American press that drew with remarkable consistency on entrenched negative images of motherhood. NAACP officials implied and others concurred that if Till's mother had asked for a $5,000 fee for public speaking engagements, she was neither a respectable woman nor a good mother, and in fact was little better than racist representations had suggested all along. Those who defended Mamie Till Bradley did so by emphasizing her vulnerability and poor judgment.[76] No one changed the terms of this debate by claiming that as a public figure working exclusively for the NAACP—she had been on an unpaid leave of absence from her job since Till's murder over two months earlier—Bradley might need or be entitled to a salary, or, more bizarre yet, might even be ambitious. Both sides in this conflict, then, reinscribed motherhood as private and femininity as that which should not penetrate politics. These were the very assumptions that Mamie Bradley's actions had troubled.

As a result, the dichotomy civil rights supporters had drawn between the "good," respectable, and maternal Mamie Till Bradley and the "bad," immoral, and cold Carolyn Bryant shifted. Polarized views of good versus bad woman endured and were now contained in opposing views of one woman, Mamie Bradley herself. Or, in the words of one headline, "What Is True Story About Mrs. Bradley?"[77]

The backdrop to this "rift over money" was the ongoing negotiation of motherhood and respectability as each informed liberal civil rights activism. From the moment that Mamie Bradley helped make her son's death a public issue, there were those who expressed concern about the money that sympathizers donated. Fears of exploitation were allayed with guarantees that funds were for the collective cause rather than for personal gain. Immediately after the funeral, for example, the *Chicago Daily Tribune* reported that "the mother" authorized the NAACP to use donations made in her behalf for legal expenses that the Till case incurred. Local NAACP branches asked churches to assume fund-raising responsibilities to ensure an air of virtue to these campaigns; the organization designated October 2 "NAACP Church Day."[78]

By mid-October, hostility toward "the sycophants, moochers, jackals and charlatans who are always ready to ply their trade of capitalizing on human outrage" and who were "as busy as a pack of vultures on a freshly killed carcass in the Till case" would not be quelled. Instead, anger about the acquittal and the overall lack of civil rights in the United States exacerbated feelings of suspicion. "It is the opinion of myself and perhaps that of thousands of other Negroes throughout the country," wrote an Ohio woman, that "if the NAACP had worked as hard presenting evidence in the Till case as they did collecting money, more would have been done to convict the suspects. . . . the NAACP [should] make publicly known the amount of money they collected and the amount to which they have participated in gathering evidence in the Till case." Proliferating rumors were evident in their denial: William Henry Huff, for example, issued a formal statement that he was not "clearing a lot of money in the unfortunate Till case"; in another instance, an editorial assured readers that Bradley "is taking her job very seriously of speaking out against the lynching of her son. . . . in spite of reports to the contrary, she is not making any profits from her appearances."[79]

During the period after the trial, representations of Bradley continued to underscore her emotionalism and dependence on men and her relative unimportance compared to the larger political forces around her: "Hear the Mississippi Story!! from the Lips and Hearts of Emmett Till's Mother and Mrs. Ruby Hurley" said one advertisement; the name "Mrs. Mamie Bradley" appeared in parentheses, in small type and below "Emmett Till's Mother." According to a "verbal agreement" made in mid-October, the NAACP exclusively would coordinate Bradley's public appearances during her unpaid leave of absence from work; the "mother of the slain boy" was to be at their disposal.[80]

Despite the emphasis on Bradley's deference, she was a public figure with something to say. At a rally in Harlem where speakers called on the government to combat a "reign of terror" in the South, she told the crowd of fifteen thousand that "you have cried enough tears for me." In late October, she went to Washington, D.C. in an unsuccessful effort to urge federal intervention into the case and to speak before the Senate Subcommittee on Constitutional Rights.[81] Many reacted to this extension of her public role with surprise, if not derision. "The demand for Mrs. Bradley at these mass meetings is astounding," wrote one black male columnist. Following Bradley's trip to Washington, a *Chicago Defender* editorial referred to "Mamie, who is really learning fast the ways of public officials."[82] The tension between two positions—grieving mother and public figure—was evident when Mamie Bradley asserted at a rally in New York that perhaps her sacrifice had not been in vain if "a little nobody like me and a little nobody like my boy can arouse the nation."[83] It was a tension that could not be sustained indefinitely.

Doubts about Mamie Bradley's role, allegations about the propriety of Till fundraising, and frustrations with NAACP campaigns for African American citizenship and government intervention were resolved conjointly through the break-up between the NAACP and Bradley. She became a scapegoat of sorts, a receptacle for anger over the trial's outcome and for overlapping anxieties about gender relations and the future of civil rights activism.

Reports that Bradley had requested a speaking fee characterized her as a "mercenary hard-hearted gold digger, seeking to capitalize on the lynching of her child" or a "greedy" woman who "had changed from a simple griefstricken mother to an arrogant celebrity full of her own importance." "Don't Need to Worry About Ma'—She's Loaded!" was the title of a sardonic letter in the *New York Amsterdam News*,

In announcements like this one, the NAACP promised that Mamie Till Bradley would speak from the heart as "Emmett Till's Mother." Courtesy of the *New York Amsterdam News*.

which described the less-than-positive transformation of one mother after Till's death: "Ordinarily, Ma is the quiet sort and legs it off to church every Sunday. . . . But ever since those two peckerwoods up and killed Mamie Bradley's boy, she's been riled up to the point of blaspheming." This fictional Ma had even "broke loose from her religion and . . . sent the rent money off to the NAACP Legal Fund."[84] With Bradley's credentials as a respectable mother jeopardized, the African American press referred to her simply as "Mamie" with far greater regularity.

Even more significantly, accounts defending Bradley depended on images of her as unable to conduct herself as a public, political, or professional player. Some argued that Bradley was "the victim of bad advice" or that the "plain, ordinary woman . . . has been misrepresented by those she trusted." Clearly, she was "ill-prepared for public life" and had been "catapulted from a humdrum existence . . . into a living martyrdom."[85] Defenders also drew attention to Bradley's emotional and physical frailty: her "nervous condition prevented her handling the business end"; she was "worn to a frazzle" according to Anne B. Crockett, "special representative" to Bradley; she had yet "to pay her own hospital bill when she suffered a nervous breakdown" (Bradley was hospitalized for "nervous fatigue" in early October). Bradley's reaction to the public rebuke proved that she was "a sensitive woman": "her almost complete withdrawal" into "semi-seclusion" followed the canceled speaking tour; the "announcement hit her hard and she hasn't recovered yet."[86]

NAACP leaders had behaved with an "obnoxious display of insensitivity" toward this "ordinary woman baffled and bewildered," claimed Bradley's defenders. A critique of the organization in a *Chicago Defender* editorial titled "Indiscreet Rebuke" carefully reinforced progressive assumptions that more healthful race relations required healthful gender relations, as defined by a middle-class white norm. Although Bradley's "alleged requests for money were seemingly greedy and conscienceless," the male-dominated organization "wield[ed] power in behalf of others" and consequently had the responsibility to "accept certain disabilities and even tenuous loyalties" and to "renounce" emotional displays and "public demonstrations of petty irritations." Disapproval of the organization indicated that with its unmanly "public demonstration" of displeasure (Wilkins had "snarled," according to *Jet*), the NAACP had departed from traditional gender roles and normative ideas about masculinity.[87]

Finally, several of Bradley's defenders argued that despite her financial needs ("It is a strain to get food for my table"), she had neither requested nor demanded $5,000. According to several accounts, Franklin Williams, west coast regional director of the NAACP, had made the offer after learning of Bradley's mounting expenses.[88] This defense positioned Bradley once again as a passive and nonconfrontational figure being done to rather than actively doing, as a woman who "wants to make it clear that she is not engaged in a fight with the NAACP," and as one who "was anxious to straighten out the mess."[89]

Bradley's defenders continued to circumscribe her actions and feelings in coverage of a press conference that she held in New York in December. By then, the Till murder was not the page-one story it had been, and the white press was largely un-interested in what seemed to be an internal dispute. Headlines in black newspa-pers—"NAACP Criticized," "Mamie Bradley Says NAACP Used Son," and "Mother of Till Bitter!"—revealed some anger on her part toward the organiza-tion. In the articles, only her father was "vehement in his condemnation" and le-gitimized any financial expectations. It was he who asserted that Roy Wilkins "was attempting to punish his daughter," that the organization was "using Emmett Till and his mother," or that "as long as my daughter can be useful to them, every-thing's all right, but the minute she asks for something, it's a different story." With the anger and the demands displaced onto a male authority figure, Bradley emerged as hurt yet remarkably conciliatory, "nonetheless hopeful" and "still in-terested in seeing justice done."[90]

At the press conference, Mamie Till Bradley released a letter she had written to Roy Wilkins after her dismissal from the NAACP. It revealed the contradictory ways in which she defied any one subject position and simultaneously relied upon and transgressed liberal conceptualizations of motherhood and citizenship:

> [T]he objective of the NAACP is of much greater concern to me than my pocketbook. I set out to trade the blood of my child for the betterment of my race; and I do not now wish to deviate from such course. I feel very bad that the opportunity to talk for the as-sociation would be taken from me. I know tht [sic] you have tried very hard and sin-cerely to see to my day-to-day financial needs. It is unfair and untrue for anyone to say otherwise. If the NAACP is willing to continue to do what it has to defray my travel and living expenses that should suffice. Please let me go forward for the NAACP. It is a duty. I would not want it said that I did anything to shirk it.[91]

Once again Bradley asserted—with some emotion—that the public cause was as important as her personal needs. She demonstrated, as she had since her son's murder, that her private and maternal grief and her public and political service could reinforce each other and did not contradict NAACP claims for black citizen-ship. Implicit was a critique of political strategies "for the betterment of the race" that segregated these positions.

Yet in this letter any rebuke was, at most, implicit. Mamie Bradley, too, relied on her authority as a respectable woman and good mother to make her bid for credibil-ity. She came across as emotional, dutiful, respectful, and conciliatory to NAACP authorities. Ultimately, there may have been no other place from which she might hope to be heard or speak with any authority. For racists, antiracists, and for Mamie Bradley herself, then, the "good mother" was a category potentially beyond criti-cism and, as such, was a viable if not effective position from which to shape liberal politics.

Mamie Till Bradley's departure from the NAACP lecture and fund-raising circuit was permanent. She returned to school in Chicago and became a public school teacher. Out of Till's death, she later explained, came a "burning . . . to push education to the limit."[92] Still, her actions following her son's murder had repercussions well beyond 1955.

Bradley, as symbol and person—the respectable woman, with an authority deriving from motherhood—posed a significant challenge to American power relations: to the racial caste system most prevalent in the South that valorized Carolyn Bryant as a way to deny black citizens rights; to dominant theories of gender roles that marginalized and depoliticized white and black women as mothers; and to dominant liberal theories of racial difference that held defeminized and emasculating black mothers responsible for racial inferiority. In laying claim to the overlapping roles of "good mother" and respectable, moral woman, Bradley resisted definitions of womanhood that either excluded black women by virtue of their race or rendered black mothers as dominating "matriarchs." She politicized and publicized motherhood and racial violence with composure and emotion, dignity and grief.

People who reached across lines of race, class, region, and gender to identify with Bradley confirmed that politicizing motherhood in these terms had subversive potential. "Womanhood without regard to color must be aroused," wrote one male New Yorker. A Canadian white woman wrote to Milam and Bryant to condemn them for violating the "joys of parenthood that are so dear to us all. Young or old, black or white." And, writing to Governor Hugh White of Mississippi, "as a white woman, a Texan, an American and the mother of a son," E. H. Johnson asked, "Since when did the testimony of strangers take priority over a mother's identification of a body—a mother who bore and raised the son. Do you think if someone took my boy and beat him to a pulp and threw him in the river, that I couldn't recognize him? . . . Think of his mother. Think of the Negro race. Think of the blot on Mississippi." She concluded by assuring White that she was not a "crackpot" but an "outraged American woman . . . taking action to see that the same justice is given for the death of a Negro boy as I would want for my own son. Do you have a son? How would you feel? Can we do less?"[93] Here, universal definitions of womanhood enabled a condemnation of Bryant and Milam and of American race relations generally.

The political mobilization of blacks that the open-casket funeral and subsequent rallies helped generate was neither local nor short-term. "It was the best advertised lynching that I had ever heard," recalled Amzie Moore, an NAACP activist in Mississippi. "Congratulations to your paper for putting the picture of the murdered Till boy on the front page," wrote one reader, "so the whole world can see what goes on inside Mississippi." One prescient reporter noted that Bradley's desire to "Let the people see" could "easily become the opening gun in a war on Dixie which can reverberate around the world."[94]

The world did see and the "war on Dixie" did escalate. As the famous and the ordinary alike construct their own memories of that period, the case often figures as a pivotal moment. The teenage Cassius Clay (later Muhammed Ali) "couldn't get Emmett out of my mind." Writing on the twenty-fifth anniversary of the *Brown* decision, the sociologist Joyce Ladner explained that "more than any other single atrocity, the *Jet* magazine photograph of Emmett Till's grotesque body left an indelible impression on many young Southern blacks who, like my sister and I, became the vanguard of the Southern student movement." Bradley's decision to "let the people see" was instrumental in the impact the case had on the American body politic, across lines of race and class.[95]

At the same time, the symbolic construction of Bradley as a "good" and "natural mother" rather than a damaging "matriarch" was fraught with contradictions and underscored the interdependence of racial liberalism and gender conservatism in this moment preceding a full-scale civil rights movement. Frequent references to Bradley as "the mother" effaced her as a decision-making person, as was evident during Till's funeral. A cross-racial definition of womanhood and motherhood relied on essentialist assumptions that women were emotional and that their identities were based upon the biology of reproduction, as was evident during the trial. And the political impact she had as a speaker and fund-raiser was predicated on her deference to the male-dominated NAACP, as was most evident during Mamie Bradley's conflict with the organization. Images of motherhood were consistently subject to conservative responses and symbolic manipulation—by racial conservatives *and* by racial liberals—and the radical potential of Bradley's position was undercut.

The reactionary responses to Mamie Till Bradley among those who rejected prejudice and discrimination suggest how race and gender shaped liberal notions of citizenship that seemed universal. It may not be surprising that many white southerners' rejection of Bradley as a "good" mother strengthened their fight *against* racial integration, or that they claimed racially exclusive rights to citizenship by propping up white motherhood. At the same time, the NAACP's initial support of Bradley as a "good" mother, and the organization's growing efforts to contain her claims to motherhood, strengthened its fight *for* racial integration; the liberal organization claimed racially inclusive rights to respectable, rational, and masculine codes of citizenship by adhering to traditional gender roles that constrained Mamie Bradley. In either case, as had been the case in New Deal and vital center liberalism, notions of citizenship for whites and blacks were gendered and relied upon meanings assigned to motherhood.

The ways in which ideas about motherhood constructed the meaning of Till's murder were dramatic, but not unique. Bradley's actions and the reactions to them enable a consideration of the political—even radical—potential of motherhood in the 1950s and a reconsideration of a paradigm that held mothers in the 1950s to be apolitical.[96] In underscoring the radical potential and political meanings of "traditional" roles, Mamie Till Bradley offers an important lens through which to consider continuities in women's activism. The radical potential of traditional roles was realized, for example, by women in the civil rights movement—the women who walked to their jobs as domestics in whites' homes during the Montgomery bus boycott, or who cooked for and fed civil rights activists.[97] And, in exposing how racial liberals relied on a discourse of motherhood to bolster a bid for civil rights, Bradley's story demonstrates the various ways in which gender shaped racial liberalism.

When Mamie Till Bradley opened her son's casket "to let the people see," she exposed more than her dead son's body. She had the courage and the determination to translate her personal pain and her family's tragedy into political terms. In negotiating her private role as a mother into the public and political sphere, she helped change the terms on which her son's death was understood and debated. In 1991, on what would have been Emmett Till's fiftieth birthday, Mamie Bradley attended a ceremony in Chicago at which sections of Seventy-First Street were renamed "Emmett Till Road."[98] As a result of Mamie Bradley, a fourteen-year-old boy was not just another statistic in the tragic history of American lynching.

CHAPTER FIVE

"Imitation" Reconsidered

Consuming Images in the Late 1950s

D irector Douglas Sirk remade the film *Imitation of Life* in 1959, when many Americans were benefiting from over a decade of economic growth ushered in by World War II, and civil rights activism was gaining momentum. The struggle for subsistence that had made the successes and sacrifices of two single mothers, one a white northern entrepreneur and the other a black southern migrant, so heartwarming to moviegoers in the 1930s seemed distant, even quaint.

Imitation of Life was a box office sensation in a time when liberal intellectuals in particular were preoccupied with cultural more than with economic issues. They focused on the seemingly ever-expanding middle class; the problems that economically disadvantaged Americans faced were of far less interest than they had been only twenty years earlier. As Arthur Schlesinger Jr. wrote in 1957, the "distinctive thing" about New Deal liberalism was the "extent to which it was economic in its basic impulse." Liberalism in the 1950s, he explained, had to grapple with other issues: the "moral and cultural" effects of "homogenization" and "blandness" in a prosperous and consumption-oriented society. Liberals needed to "seek new social inventions that will give us the benefits of a mass economy without the cost of a mass culture." Many others agreed. "Abundance for what?" asked David Riesman, a prominent sociologist, in a collection of essays which explored the meanings of affluence and consumption in the postwar United States.[1] Liberalism remained essentially optimistic. But if liberals in the 1930s had believed in the liberating potential of economic reforms, their counterparts (or older selves) in the 1950s believed that overcoming homogenization could be liberating in a prosperous society driven by consumption.

Sirk's new *Imitation of Life* opened four years after the murder of Emmett Till and five years after the Supreme Court ruling in *Brown v. Board of Education*. Many white Americans had "met" Martin Luther King Jr. and other bus boy-

111

cotters in Montgomery, Alabama, on television. Just one year earlier, they had witnessed crowds of angry whites blocking nine black students from entering a high school in Little Rock, Arkansas, and had seen a Republican president who was hardly a staunch supporter of rights for African Americans send the National Guard to enforce desegregation rulings. In 1957 Congress passed civil rights legislation; however tepid the final bill, many liberals heralded it as the first such national legislation since Reconstruction.[2] As the response to Till's murder had suggested, the outcry over violent prejudice was starting to become national, as was the fight for integration more generally.

These two themes—growing prosperity and its effects, and a growing emphasis on integration and its effects—were central to the new version of *Imitation*. Other films from this period took up questions of race relations (*Edge of the City* [1956] and *The Defiant Ones* [1958]); still others featured motherhood and domesticity in a Cold War consumer society (*Pillow Talk* [1959], and *The Manchurian Candidate* [1962]). Plenty of liberal economists, union activists, and consumer advocates were concerned about a consumer-oriented society.[3] By contrast, Sirk's remake reflected changing liberal attitudes about consumption, gender, and race *in relation to each other* in the years since the first *Imitation of Life* film was made in 1934. The new *Imitation* used an old story about maternal failure and race to explore the negative effects that consumption had in a newly affluent society. It was virtually the only Hollywood film of the era to contrast white and black mothers, and it was unique in the ways it melded motherhood, gender, and race into one narrative under the rubric of consumption.

Critics argued that the remake merely replayed old themes with inferior actors. " 'The more things change, the more they are the same,' " wrote Bosley Crowther in the *New York Times*. Audiences were far less dismissive; they were again interested in a film that joined white and black women protagonists who might (or might not) fail as mothers. "People have been swarming to see it," observed Crowther, with apparent dismay. *Imitation* was the highest-grossing moneymaker that Universal-International studio had ever had.[4]

Sirk's *Imitation of Life* struck a chord precisely because he was *not* simply retelling an old story. The film helps to explain why, in the late 1950s, so many people feared that for one reason or another they were imitating rather than living a meaningful or "real" life. (As Sirk later observed, "I would have made *Imitation of Life*, in any case, for the title".)[5] *Imitation* suggested how fears of imitation and meaninglessness were bound up with consumption in an affluent society. Virtually all the major characters choose imitation over the film's version of reality at some point in the story. Crucially, they do so as consumers. For example, whereas the original film had celebrated the white protagonist's pursuit of wealth, this zest for material success constituted her fundamental mistake and imitation in the 1959 remake. Whereas the original *Imitation* had depicted the black characters as producers, the remake positioned the black mother and daughter as consumers. Race as well as gender made consuming both a meaningful—and potentially troubling—activity in this period, and *together* shaped fears of imitation. In short, this maternal melodrama situated the dangers of imitation and the absence of an authentic life in relation to questions about consumer culture and racial integration. By doing so, *Imitation* joined seemingly unrelated issues with which liberalism was engaged in this period. It explored these themes through its depictions of motherhood and gender relations.

The relationships among gender, consumption, and race in *Imitation of Life* repeated themselves again and again in other liberal narratives. Discussions of consumer culture among liberal intellectuals were plentiful in the late 1950s, and E. Franklin Frazier's critique of the black middle class in *Black Bourgeoisie* (1957) was particularly influential. One year later, reactions to events in actress Lana Turner's own life drew popular attention to relationships between overconsumption and white maternal failure. Finally, alternative meanings of consumption developed when sit-ins as a form of political protest captured national attention in 1960. Juxtaposing intellectuals' analyses of consumer culture, *Imitation of Life*, and sit-ins suggests that as ideologies of motherhood dispersed, they helped to produce assumptions about "normal" gender relations in unlikely places and ways.

The "World of Make-Believe": Liberal Intellectuals Consider Consumption

Concerns about the potentially negative effects of consumption on Americans were not restricted to the 1950s. In the "roaring twenties," for example, intellectuals had wondered how traditional morality would survive in an expanding mass culture.[6] In the late 1950s, however, a perceived contradiction in the nature of consumption sharply divided the dominant liberal discourse. It appeared that a consumer culture was most necessary to liberal democracy, but it might also be the most dangerous feature of life in the United States.

Advocates heralded consumption as the anchor of economic growth, American democracy, and national strength. According to prevailing Keynesian economic theory, ongoing consumption increased production. It reduced the risk of depression, poverty, and labor unrest by increasing purchasing power, raising the general standard of living, and keeping unemployment rates down.[7] The purchase of consumer goods was the centerpiece of the postwar economic boom. An increasing gross national product in the mid-1950s was primarily the result of money spent (with expanding credit) on residential construction and other consumer goods. According to one estimate, Americans bought three-quarters of all the cars and appliances on earth. These and other data led some critics to conclude that consumption had social as well as economic value because it expanded equality. The "broad masses," in the view of one observer, now enjoyed "former luxuries," including "homeownership, . . . travel, recreation, and entertainment."[8]

In more instances, these broad masses now included white and black Americans.

Postwar prosperity spurred the growth of a black middle class and helped to make segregation impractical from an economic perspective. While significant disparities of income, caused by racially discriminatory hiring, did persist, the percentage of black men and women in white-collar work doubled between 1940 and 1960; the ranks of the black middle class, too, increased as a result.[9] Black as well as white Americans bought homes and automobiles and watched television with greater frequency. A number of liberal critics, though not concerned directly with race relations, noted that mass culture and consumption could enhance freedom for greater numbers of Americans.[10]

Amidst—and because of—the ongoing prosperity, doubts about the meanings of consumption in an affluent society proliferated over the course of the 1950s. An array of critics, including Dwight MacDonald and Mary McCarthy, equated consumer culture with vacuous materialism and conformity—not with American strength, ingenuity, or the absence of class conflict. Some, including Clement Greenberg and Daniel Boorstin, offered insights into the culture industry specifically—arguing that popular films, television, and popular periodicals commodified creativity and were not authentic cultural expressions emanating from individual inspiration. Instead, their popularity reflected the "homogenization of American society" that Schlesinger had warned of, and highlighted the need for "an uncompromising insistence that phoniness is phony and platitudes are platitudinous."[11]

Gender anxieties underlay both celebrations and indictments of consumption. Again and again it seemed that the "right" kind of consumerism and the "right" kind of gender roles reinforced each other. In this period even more than in earlier decades, good mothers were good, or appropriate, consumers. Their purchases strengthened democracy and the "American way of life" precisely because consuming strengthened white families in which men were the primary wage earners and traditional gender roles prevailed. For example, in the famous "Kitchen Debate" between Vice President Richard Nixon and Soviet Premier Nikita Kruschchev in 1959, the two leaders debated the merits of American capitalism versus Soviet communism by way of discussing consumer goods: televisions, washing machines, and suburban houses. Nixon asserted that a plethora of products was virtually synonymous with democracy: "Diversity, the right to choose . . . is the most important thing." Further, he added, "what we want is to make easier the life of our housewives." The Kitchen Debate demonstrated that consumption and democracy went hand in hand if and when female consumers were housewives who consumed on behalf of their families.[12] If they fit this profile, they might even work for wages outside the home and gain social approval. By the late 1950s, indictments of working married women that had been so prevalent during the Depression and in literature about "moms" began to ebb—but only when women's wage work did not reflect personal ambition. When a National Manpower Council studied married women's wage work in 1957, the committee concluded that working mothers worked to make "it possible for millions of families to buy homes, automobiles, and household appliances."[13] These and other advocates of a consumer ethos were also celebrating a certain type of family life and gender relations.

If appropriate patterns of consumption strengthened normative gender roles in healthy families, then excessive consumption might have the opposite effects. Those who were anxious about consumer culture articulated concerns about the fate of masculinity. It was "desperately hard" for a boy to "grow up to be a man" as a result of affluence and overconsumption, wrote Paul Goodman in *Growing Up Absurd*; bored and unstimulated, such a boy (like the insufficiently or excessively aggressive boy in the social science literature of the 1940s) simply did not know "how to be useful and make something of oneself." According to Schlesinger, the "crisis of American masculinity" was not just "the result of female aggression" (though "no doubt there is something in" that argument, he added). Rather, men had to recover their "individual spontaneity" and "resist the overpowering conspiracy of blandness" in mass society in order "to become men again." Others argued that as primary consumers for the family, women were responsible for a destructive emphasis on consumption because it was they who pressured men to "keep up with those Joneses."[14]

John Kenneth Galbraith, an economist who had served in the Roosevelt and Truman administrations before writing speeches for Adlai Stevenson in the 1950s, provided credibility for a liberal critique of prosperity and consumerism in *The Affluent Society* (1958). In this tract, which reached second place on the *New York Times* best-seller list—"as disturbing as it is brilliant" according to one review—Galbraith considered the problem of affluence in economic, cultural, and psychological terms. He challenged the postwar bipartisan consensus (or the "conventional wisdom," as he said) which held that unlimited economic growth was inherently a panacea.[15]

Galbraith's thesis in *The Affluent Society* was that unrestrained production as a source for economic and social security made little sense if the desire to consume newly produced goods was artificially created. "One cannot defend production as satisfying wants," he explained, "if that production creates the wants." He argued that overemphasizing the private production of unnecessary goods created the *appearance* of prosperity but in fact contributed to an economic imbalance that raised the risks of inflation and recession. As well, this system diverted energy and money from public services. "We may in due course expect our economy to choke on a surfeit of nylon seat covers and plastic doorknobs," wrote one reviewer in 1958, shortly after a recession did in fact slow down the economy.[16] Prosperity fueled by consumer culture did not offer Americans true, or authentic, strength; it only imitated economic and cultural vitality.

Galbraith, then, would hardly have endorsed the National Manpower Council's positive assessments of married women's wage work. He noted, for example, that dual wage earning was appealing to families because it met "private wants." When "both parents are engaged in private production," older children watched too much television and saw too many movies, and younger children became "the charge of the community" and a "burden on the public services" for an "appreciable part of the time."[17]

The Affluent Society did not focus on men or women or on gender relations.

Nevertheless, this critique of a consumption-oriented society relied on images of irrational desire and sensuality that were related to qualities associated with femininity. Advertising and public relations industries were not alone in seeking to "create desires—to bring into being wants that previously did not exist," Galbraith wrote. Society as a whole was enamored with the creation of private "sensuous, edifying, and lethal desires." These included "more exotic food, more erotic clothing" as well as "motion pictures, television, cars . . . narcotics, comic books, and pornography."[18]

Galbraith's and other liberal critiques perpetuated a historical opposition between two sets of associations: mass culture and femininity versus authentic culture and masculinity.[19] The imagery used by Galbraith and others reinforced the sense that too much consumption was dangerous to American citizens because it was associated with the irrational and the feminine. The problem of consumption was in part a problem of gender: to forge healthy (normative) gender relations one needed to consume properly, and to be a good consumer one needed to occupy the correct gender position. These efforts to realize the "right" degree of consumption were remarkably similar to a gendered liberal discourse in the 1940s that sought to strike a balance between too much and too little aggression.

Although a growing black middle class participated in postwar consumer culture, its role in this ethos was problematic. Black families seeking to participate in the American dream of mobility and consumption faced multiple obstacles. These included discrimination from whites and charges that their behavior undermined racial solidarity. "What's a Middle Classer?" asked a *Chicago Defender* editorial. In answering this question, the editorial indicted the African American "so-called middle class" for "adding to the racial separation" and had harsh words for lower-class blacks who "strive to be middle class with a two car garage, a bath room and a powder room."[20] It was particularly hard for black women to participate in a consumer ethos unscathed, as had been seen earlier in the decade in liberal social scientists' analyses of black middle-class "matriarchs" and in negative reactions to Mamie Till Bradley.

E. Franklin Frazier's work from the late 1950s drew even greater attention to the role of women in relation to consumption. In 1957 the acclaimed sociologist shifted his gaze from the "Negro masses"—the recent migrants from the rural South who had occupied so many pages in *The Negro Family in the United States* in 1939—to the black middle class. In *Black Bourgeoisie* Frazier argued that members of the black middle class who were too preoccupied with consumption impeded racial progress.[21]

Black Bourgeoisie was iconoclastic and hyperbolic, designed to provoke by exposing inauthenticity in the lives of black Americans. Critics noted that the black middle class was much more diverse than Frazier acknowledged. They felt that he ignored the role of monopoly capitalism and prejudice by white-owned banks in stifling the development of black businesses. They argued that he underestimated the rise of militant civil rights activism—activism in which black clergymen whom Frazier characterized as lacking racial solidarity played a crucial role. Still, praise for

Black Bourgeoisie abounded alongside criticisms and competing interpretations of its themes.[22] Frazier may have criticized the NAACP, but a review in the organization's journal, *The Crisis*, asserted that the book was "perceptive," "brilliant," and said "many, many things that need saying." Black and white journals agreed that *Black Bourgeoisie* was "one of the most provocative studies of race to appear in some time." In 1957 Frazier's study won a prestigious MacIver Award from the American Sociological Society for the best contribution to the progress of the discipline.[23]

In this slim volume, Frazier argued that the shift from the black elite to the contemporary black bourgeoisie had unfortunate repercussions. The traditional black elite, he explained, had its roots in southern light-skinned free blacks from the antebellum period and had developed from Reconstruction roughly through World War I. Its members were descended from former house slaves likely to "identify themselves with their masters" and valued education, religion, and good manners. In contrast, a more nouveau black bourgeoisie developed when "the children of black masses" with "disorganized" families "flooded" black colleges at the same time that teaching became a "source of income" rather than a vehicle for "making men." Frazier attributed this shift to migration, urbanization, and social mobility. With these, "respectability became less a question of morals and manners and more a matter of the external marks of a high standard of living."[24]

The ascendance of the black bourgeoisie was cause for concern, according to Frazier, because it was a "world of make-believe." Members labored under the myth of prosperity when they lacked a truly secure foothold in the American economy. A scattering of beauty parlors and funeral businesses and the few truly wealthy blacks in entertainment and sports industries propped up the illusion of black prosperity. In reality, too many people lived in constant debt. Members of the black bourgeoisie feigned prosperity and an interest in " 'cultural' things." In fact, they had "no real appreciation" for art or literature, preferring "poker orgies," sports, or parties.[25] The black bourgeoisie floated, rudderless and without values to anchor it. Its members were living a series of economic, personal, and cultural imitations.

Frazier infused his analysis (which anticipated Galbraith's *The Affluent Society* in certain respects) with racial specificity when he asserted that feelings of racial self-hatred caused a preoccupation with consumption. In studies of prejudice and children that had influenced Supreme Court justices in the *Brown v. Board of Education* decision, the social psychologist Kenneth Clark concluded that discrimination caused "conflicts about the individual's worth" and a "distortion in the sense of what is real."[26] Frazier maintained that such feelings of inferiority were most acute among the black bourgeoisie because its members rejected black folk and religious traditions, preferring popular diversions gleaned from white society and divested of racial meaning. Under these circumstances, "their escape into a world of make-believe" was bound to create "a feeling of emptiness . . . which causes them to constantly seek an escape in new delusions." *Black Bourgeoisie* did not simply scorn nouveau riche behavior and consumption patterns; rather, Frazier understood such behavior as self-hating and politically damaging.[27]

Frazier constructed racial self-hatred as a problem of *gender* in two ways. He depicted women as most wracked by self-hatred and as the black bourgeoisie's imitators and consumers par excellence. He also described consumption as a process that feminized black men and weakened black families. The text detailed the "unbridled extravagance" and "pathological struggle for status" in black "society" with frequent references to women's behavior: debutante balls noted for "the expensive gowns and jewels worn by the women"; wives of black men who dominated black public life because "of their ability to engage in conspicuous consumption"; and women who were "obsessed with poker in order to escape from their frustrations." He attributed women's preoccupation with "frivolities" to sexual frustration, their fears of white women, and the "ineffectual lives which they lead." In Frazier's scathing characterization, "The idle, overfed women among the black bourgeoisie are generally, to use their language, 'dripping with diamonds.' They are forever dieting and reducing only to put on more weight (which is usually the result of the food that they consume at their club meetings)."[28]

Such hostility was not incidental to this analysis. Black women were an essential part of the problem that Frazier diagnosed in the community as a whole. Because the perspective on racial self-hatred in *Black Bourgeoisie* was inherently gendered, Frazier could not conceive of the multiple jobs that black women performed in the workforce, the community, and the home, or the ways that they resisted racial stereotypes.[29] Instead, he believed that successful women produced and expressed the problem of racial inauthenticity and self-hatred.

According to *Black Bourgeoisie*, the fusion of racial self-hatred and consumption undermined black masculinity. Images associated with femininity reinforced the sense that consumption was alarming. Male consumers were "noted for their glamour" and "resemble women." They cultivated " 'personalities' " rather than the " 'masculine role,' " competed with other black men, and were often unfaithful. Even the black man who was not a glamorous consumer was a "slave" to his wife's desires and "presents a pathetic picture. He often sits at home alone, impotent physically and socially."[30]

Frazier explored the overlapping negative effects of femininity, consumption, and self-hatred in his discussion of black children. Some children "say that they had a happy family life until 'mamma took to poker,' " he wrote. He maintained that these problems would continue from one generation to the next because parents spoiled their children, purchasing them toys, clothes, and cars. With behavior that appeared loving, parents projected their own feelings of inferiority onto their children.[31] Because Frazier had already made clear that women were the worst offenders, their pathology lay at the heart of their children's deficiencies.

Consumption inspired by self-hatred wreaked havoc on positive racial identification *and* on the traditional gender relations that Frazier continued to equate in *Black Bourgeoisie*, just as he had in *The Negro Family in the United States*. Though the focus and terms of his inquiry had shifted from poor migrants to a wealthier middle class, and from anxieties about aggression to anxieties about consumption, the dangers that black women posed—both to racial progress and to black men—

persisted. In fact, because the black bourgeoisie was not "tough enough" and feared competition with whites, it had a "vested interest" in segregation. Frazier concluded that he often agreed with sociologist's Robert Park's thirty-five-year-old assessment: the not-tough-enough "Negro was 'the lady among the races.' "[32]

It is worth noting that Frazier's analysis provided a foundation for his rejections of racial prejudice *and* of red-baiting in African American communities. His critique of a consuming middle class must be seen in the context of growing civil rights activism that promoted both black autonomy and interracial cooperation; as well, when he indicted black organizations for their "middle-class values," he challenged the circumscribed conception of citizenship characteristic of Cold War liberalism. In fact, Frazier scorned the middle-class liberals, white and black, in the NAACP for "refusing to associate" with "unions or groups in which Communists might possibly be members."[33] Frazier had little patience for "sentimental and paternalistic" white liberals who criticized him for criticizing African Americans. That type of liberal "makes me sick," said Frazier. "All this Pollyanna sympathy means that the Negro will remain backward, inefficient and ignorant. Unless you make him [the Negro man] measure up to other people . . . he will never amount to anything."[34] Even when Frazier's analysis of consumption helped to constitute commitments to racial equality and cross-class solidarity, conservative gender ideologies propelled his critique forward.

In liberals' debates about consumption, white and black women occupied similar but not identical roles. Discussions that were implicitly about white Americans often concluded that women contributed to the negative effects of consumption; importantly, though, the reverse was also true: women's behavior as consumers was potentially beneficial. When they consumed properly, white women strengthened American families, masculinity, and democracy. This dichotomy between white women as good or bad consumers was far less available to black women, as Frazier's work from this period makes clear.

Imitation of Life and events that preceded production of the film offered another perspective on relationships between white and black women and consumption. If Frazier, Galbraith, or many other liberal critics of consumption needed proof that consumer culture and women together damaged families, they got it in April 1958. The drama that surrounded the actress Lana Turner and her daughter Cheryl Crane that spring in Beverly Hills showed just how intertwined white maternal failure and the gendered problem of consumption were. These events assumed further meaning in the film *Imitation of Life* in which Tuner starred and which opened one year later.

"The Most Important Performance of Her Life": Lana / Lora's Consumption, Imitation, and White Maternal Failure

In both versions of *Imitation of Life*, the daughter of a struggling but ultimately successful white woman falls in love with her mother's suitor as a result of her mother's neglect. In both, the black woman's light-skinned daughter seeks to pass as white, repudiating her race and her mother. The black protagonist dies in 1959 as painstakingly as she does in 1934, brokenhearted by her daughter's rejection.

Despite these similarities, much does change from one film to the next. The white mother, in the first version a widowed pancake magnate, becomes the aspiring actress Lora Meredith. Romance beckons to Lora not at the pinnacle of her success, as is the case in 1934, but even before she receives her first audition. In 1934 the black daughter tries to pass as white by working as a cashier; in the end, she accepts her race when she attends a segregated Negro college. In 1959 the newly named Sarah Jane tries to pass with very different behavior. And the remake does not celebrate the family that the two single mothers form. It too is an imitation—of a "real" family with a male head.

These differences point to an emphasis on appropriate femininity and normative gender roles at the heart of this new *Imitation*. The film's distinction between "real life" and "imitation" parallels its distinction between appropriate and inappropriate female behavior. The women in 1959 imitate real life when they deviate from gender mores. They do so, moreover, out of their desire to consume. The white protagonist, Lora Meredith, fails as a mother because she is compulsively drawn to a consumer culture that the film exposes as insidious. "What you're after isn't real," says the man she loves, early on, when she rejects his marriage proposal and a traditional domestic life because she wants to be an actress. In her desire for new roles and more ostentatious clothes, she neglects her daughter and chooses a ten-year loveless relationship instead of the man she truly loves. Lora's preference (until the final moments of the film) for acting and glamorous clothes over motherhood and traditional romance demonstrate that a normative heterosexual relationship and motherhood require each other, and that both require a more restrained consumerism than she exhibits.

Events in Lana Turner's life that took place before she accepted the role of Lora to reignite her flickering career reveal how and why anxieties about white maternal failure, materialism, and consumer culture intersected in *Imitation of Life*. A slippage between the character Lora Meredith and the person Lana Turner made this self-reflexive tale about imitation and white motherhood meaningful.

On April 4, 1958, Lana Turner's fourteen-year-old daughter Cheryl Crane stabbed to death Johnny Stompanato, Turner's abusive lover from whom she had tried to separate for several months. Prior to the stabbing, Crane had heard Stompanato repeatedly threaten her mother and warn that he could hire people to harm Turner, her daughter, and Turner's mother. Crane also knew that Stompanato had beaten her mother on other occasions.[35]

One week later, a jury of ten men and two women deliberated for approximately twenty minutes at a day-long inquest. They ruled that the murder had been justifiable homicide. Crane, who had been in custody since the murder, remained at Juvenile Hall until a judge declared her a ward of the court and awarded the girl's maternal grandmother physical custody.[36]

The murder and inquest generated a media explosion. Over one hundred reporters, photographers, and cameramen attended the "near-riotous" inquest. ABC was not allowed to offer live television coverage, though the local affiliate did receive permission to film the events and make radio recordings. Stompanato's connections to organized crime added another layer to this tale in which Hollywood and underworld allure converged.[37]

Like the murder of Emmett Till, this "most sensational incident," and " 'one of Hollywood's greatest scandals' " placed motherhood itself on trial.[38] Once again—though at a different location and for different reasons—what constituted authentic maternal concern was a question that observers asked to determine innocence or guilt. These questions could only be answered by considering materialism and motherhood, authenticity and artifice, and the relationship between allegedly real love versus imitations of it.

Turner, thirty-eight years old at the time of the murder, had been in the public eye for two decades. She first achieved prominence in "Sweater Girl" pinups in the late 1930s, and her star status grew after her roles in the films *Ziegfeld Girl* (1941) and *The Postman Always Rings Twice* (1946). In 1957, she received an Oscar nomination for her role as a sexually repressed single mother in *Peyton Place*. Throughout her career, observers had focused on her offscreen life as much as her onscreen roles: her sexuality and glamorous nightlife, her elaborate clothes, her fierce ambition, and, not the least, her frequent and short-lived marriages. "To her, men are like new dresses, to be donned and doffed at her pleasure," wrote Hollywood gossip columnist Hedda Hopper in 1953.[39]

In 1958 it was not surprising that the teenage Cheryl Crane's innocence or guilt hinged on reactions to Turner. National debates about juvenile delinquency in the late 1950s assumed that delinquent behavior crossed class lines and was the result of parenting. Quite aside from Lana Turner and Cheryl Crane, liberal commentators worried about adolescents for whom "everything is being done, to [whom] everything is being given . . . except a reason for living and building a socially useful life." Hollywood, or "Movietown," was a particularly "ticklish place for teenagers."[40] The circumstances surrounding Stompanato's death simply confirmed this perspective.

Two qualities were crucial to assessments of Turner: her materialism prior to the murder and her loyalty to her daughter in its aftermath. Whether accounts assumed a sympathetic or a more sneering tone (or, as was more often the case, both), all emphasized that Turner's life had been characterized by her "feckless pursuit of happiness" in the wrong places. "Can a simple girl . . . find happiness as a glamorous movie queen?" asked *Time*.[41] No, was the resounding response. Turner failed because she had "vainly sought happiness on a road cobbled with diamonds." Her rapid rise from obscurity to stardom and from working-class status to wealth reflected the American dream of mobility gone awry because the dream rested on an artificial foundation. "All the material blessings she dreamed of materialized—the high living, the mink, the diamonds, the Cadillacs, fame. Everything but love and happiness." Although Turner was an independent single mother who had supported herself, her mother, and her own daughter for years, she was not a mother whose role as consumer strengthened her family. Instead, she herself was "a high-priced commodity."[42]

Descriptions of material excesses were inseparable from discussions of the murder. It was no coincidence that the tragedy had occurred in a "mansion" in "opulent Beverly Hills," in "Lana's bedroom, lavishly furnished all in pink," and "at the foot of Lana's commodious bed." As in *Black Bourgeoisie*, descriptions of Turner sexualized her preoccupation with wealth and consumption. According to *Time*, "wanton Lana" often "took Johnny in tow, paid his bills, flashed around the town on his muscular arm."[43] While many duly noted Stompanato's abuse of Turner and his criminal record, they also implied that Turner's attraction to the "dapper Adonis of the underworld" exemplified more than poor judgment. Just as she could not tell "real" success from the "road cobbled with diamonds," so too, she could not tell a "real" man—mature, successful, and respectable—from the imitation that the lying Stompanato had offered.[44]

The question of what was real and what was artificial was even more pressing in evaluations of Turner's behavior after the murder. Frequent references to Turner as distraught yet committed to her daughter suggested that she had passed the test for authentic maternal authority—the very test that many had implied Mamie Bradley failed. Turner was "haggard and sobbing uncontrollably." "Lana Turner Breaks Into Sobs on Leaving Daughter's Hearing." "Tragedies Reflected in Lana Turner's Tears." These banner headlines indicated that the murder had cracked the facade of the sweater-girl-turned-superstar to reveal the real person beneath it: an overcome and "stricken mother" who was human after all.[45]

At the inquest, Turner's detailed hour-long testimony was the linchpin of the "justifiable homicide" verdict. "A public which knew her only as a sleek symbol of Hollywood glamour watched with squeamish fascination," explained *Life*, as Turner "went through a very real, personal ordeal." During her testimony she spoke "haltingly, constantly on the brink of collapse." Afterwards she was "overwhelmed by the crushing strain of her ordeal" and "had to be taken home" before the verdict. "She was put to bed immediately and given sedatives" when she heard that the jury ruled it was justifiable homicide. Housewives were sympathetic to Turner, according to one observer, because "they saw her fight with a woman's weapons—tears, beauty, courage and the scarred heart laid bare."[46]

Even as this discourse seemed to confirm Turner's maternal authenticity by invoking her emotional capacities, it simultaneously implied that she was engaged in a performance. Detailed descriptions of her clothes resembled chronicles of costumes, references to fans who thrilled at the sight of her at the inquest echoed accounts of Turner approaching a movie set, and photographs of the inquest duplicated a consecutive sequence of film shots. All these moves heightened the sense that the inquest was yet another performance in which the actress could shine. The inquest was "Lana's hour upon the stage"; "Lana still had one more performance to give"; her testimony was a remarkable "test role." *Life* juxtaposed photos of Turner on the stand at the Stompanato inquest with shots from three film roles in which she had testified. "As an Actress, Lots of Court Experience," explained a headline.[47]

Representations of Turner's lifestyle and of her behavior after the murder as a performance reinforced the overall sense that "Lana Turner had a daughter, Cheryl, to whom she gave gifts, money, luxurious living, expensive schooling, everything, in fact, except a normal upbringing." The consensus was that "a frightened Hollywood child of 14," simply could not "cope with a glittering, bewildering, and alcoholic world of too many fathers, too much luxury, and too much neglect."[48] In widely published comments after the inquest, the district attorney asserted that " 'Cheryl never has had a real home either with her mother or father' "; according to others, she "would be better off if she were declared a ward of the court."[49]

This perspective culminated in the lead editorial of the *Los Angeles Times* on the day after the inquest. Turner was "a simple woman, a hedonist without subtlety, who was so preoccupied with her design for living that she long ago lost the reference marks." The editorial lambasted Turner for exposing Crane to her sexual relationship with Stompanato even before the relationship became violent. Because of such maternal behavior, "the Cheryls" of the world—children of "casual divorce" who witnessed "less formal matings"—were "misplaced baggage" and psychologically crippled. In this case, "Cheryl isn't the juvenile delinquent; Lana is."[50]

On the eve of a new decade, this scandal proved just how dangerous overconsumption in an affluent society could be. This danger implicated mothers because it was their job to provide emotional security for families, and not just objects that offered the pretense of security. ("And what about a mother's love?" asks the fictional daughter in *Imitation of Life* when Lora/Lana lists the possessions which prove that her daughters has "had the best of everything.") But even this message was not clearcut. In contrast to psychosocial analyses of women that had probed unconscious feelings to illuminate social reality and "normal" families in the 1930s and 1940s, by 1958 it was unclear whether or not there was a "reality" or a norm that could be extricated from these layers of imitation and performance. Ultimately, the question of whether Turner was *in reality* a distraught and "stricken mother" or whether she was offering a highly convincing *imitation* of such a person could not be answered. Representations of her created and reinforced this conundrum.

Barely a year later, the film *Imitation* reinscribed this paradox to make its own narrative about imitation and maternal failure authentic. From the broad outlines of the story about an ambitious, materialistic, and neglectful mother/actress caught in sexual rivalry with her daughter to more specific markers—Lora Meredith's pink bedroom, the horse that she gives her daughter as a graduation present—the ironic remake of the 1930s melodrama borrowed from the "real-life drama." Sirk even shot scenes of the fictional white daughter's graduation at Cheryl Crane's school.[51]

These multiple layers of imitation crystallized in the film's dramatic confrontation between the white mother and daughter. In this scene, Lora learns that her daughter Susie is in love with her fiancee and offers to give him up. The daughter's response is, "Oh Mama, stop acting. Stop trying to shift people around as though they were pawns on a stage." These lines reflected the ways that a mother-daughter narrative in 1959 could only imitate themes of maternal self-sacrifice that the film celebrated as genuine in 1934. Even when a mother appeared to transcend artificiality and be most devoted to her child, she might still be ensnared in imitation and maternal failure. Events in Turner's own life were inextricably embedded in this message and in this narrative. This fusion constituted a discourse of white maternal failure as it was harnessed to concerns about materialism and artifice.

In *Imitation of Life*, as in Frazier's *Black Bourgeoisie*, fears about consumption and motherhood cut across lines of race. *Imitation*'s message about white maternal failure and consumption cannot be understood without attention to its message about black maternal failure, race relations, and consumption. That is because in *Imitation of Life*, excessive consumption posed a danger to healthy gender relations *and* to healthy race relations.

"No Sin in Looking Prosperous": Consuming Women, Self-Hatred, and Black Maternal Failure

In certain respects, the updated *Imitation of Life* condemned racism and endorsed integration in stronger terms than the 1934 film had. At the same time, it defined "healthy" race relations in a certain way: in terms of obedient blacks who were free from racial self-hatred and who were appropriate consumers, and in terms of respectable, "feminine" behavior on the part of women.

In the remake as in the original, the light-skinned black daughter has a problem. But in 1959 her problem is that she is as enamored with consumer culture as the white mother Lora is. The film codes Sarah Jane's desire to pass, or her imitations of whiteness, in terms of gender rather than racial deviance. To pass, she pursues a white man; she then runs away to work in sleazy nightclubs in New York and Hollywood.[52] A scantily clad Sarah Jane sings "Empty Arms" before leering men—and her shocked mother who pursues her. Her mother's outrage and propriety confirm that it is Sarah Jane's sexuality through which passing assumes such negative meaning.[53]

Sarah Jane's pattern of placing herself on display as she imitates whiteness parallels Lora's display of herself as an actress and does not only invoke the centuries-old image of the promiscuous black woman as Jezebel. She is drawn to the mecca of the industry that specializes in artifice and in which Lora is a star. The clubs in which Sarah Jane performs are no more or less artificial than the stages on which Lora performs. Both stages, and the women on them, imitate "real" life and "real" art; parallels between Lora and Sarah Jane define these scenes.[54] At the same time, Sarah Jane's efforts to pass as white confirm the links between racial self-hatred,

The black daughter in *Imitation of Life* (Susan Kohner) imitates whiteness in ways that are sexualized. As her mother and a white man watch her, she sings, "An empty purse can make a good girl bad . . . So fill me up with what I formerly had." Courtesy of the Museum of Modern Art / Film Stills Archives.

consumer culture, and gender. Her self-hating behavior takes shape in terms of gender deviance and female sexuality in ways that had not been overt in 1934. It is worth recalling that in the earlier film, a thriving consumer culture helped to solve the women's problems, and that both adult women were essentially producers for this developing consumer economy.

In the 1959 *Imitation*, a loosening of the racial order accompanies the emphasis on normative gender roles. The black mother, now Annie Johnson, sheds the dialect and Aunt Jemima-like turban of her predecessor; in the intervening twenty-five years she also acquires a last name. Although Annie does call her fellow-mother "Miss Lora," the employer/employee relationship is more ambiguous than it had been in 1934. Lora invites the woman she initially calls "Mrs. Johnson" and her daughter to stay for a night; she makes it clear that she cannot afford to pay Annie as a domestic or babysitter. Annie initially imitates the role of domestic to help Lora imitate the role of a credible actress, while, in private moments, they work together to save money for "our kitty." When the women move from a small urban flat to a sprawling country home, the black mother and daughter occupy rooms upstairs—alongside those of the white mother and daughter. The spatially segregated home of 1934 has been integrated.[55]

Annie's participation in the public sphere as an appropriate consumer is an important source for the film's (ostensibly) racially progressive stance. In the opening scene on Coney Island, under Annie's watchful eye, the two young girls enjoy the party atmosphere of the beach and the hot dogs that she buys them. It is, in part, as a result of the girls' pleasure that Lora initially allows Annie and Sarah Jane into her home. While Annie's wardrobe pales alongside Lora's, before her death she bestows her "genuine mink" and pearls to loved ones. Annie also achieves autonomy in the public sphere. When she searches for the wayward Sarah Jane, she does so independently—traveling alone and either by cab or plane. In contrast, in 1934, the black mother, ignorant about money, travels with her white boss (in a segregated car) to find her daughter.[56] And when Annie locates her daughter dancing at a seedy dive, the mild-mannered mother threatens her underage daughter's white employer with the law, cognizant of her own rights and the man's legal responsibilities.

It might seem that the two mothers in this second *Imitation* have little in common. The respectable black mother of 1959 appears to be very different from her hedonistic white counterpart as well as from dominating black matriarchs. And yet Annie is instrumental in the problems that her daughter has just as Lora sets her own daughter's problems into motion. In living with the wealthy white actress, Annie stimulates desire in Sarah Jane by surrounding her with the trappings of prosperity. "No sin in looking prosperous," she says early on, acknowledging her own penchant for imitation.[57] Annie's excessive love for her daughter is itself akin to overconsumption, as she acknowledges from her deathbed: "Tell her I know I was selfish, and if I loved her too much, I'm sorry," she says haltingly, and with her last breaths. It is she who observes that she and Lora share a great deal. "I know you meant to be a good mother, the best kind of mother. But look, I meant to be a good one, too, and I failed." With these words Annie underscores the fact that maternal failure crossed bounds of race and class. Ultimately, with regard to motherhood, which the film assigns as all women's primary role, Lora and Annie are more similar than different.[58] Both women fail as mothers because the pleasures of consumption are so alluring.

This relationship between consumption, maternal failure, and racial self-hatred emerges in a crucial scene in which Lora asks Sarah Jane to serve hors d'oeuvres as she discusses rehearsals with a film director. Sarah Jane enters the living room with tray on head, hand on hips, and an assumed dialect and subservience; much to Lora's horror, she declares, "Fetched y'all o' mess o'crawdads fo'yo', Miz Lora." The young black woman imitates the role of racial subordinate that Delilah unironically inhabits in 1934. The film invokes the racial stereotype of mammy, and through this imitation demonstrates just how discredited it is in the eyes of whites like Lora, and in the eyes of white audiences by 1959.[59] Yet Sarah Jane's inappropriate display of herself undercuts the liberal stance. Her imitation of a mammy may show that she rejects racial stereotypes, but it also demonstrates that she, *and* her mother, have erred. "Annie, did you see what she did?" asks Lora angrily. Annie fulfills Frazier's predictions when she surrounds her daughter with superficial symbols of status and raises a daughter who hates herself, is spoiled, and is disrespectful. "You weren't being colored, you were being childish," declares Lora. Sarah Jane can only reject discrimination, it seems, with immature self-hate and sexualized self-display, rather than with a developed political posture.

Annie's death and funeral at the conclusion of the film are the means through which the characters cease their imitations and inappropriate consumption *and* accept traditional gender mores. It is the moment of authenticity in a story replete with artifice. As in the original film, the funeral is elaborate; it is "the one thing I've always wanted to splurge on," says Annie earlier. Yet the "splurge of garish ostentation," as one reviewer put it, offers a glimpse of consumption untainted by imitation and racial self-hatred. Members of a large black community sing in Annie's church; others gather in the streets behind a hearse drawn by white horses. Mahalia Jackson, an internationally acclaimed singer who popularized gospel music among white audiences and who participated in civil rights demonstrations, sings "Trouble of the World" in this scene. The white characters who dominate *Imitation* only dot the landscape during the funeral, reversing the model of "integration" that prevails earlier.[60]

It is at this point that Lora and Sarah Jane learn to reject their imitations. The wayward Sarah Jane returns, now respectably attired and crying "I didn't mean it!" Lora embraces her and takes her into the back seat of the car with her own daughter, Susie. As Sarah Jane's head rests on Lora's shoulder and Susie grasps her hand, Lora is at last in the maternal position. With Annie dead and the remaining women in their proper gender roles—in the back seat of the car—Lora's long-suffering beau, Steven, looks on fondly. Here is a family with a man at last in the front seat.

Douglas Sirk acknowledged that these final moments in *Imitation* are intentionally ambiguous.[61] Given the intensity with which Lora and Sarah Jane question their designated roles, it is hard to believe that Lora will permanently renounce her career and that Sarah Jane will accept a subordinate racial status. Even if temporarily, however, the film places Lora in her "natural" gender position—a heterosexual relationship to the exclusion of her acting career—in order to prove that she might be a good woman, a good mother, and an appropriate consumer.

It should be emphasized that the narrative must eliminate Annie in order for both Lora and Sarah Jane to reform and occupy their "natural" gender and racial positions. The two mothers may play similar roles across lines of race as the *sources* of the personal/social problems that plague their families. However, the black mother is excluded, except in death, from the *solution*. Instead, her death allows for, and helps in, delineating the white woman as "normal"—a dynamic reminiscent of ways that welfare was racialized and demonized as a program for black matriarchs even as white women benefited from an expanded Social Security Act in the same period.

It is on these qualified terms—through the existence, and death, of an African

American woman who does not consume too much and still fails as a mother in many important respects—that *Imitation* affirms integration. The affirmation is cautious: it requires women to occupy specific gender roles and to be certain kinds of consumers within certain kinds of families. In other words, the quality of black family life and of gender relations are integral to such an affirmation of integration.

If *Imitation of Life* defined and left somewhat open-ended the problem of consumption as it related to gender and race, others sought to resolve these issues more thoroughly. And if the film at best offered only a tepid endorsement of racial equality, far more expansive claims for integration were emerging in other parts of the country. When *Imitation of Life* was released, the civil rights movement was at a moment of transition. The "baton was ready to pass," as Amiri Baraka put it, from an older generation of respectable African Americans (like Annie) to younger college-age African Americans (like Sarah Jane). As one critic noted, "a Negro's sympathies are with Sarah Jane, *not* Annie."[62] In 1960 this transition became evident in Greensboro, North Carolina, and elsewhere in the South. With increased civil rights activism, other meanings of consumption and gender assumed prominence. But as was the case in *Imitation of Life*, ideas about family life, appropriate gender mores, and consumption shaped positions on race relations. The credibility of public activism and political demands rested on the respectability of families and private life; this intersection continued to link gender, race, and consumption.

"A Whole Man" with "More Than a Hamburger": Sit-Ins, Consumption, and Gender

In *Black Bourgeoisie* and other work, E. Franklin Frazier analyzed depoliticized youths who were Sarah Jane's age. He targeted black colleges, declaring that "Negro schools, which had once placed great value upon the making of men or the development of a cultivated civilized person, have turned their attention to the making of money makers." Frazier believed that because college students were more interested in fraternities and sororities than in public service and serious education, they lacked a positive collective racial identity and could contribute little to desegregation efforts.[63]

But it was precisely this group of African Americans who helped to catapult civil rights into the national arena. On Monday, February 1, 1960, four male students from the North Carolina Agricultural and Technical College sat at a Woolworth's lunch counter in Greensboro, North Carolina, and asked for service. They refused to leave when employees denied their request. With this action, the four helped to launch the sit-ins that, in the words of the *Chicago Defender*, "ripped through Dixie with the speed of a rocket and the contagion of the old plague."[64] Within weeks of the initial action, sit-ins had spread to some seven other southern cities, and from Woolworth's to shopping centers, drive-ins, and drugstores; by April, seventy-eight southern or border communities had experienced sit-ins. Sit-ins gained national attention and prefigured the formation of the Student Nonviolent Coordinating Committee (SNCC) in April 1960.[65]

In sit-ins, activists who were committed to making the ideal of American democracy a reality for African Americans forged alternative meanings to the consumer ethos that so disturbed liberals in this period.[66] Black students who sat-in rejected Galbraith's argument that consumption focused attention on private life to the detriment of the public good. They rejected Frazier's assumption that consuming was a sign of racial self-hatred and inauthenticity. And they rejected the notion evident in *Imitation of Life* that consumption damaged gender relations and families. However, even as they forged alternative meanings for consumption, protesters perpetuated traditional notions about what constituted appropriate masculine and feminine behavior.

African Americans had demanded an end to discrimination based on their position as consumers well before the Greensboro students put sit-ins on the map. Among earlier examples were streetcar boycotts in the late nineteenth century and "Don't Buy Where You Can't Work" campaigns in the 1930s. In the 1940s the Congress of Racial Equality (CORE) had sponsored sit-ins, and between 1957 and 1960 sit-ins spread to at least sixteen cities. Many of these campaigns had focused on how the experience of consuming necessary goods was humiliating for African Americans, especially in relation to their roles in the workforce. By 1960, traditional strategies had shifted, and students themselves felt that they were breaking new ground. The goal of sit-ins was to request service that was not strictly "necessary"—to ask for the pleasure of a Coke after making a purchase. This strategic goal developed alongside and in relation to the growing support for nonviolent direct action among civil rights activists. A belief that extended well beyond civil rights activism explains this convergence: that consumption and democracy were inextricably linked.[67]

Many of the young activists who participated in sit-ins were among the most privileged segments of black society. They were "often referred to as the 'country club bunch,' " noted the *Chicago Defender*, and were associated with "Ivy League conservatism" according to the *New York Times*.[68] Through sit-ins, these students adapted and made political the impulses that Frazier had subjected to scathing criticism in *Black Bourgeoisie*. They did not reject the consumer ethos that he derided and to which the fictional Sarah Jane was drawn; instead they transformed its meanings. In many respects, they relied on the premise that consumption equaled happiness, which equaled freedom and revised power relations. "All I want," said one student leader, "is to come in and place my order and be served and leave a tip if I feel like it." In Washington, D.C., Howard University students marched in sympathy with protesters to their south, carrying signs that said "Pass the Bill, Not the Buck," and "Hot Dogs for All."[69] In Atlanta, lunch counter sit-ins spread to restaurants, movie theaters, and other public facilities; in cities throughout the South there were "sleep-ins" in motel lobbies, "swim-ins" or "wade-ins" at pools and beaches, and "watch-ins" at movie theaters—and other public facilities, like schools, that had less to do with consumption per se.[70]

Of course, students were demanding more than simply the right to consume like other middle-class or aspiring middle-class Americans. Several of the young leaders, in fact, were openly critical of such "bourgeoisie" behavior in their elders.[71] As Ella Baker, executive director of the Southern Christian Leadership Conference, made clear at the organizing convention for student leaders in April 1960, sit-ins were about "more than a hamburger."[72] Sit-ins represented the *use* of ideas about consumption as all-American to address racial inequities in social and economic life. To expose institutionalized racism, protesters relied on the very aspects of consumer culture that Nixon had celebrated at the Kitchen Debate. They altered aspects of a consumer-oriented society that E. Franklin Frazier criticized in *Black Bourgeoisie*, and that Sirk satirized in *Imitation of Life*. In occupying public space, activists used the depoliticized leisure associated with femininity as the crucial component of a challenge to Jim Crow. And when they targeted places of leisure and sites for the enjoyment of mass culture, they placed themselves on display in front of cameras as consumers; consumption and performance—two related qualities central to liberal discourse in this period—were crucial to their bid for equality.

The ways in which students both transformed and relied on ideas about middle-class behavior in a consumption-driven society came into sharp focus in Atlanta, the wealthiest city in the South at this time. Students at Atlanta University declared that their goal was to "secure full citizenship rights as members of this great Democracy of ours." They extended sit-ins to a comprehensive boycott of Rich's department store, a popular retail outlet where blacks could make purchases but could not use the restrooms, try on clothes in the dressing rooms, or get something to eat at the lunch counter.[73] Persuading older black consumers to stop using their Rich's credit cards was no simple feat, explained one organizer; as Frazier had observed, credit was important to many middle-class blacks. (Could Annie in *Imitation of Life* have bought her "genuine mink" without a credit card?) Yet with the slogan "Close out your charge account with segregation, open up your account with freedom," student leaders politicized qualities in an affluent society and a black bourgeoisie—a dependence on credit—that had ostensibly depoliticized middle-class blacks and whites and on which female consumers relied most.[74] They invoked the "American way" of credit card purchasing to demand racial equality and shatter middle-class complacency.

At the same time that they challenged a middle-class valorization of credit, protesters in Atlanta cultivated associations with middle-class respectability. For example, several contemporary accounts relate that Lonnie King, a senior at Morehouse College in Atlanta with a working-class background, recruited fellow-student Julian Bond because Bond had a privileged background: the light-skinned Bond had attended prep schools, had interned at *Time* magazine, and was popular among fellow students. Drawing attention to markers of middle-class status challenged Frazier's declarations that middle-class blacks were inauthentic. Protesters were also participating in an older tradition, a "politics of respectability." As studies of black reformers at the turn of the century have shown, claiming access to these markers of middle-class status had potentially subversive implications.[75]

By repeatedly evoking their own respectability, protesters linked the domestic sphere of the home to the public sphere of consumption. Many observers, for example, commented on how "polite" the young protesters were. When a white segregationist woman said that stores "have no business refusing nice, polite, young people," she responded to the ways that protesters conveyed the message that they had been "brung up" well, as Delilah had put it in the original *Imitation of Life*.[76] Demonstrators in Chapel Hill, North Carolina, made a similar point when they carried signs declaring, "We do not picket just because we want to eat. We can eat at home. . . . We do picket to protest the lack of dignity and respect shown us as human beings." It was no longer enough to be able to buy food and eat it at home. The logic of consumer-based citizenship required an extension of the right to pleasure into the public sphere, and it was there that protesters performed.[77] Signs like those in Chapel Hill and a widespread emphasis on the respectability of protesters suggested that these college students came from "good" homes. This fact legitimated their political demands. Their desire to consume was not a sign that their parents had spoiled them or raised them to hate themselves; consumption and their display of themselves in the public sphere assumed precisely the opposite meanings from those conveyed by the fictional Sarah Jane.

The ways that class and race shaped the consumer ethos in sit-ins cannot be fully understood without considering gender as well. In their use of consumption, in their use of ideas about middle-class respectability, and in their merging of public and private, protesters perpetuated dominant notions about what constituted appropriate masculine and feminine behavior. For instance, physical appearance was crucial to sit-in organizers because it helped to convey gender difference. In report after report, memoir after memoir, and from city to city, the nice clothing that protesters wore in the early years of activism is a recurring motif. When Atlanta students entered a city hall cafeteria, "we went in, very neat, neckties, and all the girls looking as sharp as they could," wrote Julian Bond. In some instances, men wore army ROTC uniforms. John Lewis, active in the Nashville sit-ins, observed that "the students were dressed like they were on the way to church or going to a big social affair." This attire was no accident. James Lawson, an activist from Nashville, gave courses on nonviolence and included strict clothing guidelines: for women to wear stockings and heels, and for men to wear coats and ties.[78] This strategy paid off when the first national news coverage of the Greensboro sit-in referred to "well dressed Negro college students."[79]

Repeated references to stockings and ties and to dresses and army uniforms suggest that the dignity and respectability evoked by clothing and good manners had intersecting gendered and class meanings. The editor of one segregationist newspaper wrote, "Here were the colored students, in coats, white shirts, ties, and one of them was reading Goethe and one was taking notes from a biology text. And here, on the sidewalk outside, was a gang of white boys come to heckle, a ragtail rabble, slack-jawed, black-jacketed."[80] In this passage as well were two models of masculinity: the first offered young black men who were restrained, yet determined, hardworking, and productive. This vision of masculinity stood in opposition to representations of white racists: they were cast as white "trash" and as unrestrained and unproductive. They resembled little more than a gang of white juvenile delinquents out of *West Side Story*, the celebrated Broadway show that opened in 1957. Similarly, the *Chicago Defender* featured a photo of the four men who staged the first sit-in dressed in ties and jackets; the caption included their majors and professional goals (pre-medical, pre-law, engineering physics). Surely such industrious young men were not sitting down at a drugstore lunch counter for lack of anything better to do; their decision to protest—"passive" as they seemed—reflected a larger maturity and independence, and as one observer put it, involved remarkable "activity."[81] Some liberal accounts of sit-ins and the students' organizational structure were rich with military metaphors in which black men assumed positions of leadership: events in Atlanta included "first skirmishes" and "field maneuvers," leaders with such titles as "Le Commandante" and "Deputy Field Commander," and "a corps of young women who serve as 'Communication Aides.' "[82]

Sit-ins also conveyed the message that protesting could restore masculinity. Protesters rejected links between self-hatred and consumption by inverting images of consuming blacks as feminized blacks. According to Franklin McCain, one of the original four Greensboro protesters, months of debates with his friends about sit-ins ended when he pounded a dresser and asked his three friends, "Are you guys chicken or not?"[83] As he sat and waited for coffee and doughnuts at the Woolworth's lunch counter, "I felt as though I had gained my manhood . . . not only gained it, but had developed quite a lot of respect for it. . . . I felt as though the manhood of a number of other black persons had been restored and had gotten some respect from just that one day." Marion Barry, a student at Fisk University, explained that he risked losing his scholarship to participate in sit-ins because "I was only part of a man, and I felt in order to be a whole man I must be an American citizen as anybody else."[84] In claiming citizenship rights, students linked consumption and mass culture not to unrestrained and sexualized femininity and self-hatred (as was the case in *Imitation of Life*), and not to effeminate black men and self-hatred (as was the case in *Black Bourgeoisie*), but to this "quiet courage" and appropriately masculine behavior.[85] Such references to manhood were not merely rhetorical because they did not exist in isolation. Together with the emphasis on clothing and respectability, they suggested that the bid for dignity in sit-ins had gendered, class, and racial dimensions that overlapped and shaped each other. This gendered protest countered segregation; it also countered a long history in which even antiracists had questioned black masculinity.

This restored sense of masculinity could include offering—and receiving—special attention to and from black women. White opponents of civil rights often subjected male and female protesters to similar verbal and physical abuse. To counter such violations, Atlanta organizers provided "special football coats for the girls, with big hoods, because there were a lot of thugs downtown throwing spitballs and stuff at them." When jailed male protesters in Atlanta were bailed out of prison, they "went over to Spelman where we could be heroes, you know, among the women."[86] Here, women were written out of the act of protesting and getting arrested and into the position of admirers. Similarly, a northern white male who traveled to Durham and Raleigh in North Carolina told of attending a mass meeting in which a black male leader with a passionate "talent for oratory" declared that "there had not been enough men on the lines that day." The leader had made the responsibility (and opportunity) of male protesters explicit: "several girls had been pushed, one had been slapped, by white men. That would never have happened had enough male students been walking. There could be no excuses; the girls needed protection, and—after all—the boys might meet their future wives 'in the movement.' "[87]

These frameworks of protest that emphasized sexual difference among black protesters undermined racial stereotypes that had remained common even, or especially, among antiracists: images of black men as feminized, of black mothers as dominating, and of black families as disorganized by maternal behavior.[88] Yet, as had been the case with Mamie Till Bradley, these challenges were double-edged. Sit-ins implied that protesting and traditional gender mores went hand in hand; the racial equality that activists demanded often required this version of "proper" gender roles and this vision of masculinity. By extension, deviations from approved masculine and feminine behavior interfered with the possibility of racial progress, and, at the very least, were not a source of heroism. As Anne Moody, a protester in Mississippi, recalled, she did not bask in the attention of admirers after her racial protest. Julian Bond and other men may have reveled in being heroes with women after their release from prison, whereas Moody went from a sit-in to a beauty shop. " 'Do you have time to wash my hair and style it?' " she asked the hairdresser, who was glad to care for Moody before her other customers.[89]

It is crucial to note that the emphasis on traditional gender roles could not diminish the significance to sit-ins of women like Ella Baker, Diane Nash, Ruby Doris Smith, and so many others whose names are known and not known. Contemporary accounts acknowledged female participation and leadership.[90] Women were active on a grassroots level ("the girls were more ardent about picketing than the boys," according to one account), as leaders (a series in the *Chicago Defender* on the "new face of young Negro America" included photos of three black women) and, crucially, as role models for younger men and women. Male and female activists recalled their own mothers as sources of inspiration. In considering women like Ruby Doris Smith and Fannie Lou Hamer, among others, one scholar has concluded that "brashness and courage" were "typical" of many black women activists in this period.[91]

Nevertheless, within the context of these protests in the early 1960s, certain expressions of femininity were more desirable than others. A firsthand account of sit-ins in Knoxville, Tennessee, detailed the contributions that a woman made as a

Jet introduced Nashville civil rights leader Diane Nash as the "Pretty Fisk coed." Courtesy of *Jet*.

leader of a sit-in but described her as a "pleasant but determined little housewife." Another woman protester may have "brought down the house" at a mass meeting but "loves—unfortunately, I think—to tantalize the assistant manager."[92] The *New York Amsterdam News* described two student leaders with gendered markers of respectability. Betty Johnson was "daughter of a Washington, D.C. dentist," and her counterpart, Lacy Streeter, was "a World War II veteran with four years of service in the Far East." *Jet* featured Diane Nash, a leader in Nashville on its cover twice in just over a year. While the stories drew attention to her negotiating skills, references to the "Pretty Fisk coed" and the "comely coed" dominated this coverage, a message that the cover photos reinforced.[93]

The paradox is that an implicit and explicit emphasis on sexual difference and normative gender mores coexisted with the enormously central role that women played in sit-ins (and in civil rights activism generally). This emphasis could and did limit women at the time; moreover, it has limited accounts of women in liberal histories of this period. As Alice Echols has explained in her analysis of scholarship on the 1960s, it can be difficult to determine the extent of women's roles and experiences because of the ways that historical work "replicates the position of women in the male-dominated movement. . . . [W]riters have managed to marginalize women more effectively than could the movements they write about."[94] Most standard accounts or canonical anthologies of the civil rights movement, for instance, do not mention what Diane Nash, in 1961, regarded as "one of the best-remembered incidents" at sit-ins in Nashville. Nash recalled how during the sit-ins, black women had entered a women's restroom marked "white." A white woman "seeking refuge" from the demonstrators could not quite believe that they had entered even this sanctuary. "Oh! Nigras everywhere!" the white woman exclaimed.[95] It is worth considering how and why some incidents—and not others—become "best remembered."

At the height of student activism, a cartoon appeared in the *Chicago Defender*. It featured two black women clad in tight skirts and high heels; the one looks at the other with an expression of puzzlement. The caption declared, "How could we join a 'boycott' . . . we're not boys."[96] Clearly, many women joined and led boycotts as well as sit-ins, yet somehow this cartoon spoke a certain kind of truth. For the gendered model of citizenship that consumer-oriented sit-ins produced, and that some liberal scholarship has duplicated, privileged masculinity.

In sum, sit-ins "re-gendered" consumption as protesters relied on already intertwined relationships between consumption, American democracy, gender, and race, and between public and private life. By choosing to consume during sit-ins, and choosing not to consume when sit-ins became boycotts, activists transformed participation in consumer culture into a vehicle for demanding state activism to correct racial inequities. In joining their roles as consumers and their demands for full citizenship, they offered a solution to the ostensible problems of consumption that liberals had outlined—its feminizing effects, its contribution to racial self-hatred, and its perpetuation of unhealthy families. Consuming became a sign of self-restraint, citizenship, and a respectable private life rather than of excessive

This cartoon and caption in the *Chicago Defender* on April 23, 1960 reflected the masculine orientation of civil rights activism in this period. Courtesy of the *Chicago Defender*.

femininity, sexuality, and dysfunctional families. In the process, consuming became a radical tool for countering discrimination instead of a symptom of those who imitated life—like Lana Turner/Lora Meredith and like Sarah Jane.

Sit-ins inverted the liberal discourse on consumption in particular kinds of ways: they linked protest in the public sphere to respectability and normative gender roles. Good manners as well as sexual difference between masculine black men and feminine black women prevailed in the public sphere, and these distinguishing features spoke to the quality of life in black families in the private sphere. If Sarah Jane's *inappropriate* display of herself in public reflected the atmosphere in which she was raised in *Imitation of Life*, protesters' *appropriate* display of themselves reflected the atmosphere in which they were raised. Sitting-in could resolve the very problems of consumption, race, and maternal failure that *Imitation of Life* had outlined.

Images of femininity as beyond or separate from protest ultimately strengthened black men's claims to citizenship. Just as Mamie Till Bradley and the fictional Annie were marginalized in narratives about politicization and racial progress based on their maternal behavior (the former by being fired and the latter by being killed), black women who were so important to sit-ins were (and, often, have remained) largely marginalized from demands for citizenship inherent in these protests. Instead, images associated with femininity and black women continued to be repositories for the ideas about racial inferiority and racial self-hatred that young activists set out to dismantle. In this way, ideas that took shape in a liberal discourse on motherhood and families underlay the gender mores evident in sit-ins. The gender dynamics underlying sit-ins further illuminate intersections between (racial) progressivism and (gender) conservatism. A consumer ethos did have subversive potential when it was harnessed to these demands for citizenship. This very subversiveness could reinforce traditional gender mores in a movement in which women were so crucial.

By considering how ideas about masculinity and femininity played a part in sit-ins, we can begin to see that a liberal discourse associated with motherhood and families had implications in events that were not explicitly about these topics. We have seen that liberal conceptions of motherhood were one arena in which ideas about families, the state, race relations, and gender mores took shape; ideologies of motherhood were never just about the private sphere. With sit-ins, we can begin to see how ideas about families, the private sphere, and motherhood spilled over beyond these parameters to affect gender relations more broadly in liberal activism. In other words, as liberal civil rights activism gained momentum, sit-ins challenged discrimination, *and* addressed the social problems that overconsumption and maternal behavior ostensibly helped to create.

In scholarship about consumption, in the film *Imitation of Life*, in the spectacle surrounding its star, and in sit-ins, key tropes and images overlapped and shaped each other. This range of liberal texts and events from the late 1950s and early 1960s used links between gender and consumption in ways that invoked gender deviance and maternal failure. Nevertheless, despite a liberal discourse that privileged masculinity, women's behavior and desires were changing. In the late 1950s—on the cusp of a national civil rights movement and the women's liberation movement—the fictional Lora Meredith expressed desires for personal and professional fulfillment that the hard-working and self-sacrificing white mother in the 1930s film could not. The fictional Annie and Sarah Jane Johnson, and activists like Diane Nash, Anne Moody, and Ruby Doris Smith Robinson were among the many black women who challenged racism, and who made political and personal claims. By 1961, greater numbers of women were in the workforce or engaging in other behavior that departed from a domestic ethos of virtuous consumption; as well, more black and white women (and men) were sitting-in, getting arrested, and engaging in other behavior that departed from earlier definitions of respectability.

As the gender conservatism and moderate racial liberalism that had constrained Mamie Till Bradley in 1955 gave way to more expansive visions of equality and opportunity, representations of black and white women as mothers fractured. By the mid-1960s, liberal activism was a resource through which many white women claimed their rights as citizens, women, and mothers—far more forcefully than did Lora Meredith or Lana Turner. Liberalism was not necessarily a resource in this manner for black women, even when government activism oriented around race relations escalated in the early 1960s. Sit-ins offer a glimpse into how and why activism oriented around remaking race relations—in which women played such an important part—had the potential to affect gender and race relations in positive ways. As a nascent civil rights movement came to dominate national political culture, this potential was seldom realized.

CHAPTER SIX

Pathologies and Mystiques

Revising Motherhood and Liberalism in the 1960s

M any Americans speak of the first half of the 1960s by recalling televised
marches and behind-the-scenes political negotiations, inspiring
speeches and legislative maneuverings, landmark publications and dramatic protests. Together, these conveyed the sense that the country was on "the
cusp of a new day of liberal activism."[1] Nowhere was this sense of possibility and
change more evident than in race relations. The sit-ins of 1960–61 galvanized college students around the country, arid a range of other direct-action protests spread
throughout the South, attracting national attention. Whether activists in SNCC,
the SCLC, CORE, and other organizations spearheaded voter registration drives in
rural Mississippi, or worked to desegregate public facilities; whether they were
sitting-in, boycotting, staging freedom rides, or marching down city streets, they
were, in the early 1960s, producing and reflecting the sense that times had changed.
The cautious and qualified racial liberalism evident in Douglas Sirk's *Imitation of
Life*—when the young Sarah Jane seemed relatively isolated in her longings for
equality and her mother seemed destined not to understand her desires—had apparently passed.

This shift was evident on a national level too. As candidate and president, John F.
Kennedy appeared to support civil rights. After becoming president in 1963, Lyndon Johnson urged passage of both the Civil Rights Act and the Economic Opportunity Act in 1964, and the Voting Rights Act in 1965. By 1965 both the president
and majorities in Congress had endorsed federal activism to remedy racial inequities. Proactive antiracism and liberalism went hand in hand in ways that they
never had before.

Indeed, racial liberalism in John F. Kennedy's New Frontier and Lyndon Johnson's Great Society looked and sounded very different from racial liberalism in
Franklin Roosevelt's New Deal. Decades of psychosocial research coupled with

139

crucial grassroots activism had helped to produce something of a liberal consensus on civil rights: a sense that because racism hurt white and black Americans and harmed American interests at home and abroad, it could not continue unchecked. This consensus was evident in civil rights legislation of 1964 and 1965, as well as in other popular and political texts that with little conflict or debate incorporated antiracism. By 1967 even interracial marriage was an appropriate topic for a mainstream Hollywood film—a source not just of controversy but of comic moments in the popular movie *Guess Who's Coming to Dinner*.[2] Although this high-water mark or consensus was limited (Kennedy approached the question of civil rights reluctantly, and neither he nor Johnson protected civil rights activists in the South from white violence or from federal surveillance, for instance), by 1964 race was no longer marginal to liberal discourse.[3] Both a president and Congress had made some commitment to federal intervention, and many Americans across the country endorsed their policies.

Race relations was not the only area in which liberal activism was ascendant in these years. In 1963, the same year that Martin Luther King Jr. had a dream that he shared with thousands at the March On Washington, Betty Friedan named the "problem that has no name" in her book *The Feminine Mystique*. Publication of this instant classic came to symbolize the birth of liberal feminism. But according to Friedan, even by 1960 discussions of white women's plight had "burst like a boil through the image of the happy American housewife."[4] Changing attitudes were already manifest in the ability of the female characters in the 1959 *Imitation of Life* to name their desires—"I want to achieve something . . . I'm going up and up and up," says Lora—even if the film then suppressed these desires.

By the mid-1960s these desires could no longer be contained as readily. Some experts in the fields of child development and female psychology continued to defend full-time stay-at-home motherhood as the only way that women could raise healthy children fit for citizenship and find personal fulfillment.[5] But this view no longer had the ideological dominance that it did in the 1940s and early 1950s. There was a sense that other options for normative white femininity and maternal success existed besides a domestic ideal. Proponents of women's work and advocates of day care quoted studies to prove that working white mothers—like Lana Turner or the fictional Lora Meredith—were not more likely to have delinquent or emotionally disturbed children and might even wreak less emotional havoc on their children's psyches than stay-at-home moms. An editor at *Harper's* magazine agreed that women's "flight from home" was neither a "neurotic rejection" of femininity nor a recipe for maternal failure.[6] On a national level, individuals and organizations were more active and inclined to make demands of the state on behalf of women. In short, liberal feminism—with its belief that women could and would realize their potential as "persons," and that federal intervention might strengthen women's equality as full citizens—was emerging.[7]

In recent years scholars have convincingly demonstrated that activism in the 1960s did not simply "erupt." They have pointed to important lines of continuity between liberal and left-oriented activism concerned with race and gender in the

1960s and challenges that varieties of groups posed in the 1950s and earlier. To understand the 1960s correctly, historians have argued, one must attend to political, intellectual, cultural, and social resistance prior to that period.[8]

In concluding, this study suggests that the opposite is also true: remapping the sixties requires attention to the *conservative* dimensions of the apparently liberal discourse that shaped this turbulent era. If the more positive political, cultural, and social changes associated with the sixties had roots in earlier decades, so too did some of the problematic aspects of the era. Liberalism's own internal contradictions and (related) conservative dimensions—particularly with regard to gender—continued into this period.[9] More specifically, the notion that certain kinds of women and mothers, black and white, posed dangers to American citizens and to the state continued to play a major role even as liberalism underwent reforms and assumed ascendancy. Indeed, the very basis of liberal activism in the 1960s developed, in part, out of an edifice that had taken shape thirty years earlier: that of the "bad mother" as the personification of pathology within the liberal welfare state.

A brief overview of two moments in the early sixties both illuminates these lines of continuity and allows important changes in liberal discourse to come into focus. The first is the release of what has come to be known as the "Moynihan report." In March 1965, Daniel Patrick Moynihan, then assistant secretary of labor and director of the Office of Policy Planning and Research, submitted to Lyndon Johnson a report on African American families. Moynihan's initially secret study, *The Negro Family: A Case for National Action*, quickly filtered out into the press and public. Publication of the report generated acrimonious debates among those committed to alleviating racial discrimination.[10]

A second important aspect of this period was the development of liberal feminism. Betty Friedan's *The Feminine Mystique* in 1963 propelled questions about discrimination against women onto the national agenda. Given the splash that this landmark book made, it is easy to overlook the fact that it was not alone in the questions it raised; *The Feminine Mystique* appeared just months after John F. Kennedy received from Esther Peterson, Women's Bureau director and assistant secretary of labor, the final report of the President's Commission on the Status of Women (PCSW). This report was based on work that over one hundred business and labor leaders, educators and scholars, and cabinet members who served on the commission's seven subcommittees had done over the course of two years. Translated into several languages and later published with related documents, the PCSW's final report included recommendations for an expanded federally and privately funded day care system, a forty-hour work week for all employees, male and female, and a more extensive unemployment insurance system for women employees.[11]

It has made sense to locate the Moynihan report and liberal feminism, as advocates expressed it in *The Feminine Mystique* and the PCSW, as prologues to narratives that unfolded and gained momentum in the late 1960s and after. Both were significant in the ways that they helped to usher in a new era. Moynihan's report triggered such a controversy that observers at the time and subsequent scholars have viewed it as that which helped to fracture the very liberal consensus on race that had been building since the 1930s, offering both advocates of black power and white moderates something to oppose.[12] Similarly, *The Feminine Mystique* and the PCSW were catalysts, enabling a more organized movement for women's liberation that came into its own in the latter half of the sixties and after.[13] Like the Moynihan report, liberal feminism became a useful target—for radical feminists in the seventies.

But the Moynihan report did not only contribute to a shift between the ascendant racial liberalism of the late 1950s and early 1960s and the eclipse of a liberal consensus on race relations in the late 1960s and early 1970s. Nor did *The Feminine Mystique* and the PCSW merely signal the demise of the happy homemaker in favor of liberal or radical feminism. These were not simply emblems of a larger sea change. To believe so is to overlook continuities within liberalism. In fact, entrenched assumptions about the political dangers of maternal failure resurfaced in these symptomatic liberal texts. Though they varied in style and in the political demands they made, the Moynihan report, *The Feminine Mystique,* and the PCSW represented black and white mothers as potential failures.

At the same time, however, the knot between mother-blaming and progressive ideas about race was beginning to unravel. It was the psychosocial dimensions of liberalism that had most centrally implicated mothers, black and white. This component of liberalism was manifest in the thirties, increasingly racialized in the forties, and consolidated in the fifties. But for a variety of reasons, by the sixties the assumption that psychologically fit citizens had to come from good families with good mothers, while damaged families and mothers produced unhealthy citizens, was starting to be discredited among liberals.[14] This shift had unexpected results. Most importantly, ideas about maternal failure that crossed lines of race had a very different impact on women, more than they had in earlier decades.

A "Tangle of Pathology": The Moynihan Report

The assistant secretary of labor, Daniel Patrick Moynihan, was one of many intellectuals who, committed to change and progress, became active in the federal government in the era of Kennedy's New Frontier. Moynihan's seventy-eight page report focused on problems that African Americans faced in the urban north. The central premise of the report was that "family structure" was *the* "fundamental problem." Black families ensnared in poverty and discrimination were "approaching complete breakdown"; they were the "principal source" of the "aberrant, inadequate, or anti-social behavior" among African Americans. Moynihan, ever the social scientist, amassed evidence to document this alleged deterioration of families and analyzed the historical roots of this breakdown. He argued that even the civil rights movement, "the most important domestic event of the postwar period," could not help "the Negro family," which was "in the deepest trouble."[15]

Throughout, Moynihan maintained that black "matriarchs" perpetuated the "tangle of pathology" in which black families were trapped. For Moynihan as for so many other liberals before him, women's behavior had crucial social, political, and

economic repercussions. Images of black women in the report reflected the cumu-
lative effects of a liberal race relations discourse that had distorted the maternal capacities of black women.[16] Moynihan repeatedly sought credibility through references to respected experts who had studied black family life—particularly E.
Franklin Frazier and contributors to a contemporary volume devoted to "the Negro American" in the prestigious journal *Daedalus*.[17] The report was replete with
scholarly citations and charts. With these data, Moynihan argued that households
headed by females were characterized by "disorganization." Rising rates of illegitimacy proved to him that disintegration was rampant on the "urban frontier"; he
speculated that promiscuity among poor black women was even greater than his
data indicated.[18]

The Negro Family essentially argued that black women who worked for wages
and reared children could not succeed in either enterprise and thereby hurt their
families. Moynihan detailed the "sad cycle" that had become familiar since literature on unemployment proliferated during the Depression. In terms similar to
those John Dollard had used nearly thirty years earlier in *Caste and Class in a
Southern Town*, Moynihan argued that women weakened and disorganized their
families because of the alleged economic power they wielded in the public sphere
combined with the personal power they wielded in the private sphere. He contrasted dominating black mothers who worked to unemployed black men who were
both unmotivated and undermined as a result of their "unusually low power."[19]

Women's "sins" were of omission and commission. Sexualized matriarchal black
mothers who had "too many children too early" neglected or dominated their children, and often did both. Moynihan reinforced images of pernicious "smother
love" (or maternal overprotection) first identified in the 1930s and 1940s and used
this concept in relation to blackness. He also warned about maternal deprivation,
especially in his critique of working mothers who deprived children "of the kind of
attention . . . which is now a standard feature of middle-class upbringing." To
highlight the social ramifications of deprivation, the report quoted authorities who
argued that children "reared in a disorganized home without a father" sought "immediate gratification" as a result of their neglect. This impulse was a "critical factor in immature, criminal, and neurotic behavior."[20]

Drawing on the work of race relations experts, Moynihan was particularly critical of black women who, "disgusted" with dependent black men, favored and encouraged their daughters over their sons. In paying excessive attention to the
"wrong" children (girls), mothers perpetuated patterns in which women were better educated, more employable, and more inclined to dominate the men in their
lives. In more direct ways than Frazier, Dollard, Kardiner and Ovesey, and others,
Moynihan expressed alarm about black women and girls who worked hard (in or
out of the home), cared for their families, and studied in school—women and girls
whose behavior under other circumstances might have received praise.[21] But this attitude was far from unprecedented. Progressive scholars had tended to laud qualities associated with initiative, ambition, and family loyalty when they saw such features in the black men or boys who were the primary focus of their studies;

whereas, both real and fictional women faced different expectations. In both versions of *Imitation of Life*, for instance, the black daughter who seeks to change her life, who is ambitious and not without talent or skill, is as suspect as the mother who helps to generate this deviant behavior. The Moynihan report exposed a common denominator between texts oriented around sons and masculinity and those oriented around daughters and femininity: in both cases, ideas about black motherhood were the site at which the parameters for acceptable masculinity and femininity were established.

Like other progressive studies that emphasized black women's maternal failure, *The Negro Family* reflected efforts to restore and preserve a certain kind of masculinity. Moynihan coded this gender identity in universal terms: "The very essence of the male animal," he wrote, "from the bantam rooster to the four-star general, is to strut." Matriarchal women were dangerous because, together with the racial caste system, they made black men submissive; they made it harder for men to be productive citizens and harder for them to strut.[22]

Given this perspective on masculinity, it is not surprising that one of the few concrete recommendations that Moynihan did make was to encourage black men to join the military. The U.S. armed forces was the "*only* experience open to the Negro American" where he was treated "as one man equal to any other man." Moreover, the "utterly masculine" military world provided black men with a much-needed "world away from women, a world run by strong men of unquestioned authority." The military was one arena through which black masculinity could be transformed; beyond the armed forces, revitalizing masculinity, patriarchy, and citizenship required revising motherhood to make black women less dominating.[23]

Efforts to qualify this argument by drawing attention to its cultural and environmental dimensions could not offset the sense that there existed a universal standard that African Americans did not meet because of their own failures. Alongside statements about the impact slavery had on black families, *The Negro Family* maintained that "disorganized" families generated patterns of behavior that were dangerous because they assumed their own momentum: "the present tangle of pathology is capable of perpetuating itself without assistance from the white world."[24]

An "Interior Marshall Plan": The Moynihan Report and Liberalism

Moynihan may have vividly described the "tangle of pathology," but what he thought the federal government should do about it was far less clear. At times *The Negro Family* seemed to advocate unprecedented government attention and legislation to address the "tangle of pathology" and the damaging effects of matriarchal families. In other instances, the report reinforced the sense that the state had little to do with black families and women's roles in these families.[25]

To some extent, *The Negro Family* was consistent with Johnson's Great Society and with efforts to expand liberalism beyond a focus on individuals. In a follow-up article to the report, Moynihan pointed to the "absurdities" of an "American social policy" that mistakenly made "the individual rather than the family . . . the object of concern."[26] One observer argued that the report contained seeds for an "aid and development program, an interior Marshall Plan." Only with a "national effort" that would include extensive work programs for Negro youth, explained the report, could black motherhood be revised and the cycle of poverty broken down.[27] This position stood in marked contrast to the liberalism characteristic of the Cold War era, which often sought to expand government activism in some areas and restrict it in others in the name of the liberal individual. It also marked a departure from psychological analyses of discrimination that dominated studies of race relations in the 1940s and 1950s—toward a more socioeconomic perspective, and toward programs that were explicitly race-conscious.

As had long been the case, advocacy for an activist liberal state proceeded in tandem with ideas about who and what "normal" men and women were. An effective welfare state, Moynihan and his supporters argued, could and should intervene into the private lives of families, but only if its policies supported male-headed families and healthy gendered distinctions between public and private that were the cornerstone to liberalism. Using data in the report to highlight the need for welfare reform, some objected strenuously to provisions that denied relief to "families with an able-bodied man in the house" because such restrictions forced "men to desert their families."[28] But with recommendations for a "national family policy," Moynihan made clear that expanding the liberal welfare state to help families meant strengthening black men, even at the expense of women. The job of the state was to understand men's needs—"what it takes for a working man to raise a family . . . and then see to it that what it takes is available." Moynihan argued that Project Headstart should not pay women to look after children of unemployed men because this practice perpetuated three problems: women's dominance, the absence of employed men as role models, and welfare dependency. "If the working class fathers of the city earned a steady $3.00 or $4.00 an hour, would we need a Project Headstart?" he asked, recommending that black men replace white and black women in the program and as public school teachers. As his ardent defenders Lee Rainwater and William Yancey explained, "Moynihan felt that . . . the government should not rest until every able-bodied Negro man was working even if this meant that some women's jobs had to be redesigned to enable men to fulfill them."[29]

Even as the Moynihan report reflected efforts to revise and expand liberalism, it also implied that individual behavior had to change before any government program could have an effect, a message conveyed especially by its focus on family disorganization and women. As Moynihan's many critics emphasized, the report allowed the federal government to retreat from a liberal civil rights agenda; if all that needed to be done had been done and the rest was up to individuals, then the report offered "a massive academic cop-out for the white conscience," wrote James Farmer, national director of the Congress of Racial Equality, because personal changes could not be legislated. Another critic pointed out that part of what made the report so alarming was that it revealed the extent to which this "ideology" was "accepted now even by some liberals."[30]

In other words, the Moynihan report reaffirmed the need for an extensive liberal welfare state while simultaneously containing its responsibility for social problems and racial inequities. As the report depicted them, black women signaled why a liberal welfare state was needed and what it could accomplish; but they also embodied what was most dangerous in and to that state. This paradox had shaped New Deal liberalism, and it had become even more pronounced in the postwar expansion of social insurance amidst simultaneous critiques of welfare. The Moynihan report followed and brought to the fore a well-established pattern within liberalism that made black women a repository for deviance and a symbol for all that could go wrong in American society. The terms and possibilities of inclusion had changed from the 1930s to the 1960s, but claims to African American citizenship continued to hinge on constructing black women as a problem.

The Negro Family adopted this familiar pattern in a moment when liberal civil rights activism had far more momentum than it had in the 1930s. For instance, the report, and significantly, even many critical reactions to it, included black men in liberal visions of citizenship. Black men's access to citizenship was more comprehensive by the mid-1960s than it had been in the 1930s when the racial "inclusion" of New Deal liberalism was so provisional; it was more comprehensive than it had been in vital center or Cold War liberalism of the 1940s and 1950s, when apparently more pressing issues of anticommunism subsumed questions of race. The Moynihan report conceptualized citizenship as that which could fully encompass black men—if their masculinity could be rehabilitated.

Further, reactions to *The Negro Family* indicated that the role of psychosocial theories was beginning to change in progressive discussions of race relations. On the one hand, because racial inequities persisted after passage of civil rights legislation, psychological explanations of prejudice and its effects remained appealing.[31] Moynihan was among those who could not relinquish what he called the "fundamental insight of psychoanalytic theory," which was that "the child learns a way of looking at life in his early years." He always assumed that "the family is the basic social unit of American life . . . adult conduct in society is learned as a child." On the other hand, by the mid-1960s, social and political analyses reflecting psychoanalytic theory had begun to lose cachet and influence, particularly among liberals. Some experts were challenging the scientific credibility of psychoanalysis altogether. Others were forging new conceptions of what constituted mental health. Psychosocial theory was becoming more oriented toward what humanistic psychologists called "selfhood" and less exclusively focused on strengthening bonds within families as the route to adjustment and mental health.[32]

These changes had particular ramifications for discussions of race. Liberal scholars now argued that prejudiced whites were part of a larger culture shaped by racism rather than individuals with personality disorders developed in dysfunctional families. Black Americans who suffered from prejudice were members of groups or cultural networks that were far larger than their individually disordered families. Some progressive experts noted that overemphasizing psychological damage made it harder to justify government programs that targeted class-based groups of people in need. The psychiatric approach, wrote two leading social scientists in 1964, "was concerned with individual, nonsocial methods of change."[33] Even *The Negro Family* highlighted class as fully as it did race and individual psychological damage, with Moynihan repeatedly emphasizing the economic opportunities that his subjects needed.

The loosening of the ties between racial progress and psychological health did not make the antiracist Moynihan less prone to mother-blaming. But it did provide more room to rework the liberal paradigm that *The Negro Family* seemed to update so effectively. Reactions to the Moynihan report, even among those who called themselves liberals, were varied and vociferous. For all of its influence, *The Negro Family* met with considerable resistance. Ironically, the report's deployments of "matriarchy" contributed to the ways in which racial liberalism became less dependent on psychosocial theories of families which highlighted maternal failure.

"New Crisis"? Reactions to Moynihan

Debates about *The Negro Family* escalated, in part because no one could dismiss the report as the idiosyncratic opinions of just one individual. Moynihan's brief study appeared to provide what its name implied: a foundation for liberal activism on the part of the federal government as a whole. The report was the blueprint for a celebrated speech that Lyndon Johnson gave at Howard University in June 1965, in which he argued that the next "battleground" for civil rights should be black poverty and the problems black families faced. He announced plans for a White House conference to address this next stage and to devise strategies for incorporating black families into the Great Society. Like Moynihan, Johnson conceptualized race relations as a social and economic problem and not as an interpersonal problem between psychologically maladjusted individuals. And like Moynihan, the president continued to associate socioeconomic and political problems with the private sphere of disorganized families. What must be understood, said Johnson at Howard University, was that "Negro poverty is not white poverty . . . there are differences—deep, corrosive, obstinate differences—radiating painful roots into the community, the family and the nature of the individual."[34]

Other national and international events affected reactions to the Moynihan report. Moynihan wrote *The Negro Family* shortly after voting rights legislation was passed; it became controversial in the same summer in which Johnson initiated a ground war in Vietnam, and just days before Watts erupted in violence. This was a time when many liberal whites were concluding that the civil rights movement had "finished its work," and that, given the seemingly more pressing issues at hand like a costly war abroad, blacks themselves must assume responsibility for their ongoing problems. "Having reacted to the movement's demands for a decade, the government had learned that it was impossible to satiate the new Negro American," wrote two Moynihan defenders in 1967. By emphasizing the need for self-reliant families, Moynihan provided credibility for this perspective among some liberals, even as his analysis also bolstered conservatives' arguments about black pathology and an over-active liberal government.[35]

In this atmosphere, personal failure, self-help, and a "self-sustaining vicious circle," as *Newsweek* put it, were often the terms through which Americans came to discuss the "next phase in the achievement of Negro equality." Mary McGrory, a prominent reporter in Washington, D.C., wrote that Johnson's speech at Howard implied that "the time had come for them [Negroes] to come to grips with their own worst problem" far more than it outlined the basis for race-conscious policies and affirmative action. Frequently, accounts of the Moynihan report concluded that promoting "self-help must realistically appear as a large part of the ultimate answer" and that "only the Negro can save his family."[36]

Meanwhile greater numbers of black activists were coming to very different kinds of conclusions: that civil rights battles had just begun, and that particularly given how the Democratic party had rejected the Mississippi Freedom Democratic Party at its convention in 1964, the administration's commitment to civil rights, antipoverty, and comprehensive social change was qualified at best. In the aftermath of Malcolm X's assassination in February 1965 and in a climate of growing black nationalism, many African Americans were deeply disturbed by the report's message that individual failure rather than systemic racism impeded racial progress. They were alarmed by the apparent retrenchment among white liberals with regard to questions of race relations. As James Farmer explained, "it has been the fatal error of American society for 300 years to ultimately blame the roots of poverty and violence . . . upon Negroes themselves."[37] Challenges to the *The Negro Family* on methodological, ideological, and historical grounds proliferated for over a decade in the popular press, among grassroots activists, and in academic journals.

Critics argued that Moynihan's emphasis on deeply rooted pathological family structures de-emphasized "*contemporary* discrimination" and confused cause and effect. Discriminatory hiring practices, they noted, contributed to high unemployment rates just as a "systematic inequality of access" to contraceptive information contributed to high illegitimacy rates. By confusing result and cause, the report had implied that "segregation and discrimination are not the terrible villains we thought they were. Rather, we are told the Negro's condition is due to his 'pathology.' "[38]

Moynihan's opponents also argued that his "norm"—the "white family" with a "high degree of stability"—was hardly universal or worthy of emulation. *The Negro Family*, they said, underestimated the incidence of pathological behaviors among whites and overestimated their frequency among African Americans.[39] In an influential critique published in *The Nation* and *The Crisis*, William Ryan, a psychologist, argued that Moynihan masked what was a "great concern apparent everywhere . . . about the 'breakdown of the American family.' " James Farmer noted that "nowhere does Moynihan suggest that there may be something wrong in an 'orderly and normal' white family structure that is weaned on race hatred and passes the word 'nigger' from generation to generation." Well after the report was released, another critic challenged Moynihan by comparing black and white mothers. Because *both* ran "the house in the absence, real or psychological, of a man," black families could not be considered in a unique crisis; suburban "white America certainly is faced" with a similar "dilemma."[40]

As the comparison between black and white women suggests, many responses to *The Negro Family*—both pro and con—replicated the gendered logic that structured its analysis of race. Discussions of the report frequently sustained the emphasis on black women's failures as the crux of the crisis; or, as one headline summarized the entire issue: "Aid to Replace Matriarchy Asked by Johnson Panel." A lengthy article in the *New York Times Magazine*, "The Absent Negro Father Haunts the Negro Family," exemplified this pattern as it explored the historical and contemporary reasons for the Negro man's "castration as a husband and father." The author applauded Moynihan for recognizing the psychological "dimensions of the crisis."[41]

Critics as well as supporters of Moynihan implicitly agreed that if black women had too much or the wrong kind of power, something was drastically wrong with "the race" as a whole. "It is a psychological truism" said one Moynihan critic, "that boys need strong male models and girls need men in their lives as children if they are to accept them readily as adults." In a photo-editorial on "A Man Around the House," *Ebony* wrote that "the heritage of matriarchy . . . once was strongly instrumental in maintaining some stability in the family" but concluded that "in this day and age it may be one of the most destructive forces in the life of the Negro family."[42] Through the late 1960s and early 1970s, many of those from across the political and ideological spectrum who challenged Moynihan's assumptions about dominant women and weak men did so by "proving" that black men were not the emasculated and deferential weaklings the report depicted. For the radical leader of the Oakland Black Panthers, Huey Newton, this meant demanding that the black man "recapture his balls" and the black woman "take care of business" at home. For scholars of black families, it meant locating traditional gender mores in African and African American history. One history of black families stated that "the most striking feature of African family and community life was the strong and dominant place in family and society assigned to and assumed by the men."[43] Especially as controversy over the report peaked in 1965–66, it was difficult to change the terms of this debate. Opponents who offered insightful criticisms of the report were among those who made black mothers part of the problem, and demanded a revision of motherhood to strengthen black masculinity.

Reactions to *The Negro Family* cast black women's wage work in the public sphere and emotional work in the private sphere as a potential problem that interfered with racial progress. Like the report itself, such discussions continued to place black women beyond or separate from evaluations of race. Black men and their role in the workforce remained the barometer for measuring racial progress. Rendering black women as suspect allowed men who supported or criticized Moynihan to claim rights as "restored" men *and* as citizens; the very terms of this debate enabled those categories to blend into each other. As a "Letter From Washington" in *The New Yorker* put it, what the country really needed was "a national policy to strengthen the ego of the Negro male."[44] This conflation of citizenship and masculinity was reminiscent of the ways that the NAACP had segregated Mamie Bradley's alleged gender deviance from the political mobilization that she had helped forge after Emmett Till's murder.

By the late 1960s the terms of this liberal discourse were publicly contested in ways that had not been apparent in the 1940s and 1950s.[45] Black women forged feminist theories that exposed both the flaws in Moynihan's liberal reasoning and the limits of his critics' arguments. In 1966 the journalist and civil rights activist Frances Beale helped found SNCC's Black Women's Liberation Committee; in an essay first published in 1970, titled "Double Jeopardy: To Be Black and Female," she challenged the "fallacious reasoning" evident in the Moynihan report and elsewhere that "in order for the Black man to be strong, the Black woman has to be weak." Beale agreed that black men had historically been "emasculated, lynched, and brutalized" but qualified her agreement by adding that "it is a gross distortion of fact to state that Black women have oppressed black men." Jean Carey Bond and Pat Peery, authors of an essay titled "Is the Black Male Castrated?," argued that "Black women, domineering or not, have not had the power in this male-dominated culture to effect a coup against anyone's manhood."[46]

In challenging liberal ideas about race relations that required certain standards of masculinity and femininity, black women also revised ideas about motherhood and race. Many unequivocally rejected the assumption that an alleged "matriarchy" had damaged men and the race as a whole. As a result of the "belief in the myth of matriarchy," wrote Linda La Rue, the "black woman has been made to feel ashamed of her strength, and so to redeem herself she has adopted from whites the belief that superiority and dominance of the male is the most 'natural' and 'normal' relationship." Mary Ann Weathers was even more direct. "Don't allow yourselves to be intimidated any longer with this nonsense about the 'Matriarchy' of black women," she declared in 1969. "Black women are not matriarchs, but we have been forced to live in abandonment and been used and abused. The myth of the matriarchy must stop, and we must not allow ourselves to be sledgehammered by it any longer."[47]

Black women did not only reject the denigration of motherhood evident in the liberal Moynihan report. They also grew increasingly critical of the pronatalism and the (apparent) celebration of motherhood among black nationalists in the late 1960s and 1970s—who were themselves were critical of Moynihan. As Beale put it, "those who are exerting their 'manhood' by telling Black women to step back into a domestic, submissive role are assuming a counter-revolutionary position. . . . Black women sitting at home reading bedtime stories to their children are just not going to make it." Toni Cade, an activist and writer, was among those who emphasized birth control as an important resource, not just for black women, but for all blacks seeking to improve their lives.[48] As black feminists attacked the liberal logic that Moynihan had employed, they also attacked the ways that critics of Moynihan had appropriated his gendered analysis of race relations. Cade's *The Black Woman*, published in 1970, was one of the first anthologies of essays and fiction by and about black women; one scholar has written that it "reflected the consciousness-raising effect of the Moynihan report."[49]

Critiques of Moynihan that attended to the gendered dimensions of his argument were not restricted to black feminists. Stokely Carmichael, a leader of SNCC and advocate of black power refuted the report: "the reason we are in the bag we are in isn't because of my mama, it's because of what they did to my mama." A "controversial" critique of Moynihan in *Dissent* noted that "pathology is in the eye of the beholder" and argued that " 'Matriarchy' is a cultural formation common to many oppressed people"—and neither cause nor symptom of pathology. Other Moynihan opponents wrote that matriarchal families reflected "powerful coping endeavors" that provided "self-help and even joy."[50]

Thus, while mother-blaming did persist in *The Negro Family* and in reactions to it, it was not as uncontested a component of liberal antiracism as it had been. Quite simply, there was no longer the same kind of liberal consensus that the healthy citizen was one who had the right kind of family and upbringing. Consequently, while images of black women as matriarchs did persist, they did not advance critiques of race relations within liberalism to the same degree. Moreover, although *Newsweek* declared that Moynihan had discovered a "New Crisis" in his discussion of black families, and others agreed, the ideas in the report were not unusual.[51] *The Negro Family* followed in a tradition of progressive psychosocial scholarship that had assumed mothers shaped their children's potential as future citizens. It consolidated a (related) tradition of progressive race relations scholarship in which black mothers caused family "disorganization" and undermined blacks' capacities as future citizens. As Rainwater and Yancey noted, Moynihan's report "seemed very much in line" with scholarship "initiated in the 1930's by such scholars as . . . John Dollard, Horace Cayton, St. Clair Drake, and others."[52]

If the ideas were old, the context in which the controversy flared was new. In 1965, when *The Negro Family* appeared, the sets of associations between families and citizenship, and between racial harmony and gender-role differentiation did not have the same power they had in earlier decades. Dollard's *Frustration and Aggression*, Adorno's *The Authoritarian Personality*, and other studies of race and prejudice embraced an assumption that circulated widely among intellectuals. They argued that the healthy citizen was psychologically fit—appropriately productive and independent yet appropriately restrained—because he came from the right kind of family and had the right kind of mother. For them as for Philip Wylie in *Generation of Vipers*, the family was the civilizing force that mediated between self and society, and the mother was the emotional force that mediated between child and future citizen. By the mid 1960s, Freudian theories that emphasized the mother-child dynamic were less dominant than they had been. Some progressive intellectuals and activists were more influenced by humanistic psychology's emphasis on the healthy self who existed separate from families, and others were increasingly interested in larger-scale social programs that accounted for class and race together.

There were only hints at this paradigm shift in *The Negro Family*. But the changing role that psychosocial theories played in liberal discourse proved to be an important resource for women who made new demands within the terms of liberalism. Liberal feminism as it developed in the early 1960s destabilized the equation between women and mothers that had characterized a psychologically oriented liberal discourse since the 1930s. Ironically, as liberal feminism reconfigured conceptions of citizenship, it used images of women as potentially bad mothers to do so.

The Feminine Mystique and Momism

Calls for women's liberation intersected with mother-blaming most apparently in *The Feminine Mystique*. Betty Friedan offered a scathing critique of Freudian theories in which images of momism had flourished. She sought to expand citizenship by freeing women from psychological definitions of femininity that were oppressive. But she depended on racially specific ideas about white women as mothers to do so. Friedan, among others who opposed the logic of momism and psychosocial theories of femininity, could not wholly extricate herself from a discourse of maternal failure.

"Women are human beings" who deserve "a share in the whole of human destiny" declared Friedan. *The Feminine Mystique* argued that the world should view women in terms of their "humanity" as opposed to their femininity and sexuality. Women afflicted with the "feminine mystique" did not meet this standard of humanity; they were trapped in the private sphere of home, domesticity, and family, and this entrapment eroded their capacities for political self-definition and citizenship. That was why the feminine mystique was such a problem. By contrast, women free of the "feminine mystique" had "fulfilled their human potential." To substantiate her claims of women's humanity, Friedan positioned women in the public sphere as independent and professional, and therefore as equal citizens. With this framework, the value of distinct gender roles that evolved out of traditional family arrangements "went out the window."[53]

Friedan both described the feminine mystique and analyzed its origins. As she did so, she honed in on the contradictions that characterized psychological theories of femininity and sexuality, of family and motherhood. Popular Freudian theories that defined women solely in terms of their femininity and in relation to their families, she argued, had created the situation in which "the mother could be blamed for almost everything." She reasoned that it made no sense to label independent or professional women frustrated, frigid, and failing to achieve a "mature" femininity, while also blaming stay-at-home mothers "for almost everything" based on their failed femininity.[54] "By some fascinating paradox," she asserted, "the massive evidence of psychological damage done to boys and girls by frustrated mothers who devoted all their days to filling children's needs was twisted by the feminine mystique to a summons to the new generation of girls to go back home and devote *their* days to filling children's needs."[55] In passages like this, *The Feminine Mystique* rejected a glorification of motherhood as the quintessential expression of femininity. Friedan derided theories of femininity that blamed " 'masculinized' " and frigid white women for men's problems.

As scholars have noted, in rejecting Freudian theories of femininity and motherhood, Friedan drew on ideas associated with humanistic psychology that gained support and credibility in the late 1950s and early 1960s.[56] Humanists like Abraham Maslow argued that psychologically healthy individuals were those who developed their own individual human potential. The "self" was their subject; liberating this individualistic self from sources of oppression—be they irrational fears and emotions like frustration and aggression, or irrational social systems and family relationships—was their goal.[57] An earlier generation of progressive thinkers who employed Freudian theories in their psychosocial analyses, like Lillian Smith or Marynia Farnham and Ferdinand Lundberg, had assumed that the right kind of family was a precondition to a healthy citizen, a strong democracy, and harmonious race relations. By contrast, Friedan adapted humanistic theories to expose the ways that the family was a source of oppression, especially for women seeking to find their true and equal selves.

And yet, even as she staked out these positions on women's humanity, individuality, and equality, Friedan relied on both the logic and imagery of momism. Fears of overbearing mothers with little to occupy their time reinforced her arguments that wage work would help women achieve their selfhood. Further, *The Feminine Mystique* claimed for women the right to be human but set this quality in direct opposition to femininity. As such, "human" was not as gender neutral a concept as it appeared. According to *The Feminine Mystique*, by failing to meet standards of humanity, women failed as women *and* as mothers. If they could not be "fully human" and fully actualized, they were bound to be bad mothers. Their maternal failure stemmed not from a failed femininity, as Freudians had argued, but from this failed humanness.

Friedan had nothing but scorn for Wylie, Farnham, Lundberg, and others whose use of Freudian theory "sounded a single, overprotective, life-restricting, future-denying note for women." She was far more critical of her predecessors than was Moynihan. Even so, the mothers in her work had much in common with mothers guilty of momism. In both instances, maternal deficiencies were responsible for men's weakness and neediness: "Is it so strange that boys who grow up with too much mother love become men who can never get enough?"[58] Another component of *The Feminine Mystique* placed Friedan in an oddly and counterintuitive alliance with Wylie and more moderate proponents of momism. She repeatedly asserted that women's frustrations and maternal failure were problems with implications for the nation's well-being. The woman who freed herself from the feminine mystique was a far better mother *and* a better citizen; indeed, as Friedan wrote in the final pages of the book, the feminine mystique took "a far greater toll on the physical and mental health of our country than any known disease." She elaborated: "If we continue to produce millions of young mothers who stop their growth and education short of identity, without a strong core of human values to pass on to their children, we are committing, quite simply, genocide, starting with the mass burial of American women and ending with the progressive dehumanization of their sons and daughters."[59]

Friedan inverted earlier models of "good" and "bad" mothers: successful mothers were those who were fully human rather than fully feminine, whereas the many who failed were insufficiently human and could not answer the question " 'who am I?' "[60] But in revising maternal success to refer to those women who were "complete and fully a part of the world," and by counterposing motherhood to citizenship, *The Feminine Mystique* retained a fear of bad mothers. In important ways, this ur-text of the women's liberation movement launched its challenge to domestic wifehood and femininity and endorsed female selfhood on the grounds of a revised and revitalized notion of women as mothers.

Friedan may well have helped launch women's liberation with her analysis of the "problem with no name," but hers was a strand of liberal feminism that was profoundly race and class specific. *The Feminine Mystique*'s crucial distinction—between the human self who could realize her potential as a citizen through meaningful work and the mother in the domestic sphere—was in fact a racial argument. The dichotomy between the home as an arena of femininity and motherhood and work as an arena of individuality and fulfillment was antithetical to many black women's experiences. Like Moynihan, Friedan did not see, in her book, how working outside the home was one way that black women, among others, offered maternal support. Like Moynihan, she maintained a focus on the need for each individual to change in ways that minimized socioeconmic issues.[61]

As feminists would repeatedly point out in the coming years, by placing so much value on women's work outside the home, *The Feminine Mystique* ignored the realities of working women's lives; it dismissed, for example, the "extreme economic exploitation that most Black women are subjected to day by day," as Frances Beale wrote.[62] Another activist, concerned with "the depth, the extent, the intensity, the importance—indeed, the suffering and depravity of the *real* oppression blacks have experienced" had little patience with "women who heretofore have suffered little more than boredom, genteel repression, and dishpan hands."[63] The cultural critic and feminist bell hooks would consolidate twenty years of criticism when she wrote in 1984 that "Friedan's famous phrase, 'the problem with no name,' often quoted to describe the condition of women in this society, actually referred to the plight of a select group of college-educated, middle- and upper-class, married white women—housewives bored with leisure, with the home, with children, with buying products, who wanted more out of life."[64] As was the case with the liberal Moynihan report, black feminists and others made clear that Friedan's call for liberal reform had a foundation that did not accommodate black women.

But liberal feminism was neither monolithic nor synonymous with Friedan and *The Feminine Mystique*. Not all liberal feminists were white, even if many white feminists like Friedan did not realize how much race defined their feminism.[65] An expression of liberal feminism nearly contemporaneous with Friedan's, the President's Commission on the Status of Women, demonstrates that the relationship between race and gender was contested from the moment that liberal feminism was taking shape and was in turn related to ideas about women and motherhood. The PCSW offers a glimpse into this productive moment and makes clear how and why ideas about race and gender, motherhood, and citizenship all intersected in liberal feminism.

"Their Full Contribution as Citizens": The President's Commission on the Status of Women

When John F. Kennedy created the PCSW in 1961, he declared that "we have by no means done enough to strengthen family life and at the same time encourage women to make their full contribution as citizens."[66] To determine how the country could use women's talents fully, members of the PCSW's seven subcommittees studied distinct aspects of women's lives. (These subcommittees were in education, civil and political rights, home and community, federal employment, private employment, protective labor legislation, social security and taxes.) Each subcommittee issued a separate report with recommendations, and four informal "consultations" met to discuss relevant topics that committees had not addressed in detail. Reports from these committees and consultations were the basis for the final PCSW report, which Kennedy received on October 11, 1963.[67]

Less than a year after the Commission delivered the report, the government had distributed eighty-three thousand copies nationally and internationally. In 1965 the report was published commercially by Charles Scribners' Sons, under the title *American Women: The Report of the President's Commission on the Status of Women and Other Publications of the Commission.* The introduction was written by the noted anthropologist Margaret Mead.[68] *American Women*'s appeal stemmed from the fact that the PCSW was emphatically not revolutionary, but did reject (certain) anachronistic assumptions, challenged (certain) gender and racial stereotypes, and recommended measures that would help women economically, socially, legally, and politically. Its recommendations ranged from revising tax codes and increasing maternity leave to offering volunteer training and home economics courses.

The PCSW adapted liberal ideologies as it made claims for women in two ways: by addressing issues of women's wage work and by demonstrating that race relations were central to liberalism and questions of women's equality. The PCSW focused on removing impediments that the twenty-four million women wage workers faced and making it easier for still more women to enter the workforce. The report countered myths about women's higher rates of absenteeism to dispel stereotypes about women's unreliability, just as race relations scholars had worked to dispel stereotypes about black men's laziness. It supported middle-class women who chose to work outside the home for "self-fulfillment" but also assumed that plenty of women, white and black, worked out of economic necessity.[69] The PCSW endorsed the Equal Pay Act in 1963; recommended equal employment opportunity for women as "the governing principle" in private employment; and called on Kennedy to issue an executive order that would make the federal government a "showcase" for equal opportunity. In all these ways the PCSW members legitimated women's rights and capacities as citizens more generally by emphasizing wage work in the public sphere. By the terms the report established, neither Mamie Bradley nor Lana Turner would have been derided as mothers based on their status as working women.[70]

Civil rights battles had both a direct and indirect impact on claims that liberals were making. From the opening lines in the "Invitation to Action" onward, the PCSW's report positioned itself as antiracist: "discrimination based on color is morally wrong and a source of national weakness. Such discrimination currently places an oppressive dual burden on millions of Negro women."[71] The Commission's recommendations for executive orders, Supreme Court rulings, and congressional action as vehicles to correct gender inequities were modeled after liberal civil rights activism, with its emphasis on government intervention. Reflecting a growing emphasis on integration, several black women and men worked on various committees.[72] As was the case in battles for civil rights, the PCSW argued that alleviating discrimination against women strengthened the country as a whole. More was at stake than "simply" the fate of those who were discriminated against.[73]

These intersections of race and gender did not necessarily strengthen the PCSW's arguments against gender or racial discrimination. Through an inconsistent blend of racial inclusion on the one hand and racial exclusion on the other, the PCSW appeared to address questions of racial inequalities while eliding these questions at precisely the points when they placed women in racial conflict with each other. The mostly white women who worked on the PCSW may well have assumed that advocacy for "women" was advocacy for all women across lines of race; this inclusive perspective marked a step forward in discussions of American women. At the same time, this assumption obscured the racial and class dimensions of liberal feminism as it developed in the PCSW. The Equal Pay Act that members supported, for example, held that wage discrimination for "equal" work was illegal but excluded workers in agriculture, households, hotels, restaurants, and laundries: the very areas where nearly three-quarters of all black women workers remained concentrated. Even when the PCSW recommended that the provisions in the Equal Pay Act be expanded, household workers still did not make it onto the list of occupations that should be included.[74] And despite occasional efforts to analyze black women's "dual burden," the PCSW largely segregated analyses of race and gender. The eight-page consultation on "problems of Negro women" was the only extended discussion of black women.[75]

This pattern of inclusion and exclusion echoed the parallel yet bifurcated treatment the white Lora and the black Annie received in Sirk's antiracist *Imitation of Life*. It was a liberal pluralism similar to that in Schlesinger's *The Vital Center*—one which seemed to accept, even celebrate, difference but still could not attend to the power dynamics between groups of people. By the mid-1960s white women were using this liberal logic which both incorporated and contained race to define their own rights as women and citizens.[76] As Friedan discussed in *The Feminine Mystique*, liberal feminists could not define these rights without also considering motherhood.

Motherhood, Race, and the "Murray Compromise"

Pauli Murray, a black lawyer and member of the PCSW committee on civil and political rights, elaborated the relationships between race, gender, and constructions
of motherhood in an analysis that shaped the Commission's stand on the Equal
Rights Amendment. Murray had been active in labor activism and the civil rights
movement for years before serving on the PCSW committee. She perceived her experience on the Commission as an "intensive consciousness-raising process leading
directly to my involvement in the new women's movement" (Murray later helped
to found NOW). Her work on the PCSW also heightened her awareness of black
"male aggressiveness against Negro women" within the civil rights movement, as
she pondered parallels between what she called "Jane Crow" and Jim Crow.[77] Murray's importance to the PCSW points to often-neglected links between the histories
of civil rights and of liberal feminism and to links between the histories of black and
white women and feminism.[78]

Disagreements over the Equal Rights Amendment had polarized women's rights
supporters since early in the century. As a result, there was a concerted effort
within the PCSW to avoid contentious debates over the amendment. With this in
mind, PCSW chair Esther Peterson delegated the question of the ERA to a single
subcommittee: the thirteen members who sat on the committee on civil and political rights had the task of devising a position that the entire Commission could accept.[79] The goal was to skirt rancorous debates between advocates of protective legislation and the ERA by accommodating tenets of both positions.

In an extensive report, Murray argued that litigation and the right test cases afforded alternatives to an equal rights amendment. Under the right circumstances,
she wrote, the Supreme Court would rule that sex discrimination violated the
"equal protection" clause of the fourteenth amendment just as racial bias did.
Women could invoke the fourteenth amendment even though it had not been designed with gender in mind because women occupied a "position comparable to
that of a racial minority."[80] An equal rights amendment was not the only way for
women to get constitutional equality, Murray explained. Legal rulings based on the
fourteenth amendment could render laws that unjustly discriminated against
women unconstitutional, thereby meeting a major premise of ERA advocates—
"equality of rights under the law for all persons." Fourteenth amendment rulings
could also preserve certain "genuinely protective" legislation that classified citizens
by sex. Under these anticipated rulings, it was not necessary to choose between
"equality" *or* "difference" because in applying the principle of "equal protection"
on a flexible case by case basis, justices could distinguish between just and unjust
difference and, when necessary, enhance equality through difference.[81]

In order to explain what constituted "just" and "unjust" difference, Murray
drew on images of motherhood *and* on the relationship between race and sex.
Motherhood, she argued, was one distinguishing factor. Statutes that protected
women workers of child-bearing age from heavy manual labor were "just" because

they protected (through "functional attributes") women who were or would be mothers, thereby freeing other women from arbitrary classifications based solely on sexual difference. By contrast, "unjust" rulings denied women "freedom of choice." The Supreme Court's 1908 ruling in *Muller v. Oregon* allowing states to pass protective legislation for women was "too sweeping," according to Murray; it had been distorted into a "separate but equal" policy toward the country's women. This was as unconstitutional, she explained, as the "separate but equal" doctrine the Court had legalized in the *Plessy v. Ferguson* case in 1896.[82]

Ultimately, the PCSW accepted Murray's proposal and her ERA compromise. ("I kept trying to put myself in the shoes of Mr. Chief Justice Warren and I could hear him agreeing with every point," wrote one enthusiastic colleague.) The final report encouraged litigation to resist discrimination against women, stating that Supreme Court rulings were "urgently needed" and that rulings under the fourteenth amendment could make "the principle of equality become firmly established in constitutional doctrine." With this, the Commission also concluded that an "amendment need not now be sought in order to establish this principle."[83]

As one scholar has observed, the "Murray compromise" over ERA was "one of the few explicit connections between the civil rights movement and the federal quest" for gender equity in the early 1960s.[84] By arguing that the fourteenth amendment could be used to curtail sex discrimination as well as the racial discrimination it was originally designed to redress in the aftermath of the Civil War, Murray harnessed civil rights activism to liberal feminism, linking racial and sexual discrimination analytically, strategically, and legally. Making race and sex discrimination legally analogous was Murray's way out of the long impasse over the ERA. But this linkage between gender and race required—and in fact, could not have been realized without—Murray's constructions of motherhood. Murray's ideas about motherhood allowed her to separate gender from motherhood *and* to integrate race and sex. For her as for others who worked on the PCSW, "women" as a category crossed lines of race. Like Friedan, Murray conceived of "woman" as a category that conferred the rights of citizenship and was not synonymous with "mother." Womanhood existed for her as distinct from those particular times when women themselves exercised their "freedom of choice" and chose to "develop their maternal and family functions primarily." She thus bracketed motherhood from citizenship and offered women (and the law) a way, ostensibly, to transcend gender. A central point of Murray's argument was that laws protecting "maternal functions" did not violate the fourteenth amendment if they were "limited in operation to that class of women who perform these functions"; citizens could be legally defined in terms of their sex if motherhood was at stake. "Few will deny that society has a legitimate interest in the effective performance of women's maternal functions . . . and that these funtions be protected and supported by enlightened governmental policies." It was based on this conception of motherhood—on the belief that society needed to protect good mothers and their offspring but that not all women would be mothers—that Murray applied "equal protection" to sex and to race. And it was on this foundation that she argued that one kind of discrimination was analogous to the other.[85]

In separating "women" from "mothers," Murray countered long-standing assumptions within liberal discourse. "Maternity legislation" she wrote, "is not sex legislation." Both she and Friedan established female selfhood as distinct from voluntary motherhood. But with this perspective Murray reshaped the racially specific model of selfhood that Friedan had formulated. The separation between womanhood and motherhood allowed Murray to analyze sex and race discrimination in relation to each other. She called for legal challenges to sex discrimination that, like *Brown*, would address the "psychological aspects of discrimination against women," and she was optimistic that the courts would dismantle sex discrimination, just as they were dismantling racial discrimination.[86]

Murray's analysis illuminated commonalities among women across lines of race and class and dispelled stereotypes of all women as always and only mothers or future mothers. As was the case for Mamie Till Bradley, in this instance constructions of motherhood had productive implications. Even so, Murray's proposal was not without its problems. Protective legislation for women continued (and continues) to divide feminists. Further, and perhaps more importantly, ideas about motherhood in the Murray compromise legitimated state regulation of women (and especially pregnant women) as a way to ensure that good mothers were those who had healthy children. Preserving the maternal functions of women who were "good" mothers and protecting against those women who were "bad" mothers remained the responsibility of the liberal state.[87] The Murray compromise implied that to resist sex discrimination, the state had to protect "maternal functions"; in other words, claims for women's equality required the state to prop up a certain type of motherhood.

Murray's analysis of the relations of race, gender, and motherhood was nuanced. Elsewhere, the PCSW was less nuanced. The final report consistently made clear that even when it made demands on behalf of women, it was not displacing their roles as wives and mothers. As the *Report of the Committee on Home and Community* reiterated, "over and above whatever role modern women play in the community . . . the care of the home and the children remains their unique responsibility . . . the care of the children is primarily the province of the mother. This is not debatable as a philosophy. It is and will remain a fact of life."[88] Even though the report encouraged women to fulfill themselves, the PCSW was even more likely than *The Feminine Mystique* to argue that doing so was important because it made women better mothers. Mothers needed the programs that the PCSW supported—from home economics courses to job training and cross-class day care facilities—precisely so that they could encourage their children to "understand their world and develop their potentialities in relation to it."[89]

Further, to the extent that black women were visible in the reports the PCSW wrote, it was often in the familiar model of matriarchy. The women in the report who needed job training programs and psychological fulfillment were largely, implicitly and explicitly, white. By contrast, in advocating more child-care facilities, the "Consultation on Problems of Negro Women" argued that when black mothers worked, their children were "not cared for properly." Another committee's report began by asserting that "traditionally, Negro families have been more matriarchal than white families" and added that this structure caused "problems to Negro children, both boys and girls, in developing their masculine and feminine roles."[90] All women, the PSCW suggested, needed to avoid the kind of behavior most evident in black women if they were to be good citizens.

In the fundamental premises of liberal feminism that *The Feminine Mystique* and the PCSW helped to formulate, situating women within the realm of motherhood was one way to make demands for women beyond the realm of motherhood. This pattern, we have seen, had more potential to help white than nonwhite women.[91] Within these foundational texts of liberal feminism, it remained difficult to see black women as citizens or as beyond motherhood. This was a point that black women would argue in the late 1960s and 1970s. As they critiqued the terms of liberal feminism, they highlighted the degree to which it privileged gender at the expense of race, and they exposed its inability to see the "double jeopardy" that Frances Beale named in 1970. In the early 1970s, the National Black Feminist Organization (NBFO), the Combahee River Collective, and individual women writers and activists addressed overt and covert racism in liberal feminism as they analyzed the interlocking systems of oppression that defined so many women's lives.

If conflating "women" with all women had political and ideological value—anticipating the "sisterhood is powerful" slogan of women's liberation, for example—it often required the PCSW to untangle racial and sexual discrimination from each other and subordinate the former to the latter. The PCSW offered the beginnings of what would become more comprehensive feminist critiques of gender and motherhood in the 1970s. But it also prefigured the ongoing limits of liberal feminism's analyses of race.

The tone of liberal feminism diverged from E. Franklin Frazier's diagnosis of "matriarchs," Philip Wylie's scorn for "moms," and popular critiques of Lana Turner and Mamie Till Bradley. Unlike the Moynihan report, liberal feminism infrequently resorted to seething indictments of women as mothers and infrequently deployed damning psychoanalytic language. Nevertheless, the liberal feminism of *The Feminine Mystique* and the PCSW neither escaped from nor wholly rejected the paradigms of momism and matriarchy.

Liberalism and Mother-blaming: The Knot Unravels

With some good reason, many Americans continue to remember the early 1960s as a time of "revolution"—social, sexual, and cultural. In this period, some of those who had been marginalized from liberal conceptions of citizenship had more room and power to assert their rights. Many factors helped to create this sense of possibility. These included the rippling effects of the civil rights movement, as protests against racism in the South developed into widespread challenges of established

authority and the status quo; the politicization of seemingly personal or cultural issues like clothes, music and hairstyles; and passage of legislation in the name of
civil rights and the Great Society.[92]

The declining credibility that psychosocial understandings of citizenship and
family played in liberalism contributed significantly to this eclectic process. Progressive intellectuals no longer assumed that political stability, psychological
health, and stable families in which gender roles were clearly defined were one and
the same; consequently, ideas about who and what constituted healthy citizens also
changed. Liberal discourse reworked relationships between private and public life
in ways that created space for new definitions of self and citizenship, of mental and
political health to develop. As the Freudian construct tying mental health to the
mother-child dyad began to crumble, liberal conceptions of the healthy citizen became less dependent on ideologies of motherhood.

In *The Vital Center* Arthur Schlesinger Jr. had analyzed American political life in
decidedly psychopolitical terms. According to the tenets of Cold War liberalism
that he and other liberal intellectuals developed, American communists were dis-
loyal and unfit citizens because they were anxious and frustrated, and because they
were feminized. By the 1960s, liberals had started to reverse this perspective, declaring that the personal and psychological dimensions of life were in fact social
and political. For Betty Friedan, women with the "feminine mystique" were not
only unhealthy citizens because of what happened in their homes; rather, the psychological oppression they experienced in their homes was itself socially caused,
and therefore political.[93]

Even given these changes, the Moynihan report and early expressions of liberal
feminism indicate that conservative ideas about gender that positioned women in
terms of motherhood and failure continued to influence liberal discourse. As had
been the case since E. Franklin Frazier and Philip Wylie made the terms "matriarchs" and "moms" commonplace, mothers who failed, black and white, still
shared a great deal. The difference was that in the 1960s even more so than in the
New Deal era, ideas about motherhood affected women's relationship to liberalism
in racially specific ways.

The Moynihan report was based on an equation between progress (in this case
racial progress), patriarchal gender arrangements, and citizenship for African
Americans. It made this equation by invoking images of black women as dangerous
mothers—images long a part of liberal discourse. By assuming that virtually all
black women were matriarchal and that they kept men, and the race, down, Moynihan drove a wedge between black men and women and offered an argument that effectively let the liberal state off the hook. *The Negro Family* maintained matriarchy
in ways that affirmed American liberalism without accounting for black women's
needs, abilities, or rights; this liberal deployment of matriarchy had few positive
implications.

With but a few exceptions, *The Negro Family* resisted the very changes in liberal
discourse outlined here, maintaining citizenship as a masculine enclave. But
Moynihan's emphasis on psychological damage, disorganized families, and mater-

nal failure helped to discredit this approach within liberalism. In the controversy the report generated, it was liberals who tended to reject the psychosocial terms of this analysis—the very terms that had helped to propel race onto the national liberal agenda by 1965. The Moynihan report thus marked the beginning of an end to a long-term trend within liberalism.

By contrast, the liberal feminism that developed in the President's Commission on the Status of Women and in *The Feminine Mystique* began to break out of those frameworks which positioned white and black women always and only in terms of motherhood. Changing conceptions of the self allowed Friedan and PCSW members to forge theories of gender equality and loosen the ties between women and mothers as they made claims for women as citizens; Friedan in particular envisioned white women who were free from the oppressiveness of the private sphere. Even when Friedan and PCSW members reasserted that motherhood was women's role, this recontainment afforded the mostly white women with whom liberal feminism was concerned certain potential. In the Commission's "Murray compromise," which used motherhood to connect race and sex discrimination, just as in *The Feminine Mystique*, ideas about motherhood allowed activist women to challenge restrictions that working women faced; to separate the categories of "motherhood" and "womanhood"; and to gesture (if fleetingly) toward cross-class and cross-racial conceptions of womanhood. Motherhood as constructed by the PCSW and *The Feminine Mystique* reveals how by the mid 1960s liberal women renegotiated the logic of "momism" to begin meeting their own needs and to affirm American liberalism.

Friedan and Moynihan both argued that families had failed to produce healthy and equal citizens. But Friedan hoped to liberate white women from dysfunctional, inegalitarian homes and family configurations. Moynihan, on the other hand, sought to restore families—albeit into a nostalgic vision that had always existed as more ideal than reality. Further, *The Negro Family* could make claims only for men who had allegedly been damaged in families and by women. Black women remained excluded from Moynihan's vision of racial liberalism and his conception of citizenship. Ultimately, then, the conservative gender ethos in *The Negro Family* undermined racial liberalism by reinforcing racist ideas about black women.

Black feminist theory as it developed in the late 1960s and 1970s critiqued the limits of these liberal paradigms. Women questioned assessments of African Americans which had effectively divorced black women from evaluations of race. They also challenged analyses like Friedan's which effectively divorced black women from evaluations of gender. They challenged the ways that liberalism had seemed to provide egalitarian language and logic but had in fact offered a vision of equality that largely excluded black women.

The arguments for greater racial and gender equity evident in the Moynihan report and liberal feminism developed in a period when racial liberalism as the consensus ideology of the nation was breaking down. It was no longer clear what roles, if any, the federal government, liberal whites, or African Americans should play in improving the lives of African Americans. By the end of the sixties, as the depth of

American racism and its institutionalized nature became virtually impossible for many Americans to ignore, appeals to liberal whites to solve the "white problem," as Lillian Smith had put it in the 1940s, were declining in frequency and influence. Instead, civil rights activists emphasized the need for black political power and called for strategies to counter racism as it existed beyond legal segregation. Fewer and fewer whites or blacks argued that ongoing discrimination was evidence of a psychological "dilemma" on the part of whites, as Gunnar Myrdal had put it.

By the late 1960s, racial liberalism and assumptions about maternal failure did not intersect in the ways that they had since the 1930s. Consequently, the impact that conservative ideas about gender had on progressive ideas about race also diminished.

Certainly, feminism played a role in the changing place occupied by ideologies of motherhood. In the late 1960s and early 1970s, feminists across lines of race and across liberal/radical divides continued to reformulate motherhood. Some feminists analyzed motherhood as central to women's gender oppression and advocated freeing women from the biological and emotional burden of mothering. Others celebrated motherhood as the symbol of women's unique power. In the aftermath of the Moynihan report, black women continued to reclaim and revalue "matriarchy," rejecting assumptions that black mothers who were either too "strong" or too "weak" were "disorganizing" to the race.[94] When women organized for welfare rights in the late 1960s and 1970s, they too analyzed both the gendered and racial bias of the liberal welfare state and its policies toward mothers. Johnnie Tillmon, the first chairwoman of the National Welfare Rights Organization, declared that Aid to Families with Dependent Children was "like a supersexist marriage. You trade in *a* man for *the* man. But you can't divorce him if he treats you bad. He can divorce you, of course, cut you off anytime he wants." Tillmon and other welfare rights advocates demonstrated how the welfare state controlled female sexuality and reproduction.[95] Regardless of their constructions of motherhood, feminists across the spectrum rejected the mother-blaming that had characterized liberal discussions of motherhood for decades. This destabilized the foundation on which the interdependence between racial liberalism and gender conservatism had rested.

Of equal if not greater significance were erosions of liberalism itself, as it faced other challenges from a diverse left and right in the late 1960s and 1970s. This is not to say that those who forged these challenges were free from gender conservatism. In fact, anti-Vietnam War activists and others on the left, as well as supporters of Barry Goldwater and others on the right, themselves emphasized normative gender roles.[96] The point is that these gender dynamics now operated in an increasingly fractured political and cultural landscape, wrested from a decreasingly dominant liberal political culture oriented around psychology. For instance, with racial liberals moving away from psychosocial analyses of race relations, conservatives made their own use of this approach. As a headline in the *Wall Street Journal* announced after riots in Watts in the summer of 1965, ". . . Husbandless Homes Spawn Young Hoodlums, Impede Reform, Sociologists Say."[97]

Radical challenges from a diverse left, a white backlash against civil rights, white liberals' dissatisfaction with allegedly dangerous militance, and the escalation of the Vietnam War all converged by the late 1960s; this convergence helped bring Richard Nixon into the White House in 1968. It may well be true that ever since that time, "American liberalism has never been the same."[98] But, sources for this fracturing were internal as well as external, embedded within the logic of liberal discourse as it had developed since the 1930s. American liberalism had repeatedly been reconfigured since the New Deal—stretched almost to the breaking point as it gradually, by the early 1960s, had become (somewhat) more racially inclusive and attentive to women's needs. But these reconfigurations did not address the contradictory configurations of race and gender out of which conceptions of liberal citizenship had developed since the 1930s. Activists on the left and the right in the late 1960s and 1970s emerged, in part, out of the limits and contradictions in liberalism itself.

Conclusion

Motherhood, Citizenship, and Political Culture

A Depression-era movie and its remake twenty-five years later, a grieving and previously unknown black mother and a glamorous actress, and scholars and intellectuals like T. W. Adorno and Daniel Patrick Moynihan may appear to have little in common. However, a preoccupation with motherhood linked these and other diverse figures and texts. *Motherhood in Black and White* has argued that ideas about motherhood helped to reconfigure liberalism from the 1930s into the 1960s. The relationship between motherhood and liberalism was based upon a widespread assumption within a psychologically oriented liberal discourse that mothers could help to shape or deform masculinity—a, if not the, crucial attribute of citizenship. As a result of this emphasis within liberalism on psychologically fit and unfit citizens, a conservative gender ethos that emphasized the potential for maternal failure played an important part in how and why race relations came to dominate the liberal agenda in the mid-twentieth century.

Liberalism—and the ideal citizen and family it envisioned—was never a fixed entity. Psychosocial political and cultural narratives about families from the 1930s first gave modern images of "bad" white and black mothers political meaning in liberal discourse. In the midst of an unprecedented economic crisis that threatened faith in capitalism and liberal democracy, affirming the viability of private life—the sphere to which the ideal family had been assigned since industrialization—became a necessary precondition to affirming the viability of public, political life. As such, normative gender relations and families with "good" mothers were intrinsic to a liberal vision of citizenship based on a family wage and male breadwinner. New Deal liberalism was a cultural and political ideology that focused on jobs and economic security alongside family stability. The ideal citizen was an independent rugged individual who could participate in collective social security programs by virtue of his position as a family's wage earner and who could benefit from the

165

safety net provided by assistance policies. Women in families helped to determine whether or not a male head of household would be able to meet this ideal—one to which black Americans had limited access.

This gendered ideal of citizenship dominant in the 1930s could not be separated from race. Because, in part, of its "universalism," New Deal liberalism drew support from racial and ethnic minorities—even as certain of its policies masked ongoing racial inequalities and suppressed racial difference per se. The cross-racial appeal of New Deal liberalism required gendered constructions of citizenship and motherhood.

In the 1940s and 1950s, questions of race came to occupy a more overt place in what came to be known as Cold War liberalism. A war against National Socialism followed by a Cold War against communism transformed racism, dangerous hatreds, and irrational aggression into pressing issues within liberal discourse. More and more liberal intellectuals and activists drew on psychological theories to argue that excessive racism not only hurt white and black Americans; it also undermined democracy—within and beyond American borders. Because this reconfigured liberal ethos emphasized the simultaneously psychological and political dimensions of racism, there was a growing sense that the federal government had to take some action to guarantee civil rights to all American citizens. This "shift in liberal sensibilities," according to one historian, had "seismic proportions."[1]

Scholars who have explored this shift and the role that psychological frameworks played in the new "liberal orthodoxy" have not sufficiently considered its gendered underpinnings.[2] Changes in liberalism were dependent on the impact of psychological frameworks, but these frameworks were in turn dependent on assumptions about what constituted "normal" gender roles and family relations. When experts exhorted white women to stop their sons from masturbating (or, alternatively, to allow them to do so), they did not seem to be addressing questions of race. Even so, the psychological perspectives they legitimated assumed that mothers and femininity could have disastrous effects on the formation of masculinity and citizenship. This same assumption—and an ensuing focus on white "moms" and black "matriarchs"—was the crucial component in psychosocial studies condemning prejudice that dominated liberal discourse in the postwar years.

Psychological perspectives inherent to liberalism in this period required a focus on family dynamics. This focus led many liberal social scientists and others to conclude that white and black women who were bad mothers helped to explain racism in whites and its negative effects in blacks. Postwar racial liberalism implicitly and explicitly employed a gendered logic that scholars associate with a celebration of white nuclear families and an eclipse in organized feminism. It was within this gendered logic that race became a more legitimate concern for mainstream postwar liberalism. And it was when this psychological narrative of family and citizenship weakened within liberalism that maternal failure no longer intersected as powerfully with progressive views of race.

Like liberalism itself, representations of motherhood within liberal discourse were not frozen in time. The specific emotional and behavioral profile of the "bad" mother underwent change. Class played a complicated and contradictory role in racialized representations of motherhood. Many liberal narratives in the 1930s defined "bad" mothers, white and black, as those whose husbands were unemployed or who had no husbands; their potential maternal failure stemmed from the fact that in the midst of an economic crisis they were neglecting their children or husbands by working or were consuming too much in light of the economic realities in their lives. This perspective on class and motherhood was consistent with New Deal liberalism's focus on economic issues and with social security legislation that bolstered the "family wage"—or benefits to working men.

By the late 1940s and 1950s, liberals viewed excessive affluence rather than poverty as a potential problem for democracy. As prosperity increased, class-based liberalism oriented around questions of economic reform had declined. Escalating attacks on white women as "moms" anticipated this shift in liberal sensibilities. It was middle-class white women who were "moms" and the "lost sex." Because their lives had changed "materially for the better but psychologically for the worse," they raised sons "unable to carry on as stalwart men" in the view of the authors of *Generation of Vipers* (1942) and *Modern Woman: The Lost Sex* (1947).[3]

Gradually if intermittently, indictments of black women as "matriarchs" also crossed lines of class. Abram Kardiner and Lionel Ovesey in *The Mark of Oppression* (1951) and E. Franklin Frazier in *Black Bourgeoisie* (1957) were among those who charged middle-class black women with "matriarchy" and who cast middle-class and poorer black women as dangerous hyperconsumers who dominated black men and weakened black families.[4] Mamie Till Bradley's status as a relatively financially secure working black woman may have afforded her access to symbols of respectability, but these same qualities made her vulnerable to criticism.

Nevertheless, the meanings of black matriarchy were never identical to those of white momism. Liberal experts linked black women's maternal pathology to feelings of racial self-hatred and thus interpreted ostensible gender disorders in black mothers as racial problems—for black men. In other words, black women's maternal failure across lines of class always stood in for racial inferiority more generally. At the same time, black women came to constitute the bounds of appropriate womanhood across lines of race. Because ideas about matriarchs encompassed gender and racial deviance, they regulated white and black women.

Crucial lines of continuity existed alongside changes in what constituted maternal failure. First and foremost, regardless of who or what bad mothers were, the effects of maternal failure remained remarkably consistent: bad mothers raised citizens unfit for democracy and undermined the liberal state. Second, as bad white moms became more associated with middle-class Americans, the already established links between black women, matriarchy, and poverty were reinforced. In the same years that Wylie's "moms" became ubiquitous and solidly (if symbolically) entrenched in the ever-expanding postwar middle class, a liberal discourse tightly spun together the web of female promiscuity, illegitimacy, and racialized welfare dependency. In this tangled knot, it seemed that any of these terms or categories went along with, or inevitably produced, the others, despite the fact that the majority of welfare recipients remained white.[5]

Paradoxically, images historically associated with black women and matriarchy—economic dependence on the state or too much economic independence, hypersexuality or masculinization, and independence from men—provided a means for demonizing black *and* white women as bad mothers. From debates about who deserved Aid to Dependent Children in the 1930s to the racialization and stigmatization of welfare in the 1940s and 1950s, from the ways that the black mothers in both *Imitation of Life* films hovered around their white counterparts and (nearly) failed their own daughters—the traits historically assigned to black women were precisely those which, to be a "good" woman and mother, one could not have. Consequently, similarities between images of motherhood across lines of race ultimately divided white and black women.

It is worth stressing that the emphasis in liberalism on traditional gender roles, along with the related notion that "good" motherhood was a precondition to healthy citizens, could have positive, and even extraordinary, implications. In the 1940s, images of restrained yet aggressive black men made gave political credibility to calls for integrated defense industries and armed forces. After white racists murdered her son in 1955, Mamie Till Bradley used interrelated ideals of families, motherhood, and citizenship in ways that politicized her position as a black mother and sparked a significant mobilization of Americans against racism. Five years later, male and female black college students who staged sit-ins throughout the South presented themselves as respectable and coming from "good" homes, and as adhering to traditional gender roles in which they preserved differences between manly men and womanly women. In these and other instances, significant, even momentous, bids for civil rights depended upon evidence of certain kinds of families and certain kinds of motherhood.

Further, it is important to respect as well as to analyze the liberal impulses that animated Americans scholars, activists, and politicians from the 1930s to the 1960s. From the male and female architects of the Social Security Act of 1935 to the NAACP leaders who fired Mamie Till Bradley, from Abram Kardiner to activists who sat-in in 1960 or attacked Moynihan in 1965—through very different methods and in very different moments, these were people who believed that American society could be more equitable or less defined by prejudice. They offered intellectual interventions and endorsed practical steps to transform what seemed an idealistic vision into a reality. Lillian Smith's was a voice of eloquence and bravery in the Jim Crow South. The men and women who worked on the President's Commission on the Status of Women in the early 1960s and who first heard Pauli Murray's idea about using the fourteenth amendment to challenge gender discrimination were palpably excited about their task and felt that they could effect positive change.

Yet the interdependence of racial liberalism and gender conservatism imposed limits on social change and activism. When Mamie Bradley ventured beyond definitions of good womanhood and good motherhood in 1955 by asking to be paid, the NAACP rejected her and exiled her from their political battles for civil rights. Douglas Sirk may have ironically affirmed integration in his 1959 remake of *Imitation of Life;* still, he could do so only by containing his white women characters and even more severely limiting the options that his black women characters had. And in 1965 Daniel Patrick Moynihan may have endorsed a stronger role for the federal government to counter the ongoing effects of racism, but that endorsement emerged from assumptions that racial inequities in the United States were largely due to "disorganized" black families in which matriarchal black mothers dominated their sons and perpetuated the "tangle of pathology." Racial health and progress remained tied to normative gender roles and good mothers. Consequently, the absence of patriarchy and bad mothers continued to assume explanatory value for racial pathology. This dynamic in liberal discourse constrained black women most specifically.

By 1965, psychosocial theories of citizenship that stigmatized motherhood were no longer a staple of liberalism. They were, however, up for grabs across the political spectrum. As liberals began to abandon a psychosocial narrative of citizenship that wed political and psychological health to maternal behavior, conservatives increasingly adopted this narrative as their own. Maternal failure, social and emotional pathology, and damaged citizens became the mantra for antiwelfare, anti-civil rights, and antifeminist postures. It was in this context that images of women as damaging mothers continued to operate within American culture into the 1970s and 1980s.[6]

Ironically, over the last twenty years liberalism's ideological cast-offs have become a pillar of the individualism upon which a bipartisan conservative consensus now rests. African American "welfare queens," working white moms, and other icons of mother-blaming certainly persist into the turn of a new century. Today as in 1965 one can find politicians and films, policies and trials that invoke images of dangerous women as bad mothers.[7] Nevertheless, from the late 1960s on, racialized ideologies of motherhood have furthered more conservative social policies and have often accompanied efforts to shrink an activist liberal state. In the 1990s, mother-blaming—whether it came from Clarence Thomas, Dan Quayle, or Bill Clinton—has gone hand in hand with a resurgent conservatism that cuts across party lines. Supporters of the "Republican revolution" of 1994–95 may have worked to dismantle social programs, remove any semblance of a safety net, and relegate liberalism to history, but it was only after 1996, under the leadership of a Democratic president committed to "ending welfare as we know it," that many of these goals were met. Today's efforts to curtail welfare to needy Americans hinge on demonizing mothers who have raised less-than-deserving citizens. Regardless of the realities structuring the lives of poor women—most are white, many live in rural areas and are working rather than consistently unemployed—the "welfare crisis" still assumes meaning through "the specter of the mythical black welfare mother, complete with a prodigious reproductive capacity and a galling laziness."[8]

In the 1980s and 1990s, liberalism became a dirty word from which many people across party lines disassociated themselves. Since 1996, a Democratic president has dismantled the welfare state, and Republicans and Democrats alike have celebrated the final passing of New Deal liberalism and a bipartisan liberal consensus. In this atmosphere, it is especially important to historicize liberalism—to explore the historical constraints affecting those who produced it, and to analyze its limits, particularly with regard to gender and race.

As scholars continue to analyze twentieth-century American cultural politics and political culture in ways that account for intersections of race and gender, attending to the related intersections of liberalism, conservatism, and radicalism is also essential. Typically useful divides—between left and right, between the years before and after World War II, between culture and politics—can obscure more than they clarify. Taking motherhood as its focus, this study displaces many commonplace divisions, analyzing how and why new visions of racial equality developed on the terrain of gender conservatism. Exploring ideologies of motherhood illuminates the paradoxical features of mid-twentieth century liberalism. And perhaps—by situating motherhood as a gendered and racial ideology that assumed varied political and cultural meanings in different hands—it does more. The liberalism that from the 1930s into the 1960s tethered mother-blaming to progressive views of race and an expansive welfare state has virtually disappeared. While a liberal consensus on race has evaporated, racialized ideologies of motherhood remain powerful. Liberalism may have abandoned a psychological view of citizenship that stigmatized motherhood as the locus of pathology, but conservatism has not. Thus ideologies of motherhood as related to conceptions of citizenship remain forceful. And the intersections of gender and race that are inherent to ideologies of motherhood continue to affect—and divide—women along lines of race. Perhaps *Motherhood in Black and White* can speak to these ongoing divisions.

NOTES

Introduction

1. See, for example, Alan Brinkley, *The End of Reform: New Deal Liberalism in Recession and War* (New York: Knopf, 1995); Lizabeth Cohen, *Making a New Deal: Industrial Workers in Chicago, 1919–1939* (New York: Cambridge University Press, 1990).

2. E. Franklin Frazier, *The Negro Family in the United States* (Chicago: University of Chicago Press, 1939); Philip Wylie, *Generation of Vipers* (New York: Holt, Rinehart and Winston, 1955 [1942]).

3. According to one SNCC worker in 1962, in every town "there is always a 'mama.' " Charles Sherrod quoted in Clayborne Carson, *In Struggle: SNCC and the Black Awakening of the 1960s* (Cambridge: Harvard University Press, 1981), p. 75; Jacqueline Jones, *Labor of Love, Labor of Sorrow: Black Women, Work and the Family from Slavery to the Present* (New York: Basic Books, 1985), p. 280.

4. See Jennifer Terry, " 'Momism' and the Making of Treasonous Homosexuals," in Molly Ladd-Taylor and Lauri Umansky, eds., *"Bad" Mothers: The Politics of Blame in Twentieth-Century America* (New York: New York University Press, 1998), pp. 169–90.

5. Important exceptions include Linda Gordon, *Pitied But Not Entitled: Single Mothers and the History of Welfare, 1890–1935* (New York: The Free Press, 1994); Regina G. Kunzel, *Fallen Women, Problem Girls: Unmarried Mothers and the Professionalization of Social Work, 1890–1945* (New Haven: Yale University Press, 1993); Ladd-Taylor and Umansky, eds., *"Bad" Mothers;* Rickie Solinger, *Wake Up Little Susie: Single Pregnancy and Race before Roe v. Wade* (New York: Routledge, 1992). For discussions of the effacement of race in feminist scholarship, see, for example, Elsa Barkley Brown, " 'What Has Happened Here': The Politics of Difference in Women's History and Feminist Politics," *Feminist Studies* 18 (summer 1992): 295–312; Evelyn Brooks Higginbotham, "African-American Women's History and the Metalanguage of Race,"*Signs* 17 (winter 1992): 251–74.

6. Scholarship on liberalism abounds—from the perspectives of political history, intellectual and cultural history, and feminist and political theory. Useful studies include Gisela Bock and Susan James, eds., *Beyond Equality and Difference: Citizenship, Feminist Politics and Female Subjectivity* (New York: Routledge, 1992); Brinkley, *End of Reform;* James Kloppenberg, *The Virtues of Liberalism* (New York: Oxford University Press, 1998); Richard Pells,

The Liberal Mind in a Conservative Age: American Intellectuals in the 1940s and 1950s (New York: Harper and Row, 1985).

7. For competing interpretations of the postwar period, see William O'Neill, *American High: The Years of Confidence, 1945–1960* (New York: The Free Press, 1986); Marty Jezer, *The Dark Ages: Life in the United States, 1945–1960* (Boston: South End Press, 1982). In *Intimate Matters: A History of Sexuality in America* (New York: Harper and Row, 1988), John D'Emilio and Estelle B. Freedman view this period as one of "sexual liberalism" because issues related to sexuality were increasingly acceptable within public discourse. They explain that this liberalism redrew and contained sexual boundaries and "raised new issues for the maintenance of sexual order" (pp. 239–300, 298). I agree, but suggest that this redrawing of sexual boundaries often itself required an emphasis on traditional gender roles; thus my terminology differs.

8. For the construction of these gender mores, see, for example, Barbara Ehrenreich, *The Hearts of Men: American Dreams and the Flight From Commitment* (New York: Anchor Books, 1983); Lynn Spigel, *Make Room for TV: Television and the Family Ideal in Postwar America* (Chicago: University of Chicago Press, 1992).

9. See, for example, Wini Breines, *Young, White and Miserable: Growing Up Female in the Fifties* (Boston: Beacon Press, 1992); Joanne Meyerowitz, ed., *Not June Cleaver: Women and Gender in Postwar America, 1945–1960* (Philadelphia: Temple University Press, 1994).

10. See, for example, John Egerton, *Speak Now against the Day: The Generation before the Civil Rights Movement in the South* (New York: Knopf, 1994); Robin D. G. Kelley, *Hammer and Hoe: Alabama Communists during the Great Depression* (Chapel Hill: University of North Carolina Press, 1990); Harvard Sitkoff, *A New Deal for Blacks: The Emergence of Civil Rights as a National Issue,* vol. 1, *The Depression Decade* (New York: Oxford University Press, 1978); Patricia Sullivan, *Days of Hope: Race and Democracy in the New Deal Era* (Chapel Hill: University of North Carolina Press, 1996).

11. Gunnar Myrdal, *An American Dilemma: The Negro Problem and Modern Democracy* (New York: Harper and Brothers, 1944).

12. See also Edward A. Strecker and Vincent T. Lathbury, *Their Mothers' Daughters* (Philadelphia: Lippincott, 1956).

13. D'Emilio and Freedman, *Intimate Matters;* Jane Gerhard, *Desiring Revolution: Second-Wave Feminism and the Rewriting of American Sexual Thought* (New York: Columbia University Press, forthcoming); Christina Simmons, "Companionate Marriage and the Lesbian Threat," *Frontiers* 4 (fall 1979): 54–59.

14. Citizenship means more than just suffrage—a right denied to many African Americans throughout much of this period. It encompasses "capacities for consent and speech, the ability to participate in a [public] dialogue," capacities that are "at odds" with both femininity and blackness. See Nancy Fraser, *Unruly Practices: Power, Discourse, and Gender in Contemporary Social Theory* (Minneapolis: University of Minnesota Press, 1989), p. 126.

15. Linda Kerber, "The Republican Mother: Women and the Enlightenment—An American Perspective," *American Quarterly* 28 (1976): 203; Kerber, *Women of the Republic: Intellect and Ideology in Revolutionary America* (Chapel Hill: University of North Carolina Press, 1980).

16. Carroll Smith-Rosenberg, "Dis-Covering the Subject of the 'Great Constitutional Discussion,' 1786–1789," *Journal of American History* 79 (December 1992): 857–65; Deborah Gray White, *Ar'n't I a Woman?: Female Slaves in the Plantation South* (New York: Norton, 1985), pp. 13–61.

17. For an account of gender and attitudes toward the poor in the nineteenth century, see Christine Stansell, *City of Women: Sex and Class in New York, 1789–1860* (Urbana: University of Illinois Press, 1987).

18. See, for example, Carol F. Karlsen, *The Devil in the Shape of a Woman: Witchcraft in Colonial New England* (New York: Norton, 1987); Gerda Lerner, *The Grimke Sisters from South Carolina: Pioneers for Woman's Rights and Abolition* (New York: Schocken Books, 1971);

Darlene Clark Hine, "Rape and the Inner Lives of Black Women in the Middle West: Preliminary Thoughts on the Culture of Dissemblance,"*Signs* 14 (summer 1989): 912–20; Nancy F. Cott, *The Grounding of Modern Feminism* (New Haven: Yale University Press, 1987).

19. Scholarship documenting the oppositional uses of women's "traditional" roles that has influenced me includes Glenda Gilmore, *Gender and Jim Crow: Women and the Politics of White Supremacy in North Carolina, 1896–1920* (Chapel Hill: University of North Carolina Press, 1996); Jacquelyn Dowd Hall, *Revolt against Chivalry: Jessie Daniel Ames and the Women's Campaign against Lynching* (New York: Columbia University Press, 1993 [1979]); Evelyn Brooks Higginbotham, *Righteous Discontent: The Women's Movement in the Black Baptist Church, 1880–1920* (Cambridge: Harvard University Press, 1993); Amy Swerdlow, *Women Strike for Peace: Traditional Motherhood and Radical Politics in the 1960s* (Chicago: University of Chicago Press, 1993).

20. Gordon, *Pitied But Not Entitled;* Linda Gordon, ed., *Women, the State and Welfare* (Madison: University of Wisconsin Press, 1990); Sonya Michel, *Children's Interests, Mothers' Rights: The Shaping of America's Child Care Policy* (New Haven: Yale University Press, 1999); Seth Koven and Sonya Michel, eds., *Mothers of a New World: Maternalist Politics and the Origins of Welfare States* (New York: Routledge, 1993); Gwendolyn Mink, *The Wages of Motherhood: Inequality in the Welfare State, 1917–1942* (Ithaca: Cornell University Press, 1995); Robyn Muncy, *Creating a Female Dominion in American Reform, 1890–1935* (New York: Oxford University Press, 1991). See also Molly Ladd-Taylor, *Mother-Work: Women, Child Welfare, and the State, 1890–1930* (Urbana: University of Illinois Press, 1994); Theda Skocpol, *Protecting Soldiers and Mothers: The Political Origins of Social Policy in the United States* (Cambridge: Harvard University Press, 1992); and the symposium "Maternalism as a Paradigm," *Journal of Women's History* 5 (fall 1993): 95–131.

21. Julia Grant, *Raising Baby by the Book: The Education of American Mothers* (New Haven: Yale University Press, 1998), pp. 10, 164–69; E. Ann Kaplan, "Mothering, Feminism and Representation: The Maternal in Melodrama and the Woman's Film, 1910–40," in Christine Gledhill, ed., *Home Is Where the Heart Is: Studies in Melodrama and the Woman's Film* (London: British Film Institute, 1987), pp. 113–37; Mari Jo Buhle, *Feminism and Its Discontents: A Century of Struggle with Psychoanalysis* (Cambridge: Harvard University Press, 1998), pp. 87–164. For discussions of the shift to a therapeutic or psychiatric ethos in the early twentieth century, see Warren Susman, " 'Personality' and the Making of Twentieth Century Culture," in *Culture as History: The Transformation of American Society in the Twentieth Century* (New York: Pantheon Books, 1984), pp. 271–85; Elizabeth Lunbeck, *The Psychiatric Persuasion: Knowledge, Gender, and Power in Modern America* (Princeton: Princeton University Press, 1994). For a discussion of this shift in relation to race, see Daryl Scott, *Contempt and Pity: Social Policy and the Image of the Damaged Black Psyche, 1880–1996* (Chapel Hill: University of North Carolina Press, 1997); for a discussion of the postwar period especially, see Ellen Herman, *The Romance of American Psychology: Political Culture in the Age of Experts* (Berkeley: University of California Press, 1995).

22. For example, see Eileen Boris, *Home to Work: Motherhood and the Politics of Industrial Homework in the United States* (New York: Cambridge University Press, 1994); Linda Kerber, "Separate Spheres, Female Worlds, Woman's Place: The Rhetoric of Women's History," *Journal of American History* 75 (June 1988): 9–39.

23. Carole Pateman, *The Disorder of Women: Democracy, Feminism and Political Theory* (Cambridge: Polity Press, 1989), esp. pp. 1–17, 179–209. The ideal of a male breadwinner in the public sphere supporting a female homemaker in the private sphere persisted despite the realities of women in the workforce.

24. Ruth Milkman, "Women's Work and the Economic Crisis: Some Lessons From the Great Depression," in Nancy Cott and Elizabeth Pleck, eds., *A Heritage of Her Own: Toward a New Social History of American Women* (New York: Simon and Schuster, 1979), pp. 507–41; Barbara Melosh, *Engendering Culture: Manhood and Womanhood in New Deal Public Art and Theater* (Washington, D.C.: Smithsonian Institution Press, 1991), pp. 16–30.

25. Daniel Patrick Moynihan, *The Negro Family: The Case for National Action* [1965], in Lee Rainwater and William L. Yancey, eds., *The Moynihan Report and the Politics of Controversy* (Cambridge: MIT Press, 1967), pp. 43–124; Betty Friedan, *The Feminine Mystique* (New York: Dell Publishing, 1963).

26. See Hazel Carby, *Reconstructing Womanhood: The Emergence of the Afro-American Woman Novelist* (New York: Oxford University Press, 1987). Excellent scholarship on the interdependence of gender and racial ideologies includes Gail Bederman, *Manliness and Civilization: A Cultural History of Gender and Race in the United States, 1880–1917* (Chicago: University of Chicago Press, 1995); Gordon, *Pitied But Not Entitled;* Louise Michele Newman, *White Women's Rights: The Racial Origins of American Feminism* (New York: Oxford University Press, 1998); Peggy Pascoe, *Relations of Rescue: The Search for Female Moral Authority in the West, 1874–1939* (New York: Oxford University Press, 1990).

27. For changing meanings of race in a multiracial and multiethnic society, see Matthew Frye Jacobson, *Whiteness of a Different Color: European Immigrants and the Alchemy of Race* (Cambridge: Harvard University Press, 1998).

28. Eileen Boris, "The Racialized Gendered State: Constructions of Citizenship in the United States," *Social Politics* 2 (summer 1995), esp. p. 163.

29. For discussions of liberalism as a constructed and changing ideology, see, for example, Brinkley, *End of Reform;* Eric Foner, "Common Origins, Different Paths," *Radical History Review* 71 (spring 1998): 6–10; Gary Gerstle, "The Protean Character of American Liberalism," *American Historical Review* 99 (October 1994): 1043–73; Kloppenberg, *Virtues of Liberalism;* Melosh, *Engendering Culture*, pp. 1–8. For an influential view of American liberalism as singular and continuous, see Louis Hartz, *The Liberal Tradition in America: An Interpretation of American Political Thought since the Revolution* (New York: Harcourt, Brace, 1955). For a view of unifying tenets within conservatism, by contrast, see Lisa McGirr, "Piety and Property: Conservatism and Right-Wing Movements in the Twentieth Century," in Harvard Sitkoff, ed., *Making Sense of the Twentieth Century: Historical Perspectives on Modern America, 1900–2000* (New York: Oxford University Press, forthcoming).

30. Bederman, *Manliness and Civilization*, p. 24.

31. For theories of discourse, see, for example, Michel Foucault, *The History of Sexuality*, vol. 1, *An Introduction* (New York: Random House, 1978 [1976]); historical analyses which employ this methodological perspective include Bederman, *Manliness and Civilization;* Carolyn Dean, *The Self and its Pleasures: Bataille, Lacan, and the History of the Decentered Subject* (Ithaca: Cornell University Press, 1992); Joan Scott, *Gender and the Politics of History* (New York: Columbia University Press, 1988); Judith R. Walkowitz, *City of Dreadful Delight: Narratives of Sexual Danger in Late-Victorian London* (Chicago: University of Chicago Press, 1992).

32. See Gordon, *Pitied But Not Entitled*, p. 2; Boris, *Home to Work*, pp. 4–9; Pateman, *Disorder of Women*, pp. 17–32, 118–40.

33. For consideration of hegemony, see also T. J. Jackson Lears, "The Concept of Cultural Hegemony: Problems and Possibilities," *American Historical Review* 90 (June 1985): 567–93. For accounts of women constructing meanings of motherhood, see Grant, *Raising Baby by the Book;* Sharon Hays, *The Cultural Contradictions of Motherhood* (New Haven: Yale University Press, 1996).

Chapter One

1. John Steinbeck, *The Grapes of Wrath* (New York: The Modern Library, 1939), p. 501.

2. Fred Matthews, "The Utopia of Human Relations: The Conflict-Free Family in American Social Thought, 1930–1960," *Journal of the History of the Behavioral Sciences* 24 (October 1988): 347; Eleanor Roosevelt, *It's Up to the Women* (New York: Frederick A. Stokes Co., 1933), p. vii.

3. Quoted in William H. Chafe, *The American Woman: Her Changing Social, Economic, and Political Roles, 1920–1970* (New York: Oxford University Press, 1972), p. 108. See also Jane Humphries, "Women: Scapegoats and Safety Valves in the Great Depression," *Review of Radical Political Economics* 8 (spring 1976): 106–08.

4. Barbara Melosh, *Engendering Culture: Manhood and Womanhood in New Deal Public Art and Theater* (Washington, D.C.: Smithsonian Institution Press, 1991), p. 1; for a discussion of challenges in the 1930s, see Alan Brinkley, *Voices of Protest: Huey Long, Father Coughlin and the Great Depression* (New York: Knopf, 1982).

5. Steinbeck, *Grapes of Wrath*, p. 467; see also p. 388.

6. For gender and citizenship, see also introduction.

7. For a discussion of liberalism and masculinity, see Carole Pateman, *The Disorder of Women: Democracy, Feminism and Political Theory* (Cambridge: Polity Press, 1989); for gender and work in the 1930s, see Ruth Milkman, "Women's Work and the Economic Crisis: Some Lessons from the Great Depression," in Nancy Cott and Elizabeth Pleck, eds., *A Heritage of Her Own: Toward a New Social History of American Women* (New York: Simon and Schuster, 1979), pp. 507–41. Unemployment peaked in 1933, when over 13 million people were officially unemployed. See Mimi Abramovitz, *Regulating the Lives of Women: Social Welfare Policy from Colonial Times to the Present* (Boston: South End Press, 1988), p. 274.

8. Julia Grant, *Raising Baby by the Book: The Education of American Mothers* (New Haven: Yale University Press, 1998), pp. 161–65; I refer to "perceived" crises in masculinity because the meanings of masculinity were never secure and were constantly being renegotiated. See Gail Bederman, *Manliness and Civilization: A Cultural History of Gender and Race in the United States, 1880–1917* (Chicago: University of Chicago Press, 1995).

9. Lizabeth Cohen, *Making a New Deal: Industrial Workers in Chicago, 1919–1939* (New York: Cambridge University Press, 1990), pp. 258–61; Nancy J. Weiss, *Farewell to the Party of Lincoln: Black Politics in the Age of FDR* (Princeton: Princeton University Press, 1983).

10. Harvard Sitkoff, *A New Deal for Blacks: The Emergence of Civil Rights as A National Issue*, vol. 1, *The Depression Decade* (New York: Oxford University Press, 1978), pp. 60–75, *Time* quoted, p. 91.

11. Sitkoff, *A New Deal for Blacks*, pp. 190–215.

12. Useful discussions of the political and cultural dimensions of New Deal liberalism include Cohen, *Making a New Deal;* Michael Denning, *The Cultural Front: The Laboring of American Culture in the Twentieth Century* (London: Verso, 1996); Stuart Kidd, "Redefining the New Deal: Some Thoughts on the Political and Cultural Perspectives of Revisionism," *Journal of American Studies* 22 (1988): 389–415; Melosh, *Engendering Culture*.

13. These uses of the term *liberalism* were not mutually exclusive; New Deal liberals argued that an active and interventionist state would guarantee individual liberty, individual opportunity, and social progress. See Theda Skocpol, "The Legacies of New Deal Liberalism," in Douglas MacLean and Claudia Mills, eds., *Liberalism Reconsidered* (Totowa, N.J.: Rowman and Allanheld Publishers, 1983), pp. 87–104.

14. Steve Fraser and Gary Gerstle, introduction to Fraser and Gerstle, eds., *The Rise and Fall of the New Deal Order, 1930–1980* (Princeton: Princeton University Press, 1989), p. xi; Alan Brinkley, *Liberalism and Its Discontents* (Cambridge: Harvard University Press, 1998), pp. 17–36.

15. Linda Gordon, *Pitied But Not Entitled: Single Mothers and the History of Welfare 1890–1935* (New York: The Free Press, 1994); Susan Ware, *Beyond Suffrage: Women in the New Deal* (Cambridge: Harvard University Press, 1981); Jacqueline Jones, *Labor of Love, Labor of Sorrow: Black Women, Work and the Family from Slavery to the Present* (New York: Basic Books, 1985), pp. 221–31; Annelise Orleck, " 'We Are That Mythical Thing Called the Public': Militant Housewives During the Great Depression," *Feminist Studies* 19 (spring 1993): 147–172; Wendy Kozol, "Madonnas of the Field: Photography, Gender, and 1930s Farm Relief," *Genders* 2 (summer 1988): 1–23; Melosh, *Engendering Culture*.

16. Jones, *Labor of Love*, pp. 200–03; Lois Scharf, *To Work and to Wed: Female Employment, Feminism, and the Great Depression* (Westport, Conn.: Greenwood Press, 1980).

17. Sitkoff, *A New Deal for Blacks;* Patricia Sullivan, *Days of Hope: Race and Democracy in the New Deal Era* (Chapel Hill: University of North Carolina Press, 1996); Donald Bogle, *Toms, Coons, Mulattoes, Mammies and Bucks: An Interpretive History of Blacks in American Films* (New York: Continuum, 1994 [1973]); Vernon Williams, *From a Caste to a Minority: Changing Attitudes of American Sociologists Toward Afro-Americans, 1896–1945* (Westport, Conn.: Greenwood Press, 1989).

18. Jones, *Labor of Love*, pp. 196–231; John A. Stanfield, *Philanthropy and Jim Crow in American Social Science* (Westport, Conn.: Greenwood Press, 1985); John B. Kirby, *Black Americans in the Roosevelt Era: Liberalism and Race* (Knoxville: University of Tennessee Press, 1980).

19. Robert Sklar, *Movie-Made America: A Cultural History of American Movies* (New York: Random House, 1975), pp. 162, 175–94; Warren Susman, *Culture as History: The Transformation of American Society in the Twentieth Century* (New York: Pantheon Books, 1984), p. 160; Lawrence Levine, "American Culture and the Great Depression," *Yale Review* 74 (winter 1985): 209.

20. The genres of woman's film and melodrama overlap despite distinctions between them. For an excellent overview, see Christine Gledhill, ed., *Home Is Where the Heart Is: Studies in Melodrama and the Woman's Film* (London: British Film Institute, 1987).

21. *New York Times*, 24 November 1934, p. 19. *Imitation of Life* (1934), screenplay by William Hulburt, directed by John Stahl, starring Claudette Colbert (Bea Pullman), Louise Beavers (Delilah).

22. *Imitation* is also among the most widely written-about films. Criticism that has shaped my thinking includes Lauren Berlant, "National Brands/National Body: *Imitation of Life*," in Hortense Spillers, ed., *Comparative American Identities: Race, Sex, and Nationality in the Modern Text* (New York: Routledge, 1991), pp. 110–40; Sandy Flitterman-Lewis, "*Imitation*(s) *of Life*: The Black Woman's Double Determination as Troubling 'Other'" [1988], in Lucy Fischer, ed., *Imitation of Life: Douglas Sirk, Director* (New Brunswick: Rutgers University Press, 1991), pp. 325–38. For the remake of *Imitation of Life* (1959), see chapter 5.

23. Sklar, *Movie-Made America*, p. 162.

24. Although the black daughter's actions hint at independent sexual desire, her "problem" remains racial rather than sexual; the film suppresses the simultaneity of these categories. See chapter 5.

25. Fannie Hurst in *Opportunity* (April 1935), quoted in James V. Hatch, ed., *Black Theater, U.S.A.: Forty-Five Plays by Black Americans, 1847–1974* (New York: The Free Press, 1974), p. 655; Mercer Cook, "*Imitation of Life* in Paris," *The Crisis* 42 (June 1935): 182; for accounts of Beavers' resistance, see *New York Amsterdam News*, 16 February 1935 (unpaginated), *Journal and Guide*, 23 February 1935 (unpaginated); and *Journal and Guide*, 2 March 1935 (unpaginated); all in Schomburg Center on Black Culture Clipping File, 1925–1974, "Louise Beavers," 000–479. See also Louise Beavers, "My Biggest Break," *Negro Digest*, December 1949, 21–22. For a more critical response, see Langston Hughes, "Limitations of Life" (1938), in Hatch, ed., *Black Theater*, pp. 656–57.

26. Berlant, "National Brands/National Body," p. 125.

27. "On the Current Screen," *Literary Digest*, 8 December 1934, 31. Even Delilah's subversive declarations ("I can't give up my baby! . . . You can't ask your mammy to do this. I ain't no white mother!") reinforce the sense that there is something essentially defining and ultimately problematic about black motherhood.

28. Although nothing explicit occurs between the white daughter and the fiancé, there is a sexual undercurrent to his "care." See E. Ann Kaplan, *Motherhood and Representation: The Mother in Popular Culture and Melodrama* (New York: Routledge, 1992), p. 167.

29. For a consideration of the staircase in 1940s films, see Mary Ann Doane, "The 'Woman's Film': Possession and Address," in Gledhill, ed., *Home Is Where the Heart Is*, pp. 287–88.

30. Delilah responds that she is 240 pounds. For a discussion of corporeality in *Imitation*, see Berlant, "National Brands/National Body." Hurst employed Zora Neale Hurston in the 1920s and alternatively treated Hurston like a peer and an employee. See Laura Hapke, *Daughters of the Great Depression: Women, Work, and Fiction in the American 1930s* (Athens: University of Georgia Press, 1995), p. 124. For a discussion of maternal nurturance masking exploitation in other contexts, see Hazel Carby, "Policing the Black Woman's Body in an Urban Context," *Critical Inquiry* 18 (summer 1992), p. 744.

31. For an analysis of the New Deal and consumption, see Alan Brinkley, *The End of Reform: New Deal Liberalism in Recession and War* (New York: Knopf, 1995), pp. 65–85.

32. *New York Times*, 24 November 1934, p. 19.

33. Robert S. Lynd, *Knowledge for What? The Place of Social Science in American Culture* (New York: Grove Press, 1964 [1939]), pp. 2, 115; Richard Wightman Fox, "Epitaph for Middletown: Robert S. Lynd and the Analysis of Consumer Culture," in T. J. Jackson Lears and Richard Wightman Fox, eds., *The Culture of Consumption: Critical Essays in American History, 1880–1980* (New York: Pantheon Books, 1983), p. 133.

34. See for example, Denning, *Cultural Front;* Melosh, *Engendering Culture;* Richard Pells, *Radical Visions and American Dreams: Culture and Social Thought in the Depression Years* (Middletown: Wesleyan University Press, 1973); William Stott, *Documentary Expression and Thirties America* (New York: Oxford University Press, 1973).

35. Gary Gerstle, "The Protean Character of American Liberalism," *American Historical Review* 99 (October 1994): 1048.

36. Essays in George Stocking, Jr., ed., *Malinowski, Rivers, Benedict and Others: Essays on Culture and Personality, History of Anthropology, vol. 4* (Madison: University of Wisconsin Press, 1986) provide an excellent overview of changes in the social sciences. See also Gerald Platt, "The Sociological Endeavor and Psychoanalytic Thought," *American Quarterly* 28 (1976): 343–359; Eli Zaretsky, introduction to William I. Thomas and Florian Znaniecki, *The Polish Peasant in Europe and America,* (Chicago: University of Chicago Press, 1984 [1918–1920]), pp. 1–53. Influential primary texts include Ernest W. Burgess, "The Family as a Unity of Interacting Personalities," *The Family* 8 (1926): 3–9; Edward Sapir, *Culture, Language and Personality*, David G. Mandelbaum, ed. (Berkeley: University of California Press, 1949); Harold D. Lasswell, *Psychopathology and Politics* (New York: Viking Press, 1960 [1930]).

37. Ruth Shonle Cavan and Katherine Howland Ranck, *The Family and the Depression: A Study of One Hundred Chicago Families* (Chicago: University of Chicago Press, 1938); Robert Cooley Angell, *The Family Encounters the Depression* (Gloucester, Mass.: Peter Smith, 1965 [1936]); Robert Lynd and Helen Lynd, *Middletown in Transition: A Study in Cultural Conflicts* (New York: Harcourt, Brace, 1937); Margaret Jarman Hagood, *Mothers of the South: Portraiture of the White Tenant Farm Woman* (New York: Norton, 1977 [1939]). This discussion also draws on Mirra Komarovsky, *The Unemployed Man and His Family* (New York: Arno Press, 1971 [1940]); Roosevelt, *It's Up to the Women;* Cora Court, "Parent Education in Nashville, Tennessee 1932–33: An Investigation of the Growth of Interest in Parent Education as Evidenced by the Experience of Parents and the Activities of Social Agencies," in Cora May Trawick Court Papers, box 3, 35v, Schlesinger Library, Radcliffe College. See also Winona Louise Morgan, *The Family Meets the Depression: A Study of a Group of Highly Selected Families* (Minneapolis: University of Minnesota Press, 1939); Samuel A. Stouffer and Paul F. Lazersfeld, *Research Memorandum on the Family in the Depression* (New York: Social Science Research Council, 1937).

38. Lynd, *Knowledge for What?*, p. 8.

39. Daryl Scott, *Contempt and Pity: Social Policy and the Image of the Damaged Black Psyche, 1880–1996* (Chapel Hill: University of North Carolina Press, 1997), pp. 58–59.

40. This discussion focuses on similarities. For an account of differences among scholars of race relations, see Scott, *Contempt and Pity*, pp. 19–56.

41. Steven Weiland, "Life History, Psychoanalysis, and Social Science: The Example of

John Dollard," *South Atlantic Quarterly* 86 (summer 1987): 272–74; John Dollard, *Caste and Class in a Southern Town* (Madison: University of Wisconsin Press, 1988 [1937]), p. xiii, 1. "Southerntown" was Indianola, Mississippi. For a discussion of theories of caste, see also W. Lloyd Warner, "American Caste and Class," *American Journal of Sociology* 42 (September 1936): 234–37. Important studies of southern black communities from this period also include Charles S. Johnson, *Shadow of the Plantation* (Chicago: University of Chicago Press, 1934); and another study of Indianola, Hortense Powdermaker, *After Freedom: A Cultural Study in the Deep South* (New York: Russell and Russell, 1968 [1939]).

42. Park in *Annals of the American Academy of Political and Social Science* 193 (1937): 210–11; *The American Political Science Review* 31 (1937): 981–83; Walter A. Jackson, "The Making of a Social Science Classic: Gunnar Myrdal's *An American Dilemma*," *Perspectives in American History*, New Series 2 (1985): 238. Largely positive reviews of *Caste and Class* appeared in *The Nation*, *The New Republic*, and the *Saturday Review of Literature*, among other places. The 1988 paperback edition includes an introduction by Daniel Patrick Moynihan.

43. Jackson, "The Making of a Social Science Classic," 243–44; Anthony E. Platt, *E. Franklin Frazier Reconsidered* (New Brunswick: Rutgers University Press, 1991), pp. 86–92, 104.

44. E. Franklin Frazier, *The Negro Family in the United States* (Chicago: University of Chicago Press, 1939). For opposing views that stressed continuities between West African and African American culture, see especially Melville J. Herskovits, "The Negro in the New World: The Statement of a Problem," *American Anthropologist* 32 (1930): 145–55. Frazier's earlier work includes *The Negro Family in Chicago* (Chicago: University of Chicago Press, 1932) and essays in G. Franklin Edwards., ed., *On Race Relations: Selected Writings* (Chicago: University of Chicago Press, 1968). For a discussion of Frazier's later work, see chapter 5.

45. *Annals of the American Academy* 207 (January 1940): 256; Burgess, Editor's Preface, *The Negro Family in the United States*, p. ix; *London Times Literary Supplement*, 11 November, 1939, p. 659; Edwards, ed., *On Race Relations*, p. xvi.

46. Footnotes in subsequent studies alone attest to the influence of these particular texts, even though both Dollard and Frazier engaged in other scholarship as well. In other words, even if Dollard and Frazier have been misread, as some scholars convincingly argue, the texts have nevertheless been influential. See, for example, Patricia Morton, *Disfigured Images: The Historical Assault on Afro-American Women* (New York: Praeger Press, 1991); Platt, *E. Franklin Frazier Reconsidered;* Scott, *Contempt and Pity;* Weiland, "Life History, Psychoanalysis, and Social Science."

47. For discussions of "organized" and "disorganized," see Frazier, *The Negro Family;* Cavan and Ranck, *The Family and the Depression;* for a discussion of "integrated" and "unintegrated," see Angell, *The Family Encounters the Depression.*

48. Lynd, *Middletown in Transition*, pp. 178, 180; Komarovsky, *The Unemployed Man and His Family*, p. 33; Hagood, *Mothers of the South*, p. 160.

49. Cavan and Ranck, *The Family and the Depression*, p. 50.

50. Angell, *The Family Encounters the Depression*, p. 4; Cavan and Ranck, *The Family and the Depression*, pp. 12–13; see also Hagood, *Mothers of the South.*

51. Cavan and Ranck, *The Family and the Depression*, p. 122; Angell, *The Family Encounters the Depression*, p. 224; Komarovsky, *The Unemployed Man and His Family*, p. 66.

52. See especially Cavan and Ranck, *The Family and the Depression*, pp. 50–60.

53. Komarovsky, *The Unemployed Man and His Family*, p. 27. See also Roger Babson, *Cheer Up!*, and psychiatrist Nathan Ackerman's comments about unemployed miners and their wives, both quoted in Levine, "American Culture and the Great Depression," pp. 206–07.

54. Cavan and Ranck, *The Family and the Depression*, p. 106.

55. For a discussion of divorce, see Lynd, *Middletown in Transition*, pp. 154, 158–60; for

a discussion of depression, see Komarovsky, *The Unemployed Man and His Family*, p. 27; for instances of learning problems, see case studies in Cora May Trawick Court Papers, box 3, folder 39; for a discussion of physical dislocations, see Cavan and Ranck, *The Family and the Depression*, pp. 100–02. See also Roosevelt, *It's Up to the Women*, pp. 1–6, 19–22, 92.

56. Lynd, *Middletown in Transition*, p. 181; see also Cavan and Ranck, *The Family and the Depression*, pp. 101–02; Roosevelt, *It's Up to the Women*, p. 3.

57. Cavan and Ranck, *The Family and the Depression*, p. 83; Grant, *Raising Baby by the Book*, pp. 168–70; Roosevelt, *It's Up to the Women*, p. 150; Morgan, *The Family Meets the Depression*, pp. 61–68; Komarovsky, *The Unemployed Man*, pp. 49–55.

58. Cavan and Ranck, *The Family and the Depression*, p. 34; Komarovsky, *The Unemployed Man and His Family*, p. 19.

59. Hagood, *Mothers of the South*, p. 243; Lynd, *Middletown in Transition*, pp. 125–26.

60. Dollard, *Caste and Class*, pp. 9, 8, 3. For his bias against southern whites, see pp. 32–33.

61. Dollard, *Caste and Class*, p. 3. Although Dollard explained (in the clause in the first ellipsis) that he later "realized that it is not from choice but from necessity that most rooms do duty as bedrooms in addition to some other function," he could not negate the power of the initial set of images that he chose to join. Dollard did argue that middle-class blacks were cleaner as well as more sexually restrained, orderly, and concerned with the law. However, by focusing extensively on the lower-class Negro, Dollard effectively suggested that the majority of African Americans fit this description. The class dimensions of his analysis were also complicated by his Freudianism: he often suggested that middle-class blacks suffered *more* from the caste system than did poorer blacks because the former were more sexually repressed and self-hating (pp. 89–93, 425–28). See also Scott, *Contempt and Pity*, pp. 27–37, 60.

62. Dollard, *Caste and Class*, pp. 99, 115.

63. Dollard, *Caste and Class*, pp. 153, 270. For more on economic independence and maternal dominance, see also Powdermaker, *After Freedom*, pp. 145–48; Johnson, *Shadow of the Plantation*, pp. 33–39.

64. Dollard, *Caste and Class*, pp. 153, 144.

65. Ibid., pp. 137, 152, 165.

66. Ibid., pp. 255, 285.

67. Ibid., pp. 276, 451. For the assertion that "by now a well-established generalization that the typical Negro family" is "matriarchal and elastic," see Powdermaker, *After Freedom*, p. 143; for her more positive assessment of its effects, see p. 197.

68. Dollard, *Caste and Class*, pp. 138, 443, 144. For Frazier's analysis of prejudice in whites, see E. Franklin Frazier, "The Pathology of Race Prejudice" [1927], in Nancy Cunard, ed., *Negro: Anthology* (London: Wishart, 1934), pp. 116–19. The trend toward analyzing the sources of prejudice increased over the course of the 1940s. For a discussion of this process see chapter 2.

69. See, for example, pp. 168–69.

70. Dollard, *Caste and Class*, pp. 287, 147.

71. Frazier, *The Negro Family in the United States*, pp. 479, 89, 95–97, 168, 163, 170, 164.

72. W. J. Gaines quoted in Frazier, *The Negro Family in the United States*, p. 90.

73. Frazier, *The Negro Family in the United States*, pp. 58, 56.

74. Ibid., pp. 121, 355; for mention of loving and devoted black mothers, see p. 143. "The Matriarchate" is the title of chapter 7; "Outlawed Motherhood" is the title of chapter 16. For a discussion of Frazier and unwed motherhood, see Regina G. Kunzel, "White Neurosis, Black Pathology: Constructing Out-of-Wedlock Pregnancy in the Wartime and Postwar United States," in Joanne Meyerowitz, ed., *Not June Cleaver: Women and Gender in Postwar America, 1945–1960* (Philadelphia: Temple University Press, 1994), pp. 304–31. For a discussion of Frazier and matriarchy, see also Scott, *Contempt and Pity*, pp. 42–51.

75. Frazier, *The Negro Family in the United States*, p. 122.

76. Ibid., p. 107; see also p. 97.

77. Ibid., pp. 288, 286–87, 289.

78. Ibid., p. 299. For an analysis of the feminization of vice in the 1920s, see Carby, "Policing Black Women's Bodies."

79. Frazier, *The Negro Family in the United States*, pp. 354, 143–44.

80. For a comprehensive discussion of depictions of black women in scholarship, see Morton, *Disfigured Images*.

81. Frazier, *The Negro Family in the United States*, pp. 269, 391, 486–88.

82. Dollard, *Caste and Class*, p. 452.

83. Frazier, *The Negro Family in the United States*, p. 299; Jones, *Labor of Love*, pp. 202–05; Elizabeth Clark-Lewis, *Living In, Living Out: African American Domestics in Washington, D.C., 1910–1940* (Washington, D.C.: Smithsonian Institution Press, 1994).

84. This analysis of New Deal policies has been influenced by Joan Scott, "Experience," in Judith Butler and Joan Scott, eds., *Feminists Theorize the Political* (New York: Routledge, 1992), pp. 22–40.

85. See, for example, Gordon, *Pitied But Not Entitled;* Gwendolyn Mink, *The Wages of Motherhood: Inequality in the Welfare State, 1917–1942* (Ithaca: Cornell University Press, 1995); Suzanne Mettler, *Dividing Citizens: Gender and Federalism in New Deal Public Policy* (Ithaca: Cornell University Press, 1998).

86. Children's Bureau director Katharine Lenroot quoted in the *New York Times*, 7 June 1935, p. 17; thirty million estimate in the *New York Times*, 10 August 1935, p. 1; "Inching Toward Social Security," *The New Republic*, 1 May 1935, p. 327. Scholarship on the development of the American welfare state is extensive. For useful overviews, see Margaret Weir, Ann Shola Orloff, and Theda Skocpol, "Introduction: Understanding American Social Politics," and Ann Shola Orloff, "The Political Origins of America's Belated Welfare State," both in Weir, Orloff, and Skocpol, eds., *The Politics of Social Policy in the United States* (Princeton: Princeton University Press, 1988), pp. 3–27, pp. 37–80. See also introduction.

87. *New York Times*, 15 August 1935, pp. 1, 4; *New York Times*, 11 August 1935, (4), p. 8.

88. *New York Times*, 25 August 1935, p. 10; *New York Times*, 13 September 1935, p. 31; Abraham Epstein, "The Social Security Act," *The Crisis* 42 (November 1935), 338.

89. Gordon, *Pitied But Not Entitled*, pp. 3–6, 293; Orloff, "The Political Origins of America's Belated Welfare State," pp. 72–73; Brinkley, *Liberalism and its Discontents*, pp. 23–24. Social Security legislation extended assumptions evident in early New Deal programs such as the Works Progress Administration (WPA) and the Civilian Conservation Corps (CCC) that had countered the "dole" by providing wage work—largely for men.

90. Nancy Fraser and Linda Gordon, "A Genealogy of *Dependency*: Tracing a Keyword of the U.S. Welfare State," *Signs* 19 (winter 1994): 321–22.

91. Gordon, "Social Insurance and Public Assistance," pp. 20–21; Hagood, *Mothers of the South*, p. 160.

92. Jones, *Labor of Love*, p. 199; George Edmund Haynes, "Lily-White Social Security," *The Crisis* 42 (March 1935): 85.

93. Scharf, *To Work and to Wed*, pp. 86–109; Abramovitz, *Regulating the Lives of Women*, p. 224; Chafe, *The American Woman*, pp. 106–8, 283 (fn. 39). According to lore in my own family, Sara Cohen and Irving Nixon eloped in March 1931. They concealed the marriage from everyone, including their parents, until the end of the school year in June because she could not afford to be fired from her job as an elementary school teacher in New Castle, Pennsylvania.

94. Jones, *Labor of Love*, pp. 218–20.

95. "The Report of the Committee on Economic Security," reprinted in Alan Pifer, ed., *50th Anniversary Issue, The Report of the Committee on Economic Security of 1935 and Other Basic Documents Relating to the Social Security Act* (Washington, D.C.: National Conference on Social Welfare, 1985), p. 36; for similar sentiments, see also Grace Abbot, *From Relief to Social Security: The Development of the New Public Welfare Services and Their Administration*, (Chicago: University of Chicago Press, 1941), pp. 210–11.

96. The Social Security Act of 1935 [1935], in Pifer, ed., *50th Anniversary Issue*, p. 85; see also Abbott, *From Relief to Social Security*, p. 279.

97. "Moral character," quoted in Winifred Bell, *Aid to Dependent Children* (New York: Columbia University Press, 1965), p. 29; Abbot, *From Relief to Social Security*, p. 276; see also Orloff, "The Political Origins of America's Belated Welfare State," pp. 74–75; Gordon, "Social Insurance and Public Insurance," pp. 48–49. According to one report, 61 percent of ADC recipients were widows in 1939, while 25 percent were divorced, deserted, or separated from partners. See Abramovitz, *Regulating the Lives of Women*, p. 319.

98. Abramovitz, *Regulating the Lives of Women*, p. 316; Gordon, *Pitied But Not Entitled*, p. 7. For efforts among women reformers to improve ADC, see Mink, *Wages of Motherhood*, pp. 134–41.

99. Jones, *Labor of Love*, pp. 224–25; Mink, *Wages of Motherhood*, p. 140. In the 1930s, while 14 to 17 percent of all ADC recipients (nationally) were black, in southern states where the black population was considerably higher, the proportion of blacks receiving ADC was considerably lower. See Bell, *Aid to Dependent Children*, p. 34. White children constituted 86 percent of the ADC caseload in 1939. See Edward D. Berkowitz, *America's Welfare State: From Roosevelt to Reagan* (Baltimore: Johns Hopkins University Press, 1991), p. 102.

100. Mary S. Larabee, quoted in Bell, *Aid to Dependent Children*, pp. 34–35, from a 1939 report.

101. With the initial shifting over of widows, 43 percent of ADC recipients moved to OAI rolls; see Abramovitz, *Regulating the Lives of Women*, p. 265. Between 1942 and 1948, the number of families on ADC with a deceased father dropped by a third, and in 1948 only 14 percent of all widowed mothers with children received ADC. See Elizabeth Alling and Agnes Leisy, "Aid to Dependent Children in a Postwar Year," *Social Security Bulletin* 13 (August 1950): 5–8. For a detailed discussion of the 1939 amendments, see Alice Kessler-Harris, "Designing Women and Old Fools: The Construction of the Social Security Amendments of 1939," in Linda K. Kerber et al., eds., *U.S. History as Women's History: New Feminist Essays* (Chapel Hill: University of North Carolina Press, 1995), pp. 87–106.

102. "Final Report of the Advisory Council on Social Security" [1937–38], in Pifer, ed., *50th Anniversary Issue*, pp. 191–92; "less than 2 percent," in "Old Age Security Programs and the 1940 Population," *Social Security Yearbook, 1940* (Washington, D.C.: Federal Security Agency, Social Security Board, 1941), p. 30, table 12. This figure rose to only 2.5 percent in 1944, several years into World War II and the increasing number of widows across the nation; see "Old Age and Survivors Insurance," *Social Security Yearbook, 1944*, annual supplement to the *Social Security Bulletin* (Washington, D.C.: Federal Security Agency, Social Security Board, 1945), p. 59.

103. Jones, *Labor of Love*, pp. 199, 210, 218–20. For resistance to the legislation among black Americans, see Kessler-Harris, "Designing Women and Old Fools," p. 103.

104. In the early 1930s, National Recovery Administration codes institutionalized unequal pay along lines of race in the industrial work force. In 1939, as a result of racially determined hiring, 74 percent of WPA workers were white men. Throughout the 1930s unemployment among African Americans exceeded that of whites by 30 to 60 percent. See Jones, *Labor of Love*, pp. 197–201; Nancy E. Rose, "Gender, Race, and the Welfare State: Government Work Programs from the 1930s to the Present," *Feminist Studies* 19 (summer 1993): 325–27.

105. "Roosevelt, the Humanitarian," *The Crisis* 43 (October 1936): 299. *The Crisis* and the black press also criticized Roosevelt. See "Editorials: No Checks on Mobs," *The Crisis* 43 (May 1936): 145. Ickes was Secretary of the Interior and had served as president of a NAACP chapter in Chicago; Alexander, a southern white reformer with a long history of interracial organizing, was director of the Farm Security Administration; Williams was deputy director of the WPA and then head of the National Youth Administration.

106. Brinkley, *The End of Reform*, pp. 165–67; Gerstle, "The Protean Character of American Liberalism," pp. 1044–45. There were exceptions to this desire not to make race a con-

crete issue: for example, the Works Progress Administration initially included a quota plan that was designed to ensure blacks opportunities. See also Sullivan, *Days of Hope*.

107. Will Alexander, "A Strategy for Negro Labor," *Opportunity* 12 (April 1934): 102; also quoted in Kirby, *Black Americans in the Roosevelt Era*, p. 55.

108. Harold Ickes, "The Negro as a Citizen," *The Crisis* 43 (August 1936): 231.

109. Foreman quoted in Kirby, *Black Americans in the Roosevelt Era*, p. 42.

110. Ickes, "The Negro as a Citizen," pp. 242, 231; Ickes quoted in Kirby, *Black Americans in the Roosevelt Era*, p. 28.

111. Sitkoff, *A New Deal for Blacks*, pp. 244–98; Brinkley, *The End of Reform;* Gerstle, "The Protean Character of American Liberalism"; Jacquelyn Dowd Hall, *Revolt against Chivalry: Jessie Daniel Ames and the Women's Campaign against Lynching* (New York: Columbia University Press, 1993 [1979]), pp. 223–53.

112. Ira Katznelson, "Was the Great Society a Lost Opportunity?" in Gerstle and Fraser, eds., *The Rise and Fall of the New Deal Order*, p. 192.

113. See, for example, Elaine Tyler May, *Homeward Bound: American Families in the Cold War Era* (New York: Basic Books, 1985); Wini Breines, *Young, White and Miserable: Growing Up Female in the Fifties* (Boston: Beacon Press, 1992); for a discussion of historical scholarship on bad mothers, see also introduction.

Chapter Two

1. *Home of the Brave* (1949), screenplay by Carl Foreman, based on the play by Arthur Laurents, directed by Mark Robson, starring James Edwards (Pete Moss). Moss discovers that he is paralyzed by guilt over the death of a white soldier who had been a childhood friend. This man defends Moss from racist white soldiers, until he too (right before his death) calls Moss "nigger." Moss must learn that his guilt is universal—that of the soldier who survives his buddy's death. The racial power dynamics between him and his friend, he must conclude, are irrelevant. Discussions of *Home of the Brave* include Ralph Ellison, *Shadow and Act* (New York: Random House, 1972 [1949]), p. 278; Thomas Pauly, "Black Images and White Culture during the Decade before the Civil Rights Movement," *American Studies* 31 (fall 1990): 101–19; Michael Rogin, *Blackface, White Noise: Jewish Immigrants in the Hollywood Melting Pot* (Berkeley: University of California Press, 1996), pp. 228–50; Judith Smith, *Popular Promises: Fictions of Family and Social Identity in Postwar American Culture* (New York: Columbia University Press, forthcoming).

2. For discussions of racism as un-American, see ibid.; see also Mary L. Dudziak, "Desegregation as a Cold War Imperative," *Stanford Law Review* 41 (November 1988): 61–120; Ben Keppel, *The Work of Democracy: Ralph Bunche, Kenneth B. Clark, Lorraine Hansberry and the Cultural Politics of Race* (Cambridge: Harvard University Press, 1995).

3. For a discussion of race and codes of masculinity, see Hazel Carby, "Policing the Black Woman's Body in an Urban Context," *Critical Inquiry* 18 (summer 1992): 738–55; Hazel Carby, *Race Men* (Cambridge: Harvard University Press, 1998).

4. Philip Wylie, *Generation of Vipers* (New York: Holt, Rinehart and Winston, 1955 [1942]), pp. ix–xii, 210, 208, 209, 201, 213, 216. For biographical information on Wylie, see Clifford P. Bendau, *Still Worlds Collide: Philip Wylie and the End of the American Dream* (San Bernadino: Borgo Press, 1980), pp. 24–31; Truman Frederick Keefer, *Philip Wylie* (Boston: Twayne Publishers, 1977), pp. 95–108.

5. Ferdinand Lundberg and Marynia F. Farnham, *Modern Woman: The Lost Sex* (New York: Harper and Brothers, 1947), pp. 23, 298. When *Generation* and *Modern Women* discussed daughters, they stressed the fact that daughters of modern women or moms were likely to become bad mothers themselves.

6. Wylie, *Generation*, pp. 31, ix–xii; Lundberg in the *New York Times*, 20 November 1949, p. 80. For accounts of the reception and influence of *Generation*, see Mari Jo Buhle,

Feminism and Its Discontents: A Century of Struggle with Psychoanalysis (Cambridge: Harvard University Press, 1998), pp. 125–30; *New York Times*, 3 July 1949, VII, p. 9. For accounts of the influence of Farnham and Lundberg (even among critics), see the *New York Times*, 30 September 1951, VII, p. 24; *Marriage and Family Living* 9 (1947): 75; Leila J. Rupp and Verta Taylor, *Survival in the Doldrums: The American Women's Rights Movement, 1945 to the 1960s* (Columbus: Ohio State University Press, 1990), pp. 18–22.

7. For discussions of unfit soldiers and damaged veterans, see Edward Strecker, *Their Mothers' Sons: The Psychiatrist Examines an American Problem* (Philadelphia: Lippincott, 1946); Herbert Kupper, *Back to Life: The Emotional Adjustment of Our Veterans* (New York: L. B. Fischer, 1945); Sonya Michel, "Danger on the Home Front: Motherhood, Sexuality, and Disabled Veterans in American Postwar Films," *Journal of the History of Sexuality* 3 (July 1992): 109–28. For insight into the relationship between mothering and communism, see Michael Rogin, "Kiss Me Deadly: Communism, Motherhood, and Cold War Movies," *Representations* 6 (spring 1984): 1–36. Amram Scheinfeld was an important popularizer of "momism"; see his "Are American Moms a Menace?" *Ladies' Home Journal*, November 1945, 36. On debates about working mothers, see Sonya Michel, *Children's Interests/Mothers' Rights: The Shaping of America's Child Care Policy* (New Haven: Yale University Press, 1999), pp. 150–72.

8. For a discussion of mothers and indulgence, see Strecker, *Their Mothers' Sons*, p. 37; for a discussion of emotional repression, see Farnham and Lundberg, *Modern Woman*, pp. 305–06; for discussions of hyperconsumers, see Wylie, *Generation*, pp. 210–13, Farnham and Lundberg, *Modern Woman*, p. 16; for a discussion of underconsumption, see Strecker, *Their Mothers' Sons*, p. 40. See also Talcott Parsons, "The Kinship System of the Contemporary United States," *American Anthropologist* (January–March 1943): 22–38, especially p. 36.

9. For an influential study of maternal overprotection, see David M. Levy, *Maternal Overprotection* (New York: Columbia University Press, 1943); for his earlier work, see Levy, "Fingersucking and Accessory Movements in Early Infancy: An Etiological Study," *American Journal of Psychiatry* 7 (1928): 881–918; Levy, "Primary Affect Hunger," *American Journal of Psychiatry* 94 (1937): 643–52. For influential studies of maternal rejection or deprivation, see Margaret Ribble, *The Rights of Infants: Early Psychological Needs and Their Satisfaction* (New York: Columbia University Press, 1943); John Bowlby, *Maternal Care and Mental Health*, 2d ed. (Geneva: World Health Organization, monograph series no. 2, 1951); and Rene Spitz and K. Wolf, "Anaclytic Depression," *Psychoanalytic Study of the Child* 2 (1946): 313–42. For explication of psychiatrists' theories, see Diane Eyer, *Mother-Infant Bonding: A Scientific Fiction* (New Haven: Yale University Press, 1992), pp. 47–72.

10. Farnham and Lundberg, *Modern Woman*, pp. 265, 275. Here they relied on Helene Deutsch, *The Psychology of Women: A Psychoanalytic Interpretation* (New York: Grune and Stratton, 1944–45).

11. For considerations of mother-blaming in terms of reaction or conservatism, see, for example, Sara Evans, *Born for Liberty: A History of Women in America* (New York: The Free Press, 1988), pp. 238–39; Cynthia Harrison, *On Account of Sex: The Politics of Women's Issues, 1945–1968* (Berkeley: University of California Press, 1988), pp. 24–25; Joanne Meyerowitz, "Beyond The Feminine Mystique: A Reassessment of Postwar Mass Culture, 1946–1958," in Meyerowitz, ed., *Not June Cleaver: Women and Gender in Postwar America, 1945–1960* (Philadelphia: Temple University Press, 1994), pp. 229–62.

12. Ashley Montagu, *The Natural Superiority of Women* (New York: Collier, 1974 [1952]), p. 183, emphasis in the original. For discussions of the celebration of motherhood, see May, *Homeward Bound*, pp. 135–45; George Lipsitz, *Time Passages: Collective Memory and American Popular Culture* (Minneapolis: University of Minnesota Press, 1990), pp. 77–96.

13. *Newsweek*, 10 October 1955, 8, emphasis in original.

14. "Goodbye Mammy, Hello Mom," *Ebony*, March 1947, 36, quoted in Jacqueline Jones, *Labor of Love, Labor of Sorrow: Black Women, Work and the Family from Slavery to the*

Present (New York: Basic Books, 1985), p. 271; *Chicago Defender,* 15 October 1955, p. 3; for the celebration of good mothers, see also chapter 4.

15. Farnham and Lundberg supported a "federal department of welfare" that included subsidies to families (*Modern Woman,* pp. 359, 364), and in later editions Wylie criticized McCarthyism as "the rule of unreason . . . one with momism" (*Generation,* p. 196).

16. John Dollard, Leonard W. Doob, Neal E. Miller, O. H. Mower, Robert R. Sears, in collaboration with Clellan S. Ford, Carl Iver Hovland, and Richard T. Sollenberger, *Frustration and Aggression* (New Haven: Yale University Press, 1974 [1939]), p. 1, emphasis in original.

17. *New York Times Book Review,* 16 April 1939, 26; see also *Survey* 75 (August 1939): 259–60. More critical appraisals include those offered by Harold Lasswell, *American Political Science Review* 33 (1939): 1133–134; and Karl Menninger, *The New Republic,* 8 January 1940, 57–58. For a discussions of the influence of this paradigm, see Fred Matthews, "The Utopia of Human Relations: The Conflict-Free Family in American Social Thought, 1930–1960," *Journal of the History of the Behavioral Sciences* 24 (October 1988): 343–62; William Graebner, "The Unstable World of Benjamin Spock: Social Engineering in a Democratic Culture, 1917–1950," *Journal of American History* 67 (December 1980): 614–16; Ellen Herman, *The Romance of American Psychology: Political Culture in the Age of Experts* (Berkeley: University of California Press, 1995), pp. 36–38.

18. Dollard et al., *Frustration and Aggression,* p. 142, emphasis in original. Harold Lasswell's *Psychopathology and Politics* (New York: Viking Press, 1960 [1930]) was an important precursor to *Frustration and Aggression.*

19. Erik Erikson, *Childhood and Society* (New York: Norton, 1963 [1950]); Benjamin Spock, *Baby and Child Care* (New York: Hawthorn Books, 1968 [1946]), p. 337; Graebner, "The Unstable World of Benjamin Spock," pp. 612–29. Until the 1976 edition, the majority of Spock's examples referred to male children and female parents specifically. See Nancy Pottishman Weiss, "Mother, The Invention of Necessity: Dr. Benjamin Spock's *Baby and Child Care,*" *American Quarterly* 29 (1977): 519–46. For another "permissive" text, see Arnold Gesell and Frances L. Ilg, *Infant and Child in the Culture of Today: The Guidance of Development in Home and Nursery School* (New York: Harper and Brothers, 1943). For discussions of national character studies and mother-blaming, see Geoffrey Gorer, *The American People: A Study in National Character* (New York: Norton, 1948); Margaret Mead, *And Keep Your Powder Dry* (New York: Morrow, 1965 [1942]), especially pp. 80–99.

20. Strecker, *Their Mothers' Sons.*

21. Race relations also became more central to scholarly research as thousands of African Americans migrated from the South. See Keppel, *Work of Democracy,* p. 112.

22. See Smith, *Popular Promises*; Elisabeth Young-Bruehl, *The Anatomy Of Prejudices* (Cambridge: Harvard University Press, 1996). For example, the film version of *Home of the Brave* was based on a play in which the victim/protagonist was a Jewish soldier.

23. Elazar Barkan, *The Retreat of Scientific Racism: Changing Concepts of Race in Britain and the United States Between the World Wars* (Cambridge: Cambridge University Press, 1992), pp. 344–45.

24. Betsy Emmons, "The Psychiatrists Look at Race Hate," *Negro Digest,* July 1948, 25, emphasis in original.

25. Gary Gerstle, "The Protean Character of American Liberalism," *American Historical Review* 99 (October 1994): 1069–71.

26. Buhle, *Feminism and Its Discontents,* pp. 122–24.

27. T. W. Adorno, Else Frenkel-Brunswick, Daniel J. Levinson, R. Nevitt Sanford, in collaboration with Betty Aron, Maria Hertz Levinson, and William Morrow, *The Authoritarian Personality* (New York: Harper and Brothers, 1950; The American Jewish Committee Social Studies Series: Publication No. 3); Gunnar Myrdal, *An American Dilemma* (New York: Harper and Brothers, 1944). See also Wilhelm Reich, *The Mass Psychology of Fascism,* trans. Vincent R. Carfango (New York: Simon and Schuster, 1970 [1933]); Erich Fromm, *Escape From Freedom* (New York: Avon, 1969 [1941]). For a comprehensive discussion of the Frank-

furt School, see Martin Jay, *The Dialectical Imagination: A History of the Frankfurt School and the Institute of Social Research, 1923–1950* (Boston: Little, Brown, 1973); Martin Jay, *Permanent Exiles: Essays on Intellectual Migration from Germany to America* (New York: Columbia University Press, 1985). For a discussion of the influence of psychology and *The Authoritarian Personality*, see Philip Gleason, "Americans All: World War II and the Shaping of American Identity," *Review of Politics* 43 (October 1981): 495–500.

28. Charles Johnson, *Growing Up in the Black Belt: Negro Youth in the Rural South* (New York: Schocken Books, 1967 [1941]); Horace Cayton and St. Clair Drake, *Black Metropolis: A Study of Negro Life in a Northern City* (New York: Harper and Row, 1962 [1945]); Abram Kardiner and Lionel Ovesey, *Mark of Oppression: Explorations in the Personality of the American Negro* (Cleveland: Meridian Books, 1962 [1951]).

29. See, for example, Klyde Kluckhohn and Henry Murray, eds., *Personality in Nature, Society, and Culture* (New York: Knopf, 1967 [1948]).

30. This chapter focuses on areas of overlap; it is on the basis of these overlaps that I locate the Marxist cultural critic T. W. Adorno on a liberal spectrum. For a related framework, see Thomas Schaub, *American Fiction in the Cold War* (Madison: University of Wisconsin Press, 1991), pp. 16–18; see also Keppel, *Work of Democracy*, pp. 98–105. For considerations of differences between scholars, see Victor Barnouw, *Culture and Personality* (Homewood, Ill.: The Dorsey Press, 1973 [1963]), pp. 23–40; Walter Jackson, *Gunnar Myrdal and America's Conscience: Social Engineering and American Liberalism, 1938–1987* (Chapel Hill: University of North Carolina Press, 1990); Daryl Scott, *Contempt and Pity: Social Policy and the Image of the Damaged Black Psyche, 1880–1996* (Chapel Hill: University of North Carolina Press, 1997).

31. Emmons, "The Psychiatrists Look at Race Hate," p. 25.

32. Walter Jackson, "The Making of a Social Science Classic: Gunnar Myrdal's *An American Dilemma*," *Perspectives in American History*, New Series 2 (1985): 221–67.

33. Myrdal, *An American Dilemma*, p. 1022, emphasis in original; Jackson, "The Making of a Social Science Classic," p. 221. Positive reviews of *An American Dilemma* include Robert Lynd, "Prison for American Genius," *Saturday Review of Literature*, 22 April 1944, 5–7, 27; E. Franklin Frazier, "Race: An American Dilemma," *The Crisis* 51 (1944): 105–06, 129. For a critique, see Oliver Cox, "An American Dilemma: A Mystical Approach to the Study of Race Relations," in Cox, *Caste, Class, and Race* (New York: Monthly Review Press, 1959 [1948]), pp. 509–38. For a discussion of the "Negro Problem" as a paradigm, see Patricia Morton, *Disfigured Images: The Historical Assault on Afro-American Women* (New York: Praeger, 1991). For indications that the "Negro problem" was an ongoing paradigm, see Charles Glicksberg, "Science and the Race Problem," *Phylon* 12 (1951): 319–27.

34. Myrdal, *An American Dilemma*, p. 1003.

35. Myrdal, *An American Dilemma*, pp. 1004–05; Jackson, "The Making of a Social Science Classic."

36. Max Horkheimer and Samuel H. Flowerman, "Foreword to Studies in Prejudice," in Adorno et al., *The Authoritarian Personality*, p. v; *The Authoritarian Personality*, p. 603. See also Helen V. McLean, "Psychodynamic Factors in Racial Relations," *Annals of the American Academy of Political and Social Science* 244 (March 1946): 159–66; Arnold Rose, "Intergroup Anxieties in a Mass Society," *Phylon* 12 (1951): 305–18; and Ronald Lippitt and Marian Radke, "New Trends in the Investigation of Prejudice," *Annals of the American Academy of Political and Social Science* 22 (March 1946): 167–76.

37. *The Christian Century*, 26 April 1950, 532; Young-Bruehl, *The Anatomy of Prejudices*, p. 56; Herbert Hyman and Paul B. Sheatsley, " 'The Authoritarian Personality': A Methodological Critique," in Richard Christie and Marie Jahoda, eds., *Studies in the Scope and Method of "The Authoritarian Personality"* (Glencoe, Ill.: Free Press, 1954), p. 50.

38. Gordon Allport, *The Nature of Prejudice* (Reading: Addison-Wesley, 1979 [1954]); Keppel, *Work of Democracy*, pp. 125, 275, fn. 90. For an earlier synthesis, see Robin M. Williams, *The Reduction of Intergroup Tensions: A Survey of Research on Problems of Ethnic, Racial, and Religious Group Tensions* (New York: Social Science Research Council, 1947).

39. Adorno et al., *The Authoritarian Personality*, pp. 366–67; Allport, *The Nature of Prejudice*, p. 298, emphasis in original. See also R. Blake and W. Dennis, "The Development of Stereotypes Concerning the Negro," *Journal of Abnormal and Social Psychology* 38 (1943): 525–31.

40. This discourse often cast prejudiced girls simply as future mothers. See *The Authoritarian Personality*, pp. 365, 368.

41. Adorno et al., *The Authoritarian Personality*, pp. 359, 371.

42. Ibid., p. 367.

43. Ibid., p. 371; Spock, *Baby and Child Care*, p. 7; Graebner, "The Unstable World of Benjamin Spock." In this period, Spock was mostly unconcerned with race relations specifically.

44. Adorno et al., *The Authoritarian Personality*, pp. 359, 365. For discussions of American fatherhood, see Barbara Ehrenreich, *The Hearts of Men: American Dreams and the Flight from Commitment* (Garden City: Anchor Press, 1983); Robert Griswold, *Fatherhood in America* (New York: Basic Books, 1993), pp. 185–218.

45. Allport, *The Nature of Prejudice*, p. 361; Rose, "Intergroup Anxieties in a Mass Society," p. 313.

46. Anne C. Loveland, *Lillian Smith, a Southerner Confronting the South: A Biography* (Baton Rouge: Louisiana State University Press, 1986), pp. 1–105; Roseanne V. Camacho, "Race, Region, and Gender in a Reassessment of Lillian Smith," in Virginia Bernhard et al., eds., *Southern Women: Histories and Identities* (Columbia: University of Missouri Press, 1992), pp. 157–76; Margaret Rose Gladney, ed., *How Am I To Be Heard: Letters of Lillian Smith* (Chapel Hill: University of North Carolina Press, 1993); Lillian Smith, *Strange Fruit* (New York: Reynal and Hitchcock, 1944).

47. Lillian Smith, "Addressed to White Liberals," *The New Republic*, 18 September 1944, 331–33.

48. Ibid., p. 331.

49. Ibid., pp. 331–32; see also Smith, "Are We Not All Confused?" *South Today* 7 (Spring 1942): 30–34. For the views of other southern liberals, see Virginius Dabney, "Nearer and Nearer the Precipice," *The Atlantic Monthly*, January 1943, 94–100; Loveland, *Lillian Smith*, pp. 38–63; Morton Sosna, *In Search of the Silent South: Southern Liberals and the Race Issue* (New York: Columbia University Press, 1977), pp. 121–39, 184–97.

50. Smith, "Addressed to White Liberals," p. 332. See also Glicksberg, "Science and the Race Problem," p. 323; Melville Herskovits, *The Myth of the Negro Past* (New York: Harper and Brothers, 1941).

51. Lillian Smith, *Killers of the Dream* (New York: Anchor Books, 1963 [1949]), p. 128. Similar themes are explored in James W. Largen, "White Boy in Georgia," *Negro Digest*, June 1951, 67–75.

52. Smith, *Killers of the Dream*, pp. 17, 73, 100, 132–33, 70, 69, 132, 109, 112–13. Not surprisingly, Smith wrote a positive review of *Caste and Class in a Southern Town*. See Loveland, *Lillian Smith*, p. 28.

53. Smith, *Killers of the Dream*, p. 104.

54. Bucklin Moon, "A Passionate Cry for Brotherhood," *New York Times Book Review*, 23 October 1949, 3; Kate Leonard, "Jim Crow: Killers of the Dream," *Labor Action*, 30 October 1950 (unpaginated), in Schomburg Center on Black Culture Clipping File, 1925–1974 (SCBCCF, "Lillian Smith") 002–598–2; Ralph McGill, "Miss Smith and Freud," *Atlanta Constitution*, 24 November 1949 (unpaginated), SCBCCF, "Lillian Smith."

55. Gladney, ed., *How Am I To Be Heard*, p. 99; Smith, *Killers of the Dream*, pp. 122, 134. For Farnham and Lundberg on feminism, see *Modern Woman*, pp. 140–67. See also Erikson, *Childhood and Society*, pp. 289–91.

56. Jackson, *Gunnar Myrdal and America's Conscience*, p. 290; Herman, *The Romance of American Psychology*, p. 178.

57. Johnson, *Growing Up in the Black Belt*, p. 328. Johnson's *The Collapse of Cotton Tenancy: Summary of Field Studies and Statistical Surveys, 1933–35*, with Edwin Embree and Will Alexander (Chapel Hill: University of North Carolina Press, 1935), helped to bring

about the creation of the Farm Security Administration. See Jackson, "The Making of a Social Science Classic," p. 242; Morton, *Disfigured Images*, pp. 74–76; Richard Robbins, "Charles S. Johnson," in James Blackwell and Morris Janowitz, eds., *Black Sociologists: Historical and Contemporary Perspectives* (Chicago: University of Chicago Press, 1974), pp. 56–84; and Scott, *Contempt and Pity*, pp. 35, 63–66. For similar approaches, see Allison Davis et al., *Deep South: A Social Anthropological Study of Case and Class* (Los Angeles: Center for Afro-American Studies, UCLA, 1988 [1941]). For another American Youth Council-sponsored study, see E. Franklin Frazier, *Negro Youth at the Crossways: Their Personality Development in the Middle States* (Washington, D.C.: American Council on Education, 1940).

58. Richard Wright, introduction to Drake and Cayton, *Black Metropolis*, p. xviii; James B. McKee, *Sociology and the Race Problem: The Failure of a Perspective* (Urbana: University of Illinois Press, 1993), p. 214. For studies oriented around demographics in conjunction with other aspects of black life, see also Charles Johnson, *Patterns of Negro Segregation* (New York: Harper and Brothers, 1943); W. Lloyd Warner, Buford H. Junker, and Walter A. Adams, *Color and Human Nature: Negro Personality Development in a Northern City* (Washington, D.C.: American Council on Education, 1940). Positive reviews of *Black Metropolis* appeared in the *American Sociological Review*, the *Journal of Negro Education*, and the *Journal of Negro History*.

59. William C. Manson, *The Psychodynamics of Culture: Abram Kardiner and Neo-Freudian Anthropology* (New York: Greenwood Press, 1988), pp. xi–xiv, 63–68; Erikson, *Childhood and Society*, pp. 241–46. Kardiner's early work includes *The Individual and His Society: The Psychodynamics of Primitive Social Organization* (New York: Columbia University Press, 1939), and (with Ralph Linton, Cora DuBois, and James West) *The Psychological Frontiers of Society* (New York: Columbia University Press, 1945). Other studies of Negro personalities with a strong psychoanalytic focus include Allison Davis and John Dollard, *Children of Bondage: The Personality Development of Negro Youth in the Urban South* (Washington, D.C.: American Council on Education, 1940); McLean, "Psychodynamic Factors in Race Relations."

60. McKee, *Sociology and the Race Problem*, p. 213; Scott, *Contempt and Pity*, pp. 36, 100–01, 28–55.

61. Ray E. Baber, "Sociological Differences in Family Stability," *Annals of the American Academy of Political and Social Science* (November 1950): 35.

62. Wright, introduction, p. xxvi, emphasis in original.

63. Kardiner and Ovesey, *Mark of Oppression*, p. 11.

64. Kardiner and Ovesey, *Mark of Oppression*, p. 95; Johnson, *Growing Up in the Black Belt*, pp. 19, 99.

65. Johnson, *Growing Up in the Black Belt*, p. 99. Johnson did qualify this assessment of men in disorganized families, commenting that "this does not mean, however, that all members of this group are morally disorganized"; see also Drake and Cayton, *Black Metropolis*, pp. 585–87; Kardiner and Ovesey, *Mark of Oppression*, p. 109.

66. Kardiner and Ovesey, *Mark of Oppression*, pp. 385, 381. For observations about the feminization of black men, see also Drake and Cayton, *Black Metropolis*, pp. 517, 587.

67. Kardiner and Ovesey, *Mark of Oppression*, p. 97.

68. Johnson, *Growing Up in the Black Belt*, p. 58; Myrdal, *An American Dilemma*, p. 933; Drake and Cayton, *Black Metropolis*, p. 583. See also Kardiner and Ovesey, *Mark of Oppression*, pp. 54–55; Maurice Davie, *Negroes in American Society* (New York: McGraw-Hill, 1949), p. 208; and Drake and Cayton, *Black Metropolis*, p. 592.

69. Kardiner and Ovesey, *Mark of Oppression*, pp. 198–99; Drake and Cayton, *Black Metropolis*, p. 584; see also Kardiner and Ovesey, *Mark of Oppression*, pp. 251, 142.

70. Myrdal, *An American Dilemma*, p. 934. Myrdal noted that "a 'normal' family consists of at least husband and wife, living together, with or without children" (p. 364). There were exceptions to this conflation of dominant women and disorganized families, particularly in the work of Charles Johnson. See *Growing Up in the Black Belt*, pp. 11, 19.

71. Drake and Cayton, *Black Metropolis*, p. 608; Kardiner and Ovesey, *Mark of Oppres-*

sion, p. 161; Johnson, *Growing Up in the Black Belt*, pp. 79–80; Kardiner and Ovesey, *Mark of Oppression*, p. 137. For positive assessments of leisure and consumption, see Drake and Cayton, *Black Metropolis*, p. 387.

72. Kardiner and Ovesey, *Mark of Oppression*, p. 304; Erikson, *Childhood and Society*, p. 242. In this discussion of "black identity," Erikson argued that black mothers offered their babies "enough oral and sensory surplus for a lifetime," only to subject them to "a violently sudden and cruel cleanliness training" (pp. 241–46).

73. In *Caste and Class in a Southern Town*, John Dollard maintained this perspective, even when he argued that respectable middle-class blacks were more emotionally repressed. In *The Negro Family in the United States*, E. Franklin Frazier offered some criticisms of middle-class blacks. For more on Dollard and Frazier, see chapter 1.

74. Johnson, *Growing Up in the Black Belt*, p. 58; Drake and Cayton, *Black Metropolis*, p. 389, emphasis in original. See also Johnson, *Growing Up in the Black Belt*, pp. 63–64; 73–75, 80–98; Myrdal, *An American Dilemma*, pp. 931, 956–57. In 1953 Johnson and his family received the "Family of the Year" award at a Mother's Day celebration at Fisk University. See *Pittsburgh Courier*, 11 April 1954, p. 11.

75. For class and respectability among black reformers early in the century, see especially Kevin Gaines, *Uplifting The Race: Black Leadership, Politics, and Culture in the Twentieth Century* (Chapel Hill: University of North Carolina Press, 1996).

76. Johnson, *Growing Up in the Black Belt*, pp. 88–90; Drake and Cayton, *Black Metropolis*, p. 667. In other instances, Drake and Cayton contrasted stable middle-class families with disorganized and violent arrangements among the black poor (pp. 564–70).

77. Kardiner and Ovesey, *Mark of Oppression*, pp. 65, 210, 214–23; for a less critical perspective on women choosing spouses for "practical" reasons, see Johnson, *Growing Up in the Black Belt*, pp. 236–37. For more on consumption and motherhood, see chapter 5.

78. Kardiner and Ovesey, *Mark of Oppression*, p. 221. For a discussion of self-hatred and color consciousness in women, see also Johnson, *Growing Up in the Black Belt*, p. 97.

79. Erikson, *Childhood and Society*, pp. 241–46. By contrast, when black women did not identify with whiteness, "the children themselves learn to disavow their sensual and overprotective mothers as temptations and a hindrance to the formation of a more American personality." Like Dollard, Erikson noted that blacks and other immigrant groups were "privileged in the enjoyment of a more sensual early childhood" (p. 245).

80. Johnson, *Growing Up in the Black Belt*, p. 4; Drake and Cayton, *Black Metropolis*, pp. 583, 592; Myrdal, *An American Dilemma*, p. 931. For a consideration of families with successful male heads, see also Johnson, *Growing Up in the Black Belt*, pp. 58–68.

81. Kardiner and Ovesey, *Mark of Oppression*, pp. 69–70; see also Myrdal, *An American Dilemma*, pp. 957–58.

82. Carby, "Policing the Black Woman's Body," pp. 739–41.

83. Michael Rogin, " 'Democracy and Burnt Cork': The End of Blackface, the Beginning of Civil Rights," *Representations* 46 (spring 1994): 9.

84. Johnson, *Growing Up in the Black Belt*, p. 327; Drake and Cayton, *Black Metropolis*, p. 763; also quoted in McKee, *Sociology and the Race Problem*, p. 215; Kardiner and Ovesey, *Mark of Oppression*, "Advice to Reader" (unpaginated), p. 387.

85. Jane Gerhard, *Desiring Revolution: Second-Wave Feminism and the Rewriting of American Sexual Thought* (New York: Columbia University Press, forthcoming).

Chapter Three

1. Arthur M. Schlesinger, Jr., *The Vital Center: The Politics of Freedom* (New York: Da Capo Press, 1988 [1949]), p. 1; Mary Sperling McAuliffe, *Crisis on the Left: Cold War Politics and American Liberals, 1947–1954* (Amherst: University of Massachusetts Press, 1978), p. 67; Jonathan Daniels, "Ready To Be Radical," *Saturday Review of Literature*, 10 Septem-

ber 1949, 12. Scholars tend to use the terms *Cold War, anticommunist, postwar*, and *vital center liberalism* interchangeably. This chapter refers to *anticommunist* and *vital center liberalism* as terms that refer to liberals' assessments of communism, but uses *Cold War* and *postwar liberalism* as broader terms.

2. See also Lionel Trilling, *The Liberal Imagination: Essays on Literature and Society* (New York: Harcourt Brace Jovanovich, 1979 [1950]); Reinhold Niebuhr, *The Children of Light and the Children of Darkness: A Vindication of Democracy and a Critique of Its Traditional Defense* (New York: Charles Scribner's Sons, 1947 [1944]). Scholarship on this postwar liberal consensus includes Gary Gerstle, "Race and the Myth of the Liberal Consensus," *Journal of American History* 82 (September 1995): 579–86; Alonzo L. Hamby, "The Vital Center, the Fair Deal, and the Quest for a Liberal Political Economy," *American Historical Review* 77 (June 1972): 653–78; Godfrey Hodgson, *America in Our Time: From World War II to Nixon, What Happened and Why* (New York: Vintage Books, 1978), pp. 67–98; James Nuechterlein, "Arthur M. Schlesinger, Jr., and the Discontents of Postwar American Liberalism," *Review of Politics* 39 (January 1977): 3–40.

3. Schlesinger, *Vital Center*, p. 1.

4. Robert Griffith, "Forging America's Postwar Order: Domestic Politics and Political Economy in the Age of Truman," in Michael J. Lacey, ed., *The Truman Presidency* (New York: Cambridge University Press, 1989), pp. 57–88; Schlesinger, *Vital Center*, pp. 1–2. For a discussion of foreign and domestic policy in relation to each other, see Nikhil Pal Singh, "Culture/Wars: Recoding Empire in an Age of Democracy," *American Quarterly* 50 (September 1998): 471–522; Penny M. Von Eschen, *Race against Empire: Black Americans and Anticolonialism, 1937–1957* (Ithaca: Cornell University Press, 1997).

5. Henry Steele Commager, "The Survival of Liberalism in Our World," *New York Herald Tribune Weekly Book Review*, 11 September 1949, 1, 17; Ellen Herman, *The Romance of American Psychology: Political Culture in the Age of Experts* (Berkeley: University of California Press, 1995), pp. 124–35.

6. Studies of postwar liberalism tend to be oriented around either party politics and economics, or cultural dimensions, or gender relations, or racial politics and social movements. See, for example, Alan Brinkley, *The End of Reform: New Deal Liberalism in Recession and War* (New York: Knopf, 1995); Kent M. Beck, "What Was Liberalism in the 1950s?" *Political Science Quarterly* 102 (summer 1987): 233–58; Richard Pells, *The Liberal Mind in a Conservative Age: American Intellectuals in the 1940s and 1950s* (New York: Harper and Row, 1985); Thomas Schaub, *American Fiction in the Cold War* (Madison: University of Wisconsin Press, 1991); for a discussion of postwar anxieties about gender and race in relation to each other, see William H. Chafe, "Postwar American Society: Dissent and Social Reform," in Lacey, ed., *The Truman Presidency*, pp. 156–73.

7. Edward D. Berkowitz, *America's Welfare State: From Roosevelt to Reagan* (Baltimore: Johns Hopkins University Press, 1991), p. 64.

8. For discussions of resistance to liberal activism, see Griffith, "Forging America's Postwar Order"; Edwin Amenta and Theda Skocpol, "Redefining the New Deal: World War II and the Development of Social Provision in the United States," in Margaret Weir, Ann Shola Orloff, and Theda Skocpol, eds., *The Politics of Social Policy in the United States* (Princeton: Princeton University Press, 1988), pp. 81–122. For details of new policies, see "Public Assistance," in *Annual Report of the Federal Security Agency, Social Security Administration, 1950* (Washington, D.C.: Government Printing Office, 1951), p. 34; Robert Ball, "The 1939 Amendments to the Social Security Act and What Followed," in Alan Pifer, ed., *50th Anniversary Edition, The Report of the Committee on Economic Security of 1935 and Other Basic Documents Relating to the Development of the Social Security Act* (Washington, D.C.: National Conference on Social Welfare, 1985), pp. 168–69; Arthur J. Altemeyer, *The Formative Years of Social Security* (Madison: University of Wisconsin Press, 1966), p. 7.

9. Alan Brinkley, "The New Deal and the Idea of the State," in Steve Fraser and Gary Gerstle, eds., *The Rise and Fall of the New Deal Order, 1930–1980* (Princeton: Princeton

University Press, 1989), p. 112; see also Brinkley, *Liberalism and Its Discontents* (Cambridge: Harvard University Press, 1998), pp. 89–93.

10. Michael J. Lacey, "Introduction and Summary," in Lacey, ed., *The Truman Presidency*, p. 5; McAuliffe, *Crisis on the Left*, p. 70.

11. Wilbur Cohen, "The Social Security Act Amendments of 1950," *Public Welfare* 8 (December 1950): 226–29; Alonzo Hamby, *Liberalism and Its Challengers: FDR to Reagan* (New York: Oxford University Press, 1985), p. 64; Berkowitz, *America's Welfare State*, pp. 55–65; *New Republic*, 3 July 1950, 6. The 1950s' provisions included self-employed workers who were not farmers but excluded the majority of agricultural workers who were seasonally employed.

12. Elizabeth Alling and Agnes Leisy, "Aid to Dependent Children in a Postwar Year," *Social Security Bulletin* 13 (August 1950): 12. Because this ostensibly child-centered program tested the eligibility of parents, I refer to the women heads of households as recipients.

13. Daniel Reed, Extension of Remarks, *Congressional Record* (10 October 1949), 81st Cong., 95, pt. 16:A6143; Clifford Brenner, "Illegitimacy and Aid to Dependent Children," *Public Welfare* 8 (October 1950): 177; Mimi Abramovitz, *Regulating the Lives of Women: Social Welfare Policy from Colonial Times to the Present* (Boston: South End Press, 1988), p. 322; see also Maurine McKeany, *The Absent Father and Public Policy in the Program of Aid to Dependent Children* (Berkeley: University of California Press, 1960), pp. 41–68.

14. Fred H. Steininger, "Desertion and the ADC Program," *Public Welfare* 5 (October 1947): 238. For a contemporary assessment of the psychological harm of eligibility conditions, see Grace M. Marcus, "Reappraising Aid to Dependent Children as a Category," *Social Security Bulletin* 8 (1945): 3–5.

15. Virginia Millsip, "What ADC Has Meant for Children," *Public Welfare* 6 (September 1948): 173; Steininger, "Desertion and the ADC Program," p. 235. See also Alton A. Linford, "Social Security: Prop or Pillow?" *Social Work Journal* 29 (April 1948): 55–62; "Does the ADC Program Need Defining?," *Public Welfare* 6 (May-June 1948): 97. For discussions of ongoing support of ADC, see Riley Mapes, "The Mother's Employment—Whose Decision in ADC?" *Public Welfare* 8 (April 1950): 74; Henry F. and Katharine Pringle, "The Case for Federal Relief," *Saturday Evening Post*, 19 July 1952, 80; Blanche Saunders, "ADC—A Good Investment," *Public Welfare* 8 (May 1950): 108–10. Comprehensive accounts include Winifred Bell, *Aid to Dependent Children* (New York: Columbia University Press, 1965); Michael B. Katz, *In the Shadow of the Poorhouse: A Social History of Welfare in America* (New York: Basic Books, 1986); Gwendolyn Mink, *Welfare's End* (Ithaca: Cornell University Press, 1998), especially pp. 33–40.

16. Jane M. Hoey, "Public Assistance in 1948," *Journal of Social Casework* 29 (April 1948): 127; Alling and Leisy, "Aid to Dependent Children in a Postwar Year," p. 3; Saul Kaplan, "Public Assistance Costs," *Public Welfare* 7 (March 1949): 57–60. According to one estimate, the ADC caseload increased from 901,560 in 1942 to 1,176,196 in 1948 (Bell, *Aid to Dependent Children*, p. 208, fn. 24); the cost of the program rose from $133 million in 1940 to $994 million in 1960 (Abramovitz, *Regulating the Lives of Women*, p. 319).

17. *Social Security Bulletin* 13 (December 1950); Linford, "Social Security," pp. 55–62.

18. Rickie Solinger, *Wake Up Little Susie: Single Pregnancy and Race Before Roe v. Wade* (New York: Routledge, 1992), pp. 29–30; Alling and Leisy, "Aid to Dependent Children in a Postwar Year."

19. Mildred Stoves, "Ten Years of ADC in Tennessee," *Public Welfare* 6 (February 1948): 33; Jacob Panken, as told to Hal Burton, "I Say Relief Is Ruining Families," *Saturday Evening Post*, 30 September 1950, 25.

20. David H. Stevens, "Maine Revives Responsibility of Relatives," *Public Welfare* 6 (July 1948): 122; Bell, *Aid to Dependent Children*, pp. 87–92; Brenner, "Illegitimacy and Aid to Dependent Children," pp. 174–78; see also "Public Assistance Conferences on 'Law Enforcement' Amendment," *Social Security Bulletin* 14 (September 1951): 8, 11.

21. Paul Molloy, "The Relief Chiselers Are Stealing Us Blind," *Saturday Evening Post*, 8 September 1951, 143; Panken, "I Say Relief Is Ruining Families," p. 114; Charlotte Towle, "Economic Aspects of the Reunited Family," *Social Service Review* 20 (September 1946): 350.

22. Molloy, "The Relief Chiselers Are Stealing Us Blind," p. 144; Towle, "Economic Aspects of the Reunited Family," p. 351.

23. In the 1950s, as a result of discriminatory hiring practices and unequal wages, black men earned on average half as much as white men. See Jacqueline Jones, *Labor of Love, Labor of Sorrow: Black Women, Work, and the Family from Slavery to the Present* (New York: Basic Books, 1985), p. 261.

24. Linford, "Social Security," pp. 59, 57.

25. Specific variations are beyond the scope of this general overview but are worthy of further research.

26. Quoted in Molloy, "The Relief Chiselers Are Stealing Us Blind," p. 144.

27. Brenner, "Illegitimacy and Aid to Dependent Children," p. 174.

28. Over the course of the 1950s, eighteen states tried to enact policies denying aid to an unmarried woman who had more than one child; three succeeded. See Bell, *Aid To Dependent Children*, pp. 66–67, 118; Abramovitz, *Regulating the Lives of Women*, pp. 323–25; "Source Materials: The 'Suitable-Home' Requirement," *Social Service Review* 35 (June 1961): 203–14. For an account of resistance to these provisions, see Hoey, "Public Assistance in 1948."

29. E. Franklin Frazier, *The Negro Family in the United States* (Chicago: University of Chicago Press, 1939); Gunnar Myrdal, *An American Dilemma* (New York: McGraw-Hill, 1964 [1944]); see chapter 2.

30. Alling and Leisy, "Aid to Dependent Children in a Postwar Year," p. 8; Solinger, *Wake Up Little Susie*, pp. 22, 49. In 1953, 63 percent of ADC recipients were white; this gap did not narrow until the 1960s. See "Fact Book: The Negro Family in the Modern Urban Community," prepared for the National Urban League Annual Conference, 1956, Cincinnati, Ohio (National Urban League: Department of Research and Community Project, 1956), p. 26, in Schomburg Center on Black Culture Clipping File, 1925–1974, (SCBCCF) "Family, Chronology, 1951–1956," 001, 716–2. The majority of nonwhite recipients were black.

31. Alling and Leisy, "Aid to Dependent Children in a Postwar Year," pp. 3–5; Bell, *Aid to Dependent Children*, p. 55; Solinger, *Wake Up Little Susie*, p. 18; Gwendolyn Mink, *The Wages of Motherhood: Inequality in the Welfare State, 1917–1942* (Ithaca: Cornell University Press, 1995), pp. 145–50. For the decline in widows receiving ADC, see Katherine Rickey, "Is Aid to Dependent Children Effective?" *Public Welfare* 5 (November 1947): 250. Between 1948 and 1953, the number of widowed mothers on ADC dropped by 25 percent and the number of unwed mothers, black and white, on ADC rose by nearly 58 percent. See Abramovitz, *Regulating the Lives of Women*, p. 321.

32. Millsip, "What ADC Has Meant for Children," p. 174; see also Molloy, "The Relief Chiselers Are Stealing Us Blind."

33. Millsip, "What ADC Has Meant for Children," p. 174; Molloy, "The Relief Chiselers Are Stealing Us Blind," pp. 32, 142.

34. Quoted in Bell, *Aid to Dependent Children*, pp. 67, 64, 46; Jones, *Labor of Love*, p. 263.

35. Quoted in Bell, *Aid to Dependent Children*, p. 97.

36. "Fact Book: The Negro Family in the Modern American Community," p. 26.

37. Bell, *Aid to Dependent Children*, pp. 68, 111–14; Phyliss Osborn, "Aid to Dependent Children—Realities and Possibilities," *Social Service Review* 28 (June 1954): 154; see also p. 161.

38. Mink, *Welfare's End*, p. 37. For debates about women and work, see Irene M. Josselyn and Ruth Schley Goldman, "Should Mothers Work," *Social Service Review* 23 (March 1949): 74–87; "Negro Women Workers," *Social Service Review* 24 (June 1950): 255–56.

39. Brenner, "Illegitimacy and Aid to Dependent Children," pp. 174–78; Bell, *Aid to Dependent Children*, pp. 87–92. For discussions of desertion time minimums and court-action requirements, see Alling and Leisy, "Aid to Dependent Children in a Postwar Year," p. 11; U.S. Congress, *Issues in Social Security*, p. 304. The Supreme Court struck down "substitute father" rules in Alabama in 1968. See Mink, *Welfare's End*, p. 142, fn. 8.

40. Virginia Franks, "Shall We Sneak Up on Our Clients?" *Public Welfare* 9 (May 1951): pp. 106.

41. Alling and Leisy, "Aid to Dependent Children in a Postwar Year," p. 5; Bell, *Aid to Dependent Children*, pp. 55–58, 184–86; Solinger, *Wake Up Little Susie*, p. 43.

42. *Arkansas Gazette*, 1 September 1959, quoted in Bell, *Aid to Dependent Children*, p. 68.

43. Mary McLeod Bethune, "Certain Unalienable Rights," in Rayford Logan, ed., *What the Negro Wants* (New York: Agathon Press, 1969 [1944]), p. 255. See also *Children in a Democracy: Preliminary Statements Submitted to the White House Conference on Children in a Democracy* (Washington, D.C., 1940); Philip Gleason, "Americans All: World War II and the Shaping of American Identity," *Review of Politics* 93 (October 1981): 483–518.

44. Hubert M. Humphrey, "Yes: Civil Rights Affect Standing of U.S. Throughout World," *Daily Compass*, 13 February 1950, (unpaginated), in SCBCCF, "Civil Rights: Legislation: Chronology, 1938–1953," 001, 015–1.

45. Dissenting perspectives on citizenship in this period came from Mary McLeod Bethune, Ella Baker, and Constance Baker Motley, among others.

46. Social histories of race relations in these years include Richard M. Dalfiume, "The 'Forgotten Years' of the Negro Revolution," *Journal of American History* 55 (June 1968): 90–106; John Egerton, *Speak Now against the Day: The Generation before the Civil Rights Movement in the South* (New York: Knopf, 1994); Thomas Sugrue, *The Origins of the Urban Crisis: Race and Inequality in Postwar Detroit* (Princeton: Princeton University Press, 1996).

47. Merl E. Reed, *Seedtime for the Modern Civil Rights Movement: The President's Committee on Fair Employment Practice, 1941–1946* (Baton Rouge: Louisiana State University Press, 1991).

48. John Bracey Jr. and August Meier, "Allies or Adversaries?: The NAACP, A. Philip Randolph and the 1941 March on Washington," *Georgia Historical Quarterly* 75 (spring 1991): 1–17; Lucy G. Barber, "Marches On Washington, 1894–1963: National Political Demonstrations and American Political Culture," (Ph.D. diss., Brown University, 1996), pp. 251–362; Herbert Garfinkel, *When Negroes March* (Glencoe, Ill.: The Free Press, 1959). Walter White later wrote that he used the number 100,000 in his meeting with Roosevelt even though he thought the march might draw far fewer people. See Walter White, *A Man Called White* (New York: Arno Press, 1969 [1948]), pp. 189–92.

49. "Call to Negro America," quoted in Barber, "Marches On Washington," p. 299. See also *Chicago Defender*, 28 June 1941, p. 6.

50. *Baltimore Afro-American*, 14 June 1941, p. 4; *Baltimore Afro-American*, 5 July 1941, p. 12; *Chicago Defender*, 28 June 1941, p. 2.

51. Adam Clayton Powell Jr., *Marching Blacks* (New York: Dial Press, 1973 [1945]), p. 118; A. Philip Randolph, "Keynote Address to the March on Washington Movement," 26 September 1942, in Peter B. Levy, ed., *Let Freedom Ring: A Documentary History of the Modern Civil Rights Movement* (New York: Praeger Press, 1992), pp. 13–14; Powell, *Marching Blacks*, p. 147. Keeping the MOWM all-black was also a way to limit Communist Party involvement. See Garfinkel, *When Negroes March*, p. 49.

52. *Chicago Defender*, 28 June 1941, p. 14; Powell, *Marching Blacks*, p. 115.

53. Barber, "Marches On Washington," p. 300; for an account of women in the MOWM, see Melinda Chateauvert, *Marching Together: Women of the Brotherhood of Sleeping Car Porters* (Urbana: University of Illinois Press, 1998), pp. 163–74.

54. Bracey and Meier, "Allies or Adversaries?" pp. 12–13; Sitkoff, *The Struggle for Black Equality*, pp. 11–12; Richard Dalfiume, *Desegregation of the U.S. Armed Forces: Fighting on Two Fronts, 1939–1953* (New York: Columbia University Press, 1969), pp. 117–21.

55. This discussion is not focused on whether the Truman administration was good or bad for civil rights; it rather explores the similar logic evident in advances and setbacks. More comprehensive discussions include William C. Berman, *The Politics of Civil Rights in the Truman Administration* (Columbus: Ohio State University Press, 1970); Barton J. Bernstein, "The Ambiguous Legacy: The Truman Administration and Civil Rights," in Barton Bernstein, ed., *Politics and Policies of the Truman Administration* (Chicago: Quadrangle Books, 1970), pp. 296–314; Von Eschen, *Race against Empire*, pp. 96–121.

56. Chafe, "Postwar American Society," pp. 166–67; Mary L. Dudziak, "Desegregation as a Cold War Imperative," *Stanford Law Review* 41 (November 1988): 77–78.

57. President's Committee on Civil Rights, *To Secure These Rights: The Report of the President's Committee on Civil Rights* (Washington, D.C.: United States Government Printing Office, 1947), pp. x, 8, 17. Two members—attorney Sadie Alexander and philanthropist Channing Tobias—were African American; Alexander was one of two women on the committee. See Florence Murray, ed., *The Negro Handbook, 1949* (New York: Macmillan, 1949), pp. 214–15.

58. *To Secure These Rights*, pp. 100–01.

59. "Civil Rights Vital to Mental Health, Psychiatrists Declare," *P.M.*, 12 November 1947, (unpaginated), in SCBCCF, "Civil Rights—Legislation: Chronology, 1938–1953," 001, 015–1. Edward Strecker, author of *Their Mothers' Sons*, was a member of this group. Other positive reactions to *To Secure These Rights* include William L. White, "The Report That Stirred America's Conscience," *Negro Digest*, May 1951, 3–5; "Jim Crow in Handcuffs," *The New Republic*, 19 June 1950, 6–7.

60. Truman's order came after the Gillem Board (a committee of Army personnel who held hearings on African Americans and the military in 1945) issued recommendations in 1946. See Dalfiume, *Desegregation of the U.S. Armed Forces*, pp. 150–55, 165–74; E. W. Kenworthy, "The Case Against Army Segregation," *Annals of the American Academy of Political and Social Science* 275, "Civil Rights in America" (May 1951): 27–33.

61. *Pittsburgh Courier* quoted in Dalfiume, *Desegregation of the U.S. Armed Forces*, pp. 74–75; Powell, *Marching Blacks*, p. 127; "The White House Jim Crow Plan," *The Crisis* 47 (November 1940): 350; "Editorial of the Month," *The Crisis* 47 (June 1940): 180.

62. For discussions of soldiering, citizenship, and gender, see Nancy Fraser, *Unruly Practices: Power, Discourse, and Gender in Contemporary Social Theory* (Minneapolis: University of Minnesota Press, 1989); Uta G. Poiger, "Rebels with a Cause? American Popular Culture, the 1956 Youth Riots, and New Conceptions of Masculinity in East and West Germany," in Reiner Pommerin, ed., *The American Impact on Postwar Germany* (Providence: Berghahn Books, 1995), pp. 93–124.

63. Lieutenant Commander Seymour J. Schoenfeld, *The Negro in the Armed Forces: His Value and Status—Past, Present, and Potential* (Washington, D.C.: The Associated Publishers, 1945), p. 55; General Joseph T. McNarney, Commander of the Mediterranean Theater of Operations, quoted in Dalfiume, *Desegregation of the U.S. Armed Forces*, p. 149; Myrdal, *An American Dilemma*, p. 1008. White advocates of military integration were not free of prejudice; see, for example, Schoenfeld, *The Negro in the Armed Forces*, p. 54; General Douglas MacArthur, quoted in Murray, ed., *The Negro Handbook, 1949*, p. 255; Bill Mauldin, "The Negro in the Post-War Army," *Negro Digest*, July 1949, 63–65; and Lloyd Wendt, "The Navy's Debt to the Negro," *Negro Digest*, September 1949, 71–74.

64. Samuel Stouffer et al., *The American Soldier: Adjustment During Army Life*, vol. 1 (Princeton: Princeton University Press, 1949), pp. 583, 549. See also Eli Ginzberg, *The Negro Potential* (New York: Columbia University Press, 1956), pp. 68–70.

65. Will Maslow, "Prejudice, Discrimination, and the Law," *Annals of the American Academy of Political and Social Science*, 275, "Civil Rights in America" (May 1951): 13–14; Ginzberg, *The Negro Potential*, pp. 88, 76; Kenworthy, "The Case Against Army Segregation," p. 28; Advisory Board quoted in *Pittsburgh Courier*, 7 June 1947, p. 1. See also Schoenfeld, *The Negro in the Armed Forces*, p. 37.

66. W. Y. Bell Jr., "The Negro Warrior's Home Front," *Phylon* 5 (1944): 276; Stouffer et

al., *The American Soldier*, p. 595; H. C. Brearley, "The Negro's New Belligerency," *Phylon* 5 (1944): 339–345, 344.

67. Arnold M. Rose, "Psychoneurotic Breakdown Among Negro Soldiers in Combat," *Phylon* 17 (1956), pp. 61, 63; Edward Strecker, *Their Mothers' Sons: The Psychiatrist Examines an American Problem* (Philadelphia: J. B. Lippincott, 1946). See also Abram Kardiner and Lionel Ovesey, *The Mark of Oppression: Explorations in the Personality of the American Negro* (Cleveland: Meridian Books, 1962 [1951]), p. 82; Ginzberg, *The Negro Potential*, pp. 70–72; and Stouffer et al., *The American Soldier*, p. 576.

68. Quoted in Chateauvert, *Marching Together*, pp. 175–76.

69. The military as black men's source of redemption is particularly evident in Daniel Patrick Moynihan, *The Negro Family: The Case for National Action*, [1965] in Lee Rainwater and William L. Yancey, eds., *The Moynihan Report and the Politics of Controversy* (Cambridge: MIT Press, 1967). For a discussion of Moynihan, see chapter 6.

70. See Daryl Scott, *Contempt and Pity: Social Policy and the Image of the Damaged Black Psyche, 1880–1996* (Chapel Hill: University of North Carolina Press, 1997), pp. 133–36; Ben Keppel, *The Work of Democracy: Ralph Bunche, Kenneth B. Clark, Lorraine Hansberry, and the Cultural Politics of Race* (Cambridge: Harvard University Press, 1995), pp. 97–133; Waldo E. Martin, Jr., *Brown v. Board of Education: A Brief History with Documents* (Boston: Bedford/St. Martin's, 1998), pp. 19–42.

71. "Appendix to Appellants' Brief," *Brown v. Board of Education*, Topeka, Kansas, (1952), in Levy, ed., *Let Freedom Ring*, pp. 34–36; "Race Prejudice is Dying," *Life*, 19 June 1950, 34; Otto Kleinberg, a social psychologist, quoted in Keppel, *Work of Democracy*, p. 98. The social psychologist Kenneth Clark testified in *Briggs*; his study, "Effect of Prejudice and Discrimination on Personality Development" influenced Chief Justice Earl Warren significantly, though Warren also cited the work of Frazier and Myrdal.

72. Brief for the United States, *Henderson v. United States*, 339 US 816 (1950), quoted in Dudziak, "Desegregation as a Cold War Imperative," p. 107. For liberal reactions to Henderson, see "Jim Crow Doomed," *The Nation*, 17 June 1950, 589–90.

73. Even a pro-civil rights position in the Democratic platform of 1948 did not correspond with a belief in substantive change among many white Democrats. See Dudziak, "Desegregation as a Cold War Imperative," p. 79, fn. 92; Von Eschen, *Race against Empire*, pp. 113–14.

74. Martin Gardner, *Ethics* 60 (1950): 297.

75. For an analysis of the inter- and intraparty conflicts affecting perspectives on federal activism, see John Lewis Gaddis, *Strategies of Containment: A Critical Appraisal of Postwar American National Security Policy* (New York: Oxford University Press, 1982).

76. Charles Rollo, *The Atlantic Monthly*, December 1949, 92, 94.

77. Schlesinger, *The Vital Center*, pp. 11, 35; Robert J. Corber, *In the Name of National Security: Hitchcock, Homophobia, and the Political Construction of Gender in Postwar America* (Durham: Duke University Press, 1993), p. 10.

78. Elaine Tyler May, *Homeward Bound: American Families in the Cold War Era* (New York: Basic Books, 1988), p. 98.

79. Schlesinger, *Vital Center*, pp. 31, 100, 36, 40.

80. Arthur Schlesinger Jr., "The Future of Socialism: III, The Perspective Now," *Partisan Review* 14 (May–June, 1947): 229–42, p. 237.

81. Schlesinger, *Vital Center*, pp. 15, xx, 147.

82. "Hard utopianism" quoted in Harry R. Davis and Robert C. Good, eds., *Reinhold Niebuhr on Politics: His Political Philosophy and Its Application to Our Age As Expressed in His Writings* (New York: Charles Scribner's Sons, 1960), p. 13; "sentimental" in Niebuhr, *The Children of Light*, p. 11. "Hard" and "soft" imagery was quite common in this period, as was the tendency to depict political opponents as "hysterical" and therefore weak. See especially "The Hards and the Softs," *New Leader*, 20 May 1950, 30, and *The Nation*, 28 June 1952, a special edition on civil liberties.

83. Schlesinger, *Vital Center*, pp. 104, 148–49, 85, 53, 151.

84. See especially Trilling, *The Liberal Imagination*, pp. 210–28; John D'Emilio, "The Homosexual Menace: The Politics of Sexuality in Cold War American," in Kathy Peiss and Christina Simmons, eds., *Passion and Power: Sexuality in History* (Philadelphia: Temple University Press, 1989), pp. 226–40.

85. See, for example, Frank Costigliola, " 'Unceasing Pressure for Penetration': Gender, Pathology and Emotion in George Kennan's Formation of the Cold War," *Journal of American History* 83 (March 1997): 1309–339; Costigliola, "The Nuclear Family: Tropes of Gender and Pathology in the Western Alliance," *Diplomatic History* 21 (spring 1997): 163–83; Melani McAlister, *Epic Encounters: Race, Religion and Nation in U.S. Representations of the Middle East* (Berkeley: University of California Press, forthcoming).

86. McAuliffe, *Crisis on the Left*, p. 49; Steven M. Gillon, *Politics and Vision: The ADA and American Liberalism, 1947–1985* (New York: Oxford University Press, 1987).

87. Schlesinger, *Vital Center*, pp. 223, 227, 36, 222, 221.

88. Schlesinger, *Vital Center*, pp. 98, 88. See also, for example, George F. Kennan, "Long Telegram" [1946] and "The Truman Doctrine" [1947], in Thomas G. Paterson, ed., *Major Problems in Foreign Policy, Documents and Essays, vol. 2, Since 1914* (Lexington, Mass.: Heath, 1984 [1978]), pp. 295–99, pp. 308–10; see also Costigliola, " 'Unceasing Pressure,' " p. 1333.

89. Clifford quoted in William H. Chafe and Harvard Sitkoff, eds., *A History of Our Time: Readings On Postwar America* (New York: Oxford University Press, 1991 [1983]), p. 55.

90. Schlesinger, *Vital Center*, pp. 204–06, 210. See also Carroll Engelhardt, "Man in the Middle: Arthur M. Schlesinger, Jr., and Postwar American Liberalism," *South Atlantic Quarterly* 80 (spring 1981): 119–42, 125–27. As Schlesinger pointed out in his 1987 introduction to *The Vital Center*, he "was denounced by J. Edgar Hoover in 1950 as 'a stinker' " (p. xii).

91. Schlesinger, *Vital Center*, pp. 170–71. In 1947 Truman issued Executive Order 9835, establishing the first loyalty investigation. Executive Order 10241, issued in April 1951, further tightened loyalty standards. For similar imagery, see Niebuhr, *Children of Light*, p. 122; Niebuhr, *The Irony of American History*, p. 79.

92. The literature analyzing these relationships is extensive. See, for example, Andreas Huyssen, *After the Great Divide: Modernism, Mass Culture, Postmodernism* (Bloomington: Indiana University Press, 1986); Sander Gilman, "The Hottentot and the Prostitute: Toward an Iconography of Female Sexuality," in Gilman, *Difference and Pathology: Stereotypes of Sexuality, Race, and Madness* (Ithaca: Cornell University Press, 1985); see also chapters 1 and 2.

93. Schlesinger, *Vital Center*, pp. 190–91. While Reinhold Niebuhr's analyses of—and effects on—American race relations were far more complex, he too explored the psychic dimensions of prejudice. See *Children of Light*, pp. 144, 138, 141. For a discussion of Niebuhr, civil rights, and Martin Luther King Jr., see Taylor Branch, *Parting the Waters: America in the King Years, 1954–1963* (New York: Simon and Schuster, 1988), pp. 81–93.

94. Schlesinger, *Vital Center*, pp. 189–91. As evidence for the idea that most American accepted the principles spelled out by the President's Committee on Civil Rights, Schlesinger noted that Truman soundly defeated Strom Thurmond, candidate of the Dixiecrat Party, in the election of 1948, and that the "revolt of southern governors" merely "signified temper tantrums rather than a cry of conscience" (p. 190).

95. Virginius Dabney, "Nearer and Nearer the Precipice," *The Atlantic Monthly*, January 1943, 94–100.

96. McAuliffe, *Crisis on the Left*, pp. 37–46, 51–57; Corber, *In the Name of National Security*.

97. See Robert K. Merton, "Discrimination and the American Creed," in R. M. MacIver, ed., *Discrimination and National Welfare* (New York: Harper and Brothers, 1949), pp. 104–06.

98. Schlesinger, *Vital Center*, pp. 207–08; see also Trilling, *The Liberal Imagination*, pref-

ace; Oscar Handlin, "Group Life within the American Pattern," *Commentary,* 8 November 1949, 411–17; and Niebuhr, *Children of Light,* p. 123. For further discussion of these themes in liberalism, see also Engelhardt, "Man in the Middle," p. 124; Gary Gerstle, "The Protean Character of American Liberalism," *American Historical Review* 99 (October 1994): 1043–73; Gleason, "Americans All," p. 504; and Andrew Ross, *No Respect: Intellectuals and Popular Culture* (New York: Routledge, 1989), pp. 42–64.

Chapter Four

1. Henry Hampton and Steve Fayer, *Voices of Freedom: An Oral History of the Civil Rights Movement from the 1950s through the 1980s* (New York: Bantam Books, 1990), pp. 1–16; Juan Williams, *Eyes on the Prize: America's Civil Rights Years, 1954–1965* (New York: Viking Penguin, 1987), p. 43. See also Stephen Whitfield, *A Death in the Delta: The Story of Emmett Till* (New York: The Free Press, 1988); Hugh Stephen Whitaker, "A Case Study in Southern Justice: The Emmett Till Case," (M.A. Thesis, Florida State University, 1963). After the trial, journalist William Bradford Huie paid the men $3,600 to tell "the real story," and they confessed to the murder. See William Bradford Huie, *Wolf Whistle* (New York: Signet, 1959); "The Shocking Story of Approved Killing in Mississippi," *Look,* 24 January 1956, 46–49; "The Shocking Story of Approved Killing in Mississippi," *Reader's Digest,* April 1956, 57–62; and "What's Happened to the Emmett Till Killers?" *Look,* 22 January 1957, 63–68. Despite ambiguities in Huie's accounts, these are frequently assumed to be the definitive texts about the murder. This chapter focuses on how and why this murder assumed meaning; the details regarding these events—the most controversial being whether or not and for what reasons Till whistled at Carolyn Bryant—have never been clarified and are not my central concern.

2. Whitfield, *A Death in the Delta,* p. 34.

3. "Will Mississippi Whitewash the Emmett Till Slaying?" *Jet,* 22 September 1955, 8; *Greensboro Daily News,* 10 November 1955 (unpaginated), in Schomburg Center on Black Culture Clipping File, 1925–1974, "Emmett Till," 005,268 (SCBCCF, "Till").

4. Meeting of the NAACP Board of Directors, 10 October 1955, NAACP Papers, supp. to pt. 1, 1951–55, reel 1, Widener Library, Harvard University; Report of the Secretary for the Month of September 1955, NAACP Papers, supp. to pt. 1, 1951–55, reel 2; "Till Protest Meeting," *The Crisis* (November 1955): 546. The trials of the young men known as the "Scottsboro boys" generated national protests in the 1930s, but the outrage outside the South over Till's murder was more unanimous; increased media coverage and the relative silence of the Communist Party also distinguished this case from Scottsboro campaigns in the 1930s. See James Goodman, *Stories of Scottsboro* (New York: Pantheon Books, 1994).

5. Arthur M. Schlesinger Jr., *The Vital Center: The Politics of Freedom* (New York: De Capo Press, 1988 [1949]), pp. 189–91; Hampton and Fayer, *Voices of Freedom,* p. 2.

6. *Chicago Defender,* 13 August 1955, p. 1; Harvard Sitkoff, *The Struggle for Black Equality, 1954–1980* (New York: Hill and Wang, 1981), p. 23.

7. Stevenson quoted in Sara Evans, *Born for Liberty: A History of Women in America* (New York: The Free Press, 1989), p. 255.

8. Joanne Meyerowitz, "Beyond the Feminine Mystique: A Reassessment of Postwar Mass Culture, 1946–1958," and Wini Breines, "The 'Other Fifties': Beats and Bad Girls," both in Meyerowitz, ed., *Not June Cleaver: Women and Gender in Postwar America, 1945–1960* (Philadelphia: Temple University Press, 1994), pp. 229–62, 382–408; *Chicago Defender,* 15 October 1955, p. 3.

9. Mamie Till Bradley had remarried and divorced after the death of Emmett Till's father, Louis Till. In 1955 she used the name Mamie Bradley, as I do in this chapter.

10. See Ruby Hurley and Amzie Moore interviews in Howell Raines, *My Soul Is Rested:*

Movement Days in the Deep South (New York: Penguin, 1983 [1977]), pp. 131–37, 233–37; Myrlie Evers and Charles Diggs interviews in Williams, *Eyes on the Prize*, pp. 46–47, 49. Scholarship linking the murder to the movement includes Hampton and Fayer, *Voices of Freedom*, pp. 1–16 (the accompanying, critically acclaimed documentary, *Eyes on the Prize*, begins with a segment on the Till murder); William Simpson, "Reflections on a Murder: The Emmett Till Case," in Frank Allen Dennis, ed., *Southern Miscellany: Essays in History in Honor of Glover Moore* (Jackson: University Press of Mississippi, 1981), pp. 177–200; Whitfield, *A Death in the Delta*, p. 107.

11. Whitaker, "A Case Study in Southern Justice," p. 127; Simpson, "Reflections on a Murder," p. 181; Whitaker, "A Case Study in Southern Justice," pp. 119–21; Gunnar Myrdal, *An American Dilemma* (New York: Harper and Brothers, 1944), p. 1003.

12. Simpson, "Reflections on a Murder"; Whitaker, "A Case Study in Southern Justice"; Whitfield, *A Death in the Delta*.

13. For what is perhaps the most troubling reading of gender and race in the Till case, see Susan Brownmiller, *Against Our Will: Men, Women and Rape* (New York: Simon and Schuster, 1975), pp. 245–48. For a response, see Angela Davis, *Women, Race and Class* (New York: Random House, 1981), pp. 172–201. For a recent erasure of Bradley, see Ronald Turner, "Remembering Emmett Till," *Howard Law Journal* 39 (spring 1995): 411–31.

14. For discussions of related maternal activism in other periods, see Richard B. Sherman, *The Case of Odell Waller and Virginia Justice, 1940–1942* (Knoxville: University of Tennessee Press, 1992); *New York Times*, 12 April 1999, p. 1.

15. See Myrl C. Boyle, "Which Are You First of All, Wife or Mother?" *Parents' Magazine*, August 1955, 35, 77–79, 82; Herman N. Bundesen, "The Overprotective Mother," *Ladies' Home Journal*, March 1950, 243–44; Elizabeth B. Hurlock, "Mothering Does Not Mean Smothering," *Today's Health* 33 (September 1955): 60–61. For discussion of motherhood, see also chapter 2.

16. Elaine Tyler May, *Homeward Bound: American Families in the Cold War Era* (New York: Basic Books, 1985), pp. 140–50; Rickie Solinger, *Wake Up Little Susie: Single Pregnancy and Race Before Roe v. Wade* (New York: Routledge, 1992).

17. *Chicago Tribune Magazine of Books*, 4 September 1955, 1; Ashley Montagu, "The Natural Superiority of Women," *Ladies' Home Journal*, July 1952, 36–37, 61–62.

18. This suburban ethos in fact relied on an economic expansion that required working women's labor outside the home.

19. George Lipsitz, *Time Passages: Collective Memory and American Popular Culture* (Minneapolis: University of Minnesota Press, 1990), p. 77; "The American Woman," *Look*, 16 October 1956, 35; also quoted in Evans, *Born for Liberty*, p. 249, emphasis added.

20. At the time of the alleged incident between Emmett Till and Carolyn Bryant, Roy Bryant was working in Texas. J. W. Milam rented out mechanical cotton pickers and was more financially secure. See Whitfield, *A Death in the Delta*, pp. 16–23; Huie, *Wolf Whistle*, pp. 17–19. For a discussion of whiteness as a compensatory wage in the nineteenth century, see David R. Roediger, *The Wages of Whiteness: Race and the Making of the American Working Class* (London: Verso, 1991).

21. Patricia Morton, *Disfigured Images: The Historical Assault on Afro-American Women* (New York: Prager, 1991), p. 76.

22. Whitfield, *A Death in the Delta*, p. 15; Williams, *Eyes on the Prize*, p. 41. Although black women's yearly pay was still less than half that of white women's (itself less than two-thirds that of white men), the percentage of black women working as domestics declined from 60 percent in 1940 to 42 percent in 1950. See Jacqueline Jones, *Labor of Love, Labor of Sorrow: Black Women, Work, and the Family From Slavery to the Present* (New York: Basic Books, 1985), p. 261; Sitkoff, *The Struggle for Black Equality*, p. 18; Paula Giddings, *When and Where I Enter: The Impact of Black Women on Race and Sex in America* (New York: Bantam Books, 1984), p. 241.

23. "Death in Mississippi," *Commonweal*, 23 September 1955, 603–04.

24. *Chicago Defender*, 5 November 1955, p. 14, emphasis added; *Pittsburgh Courier*, 20 August 1955, p. 9.

25. These ideas about middle-class women would culminate in E. Franklin Frazier, *Black Bourgeoisie* (New York: The Free Press, 1965 [1957]). For discussion of Frazier, black women, and consumption, see chapter 5.

26. Hampton and Fayer, *Voices of Freedom*, p. 5; *Chicago Daily Tribune*, 2 September 1955, p. 2.

27. Hampton and Fayer, *Voices of Freedom*, p. 5; *Pittsburgh Courier*, 10 September 1955, p. 1. The exact words Bradley used vary slightly from one account to the next, but the message remains consistent in every report. For Bradley's declaration that "I wanted the whole world to see what I had seen," see Hampton and Fayer, *Voices of Freedom*, p. 6.

28. *Chicago Defender*, 17 September 1955, p. 2; *Chicago Defender*, 10 September 1955 p. 1; *Chicago Daily Tribune*, 4 September 1955, p. 2. For an account of the impact of the service, see "Chicago Boy," *The Nation*, 17 September 1955, 235. For estimates of 10,000, see "Mississippi: The Accused," *Newsweek*, 19 September 1955, 38; for other figures see *Chicago Daily Tribune*, 4 September 1955, p. 2 (40,000); *Chicago Defender*, 10 September 1955, p. 1; and *New York Amsterdam News,* 10 September 1955, p. 1 (50,000); *Pittsburgh Courier,* 10 September 1955, p. 1; "Nation Horrified by Murder of Kidnapped Chicago Youth," *Jet*, 15 September 1955, pp. 6–9 (600,000).

29. *Chicago Defender,* 17 September 1955, p. 9.

30. Ibid.; *Baltimore Afro-American*, 17 September 1955, p. 1; *Chicago Defender,* 1 October 1955, p. 4; *Chicago Defender,* 10 September 1955, p. 5; *Baltimore Afro-American*, 10 September 1955, pp. 1, 2.

31. "Mississippi: The Place, The Acquittal," *Newsweek*, 3 October 1955, 24; *Chicago Defender*, 1 October 1955, p. 4; *Pittsburgh Courier*, 17 September 1955, p. 1. Whether or not the teenaged Till was a boy or a man and what black masculinity and sexuality meant also shaped representations of both Till and Bradley. For images of Till as a man, see Huie, *Wolf Whistle*; for the characterization of Till as an all-American boy, see "Death in Mississippi," p. 603; for a view of Till as young, innocent, and anything but masculine, see Adam Clayton Powell, quoted in *New York Amsterdam News*, 15 October 1955, p. 1; *Chicago Defender*, 10 September 1955, p. 1.

32. "Mississippi: The Accused," p. 38; *Pittsburgh Courier,* 29 October 1955, p. 9. See also "Notes," *The New Republic,* 3 October 1955, p. 2. For a discussion of the murder and anti-colonialism, see "L'affaire Till in the French Press," *The Crisis* (December 1955): 596–602.

33. *Chicago Defender*, 17 September 1955, p. 9; *New York Amsterdam News,* 1 October 1955, p. 7; "In Memoriam, Emmett Till," *Life,* 10 October 1955, 48. Bradley's status as a widow also deflected attention away from her second marriage and divorce. According to several sources, however, Bradley and Louis Till had divorced before he entered the army. See Whitfield, *A Death in the Delta*, p. 15.

34. *New York Amsterdam News*, 1 October 1955, p. 7.

35. Jones, *Labor of Love*, p. 272; Paul Molloy, "The Relief Chiselers Are Stealing Us Blind," *Saturday Evening Post*, 8 September 1951, 32–33, 142–44.

36. Black women were not among those who defended Till by addressing sexuality. See *Pittsburgh Courier,* 1 October 1955, p. 6. For a discussion of the historical effacement of black female sexuality, see Darlene Clark Hine, "Rape and the Inner Lives of Black Women in the Middle West: Preliminary Thoughts on the Culture of Dissemblance," *Signs* 14 (summer 1989): 912–20.

37. *Chicago Defender,* 1 October 1955, p. 2; *Chicago Defender,* 8 October 1955, p. 2.

38. *Chicago Tribune*, 7 September 1955, p. 5; *Chicago Defender*, 10 September 1955, p. 1; *Chicago Defender*, 17 September 1955, p. 4.

39. The *Eyes on the Prize* documentary does draw attention to Bradley's role. According to an accompanying text, "in vengeance" Bradley "declared" that the world would see her

son's corpse. This language and other descriptions of her as overly emotional diminish the *political* significance of her actions. See Williams, *Eyes on the Prize*, pp. 43–44. See also "30 Years Ago: How Emmett Till's Lynching Launched Civil Rights Drive," *Jet*, 17 June 1985, 12–18.

40. *Chicago Defender*, 10 September 1955, p. 1; *Pittsburgh Courier*, 10 September 1955, p. 4.

41. *Memphis Commercial Appeal*, 4 September 1955, sec. II, p. 4; ibid., pp. 2, 1; *Memphis Commercial Appeal*, 7 September 1955, p. 6; *Greenville Delta-Democrat Times* quoted in Whitfield, *A Death in the Delta*, p. 29; Huie, *Wolf Whistle*, p. 26.

42. Whitaker, *A Death in the Delta*, pp. 117–19; *Chicago Defender*, 29 October 1955, p. 2; *Daily Worker*, 21 October 1955, p. 1 and *Daily Worker*, 11 October 1955 (unpaginated), both in SCBCCF, "Till"; *New York Times*, 30 October 1955, p. 87; *Jackson Daily News*, 15 October 1955, p. 1; "Extension of remarks of E. L. Forrester," *Congressional Record* (24 July 1956) 102, pt. 10: 14317. The guilt or innocence of Louis Till and the details surrounding his court-martial and hanging remain in dispute, particularly in light of the fact that in Europe during World War II, eighty-seven of the ninety-five soldiers hanged for rape and murder of civilians were African American. At least one of Till's peers in the segregated unit suggested that he had been "railroaded" by MPs enforcing "nonfraternization bans." Bradley asserted that the federal government never told her how or why her husband had died; she later noted that "Louis was never allowed to testify. . . . [T]he case was built on the testimony of what someone else said." See "GI Buddies Say Till's Dad Was 'Railroaded' in Italy," *Jet*, 3 November 1955, 4–5; *New York Amsterdam News*, 1 October 1955, p. 7; "Time Heals Few Wounds for Emmett Till's Mother," *Jet*, 9 April 1984, 55.

43. *Memphis Commercial Appeal*, 6 September 1955, pp. 1, 8; *Memphis Commercial Appeal*, 4 September 1955, sec. II, p. 4.

44. *Chicago Defender*, 17 September 1955, p. 1; Mary Cain, quoted in Ira Harkey, *The Smell of Burning Crosses: An Autobiography of a Mississippi Newspaperman* (Jacksonville, Ill.: Harris-Wolfe, 1967), p. 106.

45. Morton, *Disfigured Images*, pp. 70–72.

46. *Chicago Defender*, 17 September 1955, p. 2; *New York Amsterdam News*, 1 October 1955, p. 12, 8; *Pittsburgh Courier*, 29 October 1955, p. 9; *Pittsburgh Courier*, 22 October 1955, p. 1.

47. *Chicago Defender*, 24 September 1955, p. 1; Whitfield, *A Death in the Delta*, p. 33.

48. *Chicago Defender*, 1 October 1955, p. 1; Ruby Hurley and Medgar Evers, NAACP staff workers in Mississippi, located Amanda Bradley and Willie Reed, the two "surprise witnesses," and encouraged them to testify. Report of the Secretary for the Month of September 1955, NAACP Papers, supp. to pt. 1, 1951–55, reel 2; David Shostak, "Crosby Smith: Forgotten Witness to a Mississippi Nightmare," *Negro History Bulletin* (December 1974): 320–25.

49. *New York Times*, 22 September 1955, p. 64; Hampton and Fayer, *Voices of Freedom*, p. 11; Whitfield, *A Death in the Delta*, p. 39; *Labor Action*, 28 November 1955 (unpaginated), in SCBCCF, "Till." See also Rob F. Hall, "The Press and the Trial at Sumner," *The Worker*, 13 November 1955 (unpaginated), in SCBCCF, "Till."

50. "Mississippi: The Place, The Acquittal," p. 25; Simpson, "Reflections on a Murder," p. 192. There were six other "character witnesses" for the defense. Although 63 percent of the population in Tallahatchie County was African American, no blacks were eligible for jury service—dependent as it was on voter registration. Jury duty in Tallahatchie County was so severely restricted that only 5 percent of the county population was eligible. See Whitfield, *A Death in the Delta*, p. 35.

51. *Baltimore Afro-American*, 24 September 1955, pp. 14, 1; *Memphis Commercial Appeal*, 21 September 1955, p. 8.

52. For an account of the dangers Bradley faced, see *Memphis Commercial Appeal*, 25 September 1955, p. 1.

53. *Memphis Commercial Appeal*, 8 September 1955, p. 1; *Memphis Commercial Appeal*, 20

September 1955, p. 15. The texts of these telegrams suggest that even the men prosecuting the case were not allies of Till's family. For more on the legal team, see *Memphis Commercial Appeal*, 18 September 1955, sec. V, p. 10; Simpson, "Reflections on a Murder," pp. 185–87; Whitfield, *A Death in the Delta*, pp. 31, 41, 56.

54. *Memphis Commercial Appeal*, 21 September 1955, p. 8.

55. *Pittsburgh Courier*, 24 September 1955, pp. 1, 4; *Chicago Defender*, 1 October 1955, p. 4; "L'affaire Till in the French Press," pp. 596–602.

56. *Memphis Commercial Appeal*, 23 September 1955, p. 8; *New York Times*, 23 September 1955, p. 15; *Memphis Commercial Appeal*, 23 September 1955, p. 2; Whitfield, *A Death in the Delta*, pp. 40–42.

57. "Mississippi: The Place, The Acquittal," p. 24.

58. *Memphis Commercial Appeal*, 20 September 1955, p. 1; *Chicago Defender*, 24 September 1955, p. 2; *Memphis Commercial Appeal*, 7 September 1955, p. 1; *Memphis Commercial Appeal*, 22 September 1955, p. 33; Whitfield, *A Death in the Delta*, p. 37. Congressman Charles C. Diggs (D. Mich.) was among those at the segregated table.

59. For accounts of their subsequent economic difficulties and southerners' efforts to distance themselves from the men, see Hampton and Fayer, *Voices of Freedom*, p. 14; Raines, *My Soul Is Rested*, p. 392; and Huie, *Wolf Whistle*. See Nancy Maclean, "The Leo Frank Case Reconsidered: Gender and Sexual Politics in the Making of Reactionary Populism," *Journal of American History* (December 1991): 917–48, for how gender informed class conflicts and racial politics during this notorious murder trial in 1913.

60. Forrester, "Extension of Remarks," p. 14, 317; *Memphis Commercial Appeal*, 24 September 1955, p. 17; *Chicago Daily Tribune*, 24 September 1955, p. 2. See also *Memphis Commercial Appeal*, 24 September 1955, p. 1; *New York Times*, 24 September 1955, p. 1.

61. The state called one funeral director who testified that the body was Till's, but prosecutors made no effort to confirm the identity of the body scientifically. See Simpson, "Reflections on a Murder," pp. 189–90. For an account of Bradley's willingness to exhume the body, see *New York Times*, 30 September 1955, p. 18.

62. *New York Times*, 24 September 1955, p. 38.

63. *Chicago Defender*, 1 October 1955, p. 4.

64. "Trial By Jury," *Time*, 3 October 1955, p. 18; *Memphis Commercial Appeal*, 23 September 1955, p. 1; I. F. Stone, "The Murder of Emmett Till," in *The Haunted Fifties* (New York: Random House, 1963), p. 107.

65. For objections among African Americans to this emphasis on humility, see NAACP Correspondence: Mississippi Pressures, 1955, NAACP Papers; *Chicago Defender*, 17 September 1955, p. 9.

66. *New York Times*, 23 September 1955, p. 15; *New York Times*, 24 September 1955, pp. 1, 38.

67. *Pittsburgh Courier*, 1 October 1955, p. 4; *Chicago Defender*, 1 October 1955, p. 1; "Mississippi: The Place, the Acquittal," pp. 24, 29. Representations of Bradley as emotional did not always break down along regional or political lines. See *Memphis Commercial Appeal*, 23 September 1955, p. 35.

68. *Pittsburgh Courier*, 1 October 1955, p. 8; "L'affaire Till in the French Press," p. 600.

69. *New York Times*, 24 September 1955, p. 1, 38; *Chicago Daily Tribune*, 24 September 1955, p. 1. The similarities between Bradley's treatment and that which Anita Hill received are noteworthy. The Bryant/Milam defense team tried to "prove" a relationship between Bradley and the NAACP to discredit the "grieving mother." So, too, in the Anita Hill-Clarence Thomas hearings, hostile senators repeatedly asked Hill if she was "acting alone." Both women also faced a "damned if you do, damned if you don't" framework—which discredited them both because of their composure *and* their irrationality. See Elsa Barkley Brown, " 'What Has Happened Here': The Politics of Difference in Women's History and Feminist Politics," *Feminist Studies* 18 (summer 1992): 302–7; Toni Morrison, ed., *Race*-ing

Justice, En-*Gender*ing *Power: Essays on Anita Hill, Clarence Thomas and the Construction of Social Reality* (New York: Pantheon Books, 1992).

70. Stone, "The Murder of Emmett Till," p. 108.

71. *New York Times,* 24 September 1955, pp. 1, 38; *Pittsburgh Courier,* 1 October 1955, p. 1.

72. *New York Amsterdam News,* 8 October 1955, p. 21.

73. "Till Case Spotlights New Negro Militancy," *Labor Action,* 28 November 1955 (unpaginated), in SCBCCF, "Till"; Board of Directors Meeting, 10 October 1955, NAACP Papers, supp. to pt. 1, 1951–55, reel 1; *New York Times,* 3 October 1955, p. 19. For details about the range of contributors, see NAACP Papers, supp. to pt. 1, 1951–55, reel 2.

74. Hall, "The Press and the Trial at Sumner." See also Louis E. Burnham, *Behind the Lynching of Emmett Louis Till* (New York: Freedom Associates, 1955).

75. *Pittsburgh Courier,* 19 November 1955, p. 2; *New York Amsterdam News,* 19 November 1955, p. 1; Board of Directors Meeting, 14 November 1955, NAACP Papers, supp. to pt. 1, 1951–55, reel 1. The details of this conflict are unclear and are not my central concern. More significant to this discussion is how these events assumed meaning.

76. *Chicago Defender,* 19 November 1955, p. 2.

77. *Chicago Defender,* 26 November 1955, p. 1.

78. *Chicago Daily Tribune,* 7 September 1955, p. 5; *New York Amsterdam News,* 19 November 1955, pp. 1, 27; Report of the Secretary for the Month of September 1955, NAACP Papers, supp. to pt. 1, 1951–55, reel 2.

79. *Chicago Defender,* 15 October 1955, p. 2; *Pittsburgh Courier,* 26 November 1955, p. 12; *Pittsburgh Courier,* 29 October 1955, p. 3; *Chicago Defender,* 22 October 1955, p. 2.

80. *New York Amsterdam News,* 1 October 1955, p. 9; *Pittsburgh Courier,* 24 December 1955, p. 3; *Chicago Defender,* 22 October 1955, p. 2.

81. *Life,* 10 October 1955, 53; *Chicago Defender,* 29 October 1955, p. 1. Bradley had also sent a telegram to President Eisenhower, then recovering from a heart attack; the president did not respond. See Whitfield, *A Death in the Delta,* pp. 72–74. For an account of Washington rallies, see *New York Amsterdam News,* 29 October 1955, p. 3. For details of the attorney general's decision not to investigate the murder, see *New York Post,* 6 December 1955 (unpaginated), in SCBCCF, "Till."

82. *Pittsburgh Courier,* 29 October 1955, p. 9; *Chicago Defender,* 29 October 1955, p. 2. This editorial appears to be the first time Bradley is referred to simply as "Mamie" in the African American press; reporters and other observers had paid close attention to the titles, and lack thereof, whites had shown to blacks involved in the case.

83. *Pittsburgh Courier,* 1 October 1955, pp. 1, 4.

84. *Chicago Defender,* 26 November 1955, p. 1; *New York Amsterdam News,* 26 November 1955, p. 8.

85. *Pittsburgh Courier,* 19 November 1955, p. 2; *Chicago Defender,* 26 November 1955, p. 2; "How the Till Case Changed 5 Lives," *Jet,* 24 November 1955, 10. Chicago reporters seemed particularly intent on salvaging Mamie Bradley's reputation; perhaps to them, the city in general was potentially implicated in any scandal.

86. *New York Amsterdam News,* 19 November 1955, p. 27; *Chicago Defender,* 19 November 1955, pp. 2, 1; *Chicago Defender,* 8 October 1955, p. 1; *Chicago Defender,* 26 November 1955, pp. 1, 2. For an interesting blend of criticism and praise, see Edward Barnes Henry, "The Right View of Emmett Till's Case" (1956), pp. 15–16, pamphlet in SCBCCF, "Till."

87. *Chicago Defender,* 3 December 1955, p. 9; "How the Till Case Changed 5 Lives," p. 13.

88. *New York Amsterdam News,* 19 November 1955, pp. 1, 27; *Chicago Defender,* 19 November 1955, pp. 1, 2; *New York Amsterdam News,* 19 November 1955, pp. 1, 2. See also "How the Till Case Changed 5 Lives," pp. 10–13; *Daily Worker,* 22 November 1955 (unpaginated), in SCBCCF, "Till."

89. *Chicago Defender,* 19 November 1955, p. 2; *Pittsburgh Courier,* 24 December 1955, p. 3.

90. *Pittsburgh Courier,* 24 December 1955, pp. 3, 6; *Chicago Defender,* 24 December 1955,

p. 1. For efforts to "rehabilitate" Bradley, see also "Mamie Bradley's Untold Story, Told By Mamie Bradley, as Told to Ethel Payne," *Chicago Defender*, 21 April 1956, p. 8, and 28 April 1956, p. 10.

91. Quoted in *Pittsburgh Courier*, 24 December 1955, p. 3.

92. Studs Terkel, *Race: How Blacks and Whites Think and Feel about the American Obsession* (New York: Norton, 1992), p. 22; see also "30 Years Ago: How Emmett Till's Lynching Launched Civil Rights Drive," *Jet*, 17 June 1985, 12–18. For details of Bradley's efforts to preserve the memory of her son and to counter misrepresentations of him, see *New York Post*, 18 January 1956 (regarding a proposed movie deal), (unpaginated) in SCBCCF, "Till"; *Pittsburgh Courier*, 1 February 1958, p. 3 (for her lawsuit against *Look* and Huie).

93. *Baltimore Afro-American*, 24 September 1955, p. 4; "Inside You and Me," *The Crisis* (December 1955): 592–95.

94. Moore, in Raines, *My Soul Is Rested*, pp. 234–35; *New York Amsterdam News*, 8 October 1955, p. 10; *Pittsburgh Courier*, 10 September 1955, p. 1.

95. Clay, quoted in Whitfield, *A Death in the Delta*, p. 94; *New York Times*, 17 May 1979, p. A-23. See also Edward Strong, "The Till Case and the Negro Liberation Movement," *Political Affairs* 34 (December 1955): 35–51, esp. p. 40; Endesha Ida Mae Holland, "Memories of the Mississippi Delta," *Michigan Quarterly Review* 26 (winter 1987): 246–58; Anne Moody, *Coming of Age in Mississippi* (New York: Dell, 1968), pp. 125–29; Cloyte Murdock Larsson, "Land of the Till Murder Revisited," *Ebony*, March 1986, 53–58; Shelby Steele, "On Being Black and Middle Class," *Commentary*, January 1988, 42–47; and Michael Eric Dyson, *Reflecting Black: African American Cultural Criticism* (Minneapolis: University of Minnesota Press, 1993), pp. 194–98. For fiction and poetry that draw on Till's murder, see, among others, Gwendolyn Brooks, "A Bronzeville Mother Loiters in Mississippi. Meanwhile, a Mississippi Mother Burns Bacon," and "The Last Quatrain of the Ballad of Emmett Till," in *The Bean Eaters* (New York: Harper and Brothers, 1960), pp. 19–26; Alice Walker, "Advancing Luna—and Ida B. Wells," in *You Can't Keep a Good Woman Down* (New York: Harcourt Brace Jovanovich, 1981), pp. 85–104; Bebe Moore Campbell, *Your Blues Ain't Like Mine* (New York: G. P. Putnam's Sons, 1992); and Lewis Nordan, *Wolf Whistle: A Novel* (Chapel Hill: Algonquin Books of Chapel Hill, 1993).

96. For the political dimensions of motherhood in this period, see also Deborah A. Gerson, " 'Is Family Devotion Now Subversive?' Familialism Against McCarthyism," in Meyerowitz, ed., *Not June Cleaver*, pp. 151–76; Amy Swerdlow, *Women Strike For Peace: Traditional Motherhood and Radical Politics in the 1960s* (Chicago: University of Chicago Press, 1993).

97. Jones, *Labor of Love*, pp. 279–80.

98. Dyson, *Reflecting Black*, p. 194.

Chapter Five

1. Arthur Schlesinger Jr., "Where Does the Liberal Go from Here?" *The New York Times Magazine*, 4 August 1957, 7, 38; David Riesman, *Abundance for What? And Other Essays* (New York: Doubleday, 1964). For discussions of this shift in focus, see Richard Pells, *The Liberal Mind in a Conservative Age: American Intellectuals in the 1940s and 1950s* (New York: Harper and Row, 1985), pp. 183–261; Andrew Ross, *No Respect: Intellectuals and Popular Culture* (New York: Routledge, 1989), pp. 42–64. Assumptions about economic growth persisted despite the onset of a recession in late 1957.

2. James Patterson, *Grand Expectations: The United States, 1945–1974* (New York: Oxford University Press, 1996), p. 413.

3. Albert Johnson, "Beige, Brown or Black," *Film Quarterly* 13 (fall 1959): 38–43; Alan Brinkley, *Liberalism and Its Discontents* (Cambridge: Harvard University Press, 1998), pp. 96–100.

4. Bosley Crowther, "Screen: Sob Story Back," *New York Times*, 18 April 1959, p. 18; Crowther, "Detergent Drama," *New York Times*, 19 April 1959, (2), p. 1; Jackie Byars, *All that Hollywood Allows: Re-Reading Gender in 1950s Melodrama* (Chapel Hill: University of North Carolina Press, 1991), p. 238; *Imitation of Life* (1959), screenplay by Eleanore Griffin and Allan Scott, directed by Douglas Sirk, starring Lana Turner (Lora Meredith), Juanita Moore (Annie Johnson), Sandra Dee (the white daughter as teenager), and Susan Kohner (the black daughter as teenager).

5. Sirk, quoted in Michael Stern, "*Imitation of Life*" [1979], in Lucy Fischer, ed., *Imitation of Life: Douglas Sirk, Director* (New Brunswick: Rutgers University Press, 1991), p. 279. The film continues to strike a chord within and beyond academia. See Stephen Farber, "The Movie that Changed My Life," *Movieline*, December 1996, 63–67, 86, 95. For a bibliography of *Imitation of Life* scholarship up to 1991, see Fischer, ed., *Imitation of Life;* see also chapter 1.

6. For discussions of consumption in the 1920s, see, for example, Robert Lynd and Helen Lynd, *Middletown: A Study in Contemporary American Culture* (New York: Harcourt, Brace, 1929). Although there are important differences between "mass culture" and "popular culture," many critics in the late 1950s saw these terms as related. See, for example, Chandler Brossard, ed., *The Scene Before You: A New Approach to American Culture* (New York: Rinehart and Co., 1955); Bernard Rosenberg and David White, eds., *Mass Culture: The Popular Arts in America* (New York: Free Press, 1957).

7. Elaine Tyler May, *Homeward Bound: American Families in the Cold War Era* (New York: Basic Books, 1988), p. 167; Pells, *The Liberal Mind*, p. 165; Godfrey Hodgson, *America in Our Time* (New York: Vintage, 1976), pp. 78–82.

8. Stephen J. Whitfield, *The Culture of the Cold War* (Baltimore: Johns Hopkins University Press, 1996 [1991]), pp. 70–71; George Katona, *The Mass Consumption Society* (New York: McGraw-Hill, 1964), p. 5.

9. Jacqueline Jones, *Labor of Love, Labor of Sorrow: Black Women, Work and the Family from Slavery to the Present* (New York: Basic Books, 1985), p. 261; Harvard Sitkoff, *The Struggle for Black Equality, 1954–1980* (New York: Hill and Wang, 1981), p. 18; Paula Giddings, *When and Where I Enter: The Impact of Black Women on Race and Sex in America* (New York: William Morrow, 1984), p. 241.

10. See, for example, Gilbert Seldes, "Radio, TV, and the Common Man," *Saturday Review of Literature*, 29 August 1953, 11–12, 39–41; see also Pells, *The Liberal Mind*, pp. 219–20.

11. Schlesinger, "Where Does the Liberal Go from Here?" p. 38; Pells, *The Liberal Mind*, pp. 216–26. While critiques of popular culture predated the 1950s, they became more prevalent in this period, in part because of the influence of the Frankfurt School. For an early and influential articulation, see Clement Greenberg, "Avant-Garde and Kitsch," *Partisan Review* 6 (fall 1939): 39–49.

12. Nixon quoted in May, *Homeward Bound*, pp. 16–17; see also pp. 164–67.

13. National Manpower Council, *Womanpower: A Statement by the National Manpower Council with Chapters by the Council Staff* (New York: Columbia University Press, 1957), p. 46. Thirty percent of all married women worked in the labor force by 1960; see Susan Hartmann, "Women's Employment and the Domestic Ideal in the Early Cold War Years," in Joanne Meyerowitz, ed., *Not June Cleaver: Women and Gender in Postwar America, 1945–1960* (Philadelphia: Temple University Press, 1994), p. 86.

14. Paul Goodman, *Growing Up Absurd: Problems of Youth in the Organized System* (New York: Random House, 1960 [1956]), pp. 13–14; Arthur Schlesinger Jr., "The Crisis of American Masculinity," *Esquire*, November 1958, 63–65; William Atwood, "The American Male: Why Does He Work So Hard?" *Look*, 4 March 1958, 71; also quoted in Barbara Ehrenreich, *The Hearts of Men: American Dreams and the Flight From Commitment* (New York: Anchor Books, 1983), p. 39. For a discussion of masculinity and the social sciences, see Wini Breines, *Young, White And Miserable: Growing Up Female In The Fifties* (Boston: Beacon Press, 1992).

15. John Kenneth Galbraith, *The Affluent Society* (London: Hamish Hamilton, 1958); Pells, *The Liberal Mind*, pp. 165, 173; *New York Herald Tribune Book Review*, 1 June 1958, 3.

16. Galbraith, *The Affluent Society*, p. 119; *The Atlantic*, July 1958, 85.

17. Galbraith, *The Affluent Society*, p. 200.

18. Galbraith, *The Affluent Society*, pp. 121, 110, 109, 199. See also "Our Country and Our Culture," *Partisan Review* 19 (May–June 1952): 282–315.

19. For background on this relationship as it took shape, see Andreas Huyssen, "Mass Culture as Woman: Modernism's Other," in Huyssen, *After the Great Divide: Modernism, Mass Culture, Postmodernism* (Bloomington: Indiana University Press, 1986), pp. 44–62; Mary Louise Roberts, "Gender, Consumption, and Commodity Culture," *American Historical Review* 103 (June 1998): 817–44.

20. *Chicago Defender*, 22 October 1955, p. 2.

21. E. Franklin Frazier, *Black Bourgeoisie: The Rise of a New Middle Class* (New York: The Free Press, 1957). Frazier originally published his study in French with the title *Bourgeoisie Noire* in 1955.

22. *The Nation*, 13 April 1957, 327; *The New International* (spring 1957) (unpaginated); *The New York Post*, 12 May 1957 (unpaginated); and *Political Affairs* (July 1957) (unpaginated); all in Schomburg Center on Black Culture Clipping File, 1925–1974, "E. Franklin Frazier," 001, 833,1, and 005,268 (SCBCCF, "Frazier"); August Meier, "Some Observations on the Negro Middle Class" [1957], in Meier, *A White Scholar and the Black Community, 1945–1965: Essays and Reflections* (Amherst: University of Massachusetts Press, 1992), pp. 88–98.

23. Meier, "Some Observations on the Negro Middle Class," pp. 93, 97; *Publishers Weekly*, 18 March 1957, 47; *New York Times*, 9 March 1957 (unpaginated), SCBCCF, "Frazier."

24. Frazier, *Black Bourgeoisie*, pp. 12, 80–81.

25. Frazier, *Black Bourgeoisie*, pp. 151, 57, 208, 212.

26. Kenneth Clark, *Prejudice and Your Child* (Boston: Beacon Press, 1963 [1955]), p. 39.

27. Frazier, *Black Bourgeoisie*, pp. 131, 147–49, 213, 24–25. See also Clark, *Prejudice and Your Child*, p. 55; Dale R. Vlasek, "E. Franklin Frazier and the Problem of Assimilation," in Hamilton Cravens, ed., *Ideas In America's Cultures: From Republic to Mass Society* (Ames: Iowa State University Press, 1982), pp. 141–79.

28. Frazier, *Black Bourgeoisie*, pp. 202, 213, 202, 200, 222, 218, 230, 222. See also Louie Robinson, "The Care and Feeding of Negro Women," *Negro Digest*, September 1961, 9–12.

29. Frazier, *Black Bourgeoisie*, pp. 200–01; Jones, *Labor of Love*, pp. 268–74.

30. Frazier, *Black Bourgeoisie*, pp. 220–21.

31. Frazier, *Black Bourgeoisie*, pp. 221–23.

32. "Mike Wallace Asks E. Franklin Frazier," *New York Post*, 20 March 1958 (unpaginated), in SCBCCF, "Frazier"; Frazier, *Black Bourgeoisie*, p. 221.

33. Frazier, *Black Bourgeoisie*, pp. 103–04; Penny M. Von Eschen, *Race against Empire: Black Americans and Anticolonialism, 1937–1957* (Ithaca: Cornell University Press, 1997), pp. 149–59.

34. "Mike Wallace Asks E. Franklin Frazier."

35. As the threats persisted, the teenager got a knife. When her mother's bedroom door opened and she thought Stompanato lunged at Turner, Crane moved toward him. The knife punctured his aorta, and Stompanato died within minutes. This summary is based on the account given in Cheryl Crane with Cliff Jahr, *Detour: A Hollywood Story* (New York: Arbor House, 1988), pp. 219–26, 238; Lana Turner, *The Lady, The Legend, The Truth: Lana* (New York: Dutton, 1982); and from media accounts of the murder at the time.

36. *Los Angeles Times*, 12 April 1958, p. 1; "Cheryl—If . . . If . . . If," *Newsweek*, 21 April 1958, 36; *New York Times*, 25 April 1958, p. 21; *Los Angeles Times*, 25 April 1958, p. 1.

37. *Los Angeles Times*, 12 April 1958, p. 1; *New York Times*, 10 April 1958, p. 22. Stompanato was a longtime friend and one-time bodyguard of mobster Mickey Cohen. See *Los*

Angeles Times, 6 April 1958, p. 1. The murder received the most coverage in Los Angeles, where the *Los Angeles Times* devoted multiple front-page stories and banner headlines to it every day from 6 April to 14 April.

38. *New York Times*, 1 July 1995, p. 9; Crane, *Detour*, p. 328; obituary for Lana Turner, Morning Edition National Public Radio, 30 June 1995.

39. *New York Times*, 1 July 1995, p. 9; Richard Dyer, "Four Films of Lana Turner," [1977–78], in Dyer, *Only Entertainment* (New York: Routledge, 1992), pp. 65–98; Hopper quoted in "Death on the Pink Carpet," *Time*, 14 April 1958, 21. In 1958 Turner had been married five times to four men: to Artie Shaw (1940), to Stephen Crane (1942 and 1943–44), to Bob Topping (1948–51), and to Lex Barker (1953–57).

40. Quoted in Pells, *The Liberal Mind*, p. 206; *Chicago Defender*, 23 April 1960, p. 19.

41. "Sweater Girl Lana's Build-Up to a Tragedy," *Life*, 7 April 1958, 43; "Hollywood: The Bad and the Beautiful," *Time*, 21 April 1958, 17.

42. *Los Angeles Times*, 6 April 1958, p. 3; "Hollywood: The Bad and the Beautiful," p. 17.

43. "California: Tragic Life of A Star," *Newsweek*, 14 April 1958, 37–38; "Death on the Pink Carpet," p. 21; "Hollywood: The Bad and the Beautiful," p. 17.

44. "Sweater Girl Lana's Build-Up to a Tragedy," p. 43; *Los Angeles Times*, 6 April 1958, p. 3. The publication of love letters between Turner and Stompanato also discredited Turner's claims of abuse; see "Lana's Plea for Daughter is Real-Life Drama Triumph," *Life*, 21 April 1958, 22–23; *Los Angeles Times*, 9 April 1958, p. 1; *Los Angeles Times*, 10 April 1958, pp. 2, 24. Their final quarrel began when she found out that he was lying about his age. See "Hollywood: The Bad and the Beautiful," p. 18.

45. "California: Tragic Life of a Star," p. 38; *Los Angeles Times*, 8 April 1958, p. 3; *Los Angeles Times*, 6 April 1958, p. 3; "Sweater Girl Lana's Build-Up to a Tragedy," p. 44. Stephen Crane, Cheryl's father and Turner's ex-husband, figured prominently in accounts that highlighted traditional family loyalty in what seemed to be anything but a traditional family. See, for example, *Los Angeles Times*, 6 April 1958, p. B; *Life*, 17 April 1958, 44–45.

46. "Lana's Plea for Daughter is Real-Life Drama Triumph," p. 21; *Los Angeles Times*, 12 April 1958, p. 1. See also "Cheryl—If . . . If . . . If," p. 34.

47. *Los Angeles Times*, 12 April 1958, p. 1; "Hollywood: The Bad and the Beautiful," p. 18; *Los Angeles Times*, 12 April 1958, p. B; "Lana's Plea for Daughter is Real-Life Drama Triumph," p. 21. See also "California: Tragic Life of a Star," p. 37. Box office attendance at *Peyton Place*, which had been showing in theaters for four months and in which Turner's character testified at the trial of a female teen, jumped 32 percent after the murder. See Crane, *Detour*, p. 237.

48. "California: Death on the Pink Carpet," p. 21; "California: Tragic Life of a Star," p. 37; see also Crane, *Detour*, p. 242. Accusations that "the girl was in love" with Stompanato and that there was "jealousy between her and her mother" also undermined images of Turner as a wholesome mother. See *Los Angeles Times*, 12 April 1958, p. A; Crane, *Detour*, pp. 240–41. It is worth noting the nearly constant references to Cheryl as "child." Though she was the same age as Emmett Till at the time of his murder and was five feet seven inches tall, Crane eluded the controversy that surrounded Till's appearance—did he look like a child or a man?

49. *Los Angeles Times*, 12 April 1958, p. A; "Cheryl—If . . . If . . . If," p. 36. See also *New York Times*, 12 April 1958, p. 1; "Lana's Plea for Daughter is Real-Life Drama Triumph," p. 24. This perspective received added weight when members of Stompanato's family sued Turner for $750,000 in damages on the basis of "parental negligence." According to the suit, Turner had "failed, neglected, and refused to exercise proper or sufficient control or super-vision over Cheryl" (*New York Times*, 23 April 1958, p. 42). Turner settled the suit and paid $20,000 in what she called " 'peace money' " (Crane, *Detour*, p. 304).

50. *Los Angeles Times*, 12 April 1958, pt. III, p. 4.

51. Crane, *Detour*, p. 272. See also "Wringing Wet," *Newsweek*, 13 April 1959 (unpagi-nated) and *Commonweal*, 17 April 1959 (unpaginated), in SCBCCF, *"Imitation of Life,"*

003,242; and "Success Won't Get You Happiness, Bub" [1959], in Fischer, ed., *Imitation of Life*, pp. 237–38.

52. For a discussion of Sarah Jane's sexuality, consumption, and racial repudiations, see Lauren Berlant, "National Brands/National Body: *Imitation of Life*," in Hortense Spillers, ed., *Comparative American Identities: Race, Sex, and Nationality in the Modern Text* (New York: Routledge, 1991), esp. p. 139, fn. 44.

53. The lyrics include "an empty purse can make a good girl bad . . . so fill me up with what I formerly had."

54. Sandy Flitterman-Lewis, "*Imitation*(s) *of Life*: The Black Woman's Double Determination as Troubling 'Other' " [1988], in Fischer, ed., *Imitation of Life*, pp. 326, 332–33; Mary Ann Doane, *Femmes Fatales: Feminism, Film Theory, and Psychoanalysis* (New York: Routledge, 1991), pp. 236–38. For a discussion of the mulatta woman, see Berlant, "National Brands/National Body," pp. 113–14; for a discussion of the women's performances, see Judith Butler, "Lana's Imitation: Melodramatic Repetition and the Gender Performative," *Genders* 9 (fall 1990): 1–18.

55. Racially determined power differentials between the women and their daughters persist in the 1959 *Imitation*. In the New York apartment, Annie and Sarah Jane occupy a small back room; later, Susie attends an elite boarding school while Sarah Jane remains at home. For a consideration of Annie as subordinate, see Marina Heung, " 'What's the Matter with Sarah Jane?': Daughters and Mothers in Douglas Sirk's *Imitation of Life*" [1987], in Fischer, ed., *Imitation of Life*, pp. 302–24. The film is unclear about whether Annie is "chief maid" or whether her status is different from that of a maid. For a discussion of this ambiguity, see Michael Stern, "*Imitation of Life*," p. 280.

56. Annie rejects Steven's offer to make a train reservation for her from New York to California.

57. Annie (and Steven Archer) are "implicated in female fraudulence because of their addiction to it." See Berlant, "National Brands/National Body," p. 131.

58. For Rainer Werner Fassbinder's assessment that Annie is "brutal, wanting to possess her child because she loves her," see Fassbinder, "Imitation of Life" [1971], in Fischer, ed., *Imitation of Life*, p. 245; Byars, *All That Hollywood Allows*, p. 249. For more on the women as foils to each other, see, for example, Jeremy Butler, "*Imitation of Life* (1934 and 1959)" [1986], in Fischer, ed., *Imitation of Life*, p. 298; Heung, " 'What's the Matter with Sarah Jane?' " pp. 306–08; Lucy Fischer, "Three-Way Mirror: *Imitation of Life*," in Fischer, ed., *Imitation of Life*, pp. 16–17.

59. I would suggest that the film implicitly imagined a white liberal viewer. Discussions of audience and gender include Laura Mulvey, *Visual and Other Pleasures* (Macmillan, 1989). See also Flitterman-Lewis, "*Imitation*(s) *of Life*," pp. 50, 54–55.

60. *New York Times*, 18 April 1959, p. 18; Fischer, "Three-Way Mirror," p. 19. The self-centered Lora never imagines the existence of this community in Annie's life. "It never occurred to me that you had many friends," she says before Annie's death. "Miss Lora, you never asked," responds Annie.

61. James Harvey, "Sirkumstantial Evidence," *Film Comment* 14 (July–August 1978): 55; see also Jon Halliday, *Sirk on Sirk* (New York: Viking, 1972), p. 132.

62. Amiri Baraka, "A Critical Evaluation: *A Raisin in the Sun*'s Enduring Passion," in Lorraine Hansberry, *A Raisin in the Sun and the Sign in Sidney Brustein's Window* (New York: Vintage Books, 1995 [1986]), p. 18; Johnson, "Beige, Brown or Black," p. 43.

63. E. Franklin Frazier, "The MacIver Award Lecture: The Negro Middle Class and Desegregation," *Social Problems* (April 1957): 296; Frazier, *Black Bourgeoisie*, pp. 94–98. For a discussion of "relative deprivation" among middle-class black college students, see Ruth Searles and J. Allen Williams Jr., "Negro College Students' Participation in Sit-Ins," *Social Forces* 40 (March 1962): 216.

64. *Chicago Defender*, 26 March 1960, p. 2.

65. Students in Nashville had trained for such protests for over a year. For accounts of

sit-ins in shopping centers, drive-ins, and drugstores, see Franklin McCain in Howell Raines, *My Soul Is Rested: Movement Days in the Deep South Remembered* (New York: Putnam, 1977), p. 81; Henry Hampton and Steve Fayer, *Voices of Freedom: An Oral History of the Civil Rights Movement from the 1950s through the 1980s* (New York: Bantam Books, 1990), pp. 53–71; and Robert Weisbrot, *Freedom Bound: A History of America's Civil Rights Movement* (New York: Norton, 1990), pp. 18–44; for the figure of 78 cities, see Sitkoff, *The Struggle for Black Equality*, p. 72; for a contemporary account of numbers of protesters and their impact, see "Negro Youth's New March on Dixie," *Saturday Evening Post*, 8 September 1962, 15–19. According to the UPI, the sit-ins were one of the ten most significant events in 1960; see *Chicago Defender*, 24–30 December 1960, p. 3.

66. This discussion of sit-ins is meant to be suggestive. Comprehensive local studies and memoirs of sit-ins include William Chafe, *Civilities and Civil Rights: Greensboro, North Carolina, and the Black Struggle for Freedom* (New York: Oxford University Press, 1980); Martin Oppenheimer, *The Sit-In Movement of 1960* (Brooklyn: Carlson Publishers, 1989); Merrill Proudfoot, *Diary of a Sit-In* (Urbana: University of Illinois Press, 1990 [1962]); Miles Wolff, *Lunch at the Five and Ten, The Greensboro Sit-Ins: A Contemporary History* (New York: Stein and Day, 1970); and David Garrow, ed., *Atlanta, Georgia, 1960–1961: Sit-ins and Student Activism* (Brooklyn: Carlson Publishing, 1989). See also Taylor Branch, *Parting the Waters: America in the King Years, 1954–63* (New York: Simon and Schuster, 1988), pp. 272–312. My thoughts about this subject have also been influenced by Lizabeth Cohen, "A Consumer's Republic: The Politics of Consumption in Postwar America," presented at the workshop "Consuming Politics: How Mass Consumption Has Shaped and Been Shaped by Political Systems and Cultures," Rutgers Center for Historical Analysis, April 1993.

67. Neil McMillen, *Dark Journey: Black Mississippians in the Age of Jim Crow* (Chicago: University of Illinois Press, 1989), pp. 287–97; August Meier, "Boycotts of Segregated Street Cars, 1894–1906: A Research Note," *Phylon* 18 (1957): 296–97; Tera Hunter, *To 'Joy My Freedom: Southern Black Women's Lives and Labors after the Civil War* (Cambridge: Harvard University Press, 1997), pp. 76–97. For a discussion of students' self-perceptions, see August Meier, "Epilogue: Toward a Synthesis of Civil Rights History," in Armstead L. Robinson and Patricia Sullivan, eds., *New Directions in Civil Rights Studies* (Charlottesville: University Press of Virginia, 1991), pp. 214–15; for an analysis of consumption as a strategy, see Cohen, "A Consumer's Republic"; Louis Lomax, "The Negro Revolt against 'The Negro Leaders,' " *Harper's Magazine*, June 1960, 42, 48.

68. *Chicago Defender*, 26 March 1960, p. 2; *New York Times*, 11 April 1960, p. 25.

69. Charles Jones in *Greensboro Daily News*, 10 February 1960, quoted in Clayborne Carson, *In Struggle: SNCC and the Black Awakening of the 1960s* (Cambridge: Harvard University Press, 1981), p. 13; *Washington Post*, 7 March 1960, p. 2; *Chicago Defender*, 2 April 1960, p. 2.

70. Sitkoff, *The Struggle for Black Equality*, pp. 79–81; John Dittmer, *Local People: The Struggle for Civil Rights in Mississippi* (Urbana: University of Illinois Press, 1994), pp. 85–89, 157–69.

71. See Branch, *Parting the Waters*, p. 291; Julian Bond in Raines, *My Soul Is Rested*, p. 93. For an account of related generational tensions, see Branch, *Parting the Waters*, pp. 275–85.

72. Ella Baker quoted by Julian Bond in Raines, *My Soul Is Rested*, pp. 101–02. In Baker's report on the conference, she referred to sit-ins as being "bigger than a hamburger." See Ella Baker, "Bigger Than a Hamburger" (*Southern Patriot* 18 [1960]), in Peter B. Levy, ed., *Let Freedom Ring: A Documentary History of the Modern Civil Rights Movement* (New York: Praeger, 1992), pp. 70–71.

73. Carson, *In Struggle*, p. 14.

74. Branch, *Parting the Waters*, p. 346; Lonnie King in Raines, *My Soul Is Rested*, pp. 87–88.

75. See Weisbrot, *Freedom Bound*, p. 22; Raines, *My Soul Is Rested*, pp. 83–85. For a discussion of the politics of respectability, see, especially, Evelyn Brooks-Higginbotham, *Righ-*

teous Discontent: The Women's Movement in the Black Baptist Church, 1880–1920 (Cambridge: Harvard University Press, 1993).

76. Chafe, *Civilities and Civil Rights*, p. 127, fn. 26; see also *Atlanta Constitution*, 13 February 1960, p. 2.

77. Daniel H. Pollitt, "Dime Store Demonstrations: Events and Legal Problems of First Sixty Days," *Duke Law Journal* 315 (summer 1960): 318; Cohen, "A Consumers Republic," p. 13.

78. Bond, in Raines, *My Soul Is Rested*, p. 86; Mayer, Introduction, *Diary of a Sit-In*, p. xi; Lewis in Hampton and Fayer, eds., *Voices of Freedom*, p. 57; Branch, *Parting the Waters*, p. 275. See also Michael Walzer, "The Young: A Cup of Coffee and a Seat," *Dissent* 7 (spring 1960): 114; *New York Times*, 3 February 1960, p. 22; *New York Times*, 6 March 1960, p. 43; *Chicago Defender*, 2 April 1960, p. 3; Helen Fuller, "Southern Students Take Over: The Creation of the Beloved Community," *The New Republic*, 2 May 1960, 14. Exceptions to the emphasis on respectable clothing in this stage of civil rights activism occur when accounts focus on generational differences; see Weisbrot, *Freedom Bound*, p. 32.

79. Carson, *In Struggle*, p. 10.

80. James J. Kilpatrick, *Richmond News Leader*, quoted in Raines, *My Soul Is Rested*, p. 99.

81. *Chicago Defender*, 2 April 1960, p. 1; Walzer, "The Young," p. 116; see also *New York Amsterdam News*, 5 March 1960, p. 1. The black and white media initially reported the sit-ins "cautiously" because of assumptions that they were a "newfangled teenage rumble"; see Branch, *Parting the Waters*, p. 276.

82. C. Eric Lincoln, "The Strategy of a Sit-In" (*The Reporter* 24 [5 January 1961]), in Garrow, ed., *Atlanta, Georgia*, pp. 95–105. See also Fuller, "Southern Students Take Over."

83. Quoted in Weisbrot, *Freedom Bound*, p. 2; also in Wolff, *Lunch at the Five and Ten*, p. 16. For evidence of similar sentiments at the outset of the Montgomery bus boycott, see E. D. Nixon in Raines, *My Soul Is Rested*, p. 49.

84. McCain in Raines, *My Soul Is Rested*, p. 78; Barry quoted in Carson, *In Struggle*, p. 21.

85. *Chicago Defender*, 23 April 1960, p. 10.

86. Bond in Raines, *My Soul Is Rested*, p. 87. In Greensboro, whites pressed lit cigarettes against the backs of women protesters. For an account of other incidents directed at women see, among others, Pollitt, "Dime Store Demonstrations," pp. 323–24.

87. Walzer, "The Young," p. 116.

88. These gender ideologies also helped to transform jail terms from humiliating dangers into badges of honor and respectability across lines of class and gender. See, for example, *Chicago Defender*, 27 February 1960, p. 12; *Chicago Defender*, 26 March 1960, pp. 1–2; *New York Amsterdam News*, 5 March 1960, p. 1; "Freed After 48–Day Jail Terms," *Jet*, 19 May 1960, 20–21; and "Negro Youth's New March on Dixie," p. 17.

89. Anne Moody, *Coming to Age in Mississippi: An Autobiography of Anne Moody* (New York: Dell Publishing, 1968), p. 268.

90. See, for example, *Chicago Defender*, 2 April 1960, p. 3; *Chicago Defender*, 26 March 1960, pp. 1–2; *Chicago Defender*, 19 March 1960, p. 1; *Atlanta Constitution*, 4 February 1960, p. 12; *New York Amsterdam News*, 12 March 1960, p. 26; Fuller, "Southern Students Take Over," p. 14; for contemporary accounts of white women's participation, see, for example, *New York Times*, 2 March 1960, p. 28; *Chicago Defender*, 30 April 1960, p. 1; *Chicago Defender*, 31 December 1960–6 January 1961, pp. 3, 14; "Explosive Youth: Introduction to a Sit-In," *Look*, 3 January 1961, 36b–36d.

91. Walzer, "The Young," p. 116; *Chicago Defender*, 26 March 1960, p. 1; Chafe, *Civilities and Civil Rights*, p. 114; Cheryl Lynn Greenberg, ed., *A Circle of Trust: Remembering SNCC* (New Brunswick: Rutgers University Press, 1998), pp. 140–41; Cynthia Griggs Fleming, *Soon We Will Not Cry: The Liberation of Ruby Doris Smith Robinson* (New York: Rowman and Littlefield, 1998), p. 125. Scholarship on women's roles and gender dynamics in the civil rights movement also includes Bernice McNair Barnett, *Sisters in Struggle: Invisible Black Women in the Civil Rights Movement, 1945–1970* (London : Routledge, 1996); Vicki Crawford

et al., eds., *Women in the Civil Rights Movement: Trailblazers and Torchbearers, 1941–1965* (Brooklyn: Carlson Publishing, 1990); Sara Evans, *Personal Politics: The Roots of Women's Liberation in the Civil Rights Movement and the New Left* (New York: Vintage, 1980); Jones, *Labor of Love*, pp. 279–321; Doug McAdam, *Freedom Summer* (New York: Oxford University Press, 1988), esp. pp. 57–61, 105–110, 220–28; Charles Payne, " 'Men Led, But Women Organized': Movement Participation of Women in the Mississippi Delta," in Guida West and Rhoda Blumberg, eds., *Women and Social Protest* (New York: Oxford University Press, 1990), pp. 156–65; Belinda Robnett, *How Long? How Long? African American Women in the Struggle for Civil Rights* (New York: Oxford University Press, 1997); Mary Aikin Rothschild, *A Case of Black and White: Northern Volunteers and the Southern Freedom Summers, 1964–65* (Westport, Conn: Greenwood Press, 1982). For a discussion of consumer orientation contributing to women's activism, see Cohen, "A Consumer's Republic," pp. 17–18.

92. Proudfoot, *Diary of a Sit-In*, pp. 57, 81.

93. *New York Amsterdam News*, 5 March 1960, p. 1; "Fisk University Coed Plans Lifetime Fight With Jim Crow," *Jet*, 9 June 1960, 46–47; "Coed Quits School to Fight for Rights," *Jet*, 29 June 1961, 49.

94. Alice Echols, " 'We Gotta Get Out of this Place': Notes Toward a Remapping of the Sixties," *Socialist Review* 22 (April-June 1992): 9–33, quote on p. 11. See also Pauli Murray, "The Liberation of Black Women" [1970], in Beverly Guy-Sheftall, ed., *Words of Fire: An Anthology of African-American Feminist Thought* (New York: The New Press, 1995), p. 189; Robnett, *How Long?* p. 102.

95. Diane Nash, "Inside the Sit-Ins and Freedom Rides: Testimony of a Southern Student," in Mathew H. Ahmann, ed., *The New Negro* (Notre Dame, Ind.: Fides Publishers, 1961), pp. 47–48.

96. *Chicago Defender*, 23 April 1960, p. 10.

Chapter Six

1. Dona Cooper Hamilton and Charles V. Hamilton, *The Dual Agenda: Race and Social Welfare Policies of Civil Rights Organizations* (New York: Columbia University Press, 1997), p. 122.

2. "From Sidney With Love," *Newsweek*, 11 December 1967, 101–02; "The Current Cinema: Good Causes," *The New Yorker*, 16 December 1967, 108.

3. For accounts of a contested consensus within the administration and among African Americans, see David Garrow, *Bearing the Cross: Martin Luther King, Jr., and the SCLC* (New York: William Morrow, 1986); Henry Hampton and Steve Fayer, *Voices of Freedom: An Oral History of the Civil Rights Movement from the 1950s through the 1980s* (New York: Bantam Books, 1990), pp. 241–66; Melani McAlister, " 'One Black Allah': The Middle East in the Cultural Politics of African American Liberation, 1955–1970," *American Quarterly* 51 (September 1999): 622–56.

4. Betty Friedan, *The Feminine Mystique* (New York: Dell Publishing, 1963), p. 17. For discussions of Friedan, see especially Daniel Horowitz, *Betty Friedan and the Making of the Feminine Mystique: The American Left, the Cold War, and Modern Feminism* (Amherst: University of Massachusetts Press, 1998), pp. 197–223; Joanne Meyerowitz, "Beyond the Feminine Mystique: A Reassessment of Postwar Mass Culture, 1946–1958," in Meyerowitz, ed., *Not June Cleaver: Women and Gender in Postwar America, 1945–1960* (Philadelphia: Temple University Press, 1994), pp. 229–62.

5. See, for example, *Washington Post*, 24 May 1962, p. C24.

6. Rena Corman, "Close-up of the 'Normal' Wife," *New York Times Magazine*, 8 September 1963, 52, 54, 60, 64, 69; Marion K. Sanders, "A Proposition For Women," *Harper's*, September 1960, 43.

7. Flora Davis, *Moving the Mountain: The Women's Movement in America since 1960*

(New York: Simon and Schuster, 1991). Scholarship on women's activism before the 1960s includes Susan Lynn, *Progressive Women in Conservative Times: Racial Justice, Peace, and Feminism, 1945 to the 1960s* (New Brunswick: Rutgers University Press, 1992); Leila J. Rupp and Verta Taylor, *Survival in the Doldrums: The American Women's Rights Movement, 1945 to the 1960s* (Columbus: Ohio State University Press, 1990). For an assessment of a broad range of women's activism from the 1950s into the 1970s, see Susan M. Hartmann, *The Other Feminists: Activists in the Liberal Establishment* (New Haven: Yale University Press, 1998).

8. See for example, ibid., Maurice Isserman, *If I Had a Hammer: The Death of the Old Left and the Birth of the New Left* (New York: Basic Books, 1987); Meyerowitz, ed., *Not June Cleaver;* Horowitz, *Betty Friedan and the Making of the Feminine Mystique;* Uta G. Poiger, *Jazz, Rock, and Rebels: Cold War Politics and American Culture in a Divided Germany* (Berkeley: University of California Press, 2000).

9. See Eric Foner, "Common Origins, Different Paths," *Radical History Review* 71 (spring 1998): 6–10.

10. Daniel Patrick Moynihan, *The Negro Family: The Case for National Action* [1965], in Lee Rainwater and William L. Yancey, eds., *The Moynihan Report and the Politics of Controversy* (Cambridge: MIT Press, 1967). See also Douglas Schoen, *Pat: A Biography of Daniel Patrick Moynihan* (New York: Harper and Row, 1979), pp. 103–17; Carl Ginsburg, *Race and Media: The Enduring Life of the Moynihan Report* (New York: Institute for Media Analysis, 1989). Moynihan worked with aides Paul Barton and Ellen Broderick but was the lead author.

11. Margaret Mead and Frances Balgley Kaplan, eds., *American Women: The Report of the President's Commission on the Status of Women, and Other Publications of the Commission* (New York: Charles Scribners' Sons, 1965); Cynthia Harrison, *On Account of Sex: The Politics of Women's Issues, 1945–1968* (Berkeley: University of California Press, 1988), p. 173.

12. Robert Weisbrot, *Freedom Bound: A History of America's Civil Rights Movement* (New York: Norton, 1990), pp. 246, 186–261; Allen J. Matusow, *The Unraveling of America: A History of American Liberalism in the 1960s* (New York: Harper and Row, 1984), pp. 194–98; for a discussion of growing militance among black activists in 1964–65 and a sense of disillusion with the Democratic party even earlier, see also Hampton and Fayer, *Voices of Freedom*, pp. 267–95.

13. Friedan contributed to the PCSW subcommittee on Portrayal of Women by the Mass Media. In 1966 she, among others involved in the PCSW, founded the National Organization for Women (NOW).

14. Daryl Scott, *Contempt and Pity: Social Policy and the Image of the Damaged Black Psyche, 1880–1996* (Chapel Hill: University of North Carolina Press, 1997), p. 141.

15. Rainwater and Yancey, eds., *The Moynihan Report*, pp. 18, 43, 51, 76, 47, 50.

16. Patricia Morton, *Disfigured Images: The Historical Assault on Afro-American Women* (New York: Praeger Press, 1991), p. 4.

17. Rainwater and Yancey, eds., *The Moynihan Report*, pp. 62–65, x; "The Negro American," *Daedalus* 94 (fall 1965); "The Negro American," *Daedalus* 95 (winter 1966). Moynihan helped plan and contributed to the volumes on "The Negro American." The phrase "tangle of pathology" also appeared in Kenneth Clark, *Dark Ghetto: Dilemmas of Social Power* (New York: Harper and Row, 1965).

18. Rainwater and Yancey, eds., *The Moynihan Report*, pp. 58, 54–55. Moynihan did note that there were some black children who, though "technically illegitimate," had stable families (p. 54).

19. "Sad cycle" in Elizabeth Herzog, "Is There a 'Breakdown' of the Negro Family" [1966], in Rainwater and Yancey, eds., *The Moynihan Report*, p. 345; Rainwater and Yancey, eds., *The Moynihan Report*, pp. 67, 77–78, 71, 76.

20. Rainwater and Yancey, eds., *The Moynihan Report*, pp. 73, 71, 85; see also p. 77.

21. Thomas Pettigrew, quoted in Rainwater and Yancey, eds., *The Moynihan Report*, pp. 80, 77–80.

22. Rainwater and Yancey, eds., *The Moynihan Report*, p. 62. For the passive male

"Sambo" as a racial type, see Stanley M. Elkins, *Slavery* (Chicago: University of Chicago Press, 1959).

23. Rainwater and Yancey, eds., *The Moynihan Report*, p. 88; for more about Moynihan on extending the draft, see Thomas Meehan, "Moynihan of the Moynihan Report," *New York Times Magazine*, 31 July 1966, 5, 48–50, 54–55.

24. Rainwater and Yancey, eds., *The Moynihan Report*, pp. 62–63, 84, 93. For a related, and influential, "culture of poverty" theory, see Oscar Lewis, *The Children of Sanchez* (New York: Random House, 1961). Moynihan qualified his argument by pointing to the existence of a black middle class (pp. 51, 75), only to add that his "propositions . . . may be thought of as having a more or less general application" (p. 76).

25. *New York Times*, 12 December 1965, p. 74.

26. Daniel Patrick Moynihan, "A Family Policy for the Nation" [1965], in Rainwater and Yancey, eds., *The Moynihan Report*, pp. 390–91.

27. Rainwater and Yancey, eds., *The Moynihan Report*, pp. 149, 93; see also *Newsweek*, 9 August 1965, 35. For a discussion of the National Urban League's emphasis on federal activism in earlier periods, see Hamilton and Hamilton, *Dual Agenda*, pp. 130–45.

28. *New York Times*, 19 July 1965, p. 15; *New York Times*, 12 December 1965, p. 74; *New York Times*, 2 December 1965, p. 41. For considerations of welfare activism in this period, see Herbert J. Gans, "The Negro Family: Reflections on the Moynihan Report" [1965], in Rainwater and Yancey, eds., *The Moynihan Report*, pp. 445–57; Gwendolyn Mink, *Welfare's End* (Ithaca: Cornell University Press, 1998), pp. 14–22, 38–40, 48–61.

29. Moynihan, "A Family Policy," pp. 392–93; Meehan, "Moynihan of the Moynihan Report," p. 48; Rainwater and Yancey, "Moynihan's Strategy," in Rainwater and Yancey, eds., *The Moynihan Report*, p. 29.

30. Farmer in *New York Amsterdam News*, 18 December 1965, p. 36; William Ryan, "Savage Discovery: The Moynihan Report" [1965], in Rainwater and Yancey, eds., *The Moynihan Report*, p. 463.

31. Ellen Herman, *The Romance of American Psychology: Political Culture in the Age of Experts* (Berkeley: University of California Press, 1995), p. 208.

32. Rainwater and Yancey, eds., *The Moynihan Report*, p. 51; Sidney Hook, ed., *Psychoanalysis, Scientific Method, and Philosophy* (New York: New York University Press, 1959); Thomas Szasz, *The Myth of Mental Illness: Foundations of a Theory of Personal Conduct* (New York: Hoeber-Harber, 1961); for an overview of these changes, see Mari Jo Buhle, *Feminism and Its Discontents: A Century of Struggle with Psychoanalysis* (Cambridge: Harvard University Press, 1998), pp. 220–23; Herman, *Romance of American Psychology*, pp. 264–69.

33. Elisabeth Young-Bruehl, *The Anatomy of Prejudices* (Cambridge: Harvard University Press, 1996), pp. 88–89; Scott, *Contempt and Pity*, 141–44; Frank Riessman and S. M. Miller, quoted in Scott, *Contempt and Pity*, p. 143.

34. Lyndon Johnson, "To Fulfill These Rights: The Howard University Address" [1965], in Rainwater and Yancey, eds., *The Moynihan Report*, pp. 126–28. For discussions of the War on Poverty in relation to civil rights activism, see Weisbrot, *Freedom Bound*, pp. 154–221; Hamilton and Hamilton, *Dual Agenda*, pp. 128–42. In part as a result of controversy over the Moynihan report, the White House Conference on Civil Rights intentionally did not include black families on the agenda. See Steven F. Lawson, ed., Civil Rights during the Johnson Administration, 1963–1969, Part 4: Records of the White House Conference on Civil Rights, 1965–66, reel 19, Widener Library, Harvard University. See also *New York Times*, 25 November 1965, p. 52.

35. Rainwater and Yancey, eds., *The Moynihan Report*, pp. 15–19; 139–47, 194–214, 375–77, 14; Scott, *Contempt and Pity*, p. 157.

36. *Newsweek*, 9 August 1965, p. 35; *New York Times*, 19 July 1965, p. 1; Mary McGrory, "President Talks Frankly to Negroes" [1965], in Rainwater and Yancey, eds., *The Moynihan Report*, p. 370; *New York Times*, 19 July 1965, p. 15; C. Eric Lincoln, "The Absent Father Haunts the Negro Family," *New York Times Magazine*, 28 November 1965, 177.

37. James Farmer in *New York Amsterdam News*, 18 December 1965, p. 36. See also Rainwater and Yancey, eds., *The Moynihan Report*, pp. 199–202, 402–04.

38. Ryan, "Savage Discovery," p. 460, emphasis in original; Whitney Young, "Real Message of the Moynihan Report," *New York Amsterdam News*, 29 January 1966, p. 14; Ryan, "Savage Discovery," p. 464.

39. Rainwater and Yancey, eds., *The Moynihan Report*, p. 51; Barbara Whitaker, "Breakdown in the Negro Family: Myth or Reality," *New South* 22 (fall 1967): 39. Many also noted that Moynihan all but ignored the civil rights movement. See Frank Riessman, "In Defense of the Negro Family" [1966], in Rainwater and Yancey, eds., *The Moynihan Report*, pp. 474–78; Bayard Rustin, quoted in Rainwater and Yancey, eds., *The Moynihan Report*, p. 200.

40. Ryan, "Savage Discovery," pp. 462–63; Farmer in *New York Amsterdam News*, 18 December 1965, p. 36; Robert L. Perry, "The Black Matriarchy Controversy and Black Male Delinquency," *Journal of Afro-American Issues* 4 (summer/fall 1976): 365.

41. *New York Times*, 27 August 1965, p. 13; Lincoln, "The Absent Father," pp. 172–77.

42. Whitaker, "Breakdown in the Negro Family," p. 47; "A Man Around the House," *Ebony*, January 1966, 92–93.

43. Newton quoted in Jacqueline Jones, *Labor of Love, Labor of Sorrow: Black Women, Work and the Family from Slavery to the Present* (New York: Basic Books, 1985), p. 312; Andrew Billingsley, *Black Families in White America* (Englewood Cliffs, N.J.: Prentice Hall, 1968), p. 40; Perry, "The Black Matriarchy Controversy," p. 372. See also Baker E. Morten, "Nothing But a Man, Says Moynihan Foe," *Baltimore Afro-American*, 4 December 1965, (unpaginated) in Civil Rights During the Johnson Administration, 1963–69, Part 4, reel 19; Eldridge Cleaver, *Soul On Ice* (New York: Dell, 1968), p. 162. For a discussion of this trend in historical scholarship, see Morton, *Disfigured Images*, pp. 99–109, 125–26.

44. Richard Rovere, "Letter From Washington" [1965], in Rainwater and Yancey, eds., *The Moynihan Report*, pp. 148–49.

45. Of course, black women had rejected these assumptions in earlier periods as well. See, for example, Jones, *Labor of Love;* Paula Giddings, *When and Where I Enter: The Impact of Black Women on Race and Sex in America* (New York: William Morrow, 1984).

46. Frances Beale, "Double Jeopardy: To Be Black and Female," in Toni Cade, ed., *The Black Woman: An Anthology* (New York: New American Library, 1970), pp. 93, 92; Jean Carey Bond and Patricia Peery, "Is the Black Male Castrated?" in Cade, ed., *The Black Woman*, pp. 116–17. See also Angela Davis, "Reflections on the Black Woman's Role in the Community of Slaves," *Black Scholar* 3 (December 1971): 2–15; Jacquelyne Jackson, "But Where Are the Men?" and other essays in Gloria T. Hull, et al., eds., *All the Women Are White, All the Blacks are Men, But Some of Us Are Brave: Black Women's Studies* (New York: The Feminist Press, 1982), pp. 30–41; Joyce Ladner, *Tomorrow's Tomorrow: The Black Woman* (New York: Doubleday, 1971).

47. Linda La Rue, "The Black Movement and Women's Liberation" [1970], in Beverly Guy-Sheftall, ed., *Words of Fire: An Anthology of African-American Feminist Thought* (New York: The New Press, 1995), p. 171; Mary Ann Weathers, "An Argument for Black Women's Liberation As a Revolutionary Force" [1969], in Guy-Sheftall, ed., *Words of Fire*, p. 159.

48. Beale, "Double Jeopardy," pp. 93–94; Toni Cade, "The Pill: Genocide or Liberation," in Cade, ed., *The Black Woman*, p. 164.

49. Morton, *Disfigured Images*, p. 5. For a discussion of motherhood and black feminist theory, see Lauri Umansky, *Motherhood Reconceived: Feminism and the Legacies of the Sixties* (New York: New York University Press, 1996), pp. 77–102.

50. Carmichael quoted in Jones, *Labor of Love*, p. 313; Laura Carper, "The Negro Family and the Moynihan Report" [1966], in Rainwater and Yancey, eds., *The Moynihan Report*, pp. 471–72; Riessman, "In Defense of the Negro Family," p. 475.

51. *Newsweek*, 9 August 1965, 32.

52. Rainwater and Yancy, eds., *The Moynihan Report*, p. x.

53. Friedan, *Feminine Mystique*, pp. 60, 345; Buhle, *Feminism and Its Discontents*, p. 208. For a discussion of Friedan's emphasis on "humans" and her critique of Freudianism, see also Jane Gerhard, *Desiring Revolution: Second-Wave Feminism and the Rewriting of American Sexual Thought* (New York: Columbia University Press, forthcoming).

54. Friedan, *Feminine Mystique*, pp. 60, 180.

55. Friedan, *Feminine Mystique*, p. 184, emphasis in original.

56. Buhle, *Feminism and Its Discontents*, p. 208; Gerhard, *Desiring Revolution;* Judith Hennessee, *Betty Friedan: Her Life* (New York: Random House, 1999), pp. 81–82; Herman, *Romance of American Psychology*, pp. 290–92; Horowitz, *Betty Friedan and the Making of the Feminine Mystique*, pp. 205–07.

57. Herman, *Romance of American Psychology*, pp. 264–66.

58. Friedan, *Feminine Mystique*, pp. 116, 195.

59. Friedan, *Feminine Mystique*, p. 351.

60. Friedan, *Feminine Mystique*, p. 326.

61. Jones, *Labor of Love;* for an account of Friedan's explicit suppression of questions related to class and race, see Horowitz, *Betty Friedan and the Making of The Feminine Mystique*.

62. Beale, "Double Jeopardy," p. 98.

63. La Rue, "The Black Movement and Women's Liberation," p. 164; see also Toni Morrison, "What the Black Woman Thinks about Women's Lib," *New York Times Magazine*, 22 August 1971, 14–15, 63–64, 66.

64. bell hooks, excerpts from *Feminist Theory: From Margin to Center* [1984], in Guy-Sheftall, ed., *Words of Fire*, p. 270. For a revision of the "feminine mystique" as the prevailing paradigm for postwar women, see Meyerowitz, "Beyond the Feminine Mystique."

65. See Hartmann, *Other Feminists*, pp. 5–7, 176–206.

66. Kennedy quoted in Mead and Kaplan, eds., *American Women*, p. 16.

67. *Washington Post*, 24 May 1962, p. C24; U.S. President's Commission on the Status of Women, *Report of the Committee on Civil and Political Rights*; *Report of the Committee on Education*; *Report of the Committee on Federal Employment*; *Report of the Committee on Home and Community*; *Report of the Committee on Private Employment*; *Report of the Committee on Protective Labor Legislation*; *Report of the Committee on Social Security and Taxes*; *Four Consultations: Private Employment Opportunities, New Patterns in Volunteer Work, Portrayal of Women by the Mass Media, Problems of Negro Women* (Washington, D.C.: United States Government Printing Office, 1963). There were differences between recommendations that the Commission made in its final report and those that committees suggested; in general, the final report tended to be more moderate and wary of controversy. See Harrison, *On Account of Sex*, pp. 109–16; Mead and Kaplan, eds., *American Women*, pp. 254–67.

68. Harrison, *On Account of Sex*, p. 173.

69. Harrison, *On Account of Sex*, p. 90; Mead and Kaplan, eds., *American Women*, pp. 45–48.

70. Mead and Kaplan eds., *American Women*, p. 211; Harrison, *On Account of Sex*, p. 146. One of the Commissions four consultations focused on the problems of Negro women, and the final report supported fair labor standards to ease the pressures on all working women. See PCSW, *Four Consultations*, pp. 29–36. For the Equal Pay Act, see also Kim M. Blankenship, "Bringing Gender and Race In: U.S. Employment Discrimination Policy," *Gender and Society* 7 (June 1993): pp. 215–16; Harrison, *On Account of Sex*, pp. 89–105.

71. Mead and Kaplan, eds., *American Women*, pp. 20–21. The PCSW also noted that American Indian and Spanish-American faced multiple obstacles, but women of color who were not African American rarely came up again.

72. These included Alice Allison Dunnigan, Lorraine Hansberry, and Dorothy Height. Height, president of the National Council of Negro Women, chaired the smaller subcommittee on the "problems of Negro women." See Miriam Lynell Harris, "From Kennedy to Combahee: Black Feminist Activism from 1950 to 1980," (Ph.D. diss., University of Minnesota, 1997).

73. For discussions of liberal feminism and Title 7, see Carl M. Brauer, "Women Activists, Southern Conservatives, and the Prohibition of Sex Discrimination in Title 7 of the 1964 Civil Rights Act," *Journal of Southern History* 49 (1983): 37–56; Blankenship, "Bringing Gender and Race In"; Cynthia Deitch, "Gender, Race, and Class Politics and the Inclusion of Women in Title VII of the 1964 Civil Rights Act," *Gender and Society* 7 (June 1993): 183–203. For discussions of the PCSW and the March on Washington in 1963, see Pauli Murray, *Song in a Weary Throat: An American Pilgrimage* (New York: Harper and Row, 1987), pp. 350–54; Murray, "The Negro Woman in the Quest for Equality," undated, in Schomburg Center on Black Culture Clipping File, 1925–1974, (SCBCCF) "Women—Civil Rights," 005, 841.

74. Although domestic workers remained off the PCSW's list of occupations that should be included in the Fair Labor Standards Act, the report did suggest that "practicable means of covering at least some household workers and agricultural workers should be actively explored" with regard to unemployment insurance. See Mead and Kaplan, eds., *American Women*, pp. 211–12, 55. The Equal Pay Act excluded nearly three-quarters of black women workers and about one-third of all white women workers (most of whom were in managerial positions). See Patricia G. Zelman, *Women, Work, and National Policy: The Kennedy-Johnson Years* (Ann Arbor, Mich.: UMI Research Press, 1989), p. 32; Blankenship, "Bringing Gender and Race In," p. 215.

75. PCSW, *Report of the Committee on Home and Community*, pp. 17–18. For the consultation on the "problems of Negro women," see also Harris, "From Kennedy to Combahee," pp. 48–60.

76. For accounts of the decision in the PCSW not to add "sex" to already existing prohibitions against discrimination based on "race, creed, color or national origin," see Mead and Kaplan, eds., *American Women*, p. 49; Zelman, *Women, Work and National Policy*, pp. 28, 56–60; Harrison, *On Account of Sex*, pp. 146–51; Hugh Davis Graham, "The Origins of Affirmative Action," *Annals of American History* 523 (September 1992): 53–55.

77. Murray, *Song in a Weary Throat*, p. 348; Murray, "The Negro Woman in the Quest for Equality"; Murray, "Jane Crow and the Law: Sex Discrimination and Title 7," *George Washington Law Review* 34 (December 1965): 232–56. In one instance, Murray criticized A. Philip Randolph for speaking at the National Press Club—an organization that excluded women—days before the March On Washington. Aileen Hernandez and Shirley Chisolm were other black women involved in NOW from the outset.

78. See Hartmann, *Other Feminists*. For analyses of the links among civil rights, black and white women, and radical feminism, see especially Sara Evans, *Personal Politics: The Roots of Women's Liberation in the Civil Rights Movement and the New Left* (New York: Vintage Books, 1980); Umansky, *Motherhood Reconceived*.

79. Advocates of the ERA included the National Women's Party; opponents included Labor Department officials and union activists.

80. Murray, "A Proposal to Reexamine the Applicability of the 14th Amendment to State Laws and Practices Which Discriminate on the Basis of Sex Per Se," December 1962, pp. 10–13, in Pauli Murray papers (PM papers), box 50, folder 887, Schelsinger Library, Radcliffe College.

81. Murray, "A Proposal to Reexamine," pp. 8, 6–7, 28–29.

82. Ibid., pp. 7–9, 15.

83. Letter from Helen Gray to PM, 8 August 1963, in PM papers, box 49, folder 877, "PCSW, 1963, 1966"; Mead and Kaplan, eds., *American Women*, pp. 212, 66, see also pp. 147–50. For an account of debates that led to this consensus, see Harrison, *On Account of Sex*, pp. 130–36.

84. Harrison, *On Account of Sex*, p. 126.

85. Murray, "A Proposal to Reexamine," pp. 7–9, 17, 10.

86. Ibid., pp. 10, 21–22, 28–29.

87. For a discussion of recent implications of this framework, see Dorothy Roberts,

Killing the Black Body: Race, Reproduction, and the Meaning of Liberty (New York: Pantheon Books, 1997).

88. PCSW, *Report of the Committee on Home and Community*, p. 13.

89. Mead and Kaplan, eds., *American Women*, p. 19; PCSW, *Report of the Committee on Home and Community*, pp. 3–5. For the commission's stand on welfare issues, see PCSW, *Four Consultations*, p. 31.

90. PCSW, *Four Consultations*, pp. 30–31; see also Harris, "From Kennedy to Combahee," pp. 51–59.

91. PCSW, *Report of the Committee on Home and Community*, p. 5; see also, Mead and Kaplan, eds., *American Women*, pp. 16–17.

92. For accounts of these changes, see William H. Chafe and Harvard Sitkoff, eds., *A History of Our Time: Readings on Postwar America* (New York: Oxford University Press, 1991 [1983]), pp. 153–345; Alexander Bloom and Wini Breines, eds., *"Takin' it to the Streets": A Sixties Reader* (New York: Oxford University Press, 1995).

93. For an analysis of radicalism and the personalizaton of the political in the sixties, see Gerhard, *Desiring Revolution*; see also Matusow, *Unraveling of America*, pp. 275–325; Bloom and Breines, eds., *"Takin' It to the Streets,"* pp. 275–334.

94. Shulamith Firestone, *The Dialectic of Sex: The Case for Feminist Revolution* (New York: Bantam Books, 1971 [1970]); Adrienne Rich, *Of Woman Born: Motherhood as Experience and Institution* (New York: Norton, 1986 [1976]); Davis, "Reflections on the Black Woman's Role in the Community of Slaves"; Alice Walker, *In Search of Our Mothers' Gardens: Womanist Prose* (San Diego: Harcourt Brace Jovanovich, 1983). See also Buhle, *Feminism and its Discontents*, pp. 258–65; Umansky, *Motherhood Reconceived*.

95. Johnnie Tillmon, "Welfare is a Woman's Issue," [1972, emphasis in original], in Susan Ware, ed., *Modern American Women: A Documentary History* (New York: McGraw-Hill, 1997), p. 336.

96. Alice Echols, " 'We Gotta Get Out of this Place' ": Notes Toward a Remapping of the Sixties," *Socialist Review* 22 (April-June 1992): 12–19; Todd Gitlin, *The Sixties: Years of Hope, Days of Rage* (New York: Bantam Books, 1987); Susan E. Marshall, "Rattle on the Right: Bridge Labor in Antifeminist Organizations," in Kathleen M. Blee, ed., *No Middle Ground: Women and Radical Protest* (New York: New York University Press, 1998), pp. 155–79.

97. *Wall Street Journal*, 16 August 1965, p. 1; also quoted in Scott, *Contempt and Pity*, p. 157; for an analysis of psychological theories in the 1960s see also Herman, *Romance of American Psychology*, pp. 208–26.

98. Gary Gerstle, "The Protean Character of American Liberalism," *American Historical Review* 99 (October 1994): p. 1073; see also Ronald Radosh, *Divided They Fell: The Demise of the Democratic Party, 1964–1996* (New York: The Free Press, 1996).

Conclusion

1. Gary Gerstle, "The Protean Character of American Liberalism," *American Historical Review* 99 (October 1994): p. 1070.

2. Walter Jackson, *Gunnar Myrdal and America's Conscience: Social Engineering and Racial Liberalism, 1938–1987* (Chapel Hill: University of North Carolina Press, 1990), p. xi.

3. Philip Wylie, *Generation of Vipers* (New York: Holt, Rinehart and Winston, 1955 [1942]); Ferdinand Lundberg and Marynia F. Farnham, *Modern Woman: The Lost Sex* (New York: Harper and Brothers, 1947), pp. v, 319.

4. Abram Kardiner and Lionel Ovesey, *The Mark of Oppression: Explorations in the Personality of the American Negro* (Cleveland and New York: Meridian Books, 1962 [1951]); E. Franklin Frazier, *Black Bourgeoisie: The Rise of A New Middle Class* (New York: The Free Press, 1957). For fiction and drama by black women in the postwar years that dealt in far more nuanced ways with relationships between economic mobility and motherhood, see, for

example, Gwendolyn Brooks, *Maud Martha* (New York: Harper and Row, 1953); Ann Petry, *The Street* (Boston: Beacon Press, 1946).

5. See Rickie Solinger, *Wake Up Little Susie: Single Pregnancy and Race Before Roe v. Wade* (New York: Routledge, 1992).

6. For an influential use of momism and matriarchy to critique the welfare state, see, for example, Christopher Lasch, *Haven in a Heartless World: The Family Besieged* (New York: Basic Books, 1977).

7. For discussions of these, see for example, Katha Pollitt, *The Nation*, 27 March 1995, 408; Jane Mayer, "Comment: Motherhood Issue," *The New Yorker*, 20 March 1995, 10; "Mothers Can't Win: A Special Issue on the Joy and Guilt of Modern Motherhood," *The New York Times Magazine*, 5 April 1998.

8. Toni Morrison, ed., *Race-ing Justice, En-gendering Power: Essays on Anita Hill, Clarence Thomas, and the Construction of Social Reality* (New York: Pantheon Books, 1992); Gwendolyn Mink, *Welfare's End* (Ithaca: Cornell University Press, 1998); Rosemary L. Bray, " 'So How Did I Get Here?' " *The New York Times Magazine*, 8 November 1992, 40. See also Valerie Polakow, *Lives on the Edge: Single Mothers and Their Children in the Other America* (Chicago: University of Chicago Press, 1993); Gwendolyn Mink, ed., *Whose Welfare?* (Ithaca: Cornell University Press, 1999).

SELECTED BIBLIOGRAPHY

Primary Sources

Archival Sources:

Black Women's Oral History Project. Schlesinger Library, Radcliffe College, Cambridge, Massachusetts.

Civil Rights During the Johnson Administration, 1963–1969. Steven Lawson, ed. Part IV: Records of the White House Conference on Civil Rights, 1965–66. Widener Library, Harvard University, Cambridge, Massachusetts.

Court, Cora May Trawick. Papers. Schlesinger Library, Radcliffe College, Cambridge, Massachusetts.

Murray, Pauli. Papers. Schlesinger Library, Radcliffe College, Cambridge, Massachusetts.

NAACP. Papers. Widener Library, Harvard University, Cambridge, Massachusetts.

Schomburg Center on Black Culture. Clipping File, 1925–1974. Widener Library, Harvard University, Cambridge, Massachusetts

Journals, Newspapers, and Periodicals:

America, American Anthropologist, American Journal of Psychiatry, American Journal of Sociology, American Political Science Review, American Sociological Review, Annals of the American Academy of Political and Social Science, Atlanta Constitution, Atlantic Monthly, Baltimore Afro-American, Black Scholar, Character and Personality, Chicago Daily Tribune, Chicago Defender, Christian Century, Commentary, Commonweal, Congressional Record, Crisis, Daedalus, Dissent, Duke Law Journal, Ebony, Esquire, Ethics, Family, Film Quarterly, Harper's, Jackson Daily News, Jet, Journal of Abnormal and Social Psychology, Journal of Afro-American Issues, Journal of Negro Education, Journal of Negro History, Journal of Social Casework, Ladies' Home Journal, Life, Look, Los Angeles Times, Marriage and Family Living, Memphis Commercial Appeal, Movieline, Ms., The Nation, Negro Digest, Negro History Bulletin, New Leader, The New Republic, New South, Newsweek, New York Amsterdam News, New York Herald Tribune Book Review, New York Post, New York Times, New Yorker, Opportunity, Parents' Magazine, Partisan Review, Phylon, Pittsburgh Courier, Political Affairs, Psychiatry, Psychoanalytic Study of the Child, Public Welfare, Race, Reader's Digest, Saturday Evening Post, Saturday Review of Literature, Social Forces, Social Security Bulletin, Social Security Yearbook, Social Work Journal, South Today, Time, Today's Health.

Published Books and Pamphlets:

Abbott, Grace. *From Relief to Social Security: The Development of the New Public Welfare Services and Their Administration*. Chicago: University of Chicago Press, 1941.

Adorno, T. W., Else Frenkel-Brunswick, Daniel J. Levinson, R. Nevitt Sanford, in collaboration with Betty Aron, Maria Hertz Levinson, and William Morrow. *The Authoritarian Personality*. New York: Harper and Brothers, 1950. The American Jewish Committee Social Studies Series: Publication No. 3.

Advisory Council on Social Security. *The Status of the Social Security Program and Recommendations for Its Improvement*. Washington, D.C.: Government Printing Office, 1964.

Ahmann, Mathew, ed. *The New Negro*. Notre Dame, Ind.: Fides Publishers, 1961.

Allport, Gordon W. *The Nature of Prejudice*. Reading, Mass.: Addison-Wesley, 25th Anniversary Edition, 1979 [1954].

Altemeyer, Arthur J. *The Formative Years of Social Security*. Madison: University of Wisconsin Press, 1966.

Angell, Robert Cooley. *The Family Encounters the Depression*. Gloucester, Mass.: Peter Smith, 1965 [1936].

Billingsley, Andrew. *Black Families in White America*. Englewood Cliffs, N.J.: Prentice Hall, 1968.

Bloom, Alexander and Wini Breines, eds. *"Takin' It to the Streets": A Sixties Reader*. New York: Oxford University Press, 1995.

Bowlby, John. *Maternal Care and Mental Health*. Geneva: World Health Organization, 1951.

Brooks, Gwendolyn. *Maud Martha*. New York: Harper and Brothers, 1953.

———. *The Bean Eaters*. New York: Harper and Brothers, 1960.

Brossard, Chandler, ed. *The Scene Before You: A New Approach to American Culture*. New York: Rinehart and Co., 1955.

Burnham, Louis E. *Behind the Lynching of Emmett Louis Till*. New York: Freedom Associates, 1955.

Cade, Toni, ed. *The Black Woman: An Anthology*. New York: New American Library, 1970.

Cavan, Ruth Shonle, and Katherine Howland Ranck. *The Family and the Depression: A Study of One Hundred Chicago Families*. Chicago: University of Chicago Press, 1938.

Children in a Democracy: Preliminary Statements Submitted to the White House Conference on Children in a Democracy. Washington, D.C.: United States Government Printing Office, 1940.

Christie, Richard, and Marie Jahoda, eds. *Studies in the Scope and Method of The Authoritarian Personality*. Glencoe, Ill.: Free Press, 1954.

Clark, Kenneth B. *Dark Ghetto: Dilemmas of Social Power*. New York: Harper and Row, 1965.

———. *Prejudice and Your Child*. Boston: Beacon Press, 1963 [1955].

Cleaver, Eldridge. *Soul on Ice*. New York: Dell Publishing, 1968.

Davie, Maurice. *Negroes in American Society*. New York: McGraw-Hill, 1949.

Davis, Allison, and John Dollard. *Children of Bondage: The Personality Development of Negro Youth in the Urban South*. Washington, D.C.: American Council on Education, 1940.

Davis, Allison, et al. *Deep South: A Social Anthropological Study of Caste and Class*. Los Angeles: Center for Afro-American Studies, UCLA, 1988 [1941].

Deutsch, Helene. *The Psychology of Women: A Psychoanalytic Interpretation*. New York: Grune and Stratton, 1944.

Dollard, John, Leonard W. Doob, Neal E. Miller, O. H. Mower, Robert R. Sears, in collaboration with Clellan S. Ford, Carl Iver Hovland, and Richard T. Sollenberger. *Frustration and Aggression*. New Haven: Yale University Press, 1974 [1939].

Dollard, John. *Caste and Class in a Southern Town*. Madison: University of Wisconsin Press, 1988 [1937].

Drake, St. Clair, and Horace R. Cayton. *Black Metropolis: A Study of Negro Life in a Northern City*. New York: Harper and Row, 1962 [1945].

Edwards, G. Franklin, ed. *On Race Relations: Selected Writings.* Chicago: University of Chicago Press, 1968.

Elkins, Stanley M. *Slavery.* Chicago: University of Chicago Press, 1959.

Ellison, Ralph. *Shadow and Act.* New York: Random House, 1972.

Erikson, Erik. *Childhood and Society.* New York: Norton, 1963 [1950].

Farnham, Marynia F., and Ferdinand Lundberg. *Modern Woman: The Lost Sex.* New York: Harper and Brothers, 1947.

Firestone, Shulamith. *The Dialectic of Sex: The Case for Feminist Revolution.* New York: Morrow, 1970.

Frazier, E. Franklin. *Black Bourgeoisie: The Rise of a New Middle Class in the United States.* New York: The Free Press, 1966 [1957].

———. "The MacIver Award Lecture: The Negro Middle Class and Desegregation." *Social Problems* (April 1957): 291–301.

———. *Negro Youth at the Crossways: Their Personality Development in the Middle States.* Washington, D.C.: American Council on Education, 1940.

———. *The Negro Family in the United States.* Chicago: University of Chicago Press, 1939.

———. *The Negro Family in Chicago.* Chicago: University of Chicago Press, 1932.

———. "The Pathology of Race Prejudice." In Nancy Cunard, ed. *Negro: Anthology.* London: Wishart, 1934, [1927].

Friedan, Betty. *The Feminine Mystique.* New York: Dell Publishing, 1965 [1963].

Fromm, Erich. *Escape From Freedom.* New York: Avon, 1969 [1941].

Galbraith, John Kenneth. *The Affluent Society.* London: Hamish Hamilton, 1958.

Garfinkel, Herbert. *When Negroes March.* Glencoe, Ill.: The Free Press, 1959.

Gesell, Arnold, and Frances L. Ilg. *Infant and Child in the Culture of Today.* New York: Harper and Brothers, 1943.

Ginzberg, Eli. *The Negro Potential.* New York: Columbia University Press, 1956.

Gladney, Margaret Rose, ed. *How Am I To Be Heard? Letters of Lillian Smith.* Chapel Hill: University of North Carolina Press, 1993.

Goodman, Paul. *Growing Up Absurd: Problems of Youth in an Organized Society.* New York: Random House, 1960 [1956].

Gorer, Geoffrey. *The American People: A Study in National Character.* New York: W. W. Norton and Co., 1948.

Hagood, Margaret Jarman. *Mothers of the South: Portraiture of the White Tenant Farm Woman.* New York: W. W. Norton, 1977 [1939].

Hampton, Henry, and Steve Fayer. *Voices of Freedom: An Oral History of the Civil Rights Movement from the 1950s through the 1980s.* New York: Bantam Books, 1990.

Hansberry, Lorraine. *A Raisin in the Sun, The Sign in Sidney Brustein's Window.* New York: Vintage/Random House, 1995 [1957].

Harkey, Ira. *The Smell of Burning Crosses: An Autobiography of a Mississippi Newspaperman.* Jacksonville, Ill.: Harris-Wolfe and Co. 1967.

Hartz, Louis. *The Liberal Tradition in America: An Interpretation of American Political Thought since the Revolution.* New York: Harcourt, Brace, 1955.

Hatch, James V., ed. *Black Theater, U.S.A.: Forty-Five Plays by Black Americans, 1847–1974.* New York: The Free Press, 1974.

Herskovits, Melville. *The Myth of the Negro Past.* New York: Harper and Brothers, 1941.

Hook, Sidney, ed. *Psychoanalysis, Scientific Method, and Philosophy.* New York: New York University Press, 1959.

Huie, William Bradford. *Wolf Whistle.* New York: Signet, 1959.

Hurst, Fannie. *Imitation of Life.* New York: P. F. Collier, 1933.

Johnson, Charles, Edwin Embree, and Will Alexander. *The Collapse of Cotton Tenancy: Summary of Field Studies and Statistical Surveys, 1933–1935.* Chapel Hill: University of North Carolina Press, 1935.

Johnson, Charles. *Patterns of Negro Segregation.* New York: Harper and Brothers, 1943.

————. *To Stem This Tide: A Survey of Racial Tension Areas in the United States*. Boston and Chicago: The Pilgrim Press, 1943.

————. *Growing Up in the Black Belt: Negro Youth in the Rural South*. New York: Schocken Books, 1967 [1941].

————. *Shadow of the Plantation*. Chicago: University of Chicago Press, 1934.

Kardiner, Abram. *The Individual and His Society: The Psychodynamics of Primitive Social Organization*. New York: Columbia University Press, 1939.

Kardiner, Abram, Ralph Linton, Cora DuBois, and James West. *The Psychological Frontiers of Society*. New York: Columbia University Press, 1945.

Kardiner, Abram, and Lionel Ovesey. *The Mark of Oppression: Explorations in the Personality of the American Negro*. Cleveland and New York: Meridian Books, 1962 [1951].

Katona, George. *The Mass Consumption Society*. New York: McGraw-Hill, 1964.

Kluckhohn, Klyde, and Henry Murray, eds. *Personality in Nature, Society, and Culture*. New York: Knopf, 1967 [1948].

Komarovsky, Mirra. *The Unemployed Man and His Family*. New York: Arno Press, 1971 [1940].

Kupper, Herbert. *Back to Life: The Emotional Adjustment of Our Veterans*. New York: American Book-Stratford Press, 1945.

Ladner, Joyce. *Tomorrow's Tomorrow: The Black Woman*. New York: Doubleday, 1971.

Lasswell, Harold D. *Psychopathology and Politics*. New York: Viking Press, 1960 [1930].

Levy, David M. *Maternal Overprotection*. New York: Columbia University Press, 1943.

Levy, Peter B., ed. *Let Freedom Ring: A Documentary History of the Modern Civil Rights Movement*. New York: Praeger, 1992.

Lewis, Oscar. *The Children of Sanchez*. New York: Random House, 1961.

Lindquist, Ruth. *The Family in the Present Social Order: A Study of Needs of American Families*. Chapel Hill: University of North Carolina Press, 1931.

Logan, Rayford, ed. *What the Negro Wants*. New York: Agathon Press, 1969 [1944].

Lumpkin, Katharine Dupre. *The Family: A Study of Member Roles*. Chapel Hill: University of North Carolina Press, 1933.

Lynd, Robert S., and Helen Lynd. *Middletown*. New York: Harcourt, Brace, 1929.

————. *Middletown in Transition: A Study in Cultural Conflicts*. New York: Harcourt, Brace, 1937.

Lynd, Robert S. *Knowledge for What? The Place of Social Science in American Culture*. New York: Grove Press, 1964 [1939].

MacIver, R. M., ed. *Discrimination and National Welfare*. New York: Harper and Brothers, 1949.

Mead, Margaret. *And Keep Your Powder Dry*. New York: William Morrow and Co., 1965 [1942].

Mead, Margaret, and Frances Balgley Kaplan, eds. *American Women: The Report of the President's Commission on the Status of Women and Other Publications of the Commission*. New York: Charles Scribners' Sons, 1965.

Montagu, Ashley. *The Natural Superiority of Women*. New York: Collier, 1974 [1952].

Moody, Anne. *Coming of Age in Mississippi*. New York: Dell Publishing, 1968.

Morgan, Winona Louise. *The Family Meets the Depression: A Study of a Group of Highly Selected Families*. Minneapolis: University of Minnesota Press, 1939.

Murray, Florence, ed. *The Negro Handbook, 1949*. New York: Macmillan, 1949.

Murray, Pauli. "Jane Crow and the Law: Sex Discrimination and Title 7." *George Washington Law Review* 34 (December 1965): 232–256.

Myrdal, Gunnar. *An American Dilemma*. New York: Harper and Brothers, 1944.

National Manpower Council. *Womanpower: A Statement By the National Manpower Council With Chapters by the Council Staff*. New York: Columbia University Press, 1957.

Niebuhr, Reinhold. *The Children of Light and the Children of Darkness: A Vindication of Democracy and a Critique of Its Traditional Defense*. New York: Charles Scribners' Sons, 1947 [1944].

Niebuhr, Reinhold. *The Irony of American History*. New York: Charles Scribners' Sons, 1952.

Oppenheimer, Martin. *The Sit-In Movement of 1960*. Brooklyn: Carlson Publishers, 1989 [1963].

Parsons, Talcott. *Family, Socialization and Interaction Process*. Glencoe, Ill.: The Free Press, 1955.

Parsons, Talcott, and Kenneth B. Clark, eds. *The Negro American*. Boston: Houghton Mifflin, 1966.

Petry, Anne. *The Street*. Boston: Houghton Mifflin, 1946.

Pettigrew, Thomas F. *A Profile of the Negro American*. Toronto, New York and London: D. Van Nostrand Company, 1964.

Pifer, Alan, ed. *The Report of the Committee on Economic Security of 1935 and Other Basic Documents Relating to the Development of the Social Security Act*. Washington, D.C.: National Conference on Social Welfare, 1985.

Powdermaker, Hortense. *After Freedom: A Cultural Study in the Deep South*. New York: Russell and Russell, 1968 [1939].

Powell, Adam Clayton Jr. *Marching Blacks: An Interpretive History of the Rise of the Black Common Man*. New York: Dial Press, 1945.

President's Committee on Civil Rights. *To Secure These Rights: The Report of the President's Committee on Civil Rights*. Washington, D.C.: United States Government Printing Office, 1947.

Proudfoot, Merrill. *Diary of a Sit-In*. Urbana: University of Illinois Press, 1990 [1962].

Raines, Howell. *My Soul Is Rested: Movement Days in the Deep South Remembered*. New York: Putnam, 1977.

Rainwater, Lee, and William L. Yancey, eds. *The Moynihan Report and the Politics of Controversy*. Cambridge: MIT Press, 1967.

Reich, Wilhelm. *The Mass Psychology of Fascism*. Translated by Vincent R. Carfango. New York: Simon and Schuster, 1970 [1933].

Ribble, Margaret. *The Rights of Infants: Early Psychological Needs and their Satisfaction*. New York: Columbia University Press, 1943.

Rich, Adrienne. *Of Woman Born: Motherhood as Experience and Institution*. New York: Norton, 1986 [1976].

Riesman, David. *Abundance for What? And Other Essays*. New York: Doubleday, 1964.

Roosevelt, Eleanor. *It's Up to the Women*. New York: Frederick A. Stokes Company, 1933.

Rosenberg, Bernard, and David White, eds. *Mass Culture: The Popular Arts in America*. New York: Free Press, 1957.

Sapir, Edward. *Culture, Language and Personality*, edited by David G. Mandelbaum. Berkeley: University of California Press, 1949.

Schlesinger, Arthur M. Jr. *The Vital Center: The Politics of Freedom*. New York: De Capo Press, 1988 [1949].

Schonfeld, Seymour J. *The Negro in The Armed Forces: His Value and Status—Past, Present, and Potential*. Washington, D.C.: The Associated Press, 1945.

Smith, Lillian. *Strange Fruit*. New York: Reynal and Hitchcock Publishers, 1944.

———. *Killers of the Dream*. New York: Anchor Books, 1963 [1949].

Spock, Benjamin. *Baby and Child Care*. New York: Hawthorn Books, 1968 [1946].

Steinbeck, John. *The Grapes of Wrath*. New York: The Modern Library, 1939.

Stone, I. F. *The Haunted Fifties*. New York: Random House, 1963.

Stouffer, Samuel A., and Paul F. Lazersfeld. *Research Memorandum on the Family in the Depression*. New York: Social Science Research Council, 1937.

Strecker, Edward. *Their Mothers' Daughters*. Philadelphia: Lippincott, 1956.

———. *Their Mothers' Sons: The Psychiatrist Examines an American Problem*. Philadelphia: Lippincott, 1946.

Szasz, Thomas. *The Myth of Mental Illness: Foundations of a Theory of Personal Conduct*. New York: Hoeber-Harber, 1961.

Thomas, William I., and Florian Znaniecki. *The Polish Peasant in Europe and America*. Edited and abridged by Eli Zaretsky. Chicago: University of Chicago Press, 1984 [1918–1920].

Trilling, Lionel. *The Liberal Imagination: Essays on Literature and Society*. New York: Harcourt Brace Jovanovich, 1979 [1950].

U.S. Congress House of Representatives, *Issues in Social Security: A Report to the Committee on Ways and Means*. 79th Congress, 1st Session, 1949.

U.S. President's Commission on the Status of Women. *Four Consultations: Private Employment Opportunities, New Patterns in Volunteer Work, Portrayal of Women by the Mass Media, Problems of Negro Women*. Washington, D.C.: United States Government Printing Office, 1963.

———. *Report of the Committee on Civil and Political Rights*. Washington, D.C.: United States Government Printing Office, 1963.

———. *Report of the Committee on Education*. Washington, D.C.: United States Government Printing Office, 1963.

———. *Report of the Committee on Federal Employment*. Washington, D.C.: United States Government Printing Office, 1963.

———. *Report of the Committee on Home and Community*. Washington, D.C.: United States Government Printing Office, 1963.

———. *Report of the Committee on Private Employment*. Washington, D.C.: United States Government Printing Office, 1963.

———. *Report of the Committee on Protective Labor Legislation*. Washington, D.C.: United States Government Printing Office, 1963.

———. *Report of the Committee on Social Security and Taxes*. Washington, D.C.: United States Government Printing Office, 1963.

Warner, W. Lloyd, Buford H. Junker, and Walter A. Adams. *Color and Human Nature: Negro Personality Development in a Northern City*. Washington, D.C.: American Council on Education, 1940.

White, Walter. *A Man Called White*. New York: Arno Press, 1969 [1948].

Williams, Robin M. *The Reduction of Intergroup Tensions: A Survey of Research on Problems of Ethnic, Racial, and Religious Group Tensions*. New York: Social Science Research Council, 1947.

Wylie, Philip. *Generation of Vipers*. New York: Holt, Rinehart and Winston, 1955 [1942].

Secondary Sources

Books:

Abramovitz, Mimi. *Regulating the Lives of Women: Social Welfare Policy from Colonial Times to the Present*. Boston: South End Press, 1988.

Barkan, Elazar. *The Retreat of Scientific Racism: Changing Concepts of Race in Britain and the United States between the World Wars*. Cambridge: Cambridge University Press, 1992.

Barnett, Bernice McNair. *Sisters in Struggle: Invisible Black Women in the Civil Rights Movement, 1945–1970*. New York: Routledge, 1996.

Barnouw, Victor. *Culture and Personality*. Homewood, Ill.: Dorsey Press, 1973 [1963].

Bederman, Gail. *Manliness and Civilization: A Cultural History of Gender and Race in the United States, 1880–1917*. Chicago: University of Chicago Press, 1995.

Bell, Derrick, ed. *Shades of Brown: New Perspectives on School Desegregation*. New York: Columbia University Teachers College Press, 1980.

Bell, Winifred. *Aid to Dependent Children*. New York: Columbia University Press, 1965.

Bendau, Clifford P. *Still Worlds Collide: Philip Wylie and the End of the American Dream*. San Bernadino, Cal.: Borgo Press, 1980.

Berkowitz, Edward D. *America's Welfare State: From Roosevelt to Reagan*. Baltimore: Johns Hopkins University Press, 1991.

Berman, William C. *The Politics of Civil Rights in the Truman Administration*. Columbus: Ohio State University Press, 1970.

Bernhard, Virginia et al., eds. *Southern Women: History and Identities*. New York: Columbia University Press, 1992.

Bernstein, Barton, ed. *Politics and Policies of the Truman Administration*. Chicago: Quadrangle Books, 1970.

Blackwell, James, and Morris Janowitz, eds. *Black Sociologists: Historical and Contemporary Perspectives*. Chicago: University of Chicago Press, 1974.

Blee, Kathleen M., ed. *No Middle Ground: Women and Radical Protest*. New York: New York University Press, 1998.

Bock, Gisela, and Susan James, eds. *Beyond Equality and Difference: Citizenship, Feminist Politics and Female Subjectivity*. New York: Routledge, 1992.

Bogle, Donald. *Toms, Coons, Mulattoes, Mammies and Bucks: An Interpretive History of Blacks in American Films*. New York: Continuum, 1994 [1973].

Boris, Eileen. *Home to Work: Motherhood and the Politics of Industrial Homework in the United States*. New York: Cambridge University Press, 1994.

Branch, Taylor. *Parting the Waters: America in the King Years*. New York: Simon and Schuster, 1988.

Breines, Wini. *Young, White and Miserable: Growing Up Female in the Fifties*. Boston: Beacon Press, 1992.

Brinkley, Alan. *Liberalism and Its Discontents*. Cambridge: Harvard University Press, 1998.

———. *The End of Reform: New Deal Liberalism in Recession and War*. New York: Knopf, 1995.

———. *Voices of Protest: Huey Long, Father Coughlin and the Great Depression*. New York: Knopf, 1982.

Brownmiller, Susan. *Against Our Will Men, Women and Rape*. New York: Simon and Schuster, 1975.

Buhle, Mari Jo. *Feminism and Its Discontents: A Century of Struggle with Psychoanalysis*. Cambridge: Harvard University Press, 1998.

Butler, Judith, and Joan Scott, eds. *Feminist Theorize the Political*. New York: Routledge, 1992.

Byars, Jackie. *All That Hollywood Allows: Re-Reading Gender in 1950s Melodrama*. Chapel Hill: University of North Carolina Press, 1991.

Campbell, Bebe Moore. *Your Blues Ain't Like Mine*. New York: G. P. Putnam's Sons, 1992.

Carby, Hazel. *Race Men*. Cambridge: Harvard University Press, 1998.

———. *Reconstructing Womanhood: The Emergence of the Afro-American Woman Novelist*. New York: Oxford University Press, 1987.

Carson, Clayborne. *In Struggle: SNCC and the Black Awakening of the 1960s*. Cambridge: Harvard University Press, 1981.

Chafe, William, and Harvard Sitkoff, eds. *A History of Our Time: Readings on Postwar America*. New York: Oxford University Press, 1991 [1983].

Chafe, William. *Civilities and Civil Rights: Greensboro, North Carolina, and the Black Struggle for Freedom*. New York: Oxford University Press, 1980.

———. *The American Woman: Her Changing Social, Economic, and Political Roles, 1920–1970*. New York: Oxford University Press, 1972.

Chateauvert, Melinda. *Marching Together: Women of the Brotherhood of Sleeping Car Porters*. Urbana: University of Illinois Press, 1998.

Clark-Lewis, Elizabeth. *Living In, Living Out: African American Domestics in Washington, D.C., 1910–1940*. Washington, D.C.: Smithsonian Institution Press, 1994.

Cohen, Lizabeth. *Making A New Deal: Industrial Workers in Chicago, 1919–1939*. New York: Cambridge University Press, 1990.

Corber, Robert J. *In the Name of National Security: Hitchcock, Homophobia, and the Political Construction of Gender in Postwar America*. Durham: Duke University Press, 1993.

Cott, Nancy. *The Grounding of Modern Feminism*. New Haven: Yale University Press, 1987.

Cott, Nancy, and Elizabeth Pleck, eds. *A Heritage of Her Own: Towards a New Social History of American Women*. New York: Simon and Schuster, 1979.

Crane, Cheryl, with Cliff Jahr. *Detour: A Hollywood Story*. New York: Arbor House, 1988.

Cravens, Hamilton, ed. *Ideas in America's Cultures: From Republic to Mass Society*. Ames: Iowa State University Press, 1982.

Crawford, Vicki et al., eds. *Women in the Civil Rights Movement: Trailblazers and Torchbearers, 1941–1965*. Brooklyn: Carlson Publishing, 1990.

D'Emilio, John, and Estelle B. Freedman. *Intimate Matters: A History of Sexuality in America*. New York: Harper and Row, 1988.

Dalfiume, Richard. *Desegregation of the U.S. Armed Forces: Fighting on Two Fronts, 1939–1953*. New York: Columbia University Press, 1969.

Davis, Angela. *Women, Race and Class*. New York: Random House, 1981.

Davis, Flora. *Moving the Mountain: The Women's Movement in American Since 1960*. New York: Simon and Schuster, 1991.

Davis, Harry R., and Robert C. Good, eds. *Reinhold Niebuhr on Politics: His Political Philosophy and its Application to Our Age as Expressed in His Writings*. New York: Charles Scribners' Sons, 1960.

Dean, Carolyn J. *The Self and Its Pleasures: Bataille, Lacan, and the History of the Decentered Subject*. Ithaca: Cornell University Press, 1992.

Denning, Michael. *The Cultural Front: The Laboring of American Culture in the Twentieth Century*. London: Verso, 1996.

Dennis, Frank Allen, ed. *Southern Miscellany: Essays in History in Honor of Glover Moore*. Jackson: University Press of Mississippi, 1981.

Dittmer, John. *Local People: The Struggle for Civil Rights in Mississippi*. Urbana: University of Illinois Press, 1994.

Doane, Mary Ann. *Femme Fatales: Feminism, Film Theory, and Psychoanalysis*. New York: Routledge, 1991.

Douglas, Susan. *Where the Girls Are: Growing Up Female with the Mass Media*. New York: Times Books, 1994.

Dyer, Richard. *Only Entertainment*. New York: Routledge, 1992.

Dyson, Michael Eric. *Reflecting Black: African American Cultural Criticism*. Minneapolis: University of Minnesota Press, 1993.

Echols, Alice. *Daring to Be Bad: Radical Feminism in America, 1967–1975*. Minneapolis: University of Minnesota Press, 1989.

Egerton, John. *Speak Now against the Day: The Generation before the Civil Rights Movement in the South*. New York: Knopf, 1994.

Ehrenreich, Barbara, and Deirdre English. *For Her Own Good: 150 Years of the Experts' Advice on Women*. New York: Anchor Books, 1978.

Ehrenreich, Barbara. *The Hearts of Men: American Dreams and the Flight From Commitment*. New York: Anchor Books, 1983.

Evans, Sara. *Born for Liberty: A History of Women in America*. New York: The Free Press, 1988.

———. *Personal Politics: The Roots of Women's Liberation in the Civil Rights Movement and the New Left*. New York: Knopf, 1979.

Eyer, Diane E. *Mother-Infant Bonding: A Scientific Fiction*. New Haven: Yale University Press, 1992.

Fischer, Lucy, ed. *Imitation of Life: Douglas Sirk, Director*. New Brunswick: Rutgers University Press, 1991.

Fleming, Cynthia Griggs. *Soon We Will Not Cry: The Liberation of Ruby Doris Smith Robinson*. New York: Rowman and Littlefield, 1998.

Foucault, Michel. *The History of Sexuality, Volume 1: An Introduction*. New York: Random House, 1978 [1976].

Fraser, Steve, and Gary Gerstle, eds. *The Rise and Fall of the New Deal Order, 1930–1980*. Princeton: Princeton University Press, 1989.

Fraser, Nancy. *Unruly Practices: Power, Discourse and Gender in Contemporary Social Theory*. Minneapolis: University of Minnesota Press, 1989.

Gaddis, John Lewis. *Strategies of Containment: A Critical Appraisal of Postwar American National Security Policy*. New York: Oxford University Press, 1982.

Gaines, Kevin. *Uplifting the Race: Black Leadership, Politics, and Culture in the Twentieth Century*. Chapel Hill: University of North Carolina Press, 1996.

Garrow, David, ed. *Atlanta, Georgia, 1960–1961: Sit-ins and Student Activism*. Brooklyn: Carlson Publishing, 1989.

————. *Bearing the Cross: Martin Luther King and the SCLC*. New York: William Morrow, 1986.

Gerhard, Jane. *Desiring Revolution: Second-Wave Feminism and the Rewriting of American Sexual Thought*. New York: Columbia University Press, forthcoming.

Giddings, Paula. *When and Where I Enter: The Impact of Black Women on Race and Sex in America*. New York: William Morrow, 1984.

Gilbert, James. *A Cycle of Outrage: America's Reaction to the Juvenile Delinquent in the 1950s*. New York: Oxford University Press, 1986.

Gilman, Sander. *Difference and Pathology: Stereotypes of Sexuality, Race, and Madness*. Ithaca: Cornell University Press, 1985.

Gilmore, Glenda. *Gender and Jim Crow: Women and the Politics of White Supremacy in North Carolina, 1896–1920*. Chapel Hill: University of North Carolina Press, 1996.

Gillon, Steven. *Politics and Vision: The ADA and American Liberalism 1947–1985*. New York: Oxford University Press, 1987.

Ginsburg, Carl. *Race and Media: The Enduring Life of the Moynihan Report*. New York: Institute for Media Analysis, Inc., 1989.

Gitlin, Todd. *The Sixties: Years of Hope, Days of Rage*. New York: Bantam Books, 1987.

Gledhill, Christine, ed. *Home Is Where the Heart Is: Studies in Melodrama and the Woman's Film*. London: British Film Institute, 1987.

Goodman, James. *Stories of Scottsboro*. New York: Pantheon Books, 1994.

Gordon, Linda. *Pitied But Not Entitled: Single Mothers and the History of Welfare 1890–1935*. New York: The Free Press, 1994.

Gordon, Linda, ed. *Women, the State and Welfare*. Madison: University of Wisconsin Press, 1990.

Grant, Julia. *Raising Baby by the Book: The Education of American Mothers*. New Haven: Yale University Press, 1998.

Greenberg, Cheryl Lynn, ed. *A Circle of Trust: Remembering SNCC*. New Brunswick: Rutgers University Press, 1998.

Griswold, Robert. *Fatherhood in America*. New York: Basic Books, 1993.

Guy-Sheftall, Beverly, ed. *Words of Fire: An Anthology of African-American Feminist Thought*. New York: The New Press, 1995.

Hall, Jacquelyn Dowd. *Revolt against Chivalry: Jessie Daniel Ames and the Women's Campaign against Lynching*. New York: Columbia University Press, 1993 [1979].

Halliday, Jon. *Sirk on Sirk*. New York: Viking, 1972.

Hamby, Alonzo. *Liberalism and Its Challengers: FDR to Reagan*. New York: Oxford University Press, 1985.

Hamilton, Dona Cooper, and Charles V. Hamilton. *The Dual Agenda: Race and Social Welfare Policies of Civil Rights Organizations*. New York: Columbia University Press, 1997.

Hapke, Laura. *Daughters of the Great Depression: Women, Work, and Fiction in the American 1930s*. Athens: University of Georgia Press, 1995.

Harrison, Cynthia. *On Account of Sex: The Politics of Women's Issues, 1945–1968*. Berkeley: University of California Press, 1988.

Hartmann, Susan. *The Other Feminists: Activists in the Liberal Establishment*. New Haven: Yale University Press, 1998.

Harvey, Brett. *The Fifties: A Woman's Oral History*. New York: HarperCollins, 1993.

Hays, Sharon. *The Cultural Contradictions of Motherhood*. New Haven: Yale University Press, 1996.

Hennessee, Judith. *Betty Friedan: Her Life*. New York: Random House, 1999.

Herman, Ellen. *The Romance of American Psychology: Political Culture in the Age of Experts*. Berkeley: University of California Press, 1995.

Higginbotham, Evelyn Brooks. *Righteous Discontent: The Women's Movement in the Black Baptist Church, 1880–1920*. Cambridge: Harvard University Press, 1993.

Hodgson, Godfrey. *America in Our Time: From World War II To Nixon, What Happened and Why?* New York: Vintage Books, 1978 [1976].

Holmes, Stephen. *Passions and Constraints: On the Theory of Liberal Democracy*. Chicago: University of Chicago Press, 1995.

Horowitz, Daniel. *Betty Friedan and the Making of the Feminie Mystique: The American Left, the Cold War, and Modern Feminism*. Amherst: University of Massachusetts Press, 1998.

Hull, Gloria T., et al., eds. *All the Women Are White, All the Blacks Are Men, But Some of Us Are Brave: Black Women's Studies*. New York: The Feminist Press, 1982.

Hunter, Tera. *To 'Joy My Freedom: Southern Black Women's Lives and Labors After the Civil War*. Cambridge: Harvard University Press, 1997.

Huyssen, Andreas. *After the Great Divide: Modernism, Mass Culture, Postmodernism*. Bloomington: Indiana University Press, 1986.

Isserman, Maurice. *If I Had A Hammer: The Death of the Old Left and the Birth of the New Left*. New York: Basic Books, 1987.

Jackson, Walter. *Gunnar Myrdal and America's Conscience: Social Engineering and Racial Liberalism, 1938–1987*. Chapel Hill: University of North Carolina Press, 1990.

Jacobson, Matthew Frye. *Whiteness of a Different Color: European Immigrants and the Alchemy of Race*. Cambridge: Harvard University Press, 1998.

Jay, Martin. *Permanent Exiles: Essays on Intellectual Migration from Germany to America*. New York: Columbia University Press, 1985.

————. *The Dialectical Imagination: A History of the Frankfurt School and the Institute of Social Research, 1923–1950*. Boston: Little, Brown, 1973.

Jezer, Marty. *The Dark Ages: Life in the U.S., 1945–1960*. Boston: South End Press, 1982.

Jones, Jacqueline. *Labor of Love, Labor of Sorrow: Black Women, Work and the Family from Slavery to the Present*. New York: Basic Books, 1985.

Kaplan, E. Ann. *Motherhood and Representation: The Mother in Popular Culture and Melodrama*. New York: Routledge, 1992.

Karlsen, Carol F. *The Devil in the Shape of a Woman: Witchcraft in Colonial New England*. New York: Norton, 1987.

Katz, Michael B. *In the Shadow of the Poorhouse: A Social History of Welfare in America*. New York: Basic Books, 1988.

Keefer, Truman Frederick. *Philip Wylie*. Boston: Twayne Publishers, 1977.

Kelley, Robin D. G. *Hammer and Hoe: Alabama Communists During the Great Depression*. Chapel Hill: University of North Carolina Press, 1990.

Keppel, Ben. *The Work of Democracy: Ralph Bunche, Kenneth B. Clark, Lorraine Hansberry and the Cultural Politics of Race*. Cambridge: Harvard University Press, 1995.

Kerber, Linda, Alice Kessler-Harris, and Kathryin Kish Skylar, eds. *U.S. History as Women's History: New Feminist Essays*. Chapel Hill: University of North Carolina Press, 1995.

Kerber, Linda. *Women of the Republic: Intellect and Ideology in Revolutionary America*. Chapel Hill: University of North Carolina Press, 1980.

King, Mary. *Freedom Song: A Personal Story of the 1960s Civil Rights Movement*. New York: Morrow, 1987.

Kirby, John B. *Black Americans in the Roosevelt Era: Liberalism and Race*. Knoxville: University of Tennessee Press, 1980.

Kloppenberg, James T. *The Virtues of Liberalism*. New York: Oxford University Press, 1998.

Koven, Seth, and Sonya Michel, eds. *Mothers of a New World: Maternalist Politics and the Origins of Welfare States*. New York: Routledge, 1993.

Kunzel, Regina G. *Fallen Women, Problem Girls: Unmarried Mothers and the Professionalization of Social Work, 1890–1945*. New Haven: Yale University Press, 1993.

Lacey, Michael J., ed. *The Truman Presidency*. New York: Cambridge University Press, 1989.

Ladd-Taylor, Molly, and Lauri Umansky, eds. *"Bad" Mothers: The Politics of Blame in Twentieth-Century America*. New York: New York University Press, 1998.

Ladd-Taylor, Molly. *Mother-Work: Women, Child Welfare, and the State, 1890–1930*. Urbana: University of Illinois Press, 1994.

Lasch, Christopher. *Haven in a Heartless World: The Family Besieged*. New York: Basic Books, 1977.

Lears, T. J. Jackson, and Richard Wightman Fox, eds. *The Culture of Consumption: Critical Essays in American History 1880–1980*. New York: Pantheon Books, 1983.

Lerner, Gerda. *The Grimke Sisters from South Carolina: Pioneers for Woman's Rights and Abolition*. New York: Schocken Books, 1971.

Lipsitz, George. *Time Passages: Collective Memory and American Popular Culture*. Minneapolis: University of Minnesota Press, 1990.

Loveland, Anne C. *Lillian Smith, A Southerner Confronting the South: A Biography*. Baton Rouge: Louisiana State University Press, 1986.

Lunbeck, Elizabeth. *The Psychiatric Persuasion: Knowledge, Gender, and Power in Modern America*. Princeton: Princeton University Press, 1994.

Lynn, Susan. *Progressive Women in Conservative Times: Racial Justice, Peace, and Feminism, 1945 to 1960s*. New Brunswick: Rutgers University Press, 1992.

MacLean, Douglas, and Claudia Mills eds. *Liberalism Reconsidered*. Totowa, N.J.: Rowman and Allanheld Publishers, 1983.

Manson, William C. *The Psychodynamics of Culture: Abram Kardiner and Neo-Freudian Anthropology*. New York: Greenwood Press, 1988.

Martin, Waldo E. Jr. *Brown v. Board of Education: A Brief History with Documents*. Boston: Bedford/St.Martin's, 1998.

Matusow, Allen. *The Unraveling of America: A History of Liberalism in the 1960s*. New York: Harper and Row, 1984.

May, Elaine Tyler. *Homeward Bound: American Families in the Cold War Era*. New York: Basic Books, 1988.

McAdam, Doug. *Freedom Summer*. New York: Oxford University Press, 1988.

McAlister, Melani. *Epic Encounters: Race, Religion and Nation in U.S. Representations of the Middle East*. Berkeley: University of California Press, forthcoming.

McAuliffe, Mary Sperling. *Crisis on the Left: American Liberals, 1947–1954*. Amherst: University of Massachusetts Press, 1978.

McCoy, Donald, and Richard T. Ruetten. *Quest and Response: Minority Rights and the Truman Administration*. Lawrence: University Press of Kansas, 1973.

McKeany, Maurine. *The Absent Father and Public Policy in the Program of Aid to Dependant Children*. Berkeley: University of California Press, 1960.

McKee, James B. *Sociology and the Race Problem: The Failure of a Perspective*. Urbana: University of Illinois Press, 1993.

McMillen, Neil. *Dark Journey: Black Mississippians in the Age of Jim Crow*. Chicago: University of Illinois Press, 1989.

Meier, August. *A White Scholar and the Black Community, 1945–1965: Essays and Reflections*. Amherst: University of Massachusetts Press, 1992.

Melosh, Barbara. *Engendering Culture: Manhood and Womanhood in New Deal Public Art and Theater*. Washington, D.C.: Smithsonian Institution Press, 1991.

Mettler, Suzanne. *Dividing Citizens: Gender and Federalism in New Deal Public Policy*. Ithaca: Cornell University Press, 1998.

Meyerowitz, Joanne, ed. *Not June Cleaver: Women and Gender in Postwar America, 1945–1960.* Philadelphia: Temple University Press, 1994.

Michel, Sonya. *Children's Interests/Mother's Rights: The Shaping of America's Child Care Policy.* New Haven: Yale University Press, 1999.

Mink, Gwendolyn. *The Wages of Motherhood: Inequality in the Welfare State, 1917–1942.* Ithaca: Cornell University Press, 1995.

———. *Welfare's End.* Ithaca: Cornell University Press, 1998.

Mink, Gwendolyn, ed. *Whose Welfare?* Ithaca: Cornell University Press, 1999.

Morrison, Toni, ed. *Race-ing Justice, En-genderingPower: Essays on Anita Hill, Clarence Thomas, and the Construction of Social Reality.* New York: Pantheon Books, 1992.

Morton, Patricia. *Disfigured Images: The Historical Assault On Afro-American Women.* New York: Praeger Press, 1991.

Mulvey, Laura. *Visual and Other Pleasures.* Houndmills, Basingstoke, Hampshire: Macmillan, 1989.

Muncy, Robyn. *Creating a Female Dominion in American Reform, 1890–1935.* New York: Oxford University Press, 1991.

Murray, Pauli. *Song in a Weary Throat: An American Pilgrimage.* New York: Harper and Row, 1987.

Newman, Louise Michele. *White Women's Rights: The Racial Origins of American Feminism.* New York: Oxford University Press, 1999.

Nordan, Lewis. *Wolf Whistle: A Novel.* Chapel Hill: Algonquin Books of Chapel Hill, 1993.

O'Neill, William. *American High: The Years of Confidence, 1945–1960.* New York: The Free Press, 1986.

Pascoe, Peggy. *Relations of Rescue: The Search for Female Moral Authority in the West, 1874–1939.* New York: Oxford University Press, 1990.

Pateman, Carole. *The Disorder of Women: Democracy, Feminism and Political Theory.* Cambridge: Polity Press, 1989.

Paterson, Thomas G., ed. *Major Problems in Foreign Policy, Documents and Essays, Volume 2: Since 1914.* Lexington, Mass: D.C. Heath, 1984 [1978].

Patterson, James. *Grand Expectations: The United States, 1945–1974.* New York: Oxford University Press, 1996.

Peiss, Kathy, and Christina Simmons, eds. *Passion and Power: Sexuality and History.* Philadelphia: Temple University Press, 1989.

Pells, Richard. *Radical Visions and American Dreams: Culture and Social Thought in the Depression Years.* New York: Harper and Row, 1973.

———. *The Liberal Mind in a Conservative Age: American Intellectuals in the 1940s and 1950s.* New York: Harper and Row, 1985.

Platt, Anthony E. *E. Franklin Frazier Reconsidered.* New Brunswick: Rutgers University Press, 1991.

Poiger, Uta G. *Jazz, Rock, and Rebels: Cold War Politics and American Culture in a Divided Germany.* Berkeley: University of California Press, 2000.

Polakow, Valerie. *Lives on the Edge: Single Mothers and Their Children in the Other America.* Chicago: University of Chicago Press, 1993.

Reed, Merl E. *Seedtime for the Modern Civil Rights Movement: The President's Committee on Fair Employment Practice, 1941–1946.* Baton Rouge: Louisiana State University Press, 1991.

Roberts, Dorothy. *Killing the Black Body: Race, Reproduction, and the Meaning of Liberty.* New York: Pantheon Books, 1997.

Robinson, Armstead L., and Patricia Sullivan, eds. *New Directions in Civil Rights Studies.* Charlottesville: University Press of Virginia, 1991.

Robnett, Belinda. *How Long? How Long? African American Women in the Struggle for Civil Rights.* New York: Oxford University Press, 1997.

Roediger, David R. *The Wages of Whiteness: Race and the Making of the American Working Class.* London: Verso, 1991.

Rogin, Michael. *Blackface, White Noise: Jewish Immigrants in the Hollywood Melting Pot.* Berkeley: University of California Press, 1996.

Ross, Andrew. *No Respect: Intellectuals and Popular Culture.* New York: Routledge, 1989.

Rothschild, Mary Aikin. *A Case of Black and White: Northern Volunteers and the Southern Freedom Summers, 1964–65.* Westport, Conn.: Greenwood Press, 1982.

Rupp, Leila J., and Verta Taylor. *Survival in the Doldrums: The American Women's Rights Movement, 1945–1960s.* Columbus: Ohio State University Press, 1990.

Scharf, Lois. *To Work and to Wed: Female Employment, Feminism, and the Great Depression.* Westport, Conn.: Greenwood Press, 1980.

Schaub, Thomas. *American Fiction in the Cold War.* Madison: University of Wisconsin Press, 1991.

Schoen, Douglas. *Pat: A Biography of Daniel Patrick Moynihan.* New York: Harper and Row, 1979.

Scott, Daryl. *Contempt and Pity: Social Policy and the Image of the Damaged Black Psyche, 1880–1996.* Chapel Hill: University of North Carolina Press, 1997.

Scott, Joan. *Gender and the Politics of History.* New York: Columbia University Press, 1988.

Sherman, Richard B. *The Case of Odell Waller and Virginia Justice, 1940–1942.* Knoxville: University of Tennessee Press, 1992.

Sitkoff, Harvard. *A New Deal for Blacks: The Emergence of Civil Rights as A National Issue. Volume 1: The Depression Decade.* New York: Oxford University Press, 1978.

———. *The Struggle for Black Equality, 1954–1980.* New York: Hill and Wang, 1981.

Sitkoff, Harvard, ed. *Making Sense of the Twentieth Century: Historical Perspectives on Modern America*, 1900–2000. New York: Oxford University Press, forthcoming.

Sklar, Robert. *Movie-Made America: A Cultural History of American Movies.* New York, Random House, 1975.

Skocpol, Theda. *Protecting Soldiers and Mothers: The Political Origins of Social Policy in the United States.* Cambridge: Harvard University Press, 1992.

Smith, Judith. *Popular Promises: Fictions of Family and Social Identity in Postwar American Culture.* New York: Columbia University Press, forthcoming.

Solinger, Rickie. *Wake Up Little Susie: Single Pregnancy and Race before Roe v. Wade.* New York: Routledge, 1992.

Sosna, Morton. *In Search of the Silent South: Southern Liberals and the Race Issue.* New York: Columbia University Press, 1977.

Spigel, Lynn. *Make Room for TV: Television and the Family Ideal in Postwar America.* Chicago: University of Chicago Press, 1992.

Stanfield, John H. *Philanthropy and Jim Crow in American Social Science.* Westport, Conn.: Greenwood Press, 1989.

Stansell, Christine. *City of Women: Sex and Class in New York, 1789–1860.* Urbana: University of Illinois Press, 1987.

Stocking, George Jr., ed. *Malinowski, Rivers, Benedict and Others: Essays on Culture and Personality. History of Anthropology, Volume 4.* Madison: University of Wisconsin Press, 1986.

Stott, William. *Documentary Expression and Thirties America.* New York: Oxford University Press, 1973.

Sugrue, Thomas. *The Origins of the Urban Crisis: Race and Inequality in Postwar Detroit.* Princeton: Princeton University Press, 1996.

Sullivan, Patricia. *Days of Hope: Race and Democracy in the New Deal Era.* Chapel Hill: University of North Carolina Press, 1996.

Susman, Warren. *Culture as History: The Transformation of American Society in the Twentieth Century.* New York: Pantheon Books, 1984.

Swerdlow, Amy. *Women Strike for Peace: Traditional Motherhood and Radical Politics in the 1960s.* Chicago: University of Chicago Press, 1993.

Terkel, Studs. *Race: How Blacks and Whites Think and Feel About the American Obsession.* New York: Norton, 1992.

Turner, Lana. *Lana: The Lady, The Legend, The Truth*. New York: Dutton, 1982.

Umansky, Lauri. *Motherhood Reconceived: Feminism, Motherhood, and the Legacies of the 1960s*. New York: New York University Press, 1996.

Von Eschen, Penny M. *Race against Empire: Black Americans and Anticolonialism, 1937–1957*. Ithaca: Cornell University Press, 1997.

Walker, Alice. *You Can't Keep a Good Woman Down*. New York: Harcourt Brace Jovanovich, 1981.

———. *In Search of Our Mothers' Gardens: Womanist Prose*. New York: Harcourt Brace Jovanovich, 1983.

Walkowitz, Judith. *City of Dreadful Delight: Narratives of Sexual Danger in Late-Victorian London*. Chicago: University of Chicago Press, 1992.

Ware, Susan. *Beyond Suffrage: Women in the New Deal*. Cambridge: Harvard University Press, 1981.

Ware, Susan, ed. *Modern American Women: A Documentary History*. New York: McGraw Hill, 1997 [1972].

Weir, Margaret, Ann Shola Orloff, and Theda Skocpol, eds. *The Politics of Social Policy in the United States*. Princeton: Princeton University Press, 1988.

Weisbrot, Robert. *Freedom Bound: A History of America's Civil Rights Movement*. New York: Norton, 1990.

Weiss, Nancy J. *Farewell to the Party of Lincoln: Black Politics in the Age of FDR*. Princeton: Princeton University Press, 1983.

West, Guida, and Rhoda Blumberg, eds. *Women and Social Protest*. New York: Oxford University Press, 1990.

White, Deborah Gray. *Ar'n't I a Woman? Female Slaves in the Ante-Bellum South*. New York: Norton, 1985.

Whitfield, Stephen J. *The Culture of the Cold War*. Baltimore: Johns Hopkins University Press, 1991.

———. *A Death in the Delta: The Story of Emmett Till*. New York: The Free Press, 1988.

Williams, Juan. *Eyes on the Prize: America's Civil Rights Years, 1954–1965*. New York: Viking Penguin, 1987.

Williams, Vernon. *From a Caste to a Minority: Changing Attitudes of American Sociologists toward Afro-Americans, 1896–1945*. Westport, Conn.: Greenwood Press, 1989.

Wolff, Miles. *Lunch at the Five and Dime: The Greensboro Sit-Ins, a Contemporary History*. New York: Stein and Day, 1970.

Young-Bruehl, Elisabeth. *The Anatomy Of Prejudices*. Cambridge: Harvard University Press, 1996.

Zelman, Patricia G. *Women, Work, and National Policy: The Kennedy-Johnson Years*. Ann Arbor: UMI Research Press, 1989.

Articles, Dissertations, and Unpublished Materials:

Barber, Lucy G. "Marches on Washington, 1894–1963: National Political Demonstrations and American Political Culture." Ph.D. dissertation. Brown University, 1996.

Beck, Kent M. "What Was Liberalism in the 1950s?" *Political Science Quarterly* 102 (summer 1987): 233–58.

Bederman, Gail. " 'Civilization,' the Decline of Middle-Class Manliness, and Ida B. Wells's Anti-Lynching Campaign (1892–1894)." *Radical History Review* 52 (1992): 5–30.

Berlant, Lauren. "National Brands/National Body: *Imitation of Life*." In Hortense Spillers, ed. *Comparative American Identities: Race, Sex, and Nationality in the Modern Text*. New York: Routledge, 1991, pp. 110–140.

Blankenship, Kim. M. "Bringing Gender and Race In: U.S. Employment Discrimination Policy," *Gender and Society* 7 (June 1993): 204–26.

Boris, Eileen. "The Racialized Gender State: Constructions of Citizenship in the United States." *Social Politics* 2 (summer 1995): 160–80.

Bracey, John Jr., and August Meier. "Allies or Adversaries?: The NAACP, A. Philip Randolph and the 1941 March on Washington." *Georgia Historical Quarterly* 75 (spring 1991): 1–17.

Brauer, Carl M. "Women Activists, Southern Conservatives, and the Prohibition of Sex Discrimination in Title 7 of the 1964 Civil Rights Act." *Journal of Southern History* 49 (1983): 37–56.

Brown, Elsa Barkley. " 'What Has Happened Here': The Politics of Difference in Women's History and Feminist Politics." *Feminist Studies* 18 (summer 1992): 295–312.

Butler, Judith. "Lana's Imitation: Melodramatic Repetition and the Gender Performative." *Genders* 9 (fall 1990): 1–18.

Carby, Hazel. "Policing the Black Woman's Body in an Urban Context." *Critical Inquiry* 18 (summer 1992): 739–55.

Cohen, Lizabeth. "A Consumer's Republic: The Politics of Consumption in Postwar America." Paper presented at the Rutgers Center for Historical Analysis, April 1993.

Costigliola, Frank. "The Nuclear Family: Tropes of Gender and Pathology in the the Western Alliance." *Diplomatic History* 21 (spring 1997): 163–83.

———. " 'Unceasing Pressure for Penetration': Gender, Pathology and Emotion in George Kennan's Formation of the Cold War." *Journal of American History* 83 (March 1997): 1309–339.

Dalfiume, Richard M. "The 'Forgotten Years' of the Negro Revolution." *Journal of American History* 55 (June 1968): 90–106.

Deitch, Cynthia. "Gender, Race, and Class Politics and the Inclusion of Women in Title 7 of the 1964 Civil Rights Act." *Gender and Society* 7 (June 1993): 183–203.

Dudziak, Mary L. "Desegregation as a Cold War Imperative." *Stanford Law Review* 41 (November 1988): 61–120.

Echols, Alice. " 'We Gotta Get Out of the Place': Notes Toward Remapping the Sixties." *Socialist Review* 22 (April-June 1992): 9–33.

Engelhardt, Carroll. "Man in the Middle: Arthur M. Schlesinger, Jr., and Postwar American Liberalism." *South Atlantic Quarterly* 80 (spring 1981): 119–42.

Foner, Eric. "Common Origins, Different Paths." *Radical History Review* (spring 1998): 6–10.

Fraser, Nancy, and Linda Gordon. "A Genealogy of *Dependency*: Tracing a Keyword of the U.S. Welfare State." *Signs* 19 (winter 1994): 309–36.

Gerstle, Gary. "The Protean Character of American Liberalism." *American Historical Review* 99 (October 1994): 1043–1073.

———. "Race and the Myth of the Liberal Consensus." *Journal of American History* 82 (September 1995): 579–86.

Gleason, Philip. "Americans All: World War II and the Shaping of American Identity." *Review of Politics* 93 (October 1981): 483–518.

Graebner, William. "The Unstable World of Dr. Spock: Social Engineering in a Democratic Culture." *Journal of American History* 67 (1980): 612–29.

Hamby, Alonzo L. "The Vital Center, the Fair Deal, and the Quest for a Liberal Political Economy." *American Historical Review* 77 (June 1972): 653–78.

Harris, Miriam Lynell. "From Kennedy to Combahee: Black Feminst Activism from 1950 to 1980." Ph.D., dissertation. University of Minnesota, 1997.

Higginbotham, Evelyn Brooks. "African-American Women's History and the Metalanguage of Race." *Signs* 17 (summer 1992): 251–74.

Hine, Darlene Clark. "Rape and the Inner Lives of Black Women in the Middle West: Preliminary Thoughts on the Culture of Dissemblance." *Signs* 14 (summer 1989): 912–20.

Holland, Endesha Ida Mae. "Memories of the Mississippi Delta." *Michigan Quarterly Review* 26 (winter 1987): 246–58.

Humphries, Jane. "Women: Scapegoats and Safety Valves in the Great Depression." *Review of Radical Political Economics* 8 (spring 1976): 98–102.

Jackson, Walter A. "The Making of A Social Science Classic: Gunnar Myrdal's *An American Dilemma*." *Perspectives in American History*, New Series 2 (1985): 221–67.

Kerber, Linda. "Separate Spheres, Female Worlds, Woman's Place: The Rhetoric of Women's History." *Journal of American History* 75 (June 1988): 9–39.

———. "The Republican Ideology of the Revolutionary Generation," *American Quarterly* 37 (1985): 474–95.

———. "The Republican Mother: Women and the Enlightenment—An American Perspective." *American Quarterly* 28 (1976): 187–205.

Kidd, Stuart. "Redefining the New Deal: Some Thoughts on the Political and Cultural Perspectives of Revisionism." *Journal of American Studies* 22 (1988): 389–414.

Korstad, Robert, and Nelson Lichtenstein. "Opportunities Found and Lost: Labor, Radicals and the Early Civil Rights Movement." *Journal of American History* (December 1988): 786–811.

Kozol, Wendy. "Madonnas of the Field: Photography, Gender, and Thirties' Farm Relief." *Genders* 2 (summer 1988): 1–23.

Lears, T. J. Jackson. "The Concept of Cultural Hegemony: Problems and Possibilities." *American Historical Review* 90 (June 1985): 567–93.

Levine, Lawrence W. "American Culture and the Great Depression." *Yale Review* 74 (winter 1985): 196–223.

MacLean, Nancy. "The Leo Frank Case Reconsidered: Gender and Sexual Politics in the Making of Reactionary Populism." *Journal of American History* (December 1991): 917–948.

"Maternalism as a Paradigm." *Journal of Women's History* 5 (fall 1993): 95–131.

Matthews, Fred. "The Utopia of Human Relations: The Conflict-Free Family in American Social Thought, 1930–1960." *Journal of the History of the Behavioral Sciences* 24 (October 1988): 343–62.

McAlister, Melani. "One Black Allah': The Middle East in the Cultural Politics of African American Liberation 1955–1970." *American Quarterly* 51 (September 1999): 622–56.

Michel, Sonya. "Danger on the Home Front: Motherhood, Sexuality, and Disabled Veterans in American Postwar Films." *Journal of the History of Sexuality* 3 (July 1992): 109–28.

Nuechterlein, James. "Arthur M. Schlesinger, Jr., and the Discontents of Postwar American Liberalism." *Review of Politics* 39 (January 1977): 3–40.

Orleck, Annelise. " 'We Are That Mythical Thing Called the Public': Militant Housewives during the Great Depression." *Feminist Studies* 19 (spring 1993): 147–72.

Pauly, Thomas. "Black Images and White Culture during the Decade before the Civil Rights Movement." *American Studies* 31 (fall 1990): 101–19.

Platt, Gerald. "The Sociological Endeavor and Psychoanalytic Thought." *American Quarterly* 28 (1976): 343–59.

Poiger, Uta G. "Rebels with a Cause? American Popular Culture, the 1956 Youth Riots, and New Conceptions of Masculinity in East and West Germany." In Reiner Pommerin, ed. *The American Impact on Postwar Germany*. Providence: Berghahn Books, 1995, pp. 93–124.

Roberts, Mary Louise. "Gender, Consumption, and Commodity Culture." *American Historical Review* 103 (June 1998): 817–44.

Rogin, Michael. " 'Democracy and Burnt Cork': The End of Blackface, the Beginning of Civil Rights." *Representations* 46 (spring 1994): 1–34.

———. "Kiss Me Deadly: Communism, Motherhood, and Cold War Movies," *Representations* 6 (spring 1984): 1–36.

Rose, Nancy E. "Gender, Race, and the Welfare State Government Work Programs from the 1930s to the Present." *Feminist Studies* 19 (summer 1993): 319–42.

Selig, Michael E. "Contradiction and Reading: Social Class and Sex Class in *Imitation of Life*." *Wide Angle* 10 (1988): 14–23.

Shostak, David. "Crosby Smith: Forgotten Witness to a Mississippi Nightmare." *Negro History Bulletin* (December 1974): 320–25.

Simmons, Christina. "Companionate Marriage and the Lesbian Threat." *Frontiers* 4 (fall 1979): 54–59.

Singh, Nikhil Pal. "Culture/Wars: Recoding Empire in an Age of Democracy." *American Quarterly* 50 (September 1998): 471–522.

Smith-Rosenberg, Carroll. "Dis-Covering the Subject of the 'Great Constitutional Discussion,' 1786–1789." *Journal of American History* 79 (December 1992): 841–73.

Turner, Ronald. "Remembering Emmett Till." *Howard Law Journal* 39 (spring 1995): 411–31.

Weiland, Steven. "Life History, Psychoanalysis, and Social Science: The Example of John Dollard." *South Atlantic Quarterly* 86 (summer 1987): 269–85.

Weiss, Nancy Pottishman. "Mother, The Invention of Necessity: Dr. Benjamin Spock's *Baby and Child Care*." *American Quarterly* 29 (1977): 519–46.

Whitaker, Hugh Stephen. "A Case Study in Southern Justice: The Emmett Till Case." M.A., dissertation. Florida State University, 1963.

Index